Cognition in the Wild

Cognition in the Wild

Edwin Hutchins

The MIT Press
Cambridge, Massachusetts
London, England

Set in Helvetica and Melior by Asco Trade Typesetting Ltd., Hong Kong.
Printed and bound in the United States of America.

Library of Congress Cataloging-in-Publication Data

Hutchins, Edwin.
  Cognition in the wild / Edwin Hutchins.
     p.   cm.
  "A Bradford book."
  Includes bibliographical references and index.
  ISBN 0-262-08231-4 (HB), 0-262-58146-9 (PB)
  1. Cognition—Social aspects—Case studies. 2. Cognition and culture—Case studies. 3. Navigation—Psychological aspects. 4. Psychology, Naval. I. Title.
  BF311.H88   1994
  153—dc20   94-21562
                                                                            CIP

10   9   8   7

for Dona

Contents

Acknowledgements

This book has been a long time in the making. Its creation has been a widely distributed cognitive process. I wish to thank first those who provided me the opportunity to make the observations on which this work is based. I am grateful to the crews of the *Palau* (a pseudonym) and all the other ships I sailed upon. The commanding officer and the navigator of the *Palau* merit special recognition for allowing me to work aboard their ship. I am especially grateful to the quartermaster chief and the men of the *Palau's* Navigation Department for working with me and sharing their working lives so generously. Although I will not name them here or in the text, they know who they are and I am grateful to them.

James Tweedale, then Technical Director of the Navy Personnel Research and Development Center, generously supported the early phases of the research as an independent research project. Additional support was provided by the Office of Naval Research's Division of Psychology and Personnel Training under the guidance of Susan Chipman and Michael Shafto. My supervisor and colleague at NPRDC, James Hollan, provided a great working environment for me and helped me to organize my thinking in the early stages. Barbara Morris and Michael Goeller helped with the transcriptions and coding of the data. Colleen Siefert worked with me as a postdoc, made observations on another ship, and co-authored portions of the discussion of learning from error.

I thank the John D. and Catherine T. MacArthur Foundation for a five-year foundation fellowship that permitted me to work on this material when no suitable institutional setting existed. Perhaps more important, the fellowship gave me the courage to follow ideas that lay outside the mainstream.

Over the years in which this work developed, I profited from my involvement in the cognitive science community at the University of California at San Diego. I am especially grateful to Donald Norman, who shared many ideas with me as we ran a research laboratory and taught courses together. I am also grateful to

Aaron Cicourel, Roy D'Andrade, Rik Belew, Mike Cole, and Yrjö Engeström for helping me think through these ideas.

The preparation of the book was facilitated by the helpful comments of Bambi Schieffelin, Jacques Theureau, Everett Palmer, Nick Flor, and Christine Halverson.

My greatest debt is to my wife, Dona, who provided encouragement, support, great meals, and editorial assistance throughout the project.

The seed from which this book grew was planted in November 1980, when I spent most of a day on the navigation bridge of a U.S. Navy ship as it worked its way in from the open North Pacific, through the Straits of Juan de Fuca, and down Puget Sound to Seattle. I was aboard the ship to study what the operators of its steam propulsion plant knew and how they went about knowing it. I had spent most of the preceding week down in the bowels of the ship, observing engineering operations and talking to the boiler technicians and machinist's mates who inhabited that hot, wet, noisy tangle of boilers, pumps, and pipes called the engineering spaces. I'll admit to having felt a little claustrophobic after all that time spent below the water line, where there is no night or day and the only evidence of being at sea is the rhythmic tipping of the deck plates and sloshing of water in the bilge below one's feet as the ship rolls in the swell. A chief boiler technician confided to me that in 21 years on Navy ships he had never yet been on deck to experience either of those two most romantic seafaring events, a ship's arrival at or departure from a port.

I resolved, therefore, to take my last few hours aboard this ship on the navigation bridge, where I could see out the windows or even go out on the bridge wing to get a breath of cold fresh air. My professional rationalization for being on the bridge was that there I would be able to observe the process that generates the flurry of engine commands that always taxes the engineering crew when the ship nears the dock. And I did make a detailed record of all engine and helm commands given in the 75 minutes from the time the engines were first slowed until they were secured—there were 61 in all. But what really captured my attention was the work of the navigation team.

Three and a half years later, the project that became this book began in earnest. In the summer of 1984, I was still working for the Navy Personnel Research and Development Center in San Diego as a civilian scientist with the title Personnel Research Psychologist. By then I had participated in two successful and well-known projects. With these successes came the freedom to conduct an independent research project. I was given carte blanche to study whatever I thought was of most interest. I chose to study what I was then calling *naturally situated cognition*. Having a research position in a Navy laboratory made it possible for me to gain access to naval vessels, and my longtime love of navigation and experience as a racing yacht navigator made it easy for me to choose navigation as an activity to study afloat. I talked my way aboard a ship and set up shop on the navigation bridge. At the time, I really had no notion what an ideal subject navigation would turn out to be. When I began, I was thinking in terms of the naturally situated cognition of individuals. It was only after I completed my first study period at sea that I realized the importance of the fact that cognition was socially distributed.

A little earlier, I had been asked to write a book describing what is in cognitive anthropology for the rest of cognitive science. I began that project, but after I became disillusioned with my field I lost interest in it. The choice of naturally situated cognition as a topic came from my sense that it is what cognitive anthropology really should have been about but largely had not been. Clifford Geertz (1983) called for an "outdoor psychology," but cognitive anthropology was unable or unwilling to be that. The respondents may have been exotic, but the methods of investigation were largely borrowed from the indoor techniques of psychology and linguistics. When cognitive and symbolic anthropology split off from social anthropology, in the mid 1950s, they left society and practice behind.

As part of the cognitive revolution, cognitive anthropology made two crucial steps. First, it turned away from society by looking inward to the knowledge an individual had to have to function as a member of the culture. The question became "What does *a person* have to know?" The locus of knowledge was assumed to be inside the individual. The methods of research then available encouraged the analysis of language. But knowledge expressed or expressible in language tends to be declarative knowledge. It is what people can say about what they know. Skill went out the window of the "white room." The second turn was away from practice. In the quest to learn what people know, anthropologists lost track both of how people go about knowing what they know and of the contribution of the environments in which the knowing is accomplished. Perhaps these narrowing assumptions were necessary to get the project of cognitive anthropology off the ground. I will argue that, now that we are underway as a discipline, we should revoke these assumptions. They have become a burden, and they prevent us from seeing the nature of human cognition.

In particular, the ideational definition of culture prevents us seeing that systems of socially distributed cognition may have interesting cognitive properties of their own. In the history of anthropology, there is scarcely a more important concept than the division of labor. In terms of the energy budget of a human group and the efficiency with which a group exploits its physical environment, social organizational factors often produce group properties that differ considerably from the properties of individuals. Clearly, the same sorts of phenomena occur in the cognitive domain. Depending on their organization, groups must have cognitive properties that are not predictable from a knowledge of the properties of the individuals in the group. The emphasis on finding and describing "knowledge structures" that are somewhere "inside" the individual encourages us to overlook the fact that human cognition is always situated in a complex sociocultural world and cannot be unaffected by it.

Similar developments in the other behavioral sciences during the cognitive revolution of the late 1950s and the 1960s left a troubled legacy in cognitive science. It is notoriously difficult to generalize laboratory findings to real-world situations. The relationship between cognition seen as a solitary mental activity and cognition seen as an activity undertaken in social settings using various kinds of tools is not at all clear.

This book is about softening some boundaries that have been made rigid by previous approaches. It is about locating cognitive activity in context, where context is not a fixed set of surrounding conditions but a wider dynamical process of which the cognition of an individual is only a part. The boundaries to be softened or dissolved have been erected, primarily for analytic convenience, in social space, in physical space, and in time. Just as the construction of these boundaries was driven by a particular theoretical perspective, their dissolution or softening is driven by a different perspective—one that arose of necessity when cognition was confronted in the wild.

The phrase "cognition in the wild" refers to human cognition in its natural habitat—that is, to naturally occurring culturally constituted human activity. I do not intend "cognition in the wild" to be read as similar to Lévi-Strauss's "pensée sauvage," nor do I intend it to contrast with Jack Goody's (1977) notion of domesticated mind. Instead, I have in mind the distinction between the laboratory, where cognition is studied in captivity, and the everyday world, where human cognition adapts to its natural surroundings. I hope to evoke with this metaphor a sense of an ecology of thinking in which human cognition interacts with an environment rich in organizing resources.

The attempt is cultural in nature, giving recognition to the fact that human cognition differs from the cognition of all other animals primarily because it is intrinsically a cultural phenomenon. My aim is to provide better answers to questions like these: What do people use their cognitive abilities for? What kinds of tasks do they confront in the everyday world? Where shall we look for explanations of human cognitive accomplishment?

There is a common misconception among cognitive scientists, especially those who do their work in laboratory settings, that research conducted outside the laboratory is necessarily "applied" work. I will argue in what follows that there are many excellent reasons to look at the "real world" that are not concerned with hoped-for applications of the research findings (although funding sponsors often like to think in those terms). Pure research on the nature of real cognitive practices is needed. In this book, I emphasize practice not in order to support a utilitarian or functionalist perspective but because it is in real practice that culture is produced and reproduced. In practice we see the connection between history and the future and between cultural structure and social structure. One of my goals in writing this book is to make clear that the findings of pure research on cognition in the wild should change our ideas about the nature of human cognition in general. This is not news to anthropologists, who have been doing pure research in the form of ethnography for decades.

This book is an attempt to put cognition back into the social and cultural world. In doing this I hope to show that human cognition is not just influenced by culture and society, but that it is in a very fundamental sense a cultural and social process. To do this I will move the boundaries of the cognitive unit of analysis out beyond the skin of the individual person and treat the navigation team as a cognitive and computational system.

Chapter 1, "Welcome Aboard," attempts to locate the activity of ship navigation in the larger world of modern life. It weaves together three journeys: a movement through physical space from the "street" to the ship, a movement through social space from civilian to military life, and a movement through conceptual space from everyday notions of wayfinding to the technical domain of navigation. Both the researcher and the reader must make these journeys to arrive at the activity of navigation as practiced on the bridge of a Navy ship. Military ranks and the ways in which military identities are formed are presented here because these things affect individual's relationships to their work. An important aspect of the larger unit is that it contains computational elements (persons) who cannot be described entirely in computational terms. Who they talk to and how they talk to one another depend on these social organizational factors. This chapter also contains a discussion of the relationship of the researcher to the activity under study. (The name of the ship and the names of all the individuals mentioned in the book are pseudonyms. All the discourses reported, whether standing alone in transcript form or embedded in narrative passages were transcribed directly from audio recordings of actual events.)

Having taken navigation as it is performed by a team on the bridge of a ship as the unit of cognitive analysis, I attempt in chapter 2, "Navigation as Computation," to apply the principal metaphor of cognitive science—cognition as computation—to the operation of this system. I should note here that in doing so, I do not make any special commitment to the nature of the computations that are going on inside individuals except to say that whatever happens there is part of a larger computational system. This chapter describes the application of David Marr's notions of levels of analysis of cognitive systems to the navigation task and shows that, at the computational level, it is possible to give a single description of the computational constraints of all known technical forms of human navigation. A comparison of modern Western navigation with navigation as practiced in Micronesia shows that considerable differences between these traditions lie at the representational/algorithmic level and at the implementational level. A brief historical review of the development of modern navigation shows that the representational and implementational details of contemporary practice are contingent on complex historical processes and that the accumulation of structure in the tools of the trade is itself a cognitive process.

Chapters 3–5 explore the computational and cognitive properties of systems that are larger than an individual. The issues addressed in these chapters concern how these larger systems operate and how their cognitive properties are produced by interactions among their parts.

Chapter 3, "The Implementation of Contemporary Pilotage," describes the physical structures in which the navigation computations are implemented. This chapter elaborates a conception of computation as the propagation of representational state across a variety of media. This view of computation permits the use of a single language of description to cover cognitive and computational processes that lie inside and outside the heads of the practitioners of navigation. The first section of this chapter describes the "fix cycle" as a cognitive process. The second section describes how navigation tools are used and how local functional systems composed of a person in interaction with a tool have cognitive properties that are radically different from the cognitive properties of the person alone. The third section discusses the ways in which the computational activity can be distributed through time by precomputing not only partial results but also the means of computation. I show here how the environments of human thinking are not "natural" environments. They are artificial through and through. Humans create their cognitive powers by creating the environments in which they exercise those powers. This chapter concludes with a discussion of the relationship between the cognitive properties of the individuals performing a task and the cognitive properties of the system in which they participate.

Chapter 4, "The Organization of Team Performances," moves the boundaries of the unit of analysis even further out to consider the cognitive properties of the team as a whole. Here I note some of the problems that are encountered when cognitive activities are distributed across the members of a group. It is not the case that two or more heads are always better than one. This chapter describes the structures and processes involved in the group performance of the navigation task. The first section follows through on the application of Marr's concepts of computation to the navigation activity and discusses the properties of the activity as an explicitly computational system. The second section presents a problem in work organization encountered by the navigation team and shows why it is often difficult to apply the concepts that organize individual action to the organization of group action. The final section shows how the members of the navigation team form a flexible connective tissue that maintains the propagation of representational state in the face of a range of potentially disruptive events.

Chapter 5, "Communication," continues the theme of chapter 4 but looks at communication in more detail. It asks: How is it that patterns of communication could produce particular cognitive properties in a group? The chapter begins with a discussion of features of communication observed in the navigation team and their effects on the Team's computational properties. These observations lead to some simple hypotheses about the ways in which patterns of communication might affect the computational properties of a group. These hypotheses are explored using a computer simulation of communities of connectionist networks. The simulations lead to the surprising conclusion that more communication is not always better.

Chapters 6–8 concern learning or change in the organization of cognitive systems at several scales.

Chapter 6, "The Context of Learning," is a bridge between the descriptions of ongoing operations provided by the previous chapters and the descriptions of changes in the nature of ongoing operations provided by the following chapters. It describes the context in which novice navigators become experts. This chapter is an attempt to examine both the work that the system does in order to scaffold learning by practitioners and the opportunities for the development of new knowledge in the context of practice.

Whereas in chapter 6 I deal with the observable contexts surrounding learning, in chapter 7, "Learning in Context," I try to dissolve the boundaries of the skin and present navigation work as a system of interactions among media both inside and outside the individual. I look at learning or conceptual change as a kind of adaptation in a larger dynamical system. This chapter presents a functional notation and a framework for thinking about learning as local adaptation in a dynamic system of coordinations of representational media.

Chapter 8, "Organizational Learning," returns the focus to the larger unit of analysis: the team as a whole. It presents a case study of an incident in which the navigation team was forced to adapt to changes in its information environment. The analysis presented here examines a particular incident in which the microstructure of the development of the navigation practice can be seen clearly. It is an attempt to show the details of the kinds of processes that must be the engines of cultural change.

Chapter 9, "Cultural Cognition," attempts to pull the preceding chapters together into a coherent argument about the relationships of culture and cognition as they occur in the wild. I attempt first to illustrate the costs of ignoring the cultural nature of cognition. I argue that a new framework is needed to understand what is most characteristically human about human cognition. In order to construct a new framework, the old one must be deconstructed. I therefore provide two readings of the history of cognitive science: a history as seen by the proponents of the currently dominant paradigm and a rereading of the history of cognitive science from a sociocultural perspective. The differences between these two readings highlight a number of problems in contemporary cognitive science and give new meanings to some of the familiar events in its history.

Cognition in the Wild

1 Welcome Aboard

Narrative: A Crisis

After several days at sea, the U.S.S. *Palau* was returning to port, making approximately 10 knots in the narrow channel between Ballast Point and North Island at the entrance to San Diego Harbor. In the pilothouse or navigation bridge, two decks above the flight deck, a junior officer had the conn (i.e., was directing the steering of the ship), under the supervision of the navigator. The captain sat quietly in his chair on the port side of the pilothouse watching the work of the bridge team. Morale in the pilothouse had sagged during two frustrating hours of engineering drills conducted just outside the mouth of the harbor but was on the rise now that the ship was headed toward the pier. Some of the crew talked about where they should go for dinner ashore and joked about going all the way to the pier at 15 knots so they could get off the ship before nightfall.

The bearing recorder had just given the command "Stand by to mark time 3 8" and the fathometer operator was reporting the depth of the water under the ship when the intercom erupted with the voice of the engineer of the watch: "Bridge, Main Control. I am losing steam drum pressure. No apparent cause. I'm shutting my throttles." Moving quickly to the intercom, the conning officer acknowledged: "Shutting throttles, aye." The navigator moved to the captain's chair, repeating: "Captain, the engineer is losing steam on the boiler for no apparent cause." Possibly because he realized that the loss of steam might affect the steering of the ship, the conning officer ordered the rudder amidships. As the helmsman spun the wheel to bring the rudder angle indicator to the centerline, he answered the conning officer: "Rudder amidships, aye sir." The captain began to speak, saying "Notify," but the engineer was back on the intercom, alarm in his voice this time, speaking rapidly, almost shouting: "Bridge, Main Control, I'm going to secure number two boiler at this time. Recommend you drop the anchor!" The captain had been stopped in mid-sentence by the blaring intercom, but before the engineer could finish speaking the captain said, in a loud but cool voice, "Notify the bosun." It is standard procedure on large ships to have an anchor prepared to drop in case the ship loses its ability to maneuver while in restricted waters. With the propulsion plant out, the bosun, who was standing by with a crew forward ready to drop the anchor, was notified that he might be called into action. The falling intonation of the captain's command gave it a cast of resignation or perhaps boredom and made it sound entirely routine.

In fact, the situation was anything but routine. The occasional cracking voice, a muttered curse, or a perspiration-soaked shirt on this cool spring afternoon told the real story: the *Palau* was not fully under control, and careers and possibly lives were in jeopardy.

The immediate consequences of this event were potentially grave. Despite the crew's correct responses, the loss of main steam put the ship in danger. Without steam, it could not reverse its propeller—the only way to slow a large ship efficiently. The friction of the water on the ship's hull will eventually reduce its speed, but the *Palau* would coast for several miles before coming to a stop. The engineering officer's recommendation that the anchor be dropped was not appropriate. Since the ship was still traveling at a high rate of speed, the only viable option was to attempt to keep the ship in the deep water of the channel and coast until it had lost enough speed to safely drop anchor.

Within 40 seconds of the report of loss of steam pressure, the steam drum was exhausted. All steam-turbine-operated machinery came to a halt, including the turbine generators that produce the ship's electrical power. All electrical power was lost throughout the ship, and all electrical devices without emergency power backup ceased to operate. In the pilothouse a high-pitched alarm sounded for a few seconds, signaling an under-voltage condition for one piece of equipment. Then the pilothouse fell eerily silent as the electric motors in the radars and other devices spun down and stopped. Just outside the navigation bridge, the port wing pelorus operator watched the gyrocompass card in his pelorus swing wildly and then return to its original heading. He called in to the bearing recorder standing at the chart table: "John, this gyro just went nuts." The bearing recorder acknowledged the comment and told the pelorus operator that a breakdown was in progress: "Yeah, I know, I know, we're havin' a casualty."

Because the main steering gear is operated with electric motors, the ship now not only had no way to arrest its still-considerable forward motion; it also had no way to quickly change the angle of its rudder. The helm does have a manual backup system, located in a compartment called aftersteering in the stern of the ship: a worm-gear mechanism powered by two men on bicycle cranks. However, even strong men working hard with this mechanism can change the angle of the massive rudder only very slowly.

Shortly after the loss of power, the captain said to the navigator, who was the most experienced conning officer on board, "OK, Gator, I'd like you to take the conn." The navigator answered "Aye, sir" and, turning away from the captain, announced: "Attention in the pilothouse. This is the navigator. I have the conn." As required, the quartermaster of the watch acknowledged ("Quartermaster, aye") and the helmsman reported "Sir, my rudder is amidships." The navigator had been looking out over the bow of the ship, trying to detect any turning motion. He answered the helmsman: "Very well. Right 5 degrees rudder." Before the helmsman could reply, the navigator increased the ordered angle: "Increase your rudder right 10 degrees." (The rudder angle indicator on the helm station has two parts; one shows the rudder angle that is ordered and the other the actual angle of the rudder.) The helmsman spun the wheel, causing the indicator of the desired rudder angle to move to the right 10 degrees, but the indicator of the actual rudder angle seemed not to move at all. "Sir, I have no helm sir!" he reported.

Meanwhile, the men on the cranks in aftersteering were straining to move the rudder to the desired angle. Without direct helm control, the conning officer acknowledged the helmsman's report and sought to make contact with aftersteering by way of one of the phone talkers on the bridge: "Very well. Aftersteering, Bridge." The navigator then turned to the helmsman and said "Let me know if you get it back." Before he could finish his sentence, the helmsman responded, "I have it back, sir." When the navigator acknowledged the report, the ship was on the right side of the channel but heading far to the left of the desired course. "Very well, increase your rudder to right 15." "Aye sir. My rudder is right 15 degrees. No new course given." The navigator acknowledged—"Very well"—and then, looking out over the bow, whispered "Come on, damn it, swing!" Just then, the starboard wing pelorus operator spoke on the phone circuit: "John, it looks like we're gonna hit this buoy over here." The bearing recorder had been concentrating on the chart and hadn't quite heard. "Say again" he requested. The starboard wing pelorus operator leaned over the railing of his platform to watch the buoy pass beneath him. It moved quickly down the side of the ship, staying just a few feet from the hull. When it appeared that the *Palau* would not hit the buoy, the starboard wing pelorus operator said "Nothin' "; that ended the conversation. The men inside never knew how close they had come. Several subsequent helm commands were answered with "Sir, I have no helm." When asked by the captain how he was doing, the navigator, referring to their common background as helicopter pilots, quipped "First time I ever dead-sticked a ship, captain." (To "dead-stick" an aircraft is to fly it after the engine has died.) Steering a ship requires fine judgements of the ship's angular velocity. Even if helm response was instantaneous, there would still be a considerable lag between the time a helm command was given and the time when the ship's response to the changed rudder angle was first detectable as the movement of the bow with respect to objects in the distance. Operating with this manual system, the navigator did not always know what the actual rudder angle was, and could not know how long to expect to wait to see if the ordered command was having the desired effect. Because of the slowed response time of the rudder, the navigator ordered more extreme rudder angles than usual, causing the *Palau* to weave erratically from one side of the channel to the other.

Within 3 minutes, the diesel-powered emergency generators were brought on line and electrical power was restored to vital systems throughout the ship. Control of the rudder was partially restored, but remained intermittent for an additional 4 minutes. Although the ship still could not control its speed, it could at least now keep itself in the dredged portion of the narrow channel. On the basis of the slowing over the first 15 minutes after the casualty, it became possible to estimate when and where the *Palau* would be moving slowly enough to drop anchor. The navigator conned the ship toward the chosen spot.

About 500 yards short of the intended anchorage, a sailboat took a course that would lead it to cross close in front of the *Palau*. Normally the *Palau* would have sounded five blasts with its enormous horn to indicate disagreement with the actions taken by the other vessel. However, the *Palau*'s horn is a steam whistle, and without steam pressure it will not sound. The Navigation Department has among its equipment a small manual foghorn, basically a bicycle pump with a reed and a bell. The navigator remembered this piece of gear and instructed the keeper of the deck log to leave his post, find the manual horn, descend two levels to the flight deck, take the horn out to the bow, and sound the five warning blasts. The keeper of the deck log ran from the pilothouse, carrying a walkie-talkie to maintain communication with the bridge. The captain grabbed the microphone for the flight deck's public address system and asked "Can you hear me on the flight deck?" Men below on the deck turned and waved up at the pilothouse. "Sailboat crossing *Palau*'s bow be advised that I am not ... I have no power. You cross at your own risk. I have no power." By this time, the hull of the sailboat had disappeared under the bow of the ship and only its sails were visible from the pilothouse. In the foreground, the men on the flight deck were now running to the bow to watch the impending collision. Meanwhile, the keeper of the deck log had run down two flights of stairs, emerged from the base of the island, and begun sprinting across the nearly 100 yards that lay between the island and the bow. Before he was halfway to his goal, it was clear that by the time he would reach the bow the signal from the horn would be meaningless. The navigator turned to a junior officer who was holding a walkie-talkie and exclaimed "Just tell him to put the sucker down and hit it five times!" The message was passed, and the five feeble blasts were sounded from the middle of the flight deck. There is no way to know whether the signal was heard by the sailboat, which by then was directly ahead of the *Palau* and so close that only the tip of its mast was visible from the pilothouse. A few seconds later, the sailboat emerged, still sailing, from under the starboard bow. The keeper of the deck log continued to the bow to take up a position there in case other warnings were required.

Twenty-five minutes after the engineering casualty and more than 2 miles from where the wild ride had begun, the *Palau* was brought to anchor at the intended location in ample water just outside the bounds of the navigation channel.

The safe arrival of the *Palau* at anchor was due in large part to the exceptional seamanship of the bridge crew, especially the navigator. But no single individual on the bridge acting alone—neither the captain nor the navigator nor the quartermaster chief supervising the navigation team—could have kept control of the ship and brought it safely to anchor. Many kinds of thinking were required to perform this task. Some of them were happening in parallel, some in coordination with others, some inside the heads of individuals, and some quite clearly both inside and outside the heads of the participants.

This book is about the above event and about the kind of system in which it took place. It is about human cognition—especially human cognition in settings like this one, where the problems that individuals confront and the means of solving them are culturally structured and where no individual acting alone is entirely responsible for the outcomes that are meaningful to the society at large.

Gaining access to this field site required me, as an ethnographer, to make three journeys at once. In this first chapter I will try to weave them together, for the reader will also have to make these journeys mentally in order to understand the world of military ship navigation. The first is a journey through physical space from my home and my usual workplace to the navigation bridge of the *Palau*. This journey took me through many gates, as I moved from the street to the military base, to the ship, and within the ship to the navigation bridge. I will try to convey the spatial organization of the setting in which navigation is performed. The second journey is a trip through social space in which I moved from the civilian social world past the ship's official gatekeepers into the social organization of the Navy, and then to the ship's Navigation Department. This journey closely parallels the journey through physical space because space is so often used as an element of social organization. As the spatial journey took me to regions with narrower and narrower boundaries, so the social journey leads us through successively narrower levels of social organization. The third journey is a movement through conceptual space, from the world of everyday spatial cognition into the technical world of navigation. This third journey does not really begin until I near the end of the other two.

Through the Main Gate

A crisp salute from a young marine in dress uniform at the main gate's guard shack marked the transition from the "street" to the "base"—from the civilian realm to the military. The base is a place of close-cropped haircuts and close-cropped lawns. Here nature and the human form are controlled, arranged, disciplined, ready to make a good impression. In boot camp inductee's credo is: "If it moves, salute it. If it doesn't move, pick it up. If you can't pick it up, paint it white." The same mindset imposes an orderliness and a predictability on both the physical space and the social world of the military base.

As a civilian employee of the Navy, I was encouraged to occasionally ride a ship in order to better understand the nature of the "operational" world. But being encouraged by my own organization to ride a ship and being welcomed by the crew are two different things. From the perspectives of the people running a ship, there may be little to gain from permitting a civilian on board. Civilians, who are often ignorant of shipboard conventions, may require some tending to keep them out of trouble. They take up living space, which on many ships is at a premium, and if they do not have appropriate security clearances they may have to be escorted at all times.

The Ship

The *Palau* is an amphibious helicopter transport. Its warfare mission is to transport marines across the seas and then deliver them to the battlefields in the 25 helicopters that are carried on board. The helicopters also bring troops back to the ship, which has a small hospital and a complete operating theater. Ships of this class are often mistaken for true aircraft carriers of the sort that carry jet planes. As is the case with true aircraft carriers, the hull is capped by a large flat flight deck which creates an overhang on all sides of the ship. But this flight deck is only 592 feet long, just over half the length of a carrier deck and much too small to handle fixed-wing jets. About halfway between the bow and the stern, jutting up out of the smooth expanse of the flight deck on the starboard rail, stands a four-story structure called the island. The island occupies the rightmost 20 feet of the flight deck, which is about 100 feet wide. The ship extends 28 feet below the surface of the water and weighs 17,000 tons empty. It is pushed through the water by a single propeller driven by a 22,000-horsepower steam turbine engine.

Originally, the ships of the *Palau*'s class were planned to have been almost 200 feet longer and to have two propulsion plants and two propellers. However, budget cuts in the early 1960s led to a hasty redesign. In the original design, the off-center weight of the steel island was to be balanced by the second propulsion plant.

Unfortunately, the redesign failed to take into account the decrease in righting moment caused by the deletion of the second engine. When the hull that is now the *Palau* was launched, it capsized! It was refloated, and the steel island was replaced with an aluminum one. The ship was renamed and put into service. The aluminum island is attached to the steel deck with steel bolts. In a wet and salty environment, this forms an electrolyte that causes corrosion of the attachment points between the island and the deck. There is a standing joke among those who work in the island that someday, in a big beam swell, the ship will roll to starboard and the island will simply topple off the deck into the sea.

Two levels above the flight deck in the island is the navigation bridge. Also in the island are the air operations office, from which the helicopters are controlled, and a flag bridge where an admiral and his staff can work. The top of the island bristles with radar antennae.

The Gator Navy and the Other Navies

When I first went aboard the *Palau* it was tied up at pier 4 with several other amphibious ships. A frigate and a destroyer were tied up to an adjacent pier, but they are part of another navy within the Navy. Membership in these navies is an important component of naval identity.

Troop transport is not considered a glamorous job in the Navy. The *Palau* is part of what is called the *amphibious fleet*, the portion of the fleet that delivers marines to battlegrounds on land. The amphibious fleet is also known somewhat derogatorily as the "gator navy." The nickname is apparently derived from a reference to that amphibious reptile, the alligator. While the alligator is not a prototypical amphibian, its aggressiveness may be important in Navy culture; "salamander navy" or "frog navy" might be too disparaging.

The aviation community (the "airdales") claims to be the highest-status branch of the Navy. Most others would say that the submarine fleet (the "nukes") comes next, although the submariners consider themselves a breed apart. (They have a saying that there are only two kinds of ships in the navy: submarines and targets.) Then comes the surface fleet (the "black shoes"). Within each of these groups are subgroupings, which are also ranked. In the surface fleet the ranking descends from surface combatants (cruisers, destroyers, and frigates) to aircraft carriers, then the amphibious fleet, and finally tenders and supply ships.

While from the civilian point of view a sailor may be a sailor, in the Navy these distinctions mark important subcultural identities. The perceived differences are based on many factors, including the "glamor" of the expected mission, the sophistication of the equipment, the destructive potential, the stringency of requirements for entry into each area, the quality and extent of the training provided to the members of each community, and the general sense of the quality of the people involved. For a surface warfare officer who hopes to make a career out of the Navy and rise to a high rank, it is not good to be assigned to an amphibious ship for too long.

Ships that carry aircraft and air crewmen present a special situation with respect to these groups. Because they have aircraft they have members of the aviation community aboard, but because they are ships they must have members of the surface community aboard. The commanding officer of an aircraft carrier is always a member of the air community—a measure of the notion in the navy that the air wing is the *raison d'être* of a ship that carries aircraft. The friction between the air community and the surface community may be manifested in subtle and not-so-subtle ways. If members of the air community account for the majority of the high-ranking positions on a ship, junior surface warfare officers may complain that junior "airdales" are given more opportunities for qualification and advancement. An amphibious transport with an air wing is an even more complicated situation. Here members of the surface and air groups interact. And when marines are aboard an amphibious ship, there is also sometimes friction between the sailors and the marines.

These patterns of differentiation are present at all levels of organization in the military, from the broadest of interservice rivalries to distinctions between the occupants of adjacent spaces on the ship. Such effects are present to some degree in many social organizations, but they are highly elaborated in the military. Much of the establishment of identity is expressed in propositions like this: "We are the fighting X's. We are proud of what we are and what we do. We are unlike any other group." The unspoken inference is "If you do something else, you cannot be quite as good as we are." Identities are also signaled by insignia and emblems of various kinds. In the officer ranks, breast insignia denote which navy one is in. Aviators wear wings, submariners wear dolphins, surface warfare officers wear cutlasses.

Within each part of the surface fleet, there are strong identities associated with specific ships. Ships have stirring nationalistic or patriotic mottoes, which are often inscribed on plaques, baseball caps, t-shirts, and coffee mugs. Many ships produce yearbooks. The bond among shipmates is strongest when they are off ship. There is less of an identification with the class of one's ship, but some classes of ship are considered more advanced (less obsolete) and more glamorous than others.

The military institutionalizes competition at all levels of organization. Individuals compete with one another, and teams of individuals are pitted against other teams. Ships compete in exercises, and branches of the military compete for funding and the opportunity to participate in combat. Aboard a ship this competitiveness manifests itself in a general opinion that "we in our space know what we are doing, but the people just on the other side of the bulkhead do not." These sentiments can arise in situations where the successful completion of some task relies on cooperation between individuals in different spaces. Sometimes the larger system may fail for reasons having to do with the interactions of the units rather than with any particular unit; still, each unit needs to attach blame somewhere, and the alleged incompetence of some other unit is the easiest and most understandable explanation.

Across the Brow

A sailor standing outside a guard shack glances at the identification badge of each person passing onto the pier. Walking onto a pier between two ships of the *Palau*'s class is like walking into a deep canyon with overhanging gray walls and a dirty concrete floor. The canyon is vaguely threatening. It is noisy, and the hulls of the ships seem to box in the whine of motors and the hiss of compressed air. There are trucks and cranes on the pier, and cables are strewn across the pier and suspended in space over the narrow band of greenish water between the pier and the hulls. Floating in the water between each ship and the pier are several crude rafts called "camels" and a work barge. The camels keep the hull of the ship far enough away from the pier so that the broad flight deck flaring out at the top of the hull does not overhang the pier.

To board the *Palau*, I climbed a sort of scaffold up a few flights of gray metal stairs to a gangplank (in Navy parlance, the *brow*) that reached from the top of the scaffold to a huge hole in the side of the ship. The hole was at the level of the hangar deck (also called the *main deck*), still several levels below the flight deck. At the top of the brow was a security desk where the officer of the deck (OOD) checked the identification cards of sailors departing from and returning to the ship. Sailors stepping aboard turned to face the stern of the ship, came to attention and saluted the ship's ensign (flag), which flew on a staff over the fantail and was thus not visible from the brow.

Before visiting the ship, I had been given the NPRDC Fleet visitor's guide of basic information, which included the following instructions for proper performance of the boarding ritual: "At the top of the brow or accommodation ladder, face aft toward the colors (national ensign) and pause at attention. Then turn to the OOD, pause briefly at attention, and say, 'Request permission to come aboard, Sir.' State your name, where you are from, the purpose of your visit and the person you wish to see." This little ritual is a symbolic pledge of allegiance to the ship before boarding. Visitors to the ship wait in limbo at the security desk, neither ashore nor officially aboard, while word of their arrival is sent to their onboard host. The actual permission to go aboard must have been arranged in advance.

The ship's official gatekeeper is normally the executive officer (abbreviated XO). The commanding officer, the executive officer, and the department heads form the primary administrative structure of the ship. Every ship in the Navy is organized into a number of departments. Each department is supervised by an officer. In large departments, the department head may supervise less senior officers, who in turn supervise the enlisted personnel who do virtually all the actual work on the ship. Before embarking, I was required to convince the XO that I had something to offer the navy and that I would not cause undue aggravation while aboard. In a brief and somewhat discouraging interview with the XO, it was agreed that if the navigator was willing to tolerate my presence in his department, I could come aboard and work with the navigation team.

After getting past the XO, I made a date to have lunch with the navigator. I met him in the officer's dining area (the *wardroom*), and during our discussion we discovered a shared past. While a cadet at the Naval Academy, the navigator had served as racing tactician aboard a particular racing sloop that had been donated to the academy. The sloop was subsequently sold to a friend of mine, and I had sailed aboard it as navigator and racing tactician for 8 years. The discovery of this extraordinary coincidence helped cement our friendship and secured the navigator's permission for my work aboard the *Palau*. With my prearranged permission to sail, and with the navigator's blessing, I waited at the security desk.

An escort at the security desk and led me through the huge dark cavern of the hangar deck. We detoured around several parked helicopters and skirted forklifts and pallets of materials. We ducked through a hatch in the wall of the hangar deck and began the climb up a series of narrow steep ladders to the navigation bridge. (On a ship, floors are called *decks*, walls are called *bulkheads* or *partitions*, corridors are called *passageways*, ceilings are called *overheads*, and stairs are called *ladders*.)

Reconciling the Chart and the World

Navigation is a collection of techniques for answering a small number of questions, perhaps the most central of which is "Where am I?"

What does the word 'where' mean in this question? When we say or understand or think where we are, we do so in terms of some representation of possible positions. "Where am I?" is a question about correspondences between the surrounding world and some representation of that world.

Where am I right now as I write this? I am at my desk, in my study. The window in front of me faces the garden; the door over there leads to the hallway that leads to the remainder of the house. My house is on the Pacific coast, north of the university. I'm on the western edge of the North American continent. I'm on the planet Earth circling a minor star in the outer portion of an arm of a spiral galaxy. In every one of these descriptions, there is a representation of space assumed. Each of these descriptions of my location has meaning only by virtue of the relationships between the location described and other locations in the representation of space implied by the description. This is an absolutely fundamental problem that must be solved by all mobile organisms.

Whether the map is internal or external, whether it is a mental image of surrounding space (on whatever scale and in whatever terms) or a symbolic description of the space on a piece of paper, I must establish the correspondence of map and territory in order to answer the question "Where am I?" One of the most exciting moments in navigation is making a landfall on an unfamiliar coast. If I am making a landfall on a high island or a mountainous coast, as I approach the land, I first see just the tops of mountains, then I see the lower slopes, then the hills, and finally the features on the shoreline itself. Now, where am I? Turning to my chart, I see that I had hoped to meet the coast just to the south of a major headland. Perhaps that big hill I can see across the water on the left is that headland. And perhaps that high peak off in the haze, inland, is this peak shown on the chart. Hmm, according to the chart it is only supposed to be 500 meters high. It seems far away and higher than that. Perhaps it is something else, something too far inland to be printed on the chart.

Through considerations like these, a navigator attempts to establish a coherent set of correspondences between what is visible in the world and what is depicted on a chart. Some charts even provide small profiles showing the appearance of prominent landmarks from particular sea-level vantage points. The same sort of task confronts any of us when, for example, we walk out of the back door of a theater onto an unfamiliar street. Which way am I facing? Where am I? The question is answered by establishing correspondences between the features of the environment and the features of some representation of that environment. When the navigator is satisfied that he has arrived at a coherent set of correspondences, he might look to the chart and say "Ah, yes; I am here, off this point of land." Now the navigator knows where he is. And it is in this sense that most of us feel we know where we are. We feel that we have achieved a reconciliation between the features we see in our world and a representation of that world. Things are not out of place. They are where we expect them to be. But now suppose someone asks a navigator "How far are we from the town at the head of that bay?" To answer that question, simply having a good sense of the correspondences between what one sees and what is depicted on some representation of the local space is not enough. Now more precision is required. To answer that question the navigator needs to have a more exact determination of where he is. In particular, he needs to have a sense of his location on a representation of space in a form that will permit him to compute the answer to the question. This is *position fixing*. It is what one does when just having a sense of reconciliation between the territory and the map is not enough.

Up the Ladder

From the hangar deck the escort led the way up three steep ladders in a narrow stairwell filled with fluorescent light, stale air, and the clang of hard shoes on metal steps. The decks of a ship are numbered starting with the main deck. On most ships, the main deck is defined as the "uppermost deck that runs the length of the ship." On ships that have a flight deck above a hangar deck (this includes aircraft carriers and amphibious helicopter transports such as the *Palau*) the hangar deck is the main deck. Immediately below the main deck is the second deck, and below that the third deck, and so on down to the hold. Above the main deck, the decks are designated "levels" and are numbered 01, 02, . . . , increasing in number with altitude. We stopped periodically on deck platforms to allow sailors going down to pass. Foot traffic on ships generally moves up and forward on the starboard side and down and aft on the port side. However, the layout of the hangar deck limits the number and location of ladders, and in order to shorten the route my escort was taking me against the traffic. We climbed into a small busy foyer, and through an open hatch I caught a breath of fresh air and a glimpse of the flight deck in the sun. Men in overalls were working on the hot, rough black surface. We continued upward, now climbing inside the narrow island. One ladder pitch above the flight deck we came to the 04 level. The door leading to the flag bridge, where an admiral and his staff would work, was chained and padlocked. One more ladder brought us to the 05 level.

Military Identities

The men and women in the military are divided into two broad social classes: *officer* and *enlisted*. An officer must have a college degree and is *commissioned* (authorized to act in command). In the Navy, members of both classes believe in the reality of differences between officers and enlisted personnel. The lowest-ranking officer is superior in the command structure to the highest-ranking enlisted person. The distinction between officers and enlisted is marked by uniforms, by insignia, and by a complex set of rituals. The simplest of these rituals is the salute, of course, but the courtesies to be extended by enlisted to officers include clearing a passageway on the approach of an officer and refraining from overtaking an officer on foot until permission has been granted.

Enlisted Rates and Ratings

Enlisted personnel are classified according to pay grade (called *rate*) and technical specialization (called *rating*). As Bearden and Wedertz (1978) explain: "A rating is a Navy job—a duty calling for certain skills and attitudes. The rating of engineman, for example, calls for persons who are good with their hands and are mechanically inclined. A paygrade (such as E-4, E-5, E-6) within a rating is called a rate. Thus an engineman third class (EN3) would have a rating of engineman, and a rate of third class petty officer. The term petty officer (PO) applies to anyone in paygrades E-4 through E-9. E-1s through E-3s are called non-rated personnel."

The enlisted naval career begins with what is basically a socialization period in which the recruit is indoctrinated into basic military policy and acquires the fundamental skills of a sailor. The rates through which a recruit passes in this phase are seaman recruit, seaman apprentice, and able-bodied seaman. Once socialized, a seaman learns the skills of a particular job specialization or rating. An enlisted person is considered a real member of a rating when he becomes a petty officer (see below). The enlisted personnel in the Navigation Department are members of the quartermaster rating. They have an insignia (a ship's wheel) and an identity distinct from other ratings. They are generally considered to be relatively intelligent, although not as smart as data processing specialists. For enlisted personnel, rating insignia denote occupational fields.

A petty officers is not a kind of commissioned officer (the type of officer referred to by the unmarked term 'officer'); the label 'petty officer' simply designates an enlisted person who is a practicing members of some rating. There are two major levels of petty officer, with three rates within each. One moves through the lowest of these levels while learning the skills of the speciality of the rating. One advances through petty officer third class, petty officer second class, and petty officer first class. A petty officer third class is a novice in the speciality and may perform low-level activities in concert with others or more autonomous functions "under instruction." A petty officer first class is expected to be fully competent in the rating.

The next step up in rank moves one to the higher of the enlisted rates and is usually the most important transition of an enlisted person's career. This is the move to chief petty officer (CPO). This change in status is marked by a ritual of initiation which is shrouded in secrecy. Just what happens at a chief's initiation is supposed to be known only by chiefs. However, much of what happens apparently makes for such good story telling that it cannot be kept entirely in confidence. It is "common knowledge" that these initiations frequently include hazing of the initiate, drunkenness, and acts of special license. Making chief means more than getting a bigger pay packet or supervising more people. Chiefs have their own berthing spaces (more private that general enlisted berthing) and their own mess (eating facility). On many ships the chief's mess is reputed to be better than that of the officers. Chiefs are also important because they are the primary interface between officers and enlisted personnel. Since they typically have from 12 to 20 years of experience in their speciality, they often take part in problem-solving sessions with the officers who are their supervisors. Some chief petty officers have a considerable amount of autonomy on account of their expertise (or, perhaps, their expertise relative to the supervising officer.) Chiefs frequently talk about having to "break in" a new officer, by which they mean getting a supervising officer accustomed to the fact that the chief knows more than the officer does and is actually in charge of the space and the people in it. Officers who directly supervise lower-level enlisted personnel risk undermining the chain of command and incurring the resentment of a chief who feels that his authority has been usurped. Once one has made chief, there are still higher enlisted rates to be attained. After approximately 20 years of service a competent person may make senior chief, and after perhaps 25 years of service (being now of about the same age as a captain) one may make master chief. That is normally the end of the line for an enlisted person. There are, however, some ranks that fall between enlisted and officer. A chief may elect to become a chief warrant officer or a limited duty officer (LDO). A chief who becomes an LDO is commissioned as an ensign and may begin to rise through the officer ranks. Few chiefs take this path. As one senior chief asked rhetorically, "Why would I want to go from the top of one career to the bottom of another?"

While an enlistee may have preferences for certain ratings, the choice of a rating is not entirely up to the enlistee. Aptitude-test scores are also used to place people in various specialities. The fact that people are screened contributes to widely held stereotypes concerning the intelligence of those in various ratings. For example, boiler technicians (BTs) and machinist's mates (MMs), who run a ship's propulsion plant and who may go weeks without seeing the light of day, are often the butt of jokes about their low intelligence. Data processing specialists, on the other hand, are generally thought to be bright. The ship, as a microcosm, manifests the same patterns of competing identities that are seen among the specialties in the Navy as a whole. From the point of view of the bridge personnel there may be little apparent difference between machinist's mates and boiler technicians, but down in the propulsion spaces the perceived differences are many. Machinist mates call boiler technicians "bilge divers," while boiler technicians call machinist's mates "flange heads." Mostly, this is good-natured teasing; name calling is a way of asserting one's own identity.

At all levels of organization we see attempts to establish identity by distinguishing oneself from the other groups. This is relevant to the discussion that follows because the dynamics of the relationships among the people engaged in the task of navigation are in part constrained by these identities.

Officer Ranks

Military officers are managers of personnel and resources. In general, their job is not to get their hands dirty, but to ensure that those who do get their hands dirty are doing the right things. Unlike enlisted persons, officers do not have narrowly defined specialities. An officer pursues a career in one of the broad areas described above: air, surface, or submarine warfare. Within that area, there are subspecialties such as engineering and tactics.

Officers are initially commissioned as ensigns. Ensigns have a tough lot. They are more visible than the lowest enlisted rates, and they certainly are given more responsibility, but often a "fresh-caught" ensign knows little more about the world of the ship than the seaman recruit.

Finding One's Way Around a Ship

A ship is a complicated warren of passages and compartments. Every frame and compartment is numbered with a code that indicates which deck it is on, whether it is to port or starboard of the centerline, and where it is in the progression from stem to stern. Navigating inside a ship can be quite confusing to a newcomer. Inside the ship, the cardinal directions are *forward* and aft, port and starboard, topside and below, and inboard and outboard; north, south, east and west are irrelevant. On large ships, orientation can be a serious problem. In the early 1980's the Navy sponsored a research project to work on wayfinding in ships.

The ship is composed of a number of neighborhoods. Some are workplaces, some are residential. Some are officially dedicated to recreation, others are unofficially recreational. The fantail on some classes of ships, for example, is a place to hang out. Officers' accommodations and eating facilities are in a section of the ship called "officer country." The chief petty officers have a similar area, called "CPO country." Enlisted personnel are supposed to enter these areas only when they are on official business. They are supposed to remove their hats when entering any compartment in these neighborhoods. Some passageways inside the ship are major thoroughfares; others are alleys or culs-de-sac. A visitor quickly learns to search out alternative pathways, because corridors are frequently closed for cleaning or maintenance.

On the 05 Level

As my escort and I arrived at a small platform on the 05 level, to the right was a floor-to-ceiling partition painted flat black. Behind the partition stood an exterior doorway that led out to the starboard wing bridge. The partition forms a "light trap" that prevents light from leaking out at night when the ship is running dark. To the left was a dark corridor that led to a similar doorway on the port side of the island. Above us, the ladder continued upward one more level to the signal bridge. Ahead lay a narrow passageway. Forward along the left side of the passageway were two doors. Behind the first was the captain's at-sea cabin. He has a nicely appointed quarters below, but he takes meals and sleeps in this cabin during operations that require him to stay near the bridge. The next door opened on the charthouse. At the end of the passageway, about 25 feet away, was a door that led to the navigation bridge or pilothouse.

The charthouse is headquarters for the Navigation Department. This small room, crowded with navigation equipment, two desks, a safe, and a chart table, enjoys a luxury shared by only a few spaces on the ship: a single porthole through which natural light may enter and mix with light from the fluorescent lamps overhead. The charthouse is one of several spaces under the control of the Navigation Department. Navigation personnel not only work in these spaces, they are also responsible for keeping them clean. Since the bridge is one of the main work areas of the ship's captain, it is thought to be especially important to keep it looking nice. While in port, Navigation personnel polish the brass on the bridge. Because the captain's at-sea cabin is adjacent to the charthouse, members of the Navigation Department tend to work more quietly there than they might in other parts of the ship. Since the average age of a sailor is under 20 years, a certain amount of playful horsing around is expected in many parts of the ship, but is not tolerated on the 05 level.

The Navigation Department is responsible for all of the spaces on the 05 level with the exception of the captain's at-sea cabin. It is also responsible for the secondary or auxiliary conning station ("Secondary Conn")—a completely redundant navigation bridge located in the bow, just under the forward edge of the flight deck. Secondary Conn is manned by the ship's executive officer and a complete navigation team whenever the ship is at general quarters (battle stations). This is done because the primary navigation bridge in the island is very vulnerable if the ship comes under attack. Modern anti-ship missiles home in on electromagnetic radiation. Because the radar antennae on the top of the island are the principal sources of such radiation on the ship, the island is the most likely part to be hit by a missile. If the primary navigation bridge is destroyed, the ship can be controlled from Secondary Conn under the command of the executive officer. Secondary Conn is a space assigned to the Navigation Department and is a duty station for Navigation personnel, but it will be of little interest to us with regard to the normal practice of navigation. The ship's extensive library of charts and navigation forms is stored in this space.

The Navigation Department is supervised by the Navigator. At the time the observations reported here were made, the *Palau*'s Navigation Department consisted of the Navigator and seven enlisted men. The title "Navigator" refers to the position as head of the Navigation Department rather than to the officer's technical speciality. Though it is expected that an officer who serves as Navigator aboard any ship will know enough about navigation to supervise the working of the Navigation Department, Navigators seldom do any navigating themselves.

The work of the Navigation Department is carried out by enlisted personnel of the quartermaster rating under the direction of the Assistant Navigator (a quartermaster chief).

Navigating Large Ships

While a naval vessel is underway, a plot of its past and projected movements is maintained at all times. Such complete records are not always kept aboard merchant vessels and are not absolutely essential to the task of navigating a ship in restricted waters. It is possible for an experienced pilot to "eyeball" the passage and make judgements concerning control of the ship without the support of the computations that are carried out on the chart. Aboard naval vessels, however, such records are always kept—primarily for reasons of safety, but also for purposes of accountability. Should there be a problem, the crew will be able to show exactly where the ship was and what it was doing at the time of the mishap. Day and night, whenever a ship is neither tied to a pier nor at anchor, navigation computations are performed as frequently as is required to ensure safe navigation. During a long passage, navigation activities may be performed almost continuously for weeks or even months on end. Most of the time the work of navigation is conducted by one person working alone. However, when a ship leaves or enters port, or operates in any other environment where maneuverability is restricted, the computational requirements of the task may exceed the capabilities of any individual; then the navigation duties are carried out by a team.

The *conning officer* is nominally responsible for the decisions about the motion of the ship, but for the most part he does not make the actual decisions. Usually, such decisions are made by the Navigation Department and passed to the conning officer as recommendations, such as "Recommend coming right to 0 1 7 at this time." The conning officer considers the recommendation in the light of the ship's overall situation. If the recommendation is appropriate, he will act upon it by giving orders to the *helmsman*, who steers the ship, or to the *leehelmsman*, who controls the engines. At all times when the ship may have need of navigational information, someone from the Navigation Department is at work and ready to do whatever is required. The navigation team performs in a variety of configurations, with as few as one and as many as six members of the Navigation Department working together. In every configuration there is one individual, designated the *quartermaster of the watch*, who is responsible for the quality of the work performed and who serves as the department's official interface with other departments aboard ship.

Navigation is a specialized task which, in its ordinary operation, confronts a limited set of problems, each of which has a well-understood structure. The problem that confronts a navigator is usually not one of figuring out how to process the information in order to get an answer; that has already been worked out. The problem, in most instances, is simply to use the existing tools and techniques to process the information gathered by the system and to produce an appropriate evaluation of the ship's situation or an appropriate recommendation about how the ship should proceed in order to get where it is supposed to go.

The navigation activity is event-driven in the sense that the navigation team must keep pace with the movements of the ship. In contrast with many other decision-making settings, when something goes wrong aboard a ship, it is not an option to quit the task, to set it aside momentarily, or to start over from scratch. The work must go on. In fact, the conditions under which the task is most difficult are usually the conditions under which its correct and timely performance is most important.

The Researcher's Identity

Having said something about how naval personnel establish their own identities, I should also say something about how they and I negotiated an identity for me.

In the course of this work I made firsthand observations of navigation practice at sea aboard two aircraft carriers (the *Constellation* and the *Ranger*) and two ships of the amphibious fleet (the one known here as the *Palau* and the *Denver*). Aboard the aircraft carriers, I worked both on the navigation bridge and in the combat information center. I made a passage from San Diego to Seattle, with several stops, aboard the *Denver.* I also interviewed members of the Navigation Departments of five other ships (the *Enterprise*, the *Beleau Wood*, the *Carl Vinson*, the *Cook*, and the *Berkeley*) and had a number of informal conversations with other navigation personnel.

The events reported here come mainly from operations in the Southern California Operations (SoCalOps) area aboard the *Palau*. I also worked with the crew while the ship was in port. I logged a total of 11 days at sea over a period of 4 months. First came a week-long trip during which I observed the team, got the members used to my presence, and got to know them. During this trip, I only took notes and made a few still photos and audio tape recordings of navigation tasks and interviews with crewmen. On a later trip, I mounted a video camera with a wide-angle lens in the overhead above the chart table in the pilothouse. I placed a stereo tape recorder on the chart table, with one channel capturing the ambient noise and conversation of the pilothouse. The other channel I wired into the sound-powered phone circuit. Because the chief was both plotting positions and supervising the work of the navigation team, I wanted to be sure to capture what he said. I therefore wired him with a remote transmitter and a lavaliere microphone. I used this signal to feed the audio track on the video recording. Thus, I had one video track and three audio tracks to work with.

During my time at sea, I took a normal watch rotation. I appeared on the bridge on one occasion or another during every watch period, including the one from midnight to 4 a.m. I was accorded privileges appropriate to the military equivalent of my civilian Government Service rank: lieutenant commander. I was assigned a cabin in "officer country," took my meals in the officer's mess, and spent my waking off-watch time either in the charthouse with the navigation crew or in the wardroom with officers.

As to what they thought of me, one must begin with the understanding that for military folk the military/civilian distinction stands just below the friend/foe distinction as an element of the establishment of identity. A civilian aboard a ship is an outsider by definition. It was important that the navigator treated me as a colleague and friend, and that the captain normally addressed me as Doctor when we met. Many of the members of the navigation team were also aware that I had lunched at least once in the captain's quarters, an honor reserved for visiting VIPs.

Some evidence of what the crew thought of me is available in the video record. Early on, a number of nervous jokes were made on camera about the dangerous potential of the videotaping. In the first 5 minutes of videotaping with this crew, the assistant navigator told the navigator "Everything you say around me is getting recorded for history, for your court-martial."

On more than one occasion while he was away from the chart table, the chief of the navigation team explained my work to other members. He apparently forgot that he was being recorded. I discovered these comments weeks later while doing transcription. During my second at sea period, the chief went into the charthouse to check on the fathometer. The fathometer operator asked who I was. The conversation proceeded as follows:

Chief: He's studying navigation on big ships. He's the guy, he makes computer programs for teaching stuff. Like they got a big computer program thing they use in ASW school to teach maneuvering boards. It's all computerized. He is the one that makes it. He is the one who makes things like that. He's a psychologist and anthropologist. Works for the navy. He's a Ph.D. Makes all kinds of strange things.

Fathometer operator: He makes all kinds of strange money too.

Chief: Yeah, does he? He knows what he is doing. He's swift. He just sits and watches and records everything you're doing. Then he puts it all in data, then he starts putting it in a program. Figuring out what to do, I don't know.

My most intensive data collection was carried out on a four-day exercise during which the *Palau* left port, steamed around the operations area for two days, reentered port, and anchored in the harbor overnight. The next morning the ship left port again for another day of exercises. Finally, it entered port again and returned to its berth at the 32nd Street Naval Station. It was during the last entry to port that the crisis reported in the opening pages of this book occurred. The quality of the recording from the sound-powered phone circuit was poor until I discovered a better way to capture the signal on the last entry to port. The two entries to and exits from port were recorded from the time Sea and Anchor Detail was set until the navigation team stood down. This procedure produced video and audio tape recordings of about 8 hours of team activity. Additional recordings were made at various times during Standard Steaming Watch. In addition to the video and audio records, I took notes during these events of any aspects of the situation that I noticed that could not be fully captured on the tapes. Even with the wide-angle lens, the video camera captured only the surface of the chart table. This permitted me to identify features on the chart and even to know which buttons of a calculator were pressed, but it meant that many events of interest were not captured on tape because they occurred out of camera range.

Transcribing the tape recordings was a very difficult process. At times there were four or more conversations happening simultaneously in the pilothouse. To make matters worse, ships are noisy places. There are many kinds of equipment on the bridge that create background noises. The bosun's mate pipes various announcements from a station just aft and inboard of the chart table, and his whistle blowing and his public-address messages sometimes drown out all other sounds. Helicopters may be operating on the flight deck or in the air just outside the pilothouse. It was often necessary to listen to each of the three audio tracks separately in order to reconstruct what was being said, and still in many cases the full content of the tapes cannot be deciphered. Because of the placement of the microphones, however, the coverage of the verbal behavior of the members of the navigation team was uniformly good. Only rarely was it impossible to determine what was being said with respect to the navigation task.

I did much of the transcription myself, for three reasons. First, this is a technical domain with many specialized words in it. We know that hearing is itself a constructive process and that ambiguous inputs are often unconsciously reconstructed and cleaned up on the basis of context. Lacking context, other transcribers could not hear what I could hear in the tapes. For example, an untrained transcriber without expectations about what might be said during an anchoring detail transcribed "thirty fathoms on deck" as "thirty phantoms on deck." Navigationese is a foreign language to most people, and quality transcription cannot be expected from a transcriber who is not fluent in it. Second, since there were many speakers, the fact that I knew them personally helped me distinguish the identity of speakers where it was not clearly evident from the content of a statement who was speaking. Third, and most important, there is no better way to learn what is actually in a recording than to listen to it the many times that one must in order to produce a good transcription. (Over a period of about a year, one transcription assistant did develop enough familiarity with the subject to provide usable transcriptions.)

The fact that listening is reconstructive introduces the possibility of distortions in the data driven by my expectations. I will attempt to deal with that by making the ethnographic grounds for my interpretations explicit.

In the pilothouse I tried not to participate, but only observe. On only one occasion did I intervene, and that was a case in which I felt that by failing to speak I would put a number of people in serious danger. My intervention was a brief *sotto voce* comment to the navigator, who resolved the situation without indicating my role in it.

It was clear that I knew more about the theory of navigation than the members of the crew I was studying with the exception of the ship's navigator and the quartermaster chief. Of course, knowing the theory and knowing the nature of the practice in a particular setting are two quite different things. In no case did I know more about an individual's relation to the practice of navigation than that individual. Still, this is an unusual situation for an ethnographer. The web of constraints provided by cultural practices is important both to the people doing the task and to the researcher. For the performers, it means that the universe of possible activities is closely bounded by the constraints. For the researcher, the activities that are observed are interpreted in terms of their reflection of the constraints. My many years of studying and practicing navigation made me a particular sort of instrument, one in which the constraints of the domain were present. My interpretations of the actions of the members of the navigation team were informed by many of the same constraints that were guiding their behaviors. But there was more. Because I attempted to continually make these constraints explicit, and to conceive of them in a computational sense as well as in the operational sense required of the navigation team, my interpretations were not simply those of a native.

A few months of field work is, for an anthropologist, a rather a short visit. Many aspects of the military culture go unreported here because I am not confident about their organization and meaning on the basis of such a short exposure. I did have 5 years of employment as a civilian scientist working for the Navy, and that gave me many opportunities to observe aspects of military organization. The coverage of navigation practice is adequate, I think, because of the opportunity on my second at-sea period to videotape the navigation operations on the bridge.

How different would the story be if the observations had been made aboard another ship? I do not believe that the culture would permit it to be very different. The information processed by the navigation team may move more or less efficiently, and the individual quartermasters may have better or poorer relationships with one another, but the tasks remain, and the means of performing the tasks are standardized throughout the fleet. The crews of different ships may meet the requirements of navigation more or less capably, but they must nevertheless solve these particular tasks in the limited number of ways possible.

In fact, I made observations aboard several ships, and my colleague, Colleen Siefert, did so on yet another ship. The differences we observed across ships were minor. The ship Colleen observed had more quartermasters available and was therefore able to organize its navigation team in a slightly different way; that however, does not present a challenge to my framework or to my basic descriptions of the nature of the cognition at either the individual or the group level.

On the Bridge: Standard Steaming Watch

At the forward end of the 05 level's passageway is the door to the navigation bridge or pilothouse. It is here that the most important part of the navigation work is done. The pilothouse occupies the forward 18 feet of the 05 level of the island (see figure 1.1). Outward-canting windows extend from chest height to the overhead on both sides and the front of the pilothouse. The windows on the port side and forward overlook the flight deck. All work tables are mounted on substantial bases on a light greenish linoleum floor. The walls, the cabinets, and the equipment stands are thickly coated in light gray paint. The overhead is flat black and tangled with pipes and cables, their identities stenciled on them in white. The polished brass of ship's wheel and the controls for the engine-order telegraph stand out in the otherwise drab space.

The activities of the Navigation Department revolve around a computational ritual called the *fix cycle*. The fix cycle has two major parts: determining the present position of the ship and projecting its future position. The fix cycle gathers various bits of information about the ship's location in the world and brings them together in a representation of the ship's position. The chart is the positional consciousness of the ship: the navigation fix is the ship's internal representation of its own location.

When I first made it known to a ship's navigator that I wanted to know how navigation work was performed, he referred me to the Navigation Department Watch Standing Procedures, a document that describes the watch configurations. "It's all in here," he said.

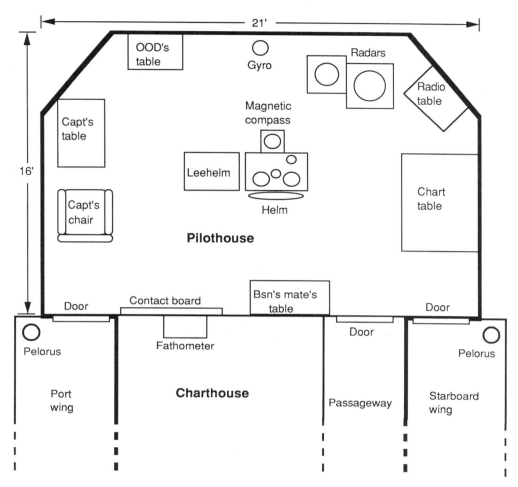

Figure 1.1 A plan view of the pilothouse and the charthouse. The members of the navigation team do most of their work at the chart table, on the wings, and in the charthouse. The heavy line represents the exterior skin of the ship. Up in the diagram is forward on the ship.

"You can read this and save yourself the trouble of standing watch." Of course it is not all in there, but the normative description in the Procedures is not a bad place to start. It is the Navigation Department's "official" version of the organization of its work. This document is one of many symbolic forms in which navigators "represent themselves to themselves and to one another" (Geertz 1983).

Because the procedures refer to objects and places that are part of shipboard navigation culture, understanding these procedures will require us to explore the environment of navigation. While conducting this exploration, we should keep in mind that the descriptions of navigation work that appear in a ship's documents and in various navigation publications must be taken as data rather than analysis.

In this section I will attempt to use the ship's documents as a guide to the task of navigation. The specifications presented in the Watch Standing Procedures describe actions to be taken and equipment and techniques to be used. First I will present the normative descriptions and try to provide the sort of background information that might be provided by a native of the navigation culture, in the hope that this will make these things meaningful to a reader who is not a practitioner of the art. Later I will present an analysis of the procedures, tools, and techniques that will be grounded in information-processing theory rather than in the world of ship navigation.

The *Palau*'s normal steaming watch procedures are introduced as follows:

While in normal steaming condition at sea, the following watch procedures will be adhered to as closely as possible, modified as necessary by situations beyond the control of the watch stander.

In normal steaming, a single quartermaster is responsible for all the navigation duties. The procedures described in the document are taken seriously, although it is recognized that it may not be possible to execute them as described in all circumstances. The normative procedures are an ideal that is seldom achieved, or seldom achieved as described.

The Primary Duty of the QMOW

When the Navigation Department is providing navigation services to the ship, a particular quartermaster is designated as the quarter master of the watch (QMOW) at all times. According to the procedures,

The Primary Duty of the QMOW is the safe navigation of the ship. To this end he shall:

(a) Fix the position of the ship by any and all methods available.

(1) All fixes will be plotted.
(2) When information is available, a fix will be plotted at least every hour, when in open ocean transit.
(3) When within Visual or Radar sight of land, a fix will be plotted at least every fifteen minutes.
  (i) Visual bearings will take priority.
  (ii) Fill in with Radar as necessary.
(4) Fixes may be obtained from any combination of the following sources:
  (i) Visual bearings

(ii) Radar ranges
(iii) Radar bearings
(iv) Fathometer (line of soundings, bottom contouring, or guyout hopping)
(v)   NavSat
(vi) Omega
(vii) Celestial observations

(5) Fixes obtained from visual or radar sources will consist of at least three LOPs.

(b) Project the ship's track by dead reckoning to a sufficient length of time that any danger presented to the ship from land, shoals or other fixed dangers, or violation of international waters will be noticed well in advance of the ship actually standing into danger or departing legal/assigned waters.

Items a and b in this document describe the two main parts of the fix cycle: fixing the ship's position and projecting its track. The procedures of dead reckoning will be explained in detail in chapter 2. The plotted fix is a residue on the chart of a process that gathers and transforms information about the ship's position. A succession of fixes is both a history of the positions of the ship and a history of the workings of the process that produced the position information. The requirement that *all* fixes be plotted ensures a complete history of positions and provides certain opportunities to detect and correct faults in the process that creates the history. The interval between fixes is set to 60 minutes in open waters and no more than 15 minutes when the ship is in visual or radar contact with land. Near land, the ship may stand into danger more quickly than when in the open ocean. Sailors know that it is not the open ocean that sinks ships, it's all that hard stuff around the edges. The increased frequency of fixes near land is intended to ensure that dangers are anticipated and avoided. Visual bearings are given priority because they are the most accurate means of fixing position. The potential sources of position information are listed roughly in order of their accuracy and reliability.

The procedure states that fixes may be obtained from any combination of a number of sources. Let us briefly consider the nature of these sources and the kinds of information they contribute to fixing the position of the ship.

Sources of Information for Position Fixing

VISUAL BEARINGS
The simplest way of fixing position, and the one that will concern us most in this book, is by visual bearings. For this one needs a chart of the region around the ship and a way to measure the

direction (conventionally with respect to north) of the line of sight connecting the ship and some landmark on the shore. The direction of a landmark from the ship is called the landmark's *bearing*. Imagine the line of sight in space between the ship and a known landmark. Although we know that one end of the line is at the landmark and we know the direction of the line, we can't just draw a line on the chart that corresponds to the line of sight between ship and landmark, because we don't know where the other end of the line is. The other end of the line is where the ship is, and that is what we are trying to discover.

Suppose we draw a line on the chart starting at the location of the symbol for the landmark on the chart and extend it past where we think the ship is—perhaps off the edge of the chart if we are really unsure. We still don't know just where the ship is, but we do know it must have been somewhere on that line when the bearing was observed. Such a line is called a *line of position* (LOP). If we have another line of position, constructed on the basis of the direction of the line of sight to another known landmark, then we know that the ship is also on that line. If the ship was on both of these lines at the same time, the only place it can have been is where the lines intersect. The intersection of two lines of position uniquely constrains the location from which the observations were made. In practice, a third line of position with respect to another landmark is constructed. The three lines of position form a triangle, and the size of that triangle is an indication of the quality of the position fix. It is sometimes said that the navigator's level of anxiety is proportional to the size of the fix triangle.

The observations of visual bearings of the landmarks (direction with respect to north) are made with a special telescopic sighting device called an *alidade*. The true-north directional reference is provided by a *gyrocompass* repeater that is mounted under the alidade. A prism in the alidade permits the image of the gyrocompass's scale to be superimposed on the view of the landmark. (The view through such a sight is illustrated in figure 1.2.) The gyrocompass repeaters are located on the wings outside the bridge. Each one is mounted on a solid metal stand just tall enough to extend above the chest-high metal railing that bounds the wing.

The most direct access to the port wing from the chart table is through a door at the back of the pilothouse just behind the captain's chair. In cold weather, the captain of the *Palau* does not permit traffic through this door. The only other way to get from the

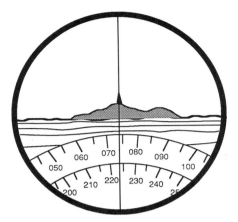

Figure 1.2 A view through an alidade. A prism inside the alidade superimposes the images of two compass scales onto whatever is seen through the telescopic sight. The inner scale is a gyrocompass repeater; the outer scale is fastened to the ship and indicates bearings relative to the ship's head.

port wing position to the chart table is to go aft on the wing to the hatch that leads to the island stairwell and then come forward through the interior passageway past the captain's at-sea cabin and the charthouse. This makes it difficult to get bearings sometimes, because it takes a long time to go around the entire 05 level.

RADAR
Radar also provides information for position fixing. The radar antenna on the ship's mast transmits pulses of radiomagnetic energy as it rotates. When the pulse strikes a solid object, the pulse reflects off the object. Some of that reflection may return to the radar antenna that transmitted it. By measuring the time required for the pulse to travel to the object and return, the radar can compute the distance to the object. This distance is called the *range* of the object. The direction in which the antenna is pointing when the reflected pulse returns gives the bearing of the object.

Radar ranges are more accurate than radar bearings, so they are given priority in position plotting. In practice, radar ranges plotted as circles of position are often combined with visual bearings to produce position fixes. The surface search radar displays are located at the front of the pilothouse on the starboard side. Each is equipped with a heavy black rubber glare shield that improves the visibility of the display in high ambient light. This glare shield prevents two or more people from looking at the scope at the same time. The surface search radar also has non-navigational uses. The officer of the deck may use the radar to observe and track other ship traffic. For this, a short range is usually desired. The navigation tasks often require a long range, and there is sometimes conflict between the two users of the scopes. It is not difficult to change from one range to another; however, in order to obtain the required information after changing ranges, the operator may have to wait for a full rotation of the radar antenna at the new range setting.

FATHOMETER

The fathometer is a device for measuring the depth of the water under a ship. It emits a pulse of sound and measures the time it takes the sound pulse to bounce off the sea bottom and return to the ship. The time delay is recorded by the movement of a pen across a piece of paper. The sound pulse is emitted when the pen is at the top of the paper. The pen moves down the paper at a constant speed and is brought into contact with the paper when the echo is detected. The distance the pen travels down the paper before making its mark is proportional to the time required for the echo to return, which is in turn proportional to the depth of the water. If the water is deep, the sound will take longer to return, and the pen will have traveled farther down the paper before coming into contact with it. The depth of the water can be read from the scale printed on the paper. Changing the scale of the fathometer to operate in deeper or shallower water is accomplished by changing the speed at which the pen travels. The paper is mounted on a motor drive that moves the paper to the side a small amount just before each pulse. This results in a continuous graphical record of the depth of the water under the ship.

The *Palau*'s fathometer is located in the charthouse, so the QMOW must leave the bridge to use it.

NAVSAT

Satellite navigation systems have now become commonplace. They are easy to use, and they provide high-quality position information. Their major drawback at the time this research was carried out was that with the number of navigation satellites then available the mean interval between fixes was about 90 minutes. After computing the ship's position from the reception of satellite signals, the satellite navigation system continuously updates the position of the ship on the basis of inputs from the gyrocompass (for direction) and the ship's log (for speed). The NavSat system aboard the *Palau* (located in the charthouse) was a box, about the size of a small suitcase that continuously displayed a digital readout of the latitude and longitude of the ship.

The fact that NavSat systems must update position with dead reckoning during the long wait between fixes puts NavSat near the bottom of the list of sources of information. With the implementation of the Global Positioning System (GPS), continuous satellite fixes are now available; the need for dead-reckoning updates of position has been eliminated. The military version of GPS is accurate to within less than a meter in three dimensions. The civilian versions are intentionally degraded to a considerably lower accuracy. GPS will very likely transform the way navigation is done, perhaps rendering most of the procedures described in this book obsolete.

OMEGA

Omega measures the phase difference between the arrival of signals from multiple stations. Omega was intended to provide accurate worldwide position-fixing capability. In practice it is unreliable. Whatever the source of the problems, they are perceived to be so serious that the following warning appears in the Watch Standing Manual.

CAUTION: Positions obtained from Omega are highly suspect, unless substantiated by information from another source. In recent years, a number of costly and embarrassing groundings have been directly attributable to trusting Omega. No drastic decisions are ever to be made on unsubstantiated Omega fixes without the explicit permission of the navigator.

If this system is considered to be so unreliable that it merits this strongly worded caution in the written procedures, what is it doing on the ship? I believe the answer involves an interaction of the organization of military research and funding with the development of technology. Omega is a system that not only went into service before all the bugs could be worked out, it has been overtaken by other superior technologies before the bugs could be worked out. Still, it was bought and paid for by the military, and can, on occasion, provide useful navigation information.

The *Palau*'s Omega is located in the charthouse.

CELESTIAL OBSERVATIONS

By measuring the angular distance of a star above the horizon, an observer can determine his distance from the point on the surface of the earth that the star is directly above. This point forms the center of a circle of position. In a celestial sight reduction, each observed celestial body defines a circle of position, and the vessel from which the observations were made must be located at the intersections of the circles of position. Celestial observations appear at the bottom of the list of sources of information. When properly performed, celestial observations provide fairly good position information.

There are, however, two major drawbacks to celestial observations. First, they can be performed only under certain meteorological circumstances. This makes celestial navigation hard to use and hard to teach. Several senior quartermasters have told me that they would like to teach celestial navigation on training missions in the Southern California operations area, but the combination of air pollution and light pollution (which makes the night sky bright, masking all but the brightest stars and obscuring the line of the horizon) produces very few occasions suitable for it. Second, the procedures are so computationally complex that, even using a specialized calculator, a proficient celestial navigator needs about half an hour to compute a good celestial position fix. Together these factors lead to infrequent practice of this skill. I believe that in the near future the only navigators who will know how to fix position by star sights will be those sailing on cruising yachts who cannot afford a thousand dollars for a SatNav system.

DRAI

The Dead Reckoning Analyzer Instrument (DRAI) is one of the most interesting navigational devices. A mechanical analog computer, it takes input from the ship's speed log and the gyrocompass and, by way of a system of motors, gears, belts, and cams, continuously computes changes in latitude and longitude. The output of the DRAI is expressed in the positions of two dials: one reads latitude and the other longitude. If these dials are set to the current latitude and longitude, the changes computed by the motions of the internal parts of the DRAI will move them so that their readings follow the latitude and longitude of the ship. The crew of the *Palau* claimed that when, properly cared for, the DRAI is quite accurate and reliable. Older versions of the DRAI, such as the one aboard the *Palau,* have been around since the 1940s. Newer versions that do the same computations electronically are installed on some of the newer ships.

PIT SWORD AND DUMMY LOG

The pit sword is a device that is extended through the hull and into the water to measure a ship's actual speed through the water. The pit sword extends several feet outside the hull and measures speed by measuring the water's distortion of a magnetic field. The speed signal generated by the pit sword is fed to speed indicators on the bridge and to all the automated instruments that do dead reckoning: the NavSat, the DRAI, and the inertial navigation systems (if present).

If the ship is operating in shallow water, the pit sword cannot be extended from the hull. In this case, or if for any other reason the pit sword cannot be used, the dummy log is used. When a ship is neither accelerating nor decelerating, its speed can be estimated fairly accurately from the rate of rotation of the propeller. The dummy log is a device that senses this rate and provides a signal that mimics what the pit sword would produce at the corresponding speed.

Both of these devices are remote from the location of the navigation team's normal activities. A display of speed through the water is available on the forward port side of the pilothouse, but it is rarely consulted by the navigation team.

CHRONOMETERS

Three traditional spring-driven clocks are kept in a special box in the *Palau*'s charthouse. Readings are recorded daily so that trends in the behavior of these chronometer's can be noted. These records are maintained while time signals are available on radio so that if time signals should become unavailable the behavior of the clocks will be known. If, for example, the log shows that a particular chronometer loses a second every day, that same rate of change will be assumed until more reliable time sources are restored.

The diversity of the many sources of navigation information and the many methods for generating constraints on the ship's position produces an important system property: the fact that positions are determined by combining information from multiple, sometimes independent, sources of information permits the navigation team to check the consistency of the multiple representations with each other. The probability that several, independently derived, representations are in agreement with one another and are in error is much smaller than the probability that any one representation is in error.

At the Chart Table

The previous section described the sources of information that the quartermaster of the watch may use while discharging his primary duty: ensuring the safe navigation of the ship. The information provided by these sources converges on the chart table, where positions are plotted and tracks are projected.

The Watch Standing Procedures specify additional constraints on the QMOW that bring us to other aspects of the navigation team's task setting:

The chart table and environs will be kept free of extraneous material at all times. Only the chart(s) in use, necessary publications, the logs of the watch, and necessary writing/plotting paraphernalia will be on the chart table.

The chart table is mounted against the starboard wall of the pilothouse, just under the large outward-canted windows. It is large enough for full-size navigation charts and tools—about 4 by 6 feet. Under the chart table are a number of locking drawers in which charts, publications, and plotting tools are stored. A locking cabinet for binoculars is mounted on the aft edge of the chart table.

Navigation Charts

The most important piece of technology in the position-fixing task is the navigation chart. A navigation chart is a specially constructed model of a real geographical space. The ship is somewhere in space, and to determine or "fix" the position of the ship is to find the point on the appropriate chart that corresponds to the ship's position in space. The lines of position derived from visual observations, radar bearings, radar ranges, celestial observations, and depth-contour matches are all graphically constructed on the chart. Latitude and longitude positions determined by NavSat, Omega, or Loran are plotted directly on the chart. A fix may be constructed from a combination of these types of information.

Navigation charts are printed on high-quality paper in color. Natural and "cultural" features are depicted in a complex symbology (see figure 1.3).

The *Palau* keeps an inventory of about 5400 charts depicting ports and coastlines around the world. A complete set of charts for current operations are kept on the chart table, and a second complete set in the table's drawers. The rest of the charts are kept in a chart library in Secondary Conn.

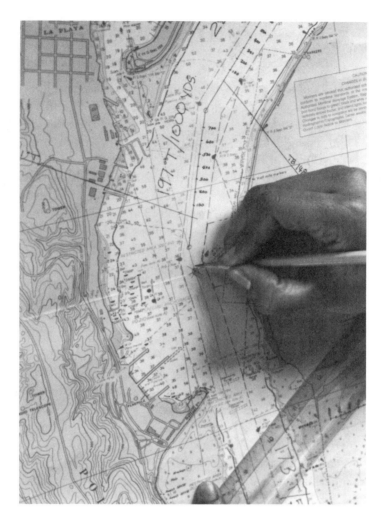

Figure 1.3 A navigation chart in use. Such a chart includes information about features both above and below the water. This chart shows the entrance to San Diego Harbor.

The Secondary Duty of the QMOW

According to the Watch Standing Procedures,

The secondary duty of the QMOW is the keeping of the logs of the watch.

Those who have experience in the merchant fleet often say that it is not necessary to do all the work of piloting in order to get a large ship into port. A good ship driver can, after all, "eyeball" the movement of the ship and get it down the channel without having positions plotted on short intervals. To say that it is possible to guide a ship down a narrow channel without maintaining the piloting record is not to say that it is easier to do it that way. Even if nothing goes wrong, the plotted and projected positions of the ship on the chart are a useful resource to the conning officer, and while it does require a navigation team to do the work of plotting positions and computing turn points, the task of the conning officer is greatly simplified by the advice he receives from the navigation team. If something does go wrong, the work of the navigation team becomes indispensable in two ways. First, depending upon what it is that goes wrong, computing the ship's position and track may become essential to the process of figuring out how to keep the ship out of trouble (see chapter 8 for an example). Second, the records kept by the navigation team—the chart, the deck log, and the bearing log—are all legal documents. If the ship is involved in a mishap, as soon as it is prudent to do so, all these documents are removed from the chart table and locked in the Executive Officer's safe. This precaution is taken to ensure that they will not be tampered with before they are turned over to a board of inquiry investigating the incident. These records may be needed to protect the navigation team, the captain, the ship, and ultimately the Navy from accusations of negligence or incompetence. The *Palau*'s Assistant Navigator offered the following justification:

You can go into San Diego by eye. But legally, you can't. If you haven't matched all the things and something happens, not necessarily to you, it don't have to. One of those buoys can float loose in the goddamn bay and rub up along side you. Boy, you better have everything covered here, because they are going to try to hang the captain. They will try to hang him. Unless he can prove with data that everything he did was right. Now ... the merchant ship wouldn't. They would just say, "We were in the middle of the channel. The damn thing hit us, and if there is an expense, fine, charge the company."

Other records are kept as well. There is a separate log for the gyrocompasses (with entries made twice daily), and another for the magnetic compasses. (The DRAI reading is also recorded in the magnetic compass log at the beginning of each watch.) There is yet another log for the ship's chronometers. A fathometer log is kept with the fathometer during maneuvers in restricted waters. A log of the ship's position is updated daily.

The Tertiary Duty of the QMOW

The tertiary duty of the quartermaster of the watch is "to give all possible aid to the Officer of the Deck in the conduct of his watch." The Officer of the Deck (OOD) is also normally the conning officer, although he may delegate this duty to a Junior Officer of the Deck. The importance of the relationship between the QMOW and the OOD is reflected in the following excerpt from the Watch Standing Procedures:

The QMOW will not leave the Bridge except to take DRAI and Fathometer readings, and collect NavSat and Omega fixes as necessary. If he leaves the bridge, he will inform the OOD, and will absent himself for as short a period of time as possible. (If a Charthouse Quartermaster is assigned, there no necessity for the QMOW to leave the bridge unless properly relieved.)

The control of the ship is a partially closed information loop. The conning officer senses the ship's situation in the world by looking out the window of the bridge. The members of the navigation team also sense the world by looking at it; in addition, however, they gather information from other sources, and from that other information they synthesize a more comprehensive and accurate representation of the situation of the ship. The navigation team uses its representation to generate advice to the conning officer, who by acting (or not acting) on that advice affects the actual situation of the ship in the world which is sensed and interpreted.

The navigation team relies on the conning officer to the extent that if the conning officer turns the ship or changes its speed in other than the recommended places then the workload of the navigation team is increased. When the quartermasters project the position of the ship into the future, the projections sometimes involve changes in course and or speed. When this is the case, the projected track is carefully planned, pre-computed, and plotted. If the ship remains on the pre-computed track, many parts of the required computation will have been performed in advance. When the ship deviates from planned track, new computations may be required to establish when and where various maneuvers are appropriate. For example, on one of the *Palau*'s departures from port an inexperienced conning officer made several turns before the recommended point. This happened because the deck of the ship is so big and so high off the water that from the point of view of the navigation bridge the surface of the water for several hundred yards in front of the ship is hidden from view. When a channel is narrow and some of the turns are tight, channel buoys disappear beneath the deck before the turn is commenced. For an inexperienced conning officer, the temptation to turn before the buoy disappears under the bow is great. Once a buoy disappears beneath the deck, it is difficult to estimate whether or not the ship will hit it. To keep the ship on track, a conning officer must be disciplined and must trust the navigation team.

The conning officer has other obligations and cannot always do what is easiest for the navigation team. On one occasion the *Palau*'s engineering department detected a rumbling noise in the propeller shaft. In order to diagnose the problem, the engineers requested 5° right rudder, then 5° left rudder, then 10° right rudder followed by 10° left rudder. The ship was slaloming along through 80° turns. This happened while the ship was out of visual and radar range of land, so its position had to be maintained by dead reckoning, a very difficult task under these conditions.

THE COMBAT INFORMATION CENTER

The navigation team also coordinates its activities with the Combat Information Center (CIC), which is located below the flight deck. Duplicate position plots are maintained by the Operations Specialists (OSs) who work in CIC. They use radar bearings and ranges to fix the position of the ship. Under conditions of reduced visibility, CIC is supposed to be the primary source of navigation advice for the conning officer. The quartermaster chief in charge of the Navigation Department on the *Palau* said the following about this shift in responsibility:

They've got a whole team down there [in CIC] and they are pretty good at what they are doing. They are supposed to be like a backup on what happens up here. They've got good radars, and for reduced visibility, they are supposed to be primary. Now the only way that is going to happen is if I drop dead. As long as I am on a ship, and this is the same thing I tell my navigator, as soon as I walk on board, *"Everything that has to do with navigation while I am on board, I'm it. I'll hand you papers to sign, I'll back you up in any way you need. You will never get in trouble, navigation is my business."* For OSs, it is a secondary business to them. There are people in my business who will let CIC take it. I won't.

I never saw this claim put to the test.

AIR BOSS

The Navigation Department provides position information to the Air Boss, who is responsible for controlling the aircraft that operate from the flight deck. The most frequent requests for information from the air boss consist of position or projected position information to be used by aircraft coming to the ship, and directions and distances to land bases for aircraft departing the ship.

Sea and Anchor Detail

Guiding a large ship into or out of a harbor is a difficult task. A ship is a massive object; its inertia makes it slow to respond to changes in propeller speed or rudder position. Putting the rudder over will have no immediate effect, but once the ship has started turning it will tend to continue turning. Similarly, stopping the engines will not stop the ship. Depending on its speed, a ship may coast without power for many miles. To stop in less distance, the propeller must be turned in the reverse direction, but even this results in only a gradual slowing. Because of this response lag, changes in direction or speed must be anticipated and planned well in advance. Depending on the characteristics and the velocity of the ship, the actions that will bring it to a stop or turn it around may need to be taken tens of seconds or many minutes before the ship arrives at the desired turning or stopping point.

In order to satisfy the OOD's need for information about the location and movement of the ship when it is near hazards, the Navigation Departments of Navy ships take on a watch configuration called Sea and Anchor Piloting Detail. Piloting waters are defined as follows in the Watch Standing Procedures:

Piloting waters—within five miles of land, shoals, or hazards to navigation, or inside of the fifty fathom curve, whichever is further from land.

Restricted waters—Inside of the outermost aid to navigation or inside of the ten fathom curve, whichever is further from land.

1. When operating within Restricted Waters, the Sea and Anchor Piloting Detail will be stationed.
2. The QMOW will ensure that all members of the Sea and Anchor Piloting Detail are called at least thirty minutes prior to entering restricted waters.
3. The Sea and Anchor Piloting Detail will consist of:
    a. The Navigator
    b. The Assistant to the Navigator
    c. Navigation Plotter
    d. Navigation Bearing Recorder/Timer
    e. Starboard Pelorus Operator
    f. Port Pelorus Operator
    g. Restricted Maneuvering Helmsman
    h. Quartermaster of the Watch
    i   Restricted Maneuvering Helmsman in After Steering
    j. Fathometer Operator

As long as the visibility is adequate for visual bearings, the primary work of the sea and anchor piloting detail is to fix the position of the ship by visual bearings. The pelorus operators stationed on the port and starboard wings, just outside the doors to the pilothouse, measure the bearings of specified landmarks and report the bearings to the bearing recorder/timer (henceforth referred to as "the recorder"), who records them in the bearing log. The recorder stands at the after edge of the chart table in the pilothouse. The bearing log is kept on the chart table, adjacent to the chart. The navigation plotter stands at the chart table and plots the recorded bearings as lines of position on the chart, thus fixing the position of the ship. The plotter also projects the future positions of the ship, and together with the recorder he chooses landmarks for the pelorus operators to use on future fixes. The restricted-maneuvering helmsman stands at the helm station in the center of the pilothouse and steers the ship in accordance with commands from the conning officer. In sea and anchor detail, the quartermaster of the watch is mainly responsible for maintaining the ship's log, in which all engine and helm commands and other events of consequence to the navigation of the ship are recorded. The quartermaster of the watch stands at the forward edge of the chart table and keeps the ships log on the chart table. The restricted-maneuvering helmsman is stationed in the after steering compartment, at the head of the rudder post in the stern of the ship. In case of a problem with the ship's wheel, the steering function can be taken over more directly by the helmsman in aftersteering. The fathometer operator is stationed in the charthouse, which is separated from the pilothouse by a bulkhead. The fathometer operator reports the depth of the water under the ship for each position fix. The navigator is responsible for the work of the navigation team but does not normally participate directly in that work. Aboard the *Palau*, even the supervision of the navigation team was done by the quartermaster chief, who acted as Assistant to the Navigator. If the crew had been more experienced, the Assistant to the Navigator would not have taken up a functional role in the performance of the task. Because the *Palau* was understaffed and the available personnel were inexperienced, however, the assistant to the navigator also served as navigation plotter.

Narrative: Sighting

In the late afternoon of a clear spring day the U.S.S. *Palau* completed several hours of engineering drills that left it alternately steaming in tight circles and lying dead in the water. The *Palau* had been at sea for a few days on local maneuvers and was now just south of the entrance to San Diego Harbor. The crew was anxious to go ashore, and going in circles and lying dead in the water when home was in plain sight was very frustrating. It was therefore something of a cause for celebration in the pilothouse when the engineering officer of the watch called the bridge on the intercom and said "Main engine warmed, ready to answer all bells." The officer of the deck acknowledged the ready state of the propulsion plant and advised the engineering officer to "stand by for 15," meaning that they should be prepared to respond to an order for 15 knots of speed. Shortly thereafter, the conning officer ordered the engine ahead standard speed. Pilothouse morale rose swiftly.

Quartermaster Second Class (QM2) John Silver stood at the chart table in the pilothouse. He was wearing a sound-powered telephone set (headphones and a collar-mounted microphone) that connected him to other members of the navigation team who were not in the pilothouse. When he learned that the ship would be getting underway again soon, he pressed the transmit button on his microphone and said "We're baggin' ass!"

On a platform on the starboard side of the ship, just outside the door to the pilothouse and about 50 feet above the surface of the water, Seaman Steve Wheeler had been leaning on the rail, studying the patches of foam that lay motionless next to the hull, and wondering when the engineering drills would end and the ship would move again. When he heard Silver's exclamation in his headphones, he looked up and began to scan the city skyline for major landmarks. Wheeler was the starboard pelorus operator, and it was his job to sight landmarks and measure their direction from the ship. A novice, he had done this job only once before, and was not sure how to identify all the landmarks, nor was he entirely clear on the procedure he was to perform.

Inside the pilothouse, Quartermaster Chief Rick Richards moved to the forward edge of the chart table and looked over the shoulder of QM2 James Smith as Smith recorded the conning officer's orders in the deck log. "Ahead standard, left 10 degrees rudder, come to course 3 0 5."

Chief Richards turned and leaned over the chart table with QM2 Silver. As happy as they were to be heading for their pier at last, they also knew it was time to begin the high-workload job of bringing the *Palau* into port. They examined the chart of the approaches to San Diego Harbor. Silver found the symbolic depictions of several important landmarks on the chart and used his fingers to draw imaginary lines from them to the last charted position of the ship. These imaginary lines represented the lines of sight from the ship to the landmarks. He checked the angles at which the lines intersected. Pointing to the chart, he said to Richards "How about these?" "Yeah, those are fine," the chief replied.

Silver was the navigation team's bearing recorder. It was his job to control the pelorus operators on the wings of the ship and record the measurements they made. Once Silver had chosen his landmarks, he assigned them to the pelorus operators: "Hey Steve, you'll be keeping Hotel del and Dive Tower as we go in, and John, you got Point Loma." Steve Wheeler answered "OK" and heard his opposite number on the port wing, Seaman John Painter, say "Aye."

Wheeler looked out across the water, found the conical red roofs of the Hotel del Coronado on the beach, and searched to the south along the strand for the building called the Dive Tower. There it was. Wheeler's hands were resting on the alidade that was mounted on a shoulder-high pedestal at his station. He quickly pointed the alidade in the rough direction of the Dive Tower and leaned down, pressing his right eye against the rubber eyepiece to look through the sight. He saw the beach and some low buildings back from the water's edge. He swung the sight left and then right until the Dive Tower came into view, then carefully rotated the sight on its pedestal until the vertical hairline in the sight fell right down the middle of the tower. Near the bottom of his field of view through the alidade, he could see a portion of the scale of a gyro-compass card. The hairline crossed the scale three small tick marks to the right of a large mark labeled 030. Another large tick mark, labeled 040, was still further to the right. Wheeler counted the little tick marks and noted that the the Dive Tower bore 033°.

Once Silver had assigned the landmarks to the pelorus operators, he wrote the name of each of the chosen landmarks at the head of a column in the bearing record log, which was lying on the chart table between him and the chart.

Silver kept an eye on his wristwatch. It was a digital model, and when he had come to his duty station several hours ago he had synchronized it with the ship's clock on the wall at the back of the pilothouse. Now he had taken the watch off his wrist and placed it on the chart table in front of him, just above the pages of his bearing record log. As the ship began to move and turn to its course for home, the plotter, Chief Richards, told Silver to take a round of bearings. It was 13 minutes and 40 seconds after 4 pm. Silver decided to make the official time of the next set of bearing observations 16:14, using the 24-hour notation standard in the military. He wrote "1614" in the time column of the bearing record log, and at 16:13:50 he said into his phone set: "Stand by to mark. Time 14."

Seaman Ron White sat on a high stool at the chart table, looking at the display of the fathometer. On the chart table in front of him was a depth sounder logbook. When he heard the "Stand by to mark" signal in his headset, he read the depth of the water under the ship from the display and reported on the phone circuit: "Fifteen fathoms." He then logged the time and the depth in his book. Silver recorded the depth in the bearing record log.

Out on the starboard wing, Wheeler heard the recorder say "Stand by to mark, time 14." As he made a small adjustment to bring the hairline to the center of the Dive Tower, he heard the fathometer operator report the depth of the water under the ship as 15 fathoms. The hairline now crossed the scale at 034°. Wheeler pressed the button on the microphone of his phone set and reported "Dive Tower, 0 3 4." That was a mistake. The bearing was correct; however, in his excitement Wheeler blurted out his bearing immediately after the fathometer operator's report. He was supposed to track the landmark and report its bearing only after the recorder gave a "mark" signal. The port pelorus operator noticed the mistake and barked, "He didn't say 'Mark'."

But by then it *was* time to mark the bearings. Wheeler's mistake was not a serious timing error; he was only a few seconds early. The important thing was to make the observations as close the "mark" time as was possible. Stopping to discuss the mistake would have been more disruptive than continuing on. There was no time for lessons or corrections now. The bearing recorder quickly restarted the procedure from its current state by giving the "mark" signal, acknowledging the premature bearing, and urging the pelorus operators to get on with their reports: "Mark it. I got Dive Tower, Steve. Go ahead." Silver then wrote "0 3 4" in the column labeled Dive Tower in the bearing record log.

The plotter, Chief Richards, was standing next to Silver, waiting for the bearings. He leaned across the chart table and read the bearing of Dive Tower even as Silver was writing it in the log. Silver noticed that Richards was craning his neck to read the bearing from the book. Softly he said "0 3 4" to Richards, whose face was close to his. As Richards moved away from the bearing log, he looked to the plotting tool in his hands and acknowledged: "Uh huh."

Chief Richards held in his hands a one-armed protractor called a *hoey*. The hoey has a circular scale of 180 degrees on it, and a straight-edged arm about 18 inches long that pivots in the center of the scale. It is used to construct lines on the chart that correspond to the lines of sight between the ship and the landmarks. Richards aligned the straightedge with the fourth tick mark to the right of the large mark labeled 030 on the scale of the hoey and turned a knob at the pivot point of the arm to lock its position with respect to the scale. He then laid the hoey on the chart and found the symbol on the chart that represented the Dive Tower. He put the point of his pencil on the symbol on the chart. Holding it there, he brought the straightedge up against the pencil point. Keeping the straightedge against the tip of the pencil and keeping the protractor scale further away from the charted location of the landmark than the anticipated location of the fix, Richards slid the hoey itself around on the chart until the directional frame of the protractor scale was aligned with the directional frame of the chart. The edge of the arm now lay on the chart along a line representing the line of sight from the ship to the landmark. Richards held the hoey firmly in place while he removed his pencil from the symbol for the landmark and drew a line segment along the protractor arm in the vicinity of the expected location of the ship on the chart. By drawing only the sections of the lines of position that were in the vicinity of the expected location of the ship, Richards kept the chart neat and avoided the creation of spurious triangles formed by the intersection of lines of position from different fixes.

While Chief Richards was plotting the line of position for the Dive Tower, the port wing pelorus operator reported the bearing of Point Loma. By the time Silver had acknowledged the port pelorus operator's report ("Three three nine, Point Loma"), Richards was ready for the next bearing. Because he was standing right next to Silver, he could hear everything that Silver said into his phone-circuit microphone. He could not hear what the pelorus operators or others on the circuit were saying to Silver or to one another; however, he could hear what Silver said, and he got the bearing to Point Loma by hearing Silver's acknowledgement.

While the port pelorus operator was making his report, "Point Loma, 3 3 9" and while Chief Richards was plotting Dive Tower, Seaman Wheeler swung his sight to the tallest spire of the Hotel del Coronado, aligned the hairline, and read the bearing from the scale. In his headset he heard the recorder acknowledge "Three 3 9, Point Loma." But he was trying not to listen, because he had his own numbers to report as soon as the phone circuit became quiet: "Hotel del, 0 2 4." Then he listened as the recorder acknowledged his report: "0 2 4, Hotel del." The report was heard and echoed without error, so Wheeler said no more.

About 30 seconds passed between the "Stand by to mark" signal and the acknowledgement of the third bearing. The pelorus operators relaxed at their stations for a minute or so while the bearings they had reported were processed by other members of the navigation team to determine the position of the ship at the time of the observations. The pelorus operators themselves did not know exactly what had been done with the bearings after they had reported them.

Less than 10 seconds after the acknowledgement of the last bearing, Chief Richards had his fix triangle constructed and was ready to label it with the time of the observations. He asked Silver "OK, what time was that?" Silver looked in the 'time' column of the bearing record log and replied "One 4," meaning 14 minutes after the hour.

With the fix plotted and labeled, Richards and Silver turned to the tasks of predicting the position of the ship at the time of the next fix (3 minutes hence) and deciding which course to take for the best approach to the harbor. Speaking slowly while plotting, Chief Richards said: "He's still turning. That's gonna put us about right here." He made a mark on the chart at the end of an arc he had drawn to represent the track of the ship through the turn. Silver looked at the projected position and determined that the same three landmarks used for the previous fix would be appropriate for the next fix.

At 16:16:50 Silver pressed the transmit button on his mike and said: "Stand by to mark. Time 1 7."

"Fifteen fathoms," said the fathometer operator.

Silver said "Mark it." The pelorus operators reported their bearings, and Silver read each one back.

"Point Loma, 3 3 8."

"3 3 8, Point Loma."

"Dive Tower, 0 3 5."

"0 3 5, Dive Tower."

"Hotel del, 0 2 4."

"0 2 4, Hotel del."

Chief Richards plotted the ship's position, but it was not as far along the track as he had projected it would be. Silver commented on the radius of the projected turn: "That was a big ellipse." Richards looked at the plot. "Oh, yeah," he said. "It's just that propulsion is coming up really slooooow. I only figured it to come up to 9, but it didn't even come up to 4." Both men laughed, and Silver said "Recompute." For half a minute they worked together silently, jointly redoing the computations of the speed calculation. They checked the lines of position for the new fix and measured the distance between the previous position and the latest one: 400 yards. Chief Richards shook his head and said "Four knots." Silver nodded and said "Right." Richards pointed to the projected track of the ship up the channel. "Four knots for the first 3 minutes," he said. "At this rate we better change the timing a little."

Navigation is the process of directing the movements of a craft from one point to another. There are many kinds of navigation. This chapter lays the foundation for the construction of an analysis of the information processing carried out by those who practice a form of navigation referred to in The Western technological culture as *surface ship piloting. Piloting* (or *pilotage*) is navigation involving determination of position relative to known geographic locations. Rather than present what passes in our cultural tradition as a description of how pilotage is done, this chapter attempts to develop a computational account of pilotage. This account of pilotage overlaps portions of the computational bases of many other forms of navigation, including celestial, air, and radio navigation. Aspects of these forms of navigation will be mentioned in passing, but the focus will be on the pilotage of surface vessels in the vicinity of land. Unless otherwise indicated, the term 'navigation' will henceforth refer to pilotage.

Having taken ship navigation as it is performed by a team on the bridge of a ship as the unit of cognitive analysis, I will attempt to apply the principal metaphor of cognitive science—cognition as computation—to the operation of this system. In so doing I do not make any special commitment to the nature of the computations that are going on inside individuals except to say that whatever happens there is part of a larger computational system. But I do believe that the computation observed in the activity of the larger system can be described in the way cognition has been traditionally described—that is, as computation realized through the creation, transformation, and propagation of representational states. In order to understand navigation practice as a computational or information-processing activity, we need to consider what might constitute an understanding of an information-processing system. Working on vision but thinking of a much wider class of information-processing systems, David Marr developed a view of what it takes to understand an information-processing system. The discussion here is based on Marr's (1982) distinctions between several levels of description of cognitive systems.

Marr's Levels of Description

In his work on vision, Marr suggests that there are several levels of description at which any information-processing system must be understood. According to Marr, the most important three levels are as follows: The first level is the computational theory of the task that the system performs. This level of description should specify what the system does, and why it does it. It should say what constraints are satisfied by the operation of the system. Here, "the performance of the [system] is characterized as a mapping from one kind of information to another, the abstract properties of this mapping are defined precisely, and its appropriateness and adequacy for the task at hand are demonstrated" (Marr 1982). Such a description is defined by the constraints the system has to satisfy in order to do what it does. The second level of description concerns the "choice of representation for the input and output and the algorithm to be used to transform one into the other." This level specifies the logical organization of the structures that encode the information and the transformations by which the information is propagated through the system from input to output. The third level concerns "the details of how the algorithm and representation are realized physically." Marr points out that there are many choices available at each level for any computational system, and that the choices made at one level may constrain what will work at other levels.

Marr intended his framework to be applied to cognitive processes that take place inside an individual, but there is no reason, in principle, to confine it to such a narrow conception of cognition. In this chapter I will attempt to apply Marr's prescription to the task of navigation.

Navigation is an activity that is recognizable across cultures, yet in each cultural tradition it is accomplished within a conceptual system that makes certain representational assumptions. In the next section, I give a *computational* account of navigation that is independent of the representational assumptions of any established tradition of navigation practice. It is an account that specifies the nature of the navigation problem and the sorts of information that are transformed in the doing of the task, yet spans the differences between even radically different traditions of navigation.

Unfortunately, the computational account by itself is quite abstract and difficult to convey in the absence of examples that embody the satisfaction of the constraints that are described. I will therefore illustrate aspects of the computational account with a few examples taken from the Western tradition of piloting. This should help the reader to understand the nature of the constraints discussed. However, these examples are inevitably grounded in the representational assumptions of the Western cultural tradition, and frequently have implications for algorithms, and will probably suggest particular implementations. The inclusion of this sort of material seems unavoidable. I will try to keep the examples as sparse as is possible and to make clear distinctions between those aspects that properly belong to the computational account and those that belong to other levels of description. The importance of keeping the computational description free of representational assumptions will become apparent in the two subsequent sections, which briefly contrast the culturally specific representations and algorithms used by our technological Western culture with those used by a nonliterate Micronesian culture to solve the navigation problem. Much of the remainder of the book can be seen as a further elaboration of the *representational/algorithmic* level of description and a thorough exploration of the *implementation* of navigation computations by navigation teams on large ships.

The implementational details have been largely ignored in the past. This may be due in part to the notion that in information-processing systems what is important is the structure of the computation, not the means of implementation. One of the most important insights of computer science is that the same program can run on many different machines—that is, the same computation can be performed many different ways. When we consider a system like ship navigation, however, the situation is complicated by a nesting of computational systems. What is the implementational level for the navigation system as a whole is the computational level for the people who operate the tools of the system. The material means in which the computation is actually performed are implementational details for the system, but they set the task constraints on the performance of the navigation staff. The distinction between what is computed by the system as a whole and what is computed by the individual navigation practitioners in the system will be developed in later chapters. For the moment, let us take it simply as a justification for attending to a level of detail that is often missing from accounts of organizations as computational systems.

A Computational Account of Navigation

In a computational sense, all systems of navigation answer the question "Where am I?" in fundamentally the same way. While the representational assumptions of the navigation systems in which this question is answered are enormously variable and wonderful in their ingenuity, all of them answer the question by combining one-dimensional constraints on position.

The surface of the sea is, of course, actually a three-dimensional surface on a nearly spherical body, the earth. As long as we are concerned only with positions on this surface, we need only two dimensions to uniquely specify a position. Thus, a minimum of two one-dimensional constraints are required to specify positions for ship navigation. Navigating in three dimensions—a rather recent activity—requires at least three one-dimensional constraints to specify position.

Lines of Position

Figure 2.1 depicts the one-dimensional constraint that is produced by a known position and a given direction. Such a combination produces a *line of position*. Thus, if we know that point B lies in a particular direction from known position A, we know that B must lie on a line extended from A in the specified direction. Given that constraint alone, however, we still don't know where point B actually is; we know only that it must lie on the line of position defined by point A and the specified direction. If, for example, we are told that a treasure is buried due east of a certain split rock, the options are considerably narrowed but we still don't know where to dig.

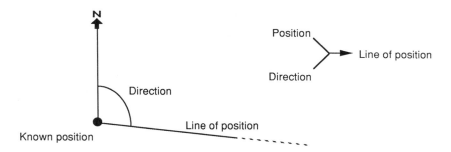

Figure 2.1   Graphical and conceptual depiction of the line-of-position constraint.

Circles of Position

Figure 2.2 shows another type of one-dimensional constraint. This one consists of a known position and a specified distance, and it defines a circle of position. If we know that point B lies some specified distance from point A, then we know that B must lie on a circle of position centered on A with a radius of the specified distance. Given this constraint alone, we cannot yet locate B; we know only that it is somewhere on the circle of position specified by the known point and the distance from the point. In practice, a circle of position is often plotted as an arc in the vicinity of the expected location of point B rather than as a complete circle.

Combining Positional Constraints: Position Fixing

One-dimensional constraints can be combined in many ways to produce two-dimensional constraints on position. Figure 2.3 shows some of the possibilities. In the Western tradition, the line-of-position constraint is the computational basis of position fixing by visual bearings and by radio direction finding (figure 2.3a). In these procedures, position is determined by finding the intersections of two or more lines of position. A radar fix is constructed from a bearing and a range (figure 2.3b). The circle-of-position constraint is the basis of celestial navigation, although the circles of position

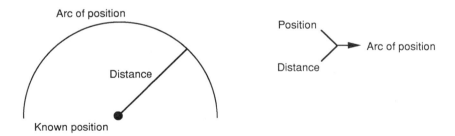

Figure 2.2 Graphical and conceptual depiction of the arc-of-position constraint.

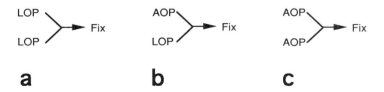

Figure 2.3 A conceptual depiction of the combinations of one-dimensional constraints.

are so large that they are treated as lines of position in the vicinity of the fix (figure 2.3c). In a celestial sight reduction, each observed celestial body defines a circle of position, and the vessel from which the observations were made must be located at the intersections of the circles of position established with respect to celestial bodies.

Systems such as Loran, Decca, and Omega measure time or phase differences between the arrival of signals from multiple stations. Consider position fixing by Loran. If stations A and B emit signals at precisely the same time, where must I be if I receive the signal from station A 3 microseconds before I receive the signal from station B? The answer is that I must be somewhere on a hyperbolic line of position that is defined by all the intersections of circles of position around A and B for which the circle of position around station A is 3 microseconds closer to station A (at the speed of light) than the circle of position around station B is to station B. Each pair of stations received provides a time difference that defines a hyperbolic line of position. The vessel's position is fixed by finding the intersection of two or more such one-dimensional lines of position. Radar combines a circle of position, expressed as a range (distance), with a line of position, expressed as a bearing (direction), to provide a two-dimensional constraint on the relative position of the object detected.

The Position-Displacement Constraint

Two other important questions in navigation are "Given that we are where we are, how shall we proceed in order to arrive at a particular somewhere else?" and "Given that we are where we are, where shall we be if we proceed in a particular way for a particular period of time?" Both of these questions concern relationships among positions. To answer the first is to use the specification of two positions to determine the relationship between them. To answer the second is to use the specification of a position and a positional relationship to determine the specification of another position. Both of these constraints are captured by a single constraining relationship that holds among positions and the spatial displacements that lie between them. Figure 2.4 describes this constraint. It simply says that the specification of any two of the items in the relationship fully constrains the specification of the third item. There is no commitment to representation or algorithm in this. Positions

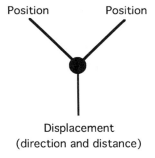

Displacement
(direction and distance)

Figure 2.4   A conceptual depiction of the position and displacement constraint.

and displacements may be represented in a wide variety of ways; however, if they are to be part of a system that does navigation, they will have to be represented in a way that satisfies this generic constraint. Things work out especially nicely if the displacement is given in the form of a direction and a distance. Then the determination of a new position from a given position and a displacement is simply the familiar case of combining the one-dimensional constraint defined by the starting position and a direction and a second one-dimensional constraint defined by the same starting position and a distance. Let me illustrate the satisfaction of this constraint with two procedures from the Western tradition, course planning and dead reckoning.

COURSE PLANNING

The fact that the specification of any two positions uniquely constrains the displacement that lies between them is the basis of course planning. If I know where I am and where I want to be, how can I determine a plan that will get me where I want to go? In some representational systems it is possible to compute a description of how to move from one position to the other from the description of the displacement between two positions. For example, on some types of nautical charts it is easy to measure the direction (course) and the distance between any two locations represented on the chart. Starting at one point and sailing the specified course for the specified distance will deliver the traveler to the other point. In this case, the representational medium, the chart, has been carefully designed so that an easily obtained description of the displacement between positions is also a description of a plan for getting from one point to the other. We tend to take this property for granted, but it is itself an impressive technical accomplishment.

To appreciate what a nice property it is that displacement on a chart is a plan for travel, one need only consider how often such is not the case. If the positions are represented as street addresses to be looked up in a phone book, for example, it may not be easy to get any description of the displacement between them at all. And if one can construct a description of the displacement from the addresses, unless the places are on the same street it is unlikely that the description by itself will be a useful plan of travel.

DEAD RECKONING

The fact that the specification of a position and a displacement uniquely constrains another position is the basis of dead reckoning. In dead reckoning the navigator monitors the motion of the vessel to determine its displacement from a previous position. If the distance and the direction of the vessel's travel can be determined, the measured displacement can be added to the previous position to determine the current position. Or a planned future displacement can be added to the current position to determine a future position. Thus, if I know where I started and in which direction and how far I have traveled, I can compute my position.

According to Bowditch (1977), the term "dead reckoning" is derived from *deduced* or *ded* reckoning, a procedure (predating modern charts) in which a ship's position was computed, or deduced, mathematically from a displacement and a known starting position. Even though modern charts permit simple graphical solutions to this problem, the term "dead reckoning" remains. And even though the representation of information and the procedure used in the computation changed with the advent of modern charts, both the old and the new version of dead reckoning are based on the satisfaction of the position-displacement constraint.

Depth-Contour Matching

There is one additional one-dimensional constraint to consider. Nautical charts sometimes have depth contours indicating lines of equal depth of water. If the depth of the water under a ship can be measured, the position of the ship can be constrained to be over a contour of that depth. This is a one-dimensional constraint although the line that defines it is usually not a straight line. The utility of this method depends on the shape of the bottom of the sea in the area. If it is a featureless plain, the constraints imposed by measured depth are weak. Almost any location on the chart will satisfy the constraint imposed by the measured depth, because the measured depth is almost everywhere the same. If there are many hills and valleys of nearly equal size, then again there may be many contours in many locations that satisfy the constraint. An inclined plane with a moderate slope is a useful bottom shape for simple contour navigation. A measurement of depth in such an area yields a one-dimensional constraint that is typically combined with other one-dimensional constraints, such as circles or lines of position, to generate an estimated position. Another useful bottom shape is encountered in the Central Pacific, where a uniform abyssal plain is dotted with small raised plateaus called *guyots*. There, one can hop from guyot to guyot, identifying them by their depths.

If the depth-measuring apparatus is more sophisticated and can match changing depth contours against patterns of changing depths rather than simply matching single depth measurements against single contours, then additional features on the bottom may provide additional constraints—enough, in fact, to permit a two-dimensional position determination from depth data alone. A similar sort of positional constraint can be achieved on land through the use of an altimeter and a topographic map of terrain that includes altitude contours.

The Distance-Rate-Time Constraint

Just one more constraint is required to complete the description of the computational core of navigation. This constraint relates distance, rate, and time. Figure 2.5 shows the form of this constraint. As with the constraint that holds among positions and displacements, the specification of any two values uniquely constrains the value of the third. The constraint on distance, rate, and time is

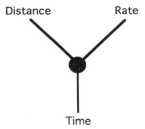

Figure 2.5 A conceptual depiction of the distance-rate-time constraint.

often used to determine the distance portion of a planned displacement in dead reckoning. This is a commonly used constraint in the Western cultural tradition outside the realm of navigation as well. It is an important part of logistical planning, for organizations and individuals alike. If I walk 4 miles per hour, how far can I get during a 50-minute lunch break? How long will it take me to drive the 118 miles to Los Angeles if I can average 50 miles per hour? If the circumference of the earth's orbit is 584 million miles, how fast is the earth moving along its orbital track?

Summary of Constraints

The computational account of navigation consists of four principal constraints. Two of them provide one-dimensional constraints on position from a given position and a component of a spatial displacement. The third relates positions and the spatial displacements that lie between them, where a displacement is composed of a pair of one-dimensional constraints (one a distance and the other a direction). The fourth constrains the relations among distance, rate, and time as descriptions of the motion of an object. Part of the art of the actual practice of navigation lies in integrating information from many kinds of simultaneous constraints to produce a single solution that satisfies them all.

Representational Assumptions of Western Navigation

This section and the next describe sets of structures that have arisen in the Western cultural tradition in terms of which the computational constraints outlined above are represented. The actual mechanics of the techniques for propagating the constraints across representational structures will be discussed in detail in a later chapter.

Units and Frames of Reference

In Western navigation, the units of direction are based on a system of angular measurement. This abstract system consists of a circle composed of 360 equal angular units called *degrees*. By convention, north is 0 degrees, east is 90 degrees, south is 180, and west is 270 degrees. Traditional magnetic compasses had 32 named compass points. If the compass rose is oriented to true north and south (as defined by the geographic poles), the directions are called *true directions*. If the compass rose is oriented to magnetic north or south (as defined by the magnetic poles), the directions are called *magnetic directions*. The magnetic north pole is currently west of Greenland, about 15° from the north geographic pole; the south magnetic pole is off the coast of Antarctica, toward Australia, about 22° from the south geographic pole. These differences between the locations of the geographic and magnetic poles cause magnetic instruments to show considerable but largely predictable and compensable errors in some locations. For finer resolution, each degree is subdivided into 60 equal minutes of arc, and each minute is further subdivided into 60 equal seconds. Thus, a second of arc is 1/1,296,000 of a full circle. It is not widely realized that the coordinates of geographic position (latitude and longitude) and the basic unit of distance in modern navigation (the nautical mile) are based on this same system of angular measurement.

GEOGRAPHIC POSITION

The coordinate system in which locations on the face of the earth are specified is based on a mapping of this circle onto the earth itself. Every location has a *latitude* and a *longitude*. The latitude of a place is its angular distance from the equator. Points on the equator itself have latitude 0°. The north and south poles, which are defined by the axis of rotation of the planet, are each a quarter of a circle away from the equator and are therefore at latitude 90°. Locations in the northern hemisphere are said to have north latitude; those in the southern hemisphere have south latitude.

A geometric plane passed through the earth such that it contains the Planet's axis of rotation will define two meridians where it intersects the earth's surface. Longitude is the angular distance of the meridian of a place from an arbitrarily selected meridian that passes through Greenwich, England.

The Greenwich or Prime meridian defines longitude 0°; its partner, stretching down the Pacific ocean on the other side of the globe, defines longitude 18°. Locations that lie in the 180° to the west of Greenwich are given west longitudes; those in the 180° to the east are given east longitude. Positions are given in terms of these two one-dimensional constraints. Global positions are specified in terms of this general system. Specific positions are fixed, as described in the examples given in the previous section, by their relation to actual locations in the immediately surrounding local space. The nautical chart is a medium in which the specification of positions can be transformed from the local to the global and vice versa.

THE NAUTICAL MILE

The nautical mile, the primary unit of distance in maritime navigation, is based on this system of angular measurement. A nautical mile is one minute of arc on the surface of the earth. Thus, there are $360 \times 60 = 21{,}600$ nautical miles around the circumference of the earth. The size of this unit has varied historically with variations in the estimation of the size of the earth. Columbus and Magellan assumed a smaller earth that had 45.3 modern nautical miles per degree of latitude. The earth turned out to be about 32 percent larger than they thought. The statute mile (now established as 5,280 feet in the United States) is a descendant of an earlier Roman mile that was also intended to be 1/21,600 of the circumference of the earth. As measurement of the earth improved and previous estimates were found to be in error, there were proposals to change the length of the mile itself and proposals to change the number of miles in a degree. For navigation at sea the easy mapping between position descriptions by angular displacement and the size of the major unit of distance is extremely useful. Having one minute of arc equal one nautical mile simplifies many computations at sea. Since this relationship would have been destroyed by changing the number of miles in a degree, the length of the nautical mile was changed. The modern nautical mile—6,076.11549 feet—is an attempt to preserve that relationship. However, the modern nautical mile is still an approximation. Because the earth is not a sphere, the length of a minute of latitude varies from about 6080.2 feet at the equator to 6108 feet at the poles. One minute of longitude at the equator is about 6087 feet. The current nautical mile is 1852 meters exactly. (Bowditch 1977)

·The *knot*, or nautical mile per hour, is the standard unit of velocity in navigation. This knot ties the circumference of the earth to the angular velocity of the earth. Because an hour is 1/24 of a day (a complete revolution of the earth), a point on the surface of the earth at the equator moves to the east at a rate of 1/24 of the circumference of the earth in nautical miles per hour. That is, 900 knots.

Charts

In the Western tradition of pilotage, virtually all computations involving position are carried out on nautical charts. While there are many other ways to represent the data and carry out the computations of navigation, the chart is the key representational artifact. The most obvious property of maps and charts is that they are spatial analogies. Positions on a map or a chart have correspondence with positions in a depicted large scale space. That is always true. But charts designed for navigation are something more than this. A navigation chart is a carefully crafted computational device.

In algebra and analytic geometry, many computations can be performed on graphs; in fact, graphs are essential in motivating the symbolic manipulations that form the real heart of computation in algebra and analytic geometry. One can compute all the points that lie between any two points by drawing a line between them. Or one can identify all the points that lie at a specified distance d from a given point by drawing a circle with radius d around the given point. Using graphs for computation, however, introduces errors, because plotted lines are less precise than the abstractions they depict (infinitely small points and truly one-dimensional lines). The infinite set of points lying between any two given points is accurately and economically represented by the equation of the line that contains the two points (and a range on x or y to constrain points to be between the reference points), and the set of points lying a specified distance from a given point is accurately and economically represented by the quadratic equation for the circle. Of course, the utility of these representations depends on the subsequent computations that they are supposed to support and the sort of computational systems that are available to carry out the computation.

It is essential to realize that a nautical chart is more akin to a coordinate space in analytic geometry than to the sort of simple map I may produce to guide a new acquaintance to my office. All maps are spatial analogies in the sense that they preserve some of the spatial relationships of the world they depict, but navigation charts depict spatial relationships in special ways that support certain specialized computations. A navigation chart is an analog computer. Clearly, all the problems that are solved on charts could be represented as equations and solved by symbol-processing techniques. Plotting a position or a course on a nautical chart is just as much a computation as solving the set of equations that represent the same constructs as the plotted points and lines. A chart contains an enormous amount of information—every location on it has a specifiable address, and the relationships of all the locations to all the others are implicitly represented.

Finally, charts introduce a perspective on the local space and on the position and motion of the vessel that is almost never achieved directly by any person. Standing over a chart, one has a "bird's-eye" view that, depending on the scale of the chart, could be duplicated with respect to the real space only from an aircraft or a satellite. Furthermore, the perspective is that of a spectator rather than that of a participant. This is one reason why establishing the correspondences between the features on a chart and the features in the local space is so difficult. In order to reconcile the chart to the territory, one must imagine how the world that is seen from a location on the surface would appear from a point of view from which it is never seen. The chart depiction assumes a very different perspective than that of the observer on the vessel. The experience of motion for the observer on the vessel is of moving through a surrounding space, while the depiction of motion on a chart is that of an object moving across a space. This other perspective created by the chart is so compelling that a navigator may have difficulty imagining his movements, especially over large spaces, from the traveler's perspective. Conversely, people who have had no experience with maps and charts may find them completely baffling.

THE COMPUTATIONAL PROPERTIES OF CHART PROJECTIONS
Not all charts are equally useful for all sorts of computations. For example, compare rhumb-line sailing with radio-beacon navigation.

Rhumb-line sailing
A *rhumb line* is a line on the surface of the earth that represents a constant direction from some location. Rhumb-line sailing refers to a form of navigation in which one sets a course to a destination and then maintains a constant heading until the destination is reached. When one is steering a ship by any sort of compass, the simplest route is a constant heading. For this task it is very useful to have a chart on which rhumb lines are straight lines. However, if one were to plot the course that would result from steering a constant heading on a globe rather than on a chart, one would produce a line that

wraps around the globe and spirals up to the pole. This line is called a *loxodrome*.

The Mercator projection overcomes this problem and transforms the spiral into a straight line. Imagine the transformation in two steps. First, the meridians of longitude that actually converge with one another at the poles of the globe are made parallel to one another, so that they are just as far apart at high latitudes as they are at the equator. This introduces a systematic distortion. At the equator there is no distortion, but with increasing latitude the east-west distance shown between the meridians on the chart exceeds by an increasing margin the distance between them on the globe. At the poles, of course, the distortion is infinite—what was zero distance between meridians where they converged at the pole of the globe would appear as a finite distance on the chart. To compensate for the effects of this distortion on direction, the parallels of latitude are expanded by the same ratio as the meridians of longitude. At the poles this would require infinite expansion, which is why the poles never appear on Mercator projections. This expansion also results in a distortion of the relative areas depicted on the chart. This distortion is more pronounced at higher latitudes. Thus, while Greenland actually has only 1/9 the area of South America, they appear to have roughly the same area on a Mercator chart.

Radio-beacon navigation
Radio beacon navigation uses radio antennae that are sensitive to direction. Such an antenna can determine the direction from which it receives a radio signal. By tuning the antenna to a station whose location is known and identifying the direction from which the signal comes, one can establish a one-dimensional position constraint. However, a radio signal does not follow a rhumb line; it takes the shortest route. These shortest routes are called *great-circle* routes. A great-circle route is defined by the intersection with the surface of the earth of a plane that contains the center of the earth and the two points on the surface between which the route is to be constructed. Great-circle routes can be approximated by stretching a piece of yarn over the surface of a globe. The meridians of longitude define great circles, and so does the equator. All the circles of latitude other than the equator define rhumb-line courses that are not great circles. While the rhumb-line course from Los Angeles to Tokyo is almost exactly due west (and the heading is constant for the entire trip), the great-circle route leaves Los Angeles heading to

the northwest and arrives in Tokyo heading to the southwest. To plot a position from radio-beacon bearings, one would like a chart on which great circles are straight lines. Over short distances, great circles approximate straight lines on all projections; however, over long distances (and radio signals travel long distances) great circles are significantly different from rhumb lines. There is no chart projection on which both rhumb lines and great circles appear as straight lines.

In addition to the properties of having rhumb lines and great circles represented as straight lines, it is easy to imagine navigation tasks in which the following would be desirable chart properties:

- true shapes of physical features
- correct angular relationships among positions
- equal area, or the representation of areas in their correct relative proportions
- constant scale values for measuring distances

Whenever the three-dimensional surface of the earth is rendered in two dimensions, some of these properties are sacrificed. For example, the Mercator projection sacrifices true shape of physical features, equal area, and constant scale values for measuring distances in the interest of providing correct angular relationship and rhumb lines as straight lines. These features are most apparent on charts of large areas. As the area of the earth's surface represented by the chart decreases, the differences between projections becomes less noticeable.

Chart projections make it clear that different representational systems have different computational properties and permit differing implementations of the computations. For example, it is *possible* to draw a great circle on a Mercator projection; it is just very difficult to compute where the points should go. On a Lambert conformal chart it is quite easy to draw a great circle, because on this projection a straight line so nearly approximates a great circle that it is more than adequate for navigational purposes. One can see the work that went into constructing a chart as part of every one of the computations that is performed on the chart in its lifetime. This computation is distributed in space and time. Those who make the chart and those who use it are not known to one another (perhaps they are not even contemporaries), yet they are joint participants in a computational event every time the chart is used.

Summary

Large-scale space is represented as small-scale space on a chart. The primary frame of reference is the system of earth coordinates. Objects that are unmoving with respect to earth coordinates are given fixed locations on the chart. Every location can be assigned an absolute address in a global coordinate system. Direction, position, and distance are all defined in terms of a single universal framework, established by applying a scheme of angular measurement to the earth itself. A universal time standard in combination with the measurement of distance yields a universal unit of rate of movement. These units are universal in the sense that their interpretations do not change with changing location or circumstances of their use. Directions, positions, distances, and rates can all be represented as numbers, and any of the first three can also be modeled in the small-scale space of a chart. Line-of-position constraints are represented as lines on a chart; circles of position are represented as circles on a chart; position-displacement constraints are represented as positions and displacements on a chart. Distance, rate, and time are represented as numbers, and computations of the constraints among them are accomplished by digital arithmetic algorithms. All the major computations in this system are based on procedures that involve measurement (which is analog-to-digital conversion), followed by digital manipulation, followed by digital-to-analog conversion in the plotting of results on a chart.

Representational Assumptions of Micronesian Navigation

The computational account presented above also describes the computations carried out by Micronesian navigators (Hutchins 1983). Micronesian navigators establish their position in terms of the intersections of one-dimensional constraints. Substantial differences between Western and Micronesian navigation become apparent as soon as we consider the representations and the algorithms that the two cultural traditions have developed to satisfy the constraints of the task. A major problem with earlier Western studies of Micronesian navigation was that the representations used in the performance of Western navigation were assumed to be the most general description. Because they failed to see the computational level at all Gladwin (1970), Lewis (1972), Sarfert (1911), and Schück (1882) attempted to interpret the representations used in

Micronesian navigation in terms of the representations used in Western navigation, rather than interpreting both sets of representations in terms of a single, more general, computational account.

This brief discussion of Micronesian navigation is inserted here in the hope that it will make the importance of the distinction between the computational and representational level of description clearer. I also hope to show that even the most commonplace aspects of thinking in Western culture, as natural as they may seem, are historically contingent. In this light, the organization of systems of cultural representations may become visible and, once noticed, may come to seem much less obvious than before. Furthermore, because the representational and implementational levels constrain each other more closely than do the computational and representational, it is useful to see the relationship between the representational level and its implementation in cultures that are technologically quite different from each other.

For more than a thousand years, long-distance non-instrumental navigation has been practiced over large areas of Polynesia and Micronesia, and perhaps in parts of Melanesia. In Polynesia, the traditional techniques atrophied and were ultimately lost in the wake of contact with colonial powers. Only the Micronesians have maintained their traditional skills, and in the past two decades they have been the wellspring of navigation knowledge for a renaissance of traditional voyaging throughout the Pacific Basin (Finney 1979, 1991; Kyselka 1987; Lewis 1976, 1978).

Without recourse to mechanical, electrical, or even magnetic devices, the navigators of the Central Caroline Islands of Micronesia routinely embark on ocean voyages that take them several days out of the sight of land. Their technique seems at first glance to be inadequate for the job demanded of it, yet it consistently passes what Lewis (1972) has called "the stern test of landfall." Of the thousands of voyages made in the memory of living navigators, only a few have ended with the loss of a canoe. Western researchers traveling with these people have found that at any time during the voyage the navigators can accurately indicate the bearings of the port of departure, the destination, and other islands off to the side of the course being steered, even though all of these may be over the horizon and out of sight. These navigators are also able to tack upwind to an unseen island while keeping mental track of its changing bearing—a feat that is simply impossible for a Western navigator without instruments.

In the neighborhood of the Caroline Islands, less than 0.2 percent of the surface is land. The surface is a vast expanse of water dotted with about two dozen atolls and low islands. Experienced navigators in these waters routinely sail their outrigger canoes up to 150 miles between islands. The knowledge required to make these voyages is not held by all, but is the domain of a small number of experts.

The world of the navigator, however, contains more than a set of tiny islands on an undifferentiated expanse of ocean. Deep below, the presence of submerged reefs changes the apparent color of the water. The surface of the sea undulates with swells born in distant weather systems, and the interaction of the swells with islands produces distinctive swell patterns in the vicinity of land. Above the sea surface are the winds and weather patterns which govern the fate of sailors. Seabirds abound, especially in the vicinity of land. Finally, at night, there are the stars. Here in the Central Pacific, away from pollution and artificial light, the stars shine brightly and in incredible numbers. All these elements in the navigator's world are sources of information. The whole system of knowledge used by a Micronesian master navigator is well beyond the scope of this book. Here I will treat only a portion of the navigators' use of celestial cues.

The most complete description of this system comes from the work of Thomas Gladwin, who worked with the navigators of Puluwat Atoll in what is now the Republic of Micronesia. Gladwin (1970) divides the pragmatics of Puluwat navigation into three parts. First one must set out in a direction such that, knowing the conditions to be expected en route, one will arrive in the vicinity of the island of destination. Second, one must hold the canoe steady on its course and maintain a running estimate of its position. Finally, when nearing the destination one must be able to locate it and head toward it.

One of the most widespread notions employed in Pacific non-instrumental navigation is the concept of the *star path*. From the point of view of the earth, the positions of the stars relative to one another are fixed. As the earth rotates about its axis, the stars appear to move across the sky from east to west. As the earth moves through its orbit around the sun, the stars that can be seen at night (that is, from the side of the earth away from the sun) change. But from any fixed location on the earth, any given star always rises from the same point on the eastern horizon and always sets into the same point in the western horizon, regardless of season. Movement to the north or south does change the azimuth of the rising and setting of any star. Within the range of the Caroline Islands navigator, however, the effects of such movements are small (on the order of 3° or less). A star path, also known as a *linear constellation* (Aveni 1981), is a set of stars all of which "follow the same path" (Gladwin 1970). That is, they all rise in succession from the same point on the eastern horizon, describe the same arc across the sky, and set into the same point on the western horizon. Star paths are typically composed of from six to ten stars fairly evenly spaced across the heavens (Lewis 1972). Thus, when one star in the linear constellation has risen too far above the horizon to serve as an indication of direction, another will soon take its place. In this way, each star path describes two directions on the horizon, one in the east and one in the west, which are visible regardless of season or time of night as long as the skies are clear. A "connect the dots" drawing of such a linear constellation is simply an arc across the sky, anchored at fixed azimuths in the east and in the west. While the stars themselves make their nightly journeys across the sky, the arcs of the linear constellations remain stationary.

Seeing the night sky in terms of linear constellations is a simple representational artifice that converts the moving field of stars into a fixed frame of reference.

This seeing is not a passive perceptual process. Rather, it is the projection of external structure (the arrangement of stars in the heavens) and internal structure (the ability to identify the linear constellations) onto a single spatial image. In this superimposition of internal and external, elements of the external structure are given culturally meaningful relationships to one another. The process is actively constructive. The positions of a few stars may suggest a relationship which, when applied, establishes the identity of yet other stars. Anyone who can identify the traditional Western constellations knows that, in the subjective experience of this seeing, not just the stars but the constellations themselves seem to be "out there." The little lines holding the stars together seem nearly visible in the sky. These relations are expressed in verbal formulas. For example, the formula "Follow the arc (of the handle of the Big

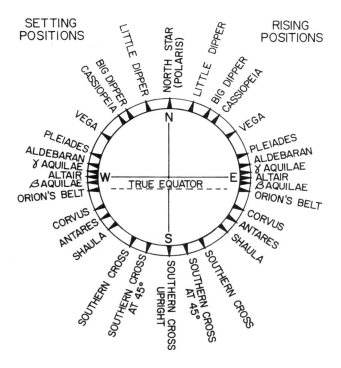

Figure 2.6   A Caroline Island sidereal compass.

Dipper) to Arcturus, and drive a spike into Spica" guides the observer's eye across the sky, constructing part of a constellation. In sky charts for amateur star watchers, the lines are drawn in on the charts—like mental training wheels—to make the constellations easier to imagine when looking at the sky.

It is known that star paths have long been used to define the courses between islands in many parts of Oceania (Lewis 1972). The navigators of the Caroline Islands have combined fourteen named star paths with the position of Polaris (the North Star) to form a sidereal compass that defines 32 directions around the circle of the horizon. Figure 2.6 shows a schematic representation of the Caroline Island sidereal compass. As can be seen, most of the recognized star bearings are named for major stars whose paths intersect the horizon at those points. Those which are not so named are the true-north bearing, named for Polaris which from the Caroline Islands is always about 8° above the northern horizon, and three bearings in the south which are defined by orientations of the Southern Cross above the horizon. Of course, the names given to these stars are not the same as the names given to them in the

Western tradition, nor are all the constellations grouped in the same way. The cardinal direction in the Micronesian system is east, at the rising point of the star Altair. It is interesting that Altair is part of a Micronesian constellation called the "Big Bird" (hence Gladwin's title *East is a Big Bird*). The Western tradition has inherited many of its star names from Arabic roots, and Altair is the brightest star in the constellation Aquila, the eagle. East was the cardinal direction in the Western tradition (consider the two meanings of the word 'orient') before the advent of the magnetic compass.

The inclusion of other stars which travel the same path guarantees that as long as the weather is clear the complete compass is available to the navigator no matter what time of year he is sailing. In fact, a practiced navigator can construct the whole compass mentally from a glimpse of only one or two stars near the horizon. This ability is crucial to the navigator's performance, because the star bearings that concern him during a voyage may not be those he can readily see. The star compass is an abstraction which can be oriented as a whole by determining the orientation of any part. During the day, the orientation of the star compass can be maintained by observing the star bearings from which the major ocean swells come and the star bearings at which the sun and the moon rise and set.

Courses between islands are defined in terms of this abstract sidereal compass. For every island in a navigator's sailing range, he knows the star point under which he must sail to reach any other island in the vicinity. Thus, the sidereal compass provides the directional reference in terms of which displacements can be specified.

The sidereal compass has a second function in navigation: the expression of distance traveled on a voyage. For every course from one island to another, a third island (over the horizon and out of sight of the first two) is taken as a reference for the expression of the distance traveled. In the language of Puluwat Atoll, this system of expressing distance traveled in terms of the changing bearing of a reference island is called *etak* (Gladwin 1970). Since he knows the star bearings for all the inter-island courses in his area, the navigator knows the star bearing of the reference island from his point of origin and the bearing of the reference island from his destination. In the navigator's conception, this reference island starts out under a particular star (at a particular star bearing) and moves back

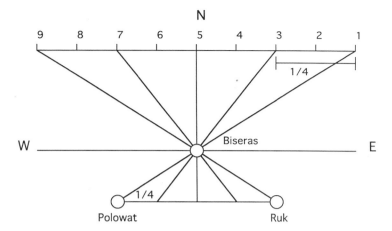

Figure 2.7 An *etak* diagram. This diagram, based on the work of the ethnographer E. Sarfert, reflects the conventional method of drawing the relationships between islands and star points for a typical voyage.

abeam of the canoe during the voyage through a succession of star bearings until the canoe reaches its destination, at which time the reference island is under the point that defines the course from the destination island to the reference island. The changing star bearing of the reference island during the voyage is illustrated in figure 2.7.

The movement of the reference island under the succession of star bearings divides the voyage conceptually into a set of segments called the *etak*s of the voyage. Each voyage has a known number of *etak* segments defined by the passage of the reference island under the star bearings.

A fundamental conception in Caroline Island navigation is that a canoe on course between islands is stationary and the islands move by the canoe. This is, of course, unlike our notion of the vessel moving between stationary islands. A passage from Gladwin (1970: 182) amplifies this:

Picture yourself on a Puluwat canoe at night. The weather is clear, the stars are out, but no land is in sight. The canoe is a familiar little world. Men sit about, talk, perhaps move around a little within their microcosm. On either side of the canoe, water streams past, a line of turbulence and bubbles merging into a wake and disappearing into the darkness. Overhead there are stars, immovable, immutable. They swing in their paths across and out of the sky but invariably come up again in the same places. You may travel for days on the canoe, but the stars will not go away or change their positions aside from their nightly trajectories from horizon to horizon. Hours go by, miles of water have flowed past. Yet the canoe is still underneath and the stars are still above. Back along the wake however, the island you left falls farther and farther behind, while the one toward which you are heading is hopefully drawing closer. You can see neither of them, but you know this is happening. You know too that there are islands on either side of you, some near, some far, some ahead, some behind. The ones that are ahead will, in due course, fall behind. Everything passes by the little canoe—everything except the stars by night and the sun in the day.

Here we have a conceptualization in which the known geography is moving past the navigator, his canoe, and the stars in the sky. Off to the side of the course being steered is the reference island. It cannot be seen because of its distance over the horizon, yet the navigator imagines it to be moving back slowly under a sequence of star points on the horizon. Observations of navigators during voyages have shown that the navigators can accurately judge the relative bearing of the reference island at any time during the voyage (Lewis 1972). Since the navigator has not actually *seen* the reference island at any point during the voyage, his ability to indicate where it lies represents an inference that could not be made in the Western system without recourse to tools.

Gladwin (1970: 184) describes the Micronesian navigator's use of this judgement as follows:

When the navigator envisions in his mind's eye that the reference island is passing under a particular star he notes that a certain number of segments have been completed and a certain proportion of the voyage has therefore been accomplished.

The navigator uses this information to estimate when he will be in the vicinity of his destination, and therefore when he should start looking for signs of land. Since land-based birds venture as far as 20 miles to sea, seeing them arrive at a fishing ground from land or seeing them depart a fishing ground for land can give information at a distance about the direction in which land lies. This information is available only in the early morning and at dusk, when the birds are moving from or to their island. A navigator who arrives at what he believes to be the vicinity of his destination at midday is therefore well advised to drop sail and wait for dusk. The danger of failing to make an accurate judgement of when land is near is that one might be close to land when no indications are available and then sail past and be far away from the destination when homing signs are available.

Because traditional Micronesian culture is nonliterate, navigators are required to commit a large body of information to memory. Riesenberg (1972) has documented some of the elaborate mnemonic devices used by navigators to organize their knowledge of geography, star courses, and etak segments. An interesting finding of Riesenberg's work is that the memorized systems of knowledge make frequent reference to islands that do not exist. Riesenberg (1972: 20) explains:

In a few instances, when unknown geographical features were mentioned and when enough courses from identifiable islands to them have been given, an attempt has been made to locate them by projecting the courses on a chart. The intersections of the projected courses generally coincide poorly with known bathymetric features.

The role of these phantom islands will be taken up in a later section of this chapter.

Some Anomalous Interpretations

The history of attempts to understand how the Micronesian navigators accomplished their way-finding feats reads like a detective story in which we know who did it but not how it was done. Each of several researchers has provided us with both useful clues and a few red herrings.

There is little dispute about the nature of course-keeping with the sidereal compass. Western accounts of the star compass go back at least to 1722 (Schück 1882), and its use seems relatively easy to observe and document. The most detailed description of the star compass of the Caroline Islands was provided by Goodenough (1953). Although his diagram reproduced above as figure 2.6 is, as far as we know, a completely accurate depiction of the stars used by the Caroline Island navigators, and although it gives the first complete tabulation of the azimuths (true bearings on the horizon) and names of the star points, it contains a potentially misleading distortion that was probably incorporated to make the compass concept more accessible to Western readers. Goodenough drew the compass as a circular compass rose, the way compasses are traditionally represented in our culture. The original records of native depictions of the star compass, however, are all box-shaped.

To date there have been two attempts to explain just how the Caroline Island navigators use the concept of *etak* to keep track of their progress on a voyage: Sarfert's (1911) and Gladwin's (1970). Sarfert's (1911: 134) description is rich and compact and bears careful consideration:

In an arbitrary voyage between two determined islands, the native captains have still a third island in mind, besides the starting point and goal of the trip. For the voyage between every pair of islands, this is a specific island. Henceforth, I will refer to this island simply as "emergency island" [Notinsel] corresponding to the purpose that it serves as a last place to flee to in case of extenuating circumstances that make it impossible to reach either the starting point or goal of the trip. This island is placed off to the side of the course. In rare situations the natives established two islands as emergency islands, specifically in such a way that one lies to the left and the other to the right of the direction of travel.

Riesenberg's (1972) discovery that the reference islands for some voyages are phantoms, however, makes the "emergency island" interpretation unlikely. No navigator would attempt to take refuge in a location known to be devoid of land. Another possibility is that knowing the location of the reference island as well as the origin and destination of the voyage allows the navigator to estimate accurately where many other islands in the area are, so that, should he need to take refuge, a choice based on the existing conditions of the wind and the sea might be made among several possible islands. The specification of the placement of the islands is no doubt important; but if they were places in which to take refuge, why would it not be just as well to have two "emergency islands" on the same side of the course?

Sarfert continues:

In figure [2.7 of this chapter—E.H.], the island Biseras, a small island of the Onona atoll, serves as emergency island in the already given voyage from Polowat to Ruk [Truk]. If the emergency island is to fulfill its purpose, the captain must be capable of determining at any moment the direction in which the island lies, and therefore the course to it, from an arbitrary point of the voyage. As far as I have experience about it, he ... does this by rather simple means:

1) The direction of the island Biseras from Polowat as well as from Ruk is known.

2) The native captain may undertake a bearing of the area during the trip by means of calculating the already-traveled distance. This is done with the aid of experience, knowledge of the normal duration of the voyage and with the help of an estimate of the speed that the canoe travels through the water. This last means, the so-called dead reckoning, was also in general used by us for the same purpose before the introduction of the log at the end of the sixteenth century.

3) To determine the bearing of the emergency island from the vantage point of the canoe, the observation must necessarily be done such that, as [figure 2.7] clearly demonstrates, it describes the emergency island Biseras, from the canoe as a visible movement on the horizon in the opposite direction of the voyage. This visible movement of the emergency island appears, with the interpretation of the horizon as a straight line, in direct relationship to the already-traversed distance. If the captain estimates, for example, the covered path as being a quarter of the total voyage length, then the emergency island must have completed likewise a quarter of its visible path along the horizon. If the total length of the visible path totals eight (etak) lines, then after one quarter of the trip they would have reached, accordingly, the third line. By means of this simple calculation, the course to the emergency island is confirmed and the captain is capable of seeking it out. (135)

The major issue raised by Sarfert's proposed calculation technique involves the method used to express the proportion of the total voyage that has been completed. It is easy enough to imagine how the navigator might represent the fact that "the emergency island must have completed a quarter of its visible path along the horizon," although it is doubtful that proportions like "a quarter" are involved. But how does the captain compute that he has covered some proportion of the total length of the voyage? Further, the expression of the movement of the emergency island in terms of the proportion of the number of *etak* segments will work only if the *etak* segments themselves are all nearly the same size.

Gladwin's descriptive model, like Sarfert's, relates the bearing of the *etak* reference island to the distance traveled. However, Sarfert believed that the navigator computed the apparent bearing of the *etak* island so that he could take refuge there, whereas Gladwin asserted that the navigator used that apparent position as an expression of the proportion of the voyage completed. Gladwin states:

When the navigator envisions in his mind's eye that the reference island is passing under a particular star he notes that a certain number of segments have been completed and a certain proportion of the voyage has therefore been accomplished. (184)

This is similar to Sarfert's proportional-derivation model, but the subtle difference raises an interesting question. What is the nature of the computation? Is it, as Sarfert maintains, that the navigator uses his estimate of the proportion of the voyage completed to establish the bearing of the reference island, or, as Gladwin maintains, that the navigator uses his estimate of the bearing of the reference island to establish the proportion of the voyage that has been accomplished? Clearly, these concepts are closely related for the navigator.

In practice, not every inter-island course is situated such that there is an island to the side of the course with the desired properties of an etak island. Gladwin notes:

If the reference island is too close, it passes under many stars, dividing the journey into a lot of segments. Worse, the segments are of very unequal length. They start out rather long (slow) and then as the canoe passes close by, they become shorter (fast) as the reference island swings under one star after another, and then at the end they are long again, a confusing effect. A distant reference island has the opposite effect making the segments approximately equal, but so few in number that they do not divide the journey into components of a useful size. (187)

The effect of having a close reference island is confusing because when a voyage is divided into segments of very different lengths the estimation of the number of segments remaining is a poor measure of the distance remaining in the voyage. Gladwin describes another situation, also noted by Sarfert, in which this same sort of confusion was bound to arise. In a discussion with the master navigator Ikuliman, Gladwin discovered that for the voyage between Puluwat and Pulusuk atolls, a distance of about 30 miles, the navigator used two *etak* islands—one to the west of the course and nearby, the other to the east and quite distant:

This case well illustrates one of the difficulties with the practice: when two reference islands are used in this way, the segments are almost certain to be markedly different in length. Ikuliman was not able to offer a good explanation for using two islands, insisting only that this is the way it is taught. When I pressed him further, he observed dryly that Puluwat and Pulusuk are so close together that a navigator does not really need to use ETAK at all in order to establish his position on this seaway, so in this case my question was irrelevant. (188)

Another feature of the system in use that seems to give rise to the same sort of conceptual difficulty is that the first two and last two segments of the voyages are all about the same length, regardless of the positioning of the reference island relative to the courses and regardless of the density of star points in the portion of the horizon through which the reference island is imagined to be moving. Gladwin states:

Upon leaving an island, one enters upon the "ETAK of sighting," a segment which lasts as long as the island remains in view, usually about 10 miles. When the island has at last disappeared, one enters the "ETAK of birds" which extends out as far as the flights of birds which sleep ashore each night. This is about twenty miles from land, making the first two and therefore also the last two, segments each about ten miles long. Having four segments of the voyage absolute in length is logically incongruous (by our criteria) with the proportional derivation of the remainder of the ETAK divisions. (188)

Again, the problem with this conception is that it interferes with the computation of the distance remaining in the voyage because it destroys the consistency of the *etak* segments as units of distance. Gladwin explored this inconsistency with his main informant, the navigator Hipour—who later sailed with Lewis to Saipan and back using the system described here (Lewis 1972, 1976, 1978). Gladwin continues:

When I tried to explore with Hipour how he resolved the discrepancy he simply replied that beyond the ETAK of birds he uses the reference island to establish distance. When I asked how he handled the problem of segments ending in different places, under the two methods, he said he did not see this as a problem. As with

*Ikuliman's answer to my "problem" over the dual reference is-
lands, this ended the discussion. (189)*

The major difficulty with Sarfert's model, and all the "problems"
that Gladwin raised with his navigator informants, spring from the
observation that *etak* segments are unsuitable units for the measurement of distance covered on a voyage. One interpretation of this
state of affairs is that what appeared to be a logical organizing
principle in navigation may be a useful description in the abstract,
but that in the exigencies of use it is not strictly adhered to.
Gladwin concludes:

*Although ETAK has for us much the quality of a systematic orga-
nizing principle or even logical construct, the Puluwat navigator
does not let logical consistency or inconsistency, insofar as he is
aware of them, interfere with practical utility. (189)*

There is, of course, another possible interpretation: that the apparent anomalies result from the unwarranted assumption that the
etak segments are units of measurement. The notion that consistent
units of measurement are necessary for accurate navigation is one
of the fundamental representational assumptions of our system of
navigation—so much so, in fact, that it is hard for us to conceive of
a system of navigation that does not rely on such units and a set of
operations for manipulating them. Yet there is no evidence in the
record that the *etak* segments perform that function, nor is there
any evidence of any set of mental arithmetic operations that would
permit a navigator to manipulate *etak* segments as though they
were units of distance.

A Conceptual Blind Spot

The following revealing incident occurred while Lewis was working with the master navigators Hipour of Puluwat and Beiong of
Pulusuk. According to Lewis:

*On one occasion I was trying to determine the identity of an island
called Ngatik—there were no charts to be consulted of course—
that lay somewhere south-west of Ponape. It has not been visited by
Central Carolinian canoes for several generations but was an ETAK
reference island for the Oroluk—Ponape voyage and as such, its
star bearings from both these islands were known to Hipour. On his
telling me what they were, I drew a diagram to illustrate that Ngatik*

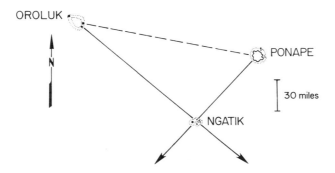

Figure 2.8   Lewis's method of determining the position of the island Ngatik.

must necessarily lie where these ETAK bearings intersected. [See figure 2.8.] Hipour could not grasp this idea at all. His concept is the wholly dynamic one of moving islands. (1972: 142)

This passage raises several important questions: Why did Lewis use the technique of drawing the intersecting bearings in order to determine the location of the island called Ngatik? Why did Lewis assume that posing the question the way he did would make sense to Hipour? Why did Hipour not grasp the idea of the intersecting bearings?

Let us consider the questions about Lewis first. The technique Lewis used is clearly an effective one for the solution of this particular problem. It establishes a two-dimensional constraint on the location of Ngatik by combining two one-dimensional constraints. It also contains some very powerful assumptions about the relation of the problem solver to the space in which the problem is being solved. First, it requires a global representation of the locations of the various pieces of land relative to each other. In addition, it requires a point of view relative to that space which we might call the "bird's-eye" view. The problem solver does not (and cannot without an aircraft) actually assume this relation to the world in which the problem is posed. We can guess that Lewis did this because it is for him a natural framework in which to pose questions and solve problems having to do with the relative locations of objects in a two-dimensional space. Western navigators make incessant use of this point of view. When a Western navigator takes a bearing of landmark, he has a real point of view on a real space. However, as soon as he leans over his chart, he is no longer conceptually on the boat; he is over the sea surface, looking down on the position of his craft in a representation of the real local space. Novice navigators sometimes find this change of viewpoint disorienting, especially if the orientation of the chart does not happen to correspond to the orientation of objects in the world.

Beiong was also puzzled by Lewis's assertion, and in reaching an understanding of it he provides us with an important insight into the operation of the Micronesian conceptual system:

He eventually succeeded in achieving the mental tour de force of visualizing himself sailing simultaneously from Oroluk to Ponape and from Ponape to Oroluk and picturing the ETAK bearings to Ngatik at the start of both voyages. In this way he managed to comprehend the diagram and confirmed that it showed the island's position correctly. (143)

The nature of Beiong's understanding indicates that for the Caroline Island navigator the star bearing of an island is not simply the orientation of a line in space but *the direction of a star point from the position of the navigator*. In order to see that the star bearings would indeed intersect each other at the island, he had to imagine himself to be at both ends of the voyage at once. This allowed him to visualize the star bearing from Oroluk to Ngatik radiating from a navigator at Oroluk and the star bearing from Ponape to Ngatik radiating from a navigator at Ponape. What Hipour probably imagined when Lewis asserted that the island lies where the bearings cross must have been something like the situation depicted in figure 2.9. Contrast this with what Lewis imagined he was asserting (figure 2.8). Hipour's consternation is now perhaps more understandable. The star bearings of the *etak* island radiate out from the navigator himself. From this perspective they meet only at him. In his conception of this voyage, the *etak* island begins under one of these bearings and ends under the other. That two relative bearings might meet anywhere other than at the navigator is inconceivable.

Because the Caroline Island navigator takes a real point of view on the real local space to determine the star bearings, it does not seem likely that the mapping of *etak* segments onto an abstract representation of the expanse of water between the islands is faithful to his conception. Gladwin's (1970) statement about the navigator's noting that "a certain number of segments have been completed" and the diagrams that Lewis, Gladwin, and Sarfert use to represent the changing relative bearing of the *etak* reference island all contain two implicit assumptions: that the navigator uses

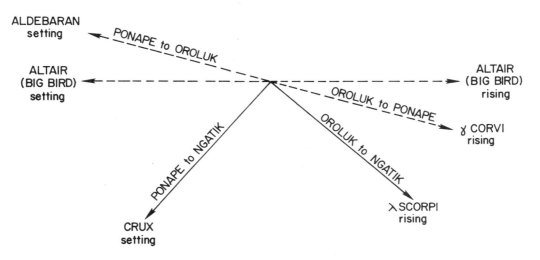

Figure 2.9 Hipour's way of thinking about star bearings. For the Micronesian navigator, all bearings originate at himself and radiate outward. This diagram puts the Micronesian conception in the Western bird's-eye perspective.

some sort of bird's-eye view of the space he is in, and that he conceives of a voyage in terms of changes in the position of his canoe in a space upon which he has an unchanging point of view. These assumptions are true of the Western navigator's conception of a voyage, but they appear not to be true of the Caroline Island navigator's conception. These assumptions are at odds with the verbal data (i.e., descriptions of the islands moving relative to the navigator) and with the behavioral data (i.e., consternation in the face of what ought to be a trivial inference).

It is tempting to criticize the Caroline Island navigators for maintaining an egocentric perspective on the voyage when the global perspective of the chart seems so much more powerful. Before concluding that the Western view is superior, consider the following thought experiment: Go at dawn to a high place and point directly at the center of the rising sun. That defines a line in space. Return to the same high place at noon and point again to the center of the sun. That defines another line in space. I assert that the sun is located in space where those two lines cross. Does that seem wrong? Do you feel that the two lines meet where you stand and nowhere else? In spite of the fact that the lines seem to be orthogonal to each other, they do cross at the sun. This is not intuitively obvious to us, because our usual way of conceiving of the

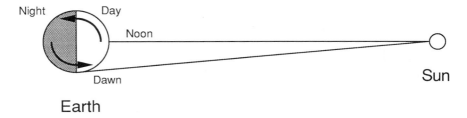

Figure 2.10 A heliocentric depiction (not to scale) of pointing at the sun at dawn and then again at noon. The sun is indeed located where the lines cross.

sun's location is not to conceive of its location at all. Rather, we think of its orientation relative to a frame defined by the horizons and the zenith on earth. The rotation of the earth is not experienced as the movement of the surface of the earth around its center, but as the movement of the celestial bodies around the earth. From a point of view outside the solar system, however, the intersection of the lines is obvious, and it is immediately apparent that the sun is in fact located where the lines cross (figure 2.10).

Our everyday models of the sun's movement are exactly analogous to the Caroline Island navigator's conception of the location of the reference island. The choice of representations limits the sorts of inferences that make sense. Because we Westerners have all been exposed to the ideas of Copernicus, we can sit down and convince ourselves that what we experience is an artifact of our being on the face of a spinning planet. That is, after all, the "correct" way to think of it, but it is not necessarily the most useful way. Modern celestial navigation is deliberately pre-Copernican precisely because a geocentric conception of the apparent movements of bodies on a rigid celestial sphere makes the requisite inferences about the positions of celestial bodies much easier to compute than they would be in a heliocentric representation. From a perspective outside the galaxy, of course, the heliocentric conception itself is seen to be a fiction which gives an improved account of the relative movements of bodies within the solar system but which is incapable of accounting for the motion of the solar system relative to the other stars in the universe. Such a "veridical cosmology" is irrelevant to any present-day navigator's concerns.

These observations place strong constraints on candidate models of how the Caroline Island navigators use the *etak* system. Viable models must not rely on arbitrary units of distance, nor should they involve a bird's-eye view of the navigator and his craft situated in some represented space.

An Alternative Model

What does the Caroline Island navigator gain by using the conception of the moving reference island? Western navigators find the use of a chart or some other model indispensable for expressing and keeping track of how much of the journey has been completed and how much remains. While the Caroline Island navigators are fully capable of imagining and even drawing charts of their island group, these conceptions are not compatible with the moving-island and star-bearing conceptions they use while navigating. Lewis's diagram was nonsense to Hipour because Hipour never takes a bird's-eye point of view when he is thinking about star bearings. In addition, even though the necessary technology is available to them, we know that the navigators carry nothing like a chart with them on their voyages.

Consider the Caroline navigator's conception in its context of use. At the outset of any voyage, the navigator imagines that the reference island is over the horizon ahead of him and to one side. It is, for him, under the point on the horizon marked by the rising or setting of a particular line of stars. During the course of the voyage, the reference island will move back along its track, remaining out of sight of the navigator. As it does so, it will assume positions under a succession of star bearings until it lies under the star bearing that marks the course from the destination to the reference island. If the helmsman has kept a straight course, then the canoe will be at the destination when this happens. An important aspect of this imagined sweep of the reference island back along its track, out of sight of the navigator, has been ignored by recent writers on Caroline navigation but was noticed by Sarfert in 1911. Sarfert was struck by the fact that the navigators conceive of the horizon as a straight line lying parallel to the course of the canoe. For a Western navigator, who normally conceives of the horizon as a circle around him, this is a puzzling observation. Why should these navigators make such a counterfactual assumption?

Sarfert realized the importance of the fact that the Caroline navigator conceives of the horizon as a straight line and imagines the apparent movement of the reference island beyond it. With this

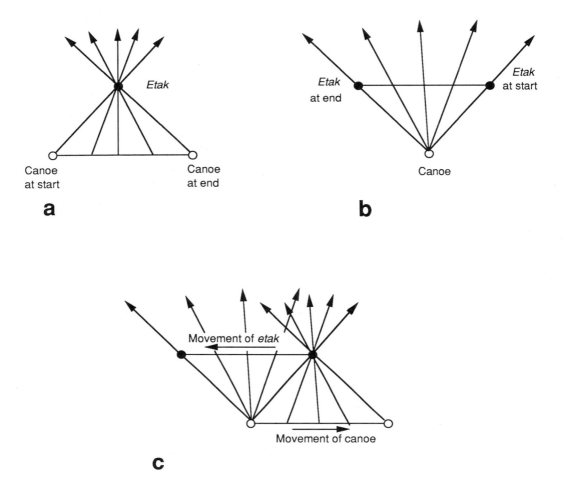

Figure 2.11 (a) The standard Western representation of the movement of the canoe and changing star bearings to the *etak* island. (b) The Micronesian representation of the same phenomenon as the movement of the *etak* island under the star bearings. (c) Illustration that the imagined movement of the *etak* island is a model of the movement of the canoe along the course

image the horizon itself becomes a line, parallel to the course steered, on which the progress of the reference island from initial bearing through a set of intermediate bearings to the final bearing is exactly proportional to the progress of the canoe from the island of departure across the sea to the goal island (figure 2.11). Of course, the navigator does not think of it from the bird's-eye perspective provided by the figure. Rather, the imagined movement of the *etak* reference island just under the horizon is a complete model of the voyage which is visualizable (but not visible) from the natural point of view of the navigator in the canoe (figure 2.12). It is a repre-

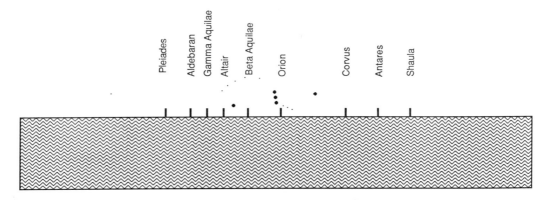

Figure 2.12 The horizon with star points as seen from the canoe. When the navigator looks at the horizon, he imagines the locations of the star bearings. In this diagram, the constellation Orion is shown rising. This serves as an anchor for the construction of the entire star compass, including points defined by stars that are not presently visible. The shaded region below the horizon represents the water between the canoe and the horizon.

sentation of the spatial extent of the voyage, and of one's progress along it, that does not require either the construction of a map or a change of viewpoint. The straight-line-horizon conception is essential to the transformation of angular displacement into linear displacement.

The image of the *etak* reference island moving along just below the horizon can be quite naturally tied to the passage of time. Part of the knowledge that a navigator has about every voyage is the amount of time he can expect the trip to take under various conditions. Suppose that the navigator knows for a particular voyage that, under favorable conditions, he will arrive at his goal after one day of sailing. If he leaves his island of departure at noon (a common departure time), he can estimate that he will arrive at his destination at about noon on the following day. In terms of the movement of the reference island, this means that the island will move from a position under the initial bearing to a position under the final bearing in one day (figure 2.13). Still assuming a normal rate of travel, he can associate other times during the voyage with other bearings of the reference island (figure 2.14). In so doing, he not only has a visual image that represents the extent of the voyage in space; he also has one that represents the voyage and its subparts in time. If the sailing conditions are as expected, the task of determining where the reference island is positioned over the horizon at any point in time is trivial. All the navigator need do is determine

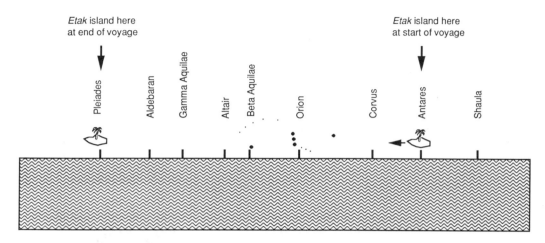

Figure 2.13   The superimposition of starting and ending bearings on the star points. The star bearing of the *etak* island at the start of the voyage is under the star point defined by Antares. At the end of the voyage the star bearing of the *etak* island is under the Pleiades. The *etak* is imagined to move along beyond the horizon from the star point defined by Antares to the star point defined by the Pleiades.

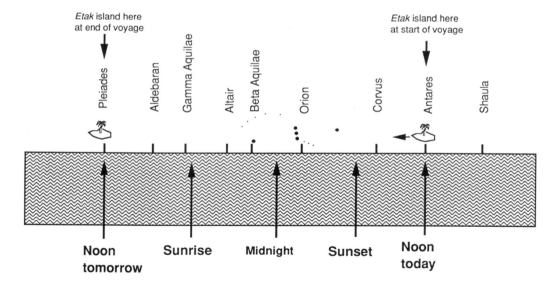

Figure 2.14   Temporal landmarks superimposed on star points and the image of the *etak* island. The expected duration of the voyage is mapped uniformly onto the space defined by the starting and ending star bearings of the *etak* island.

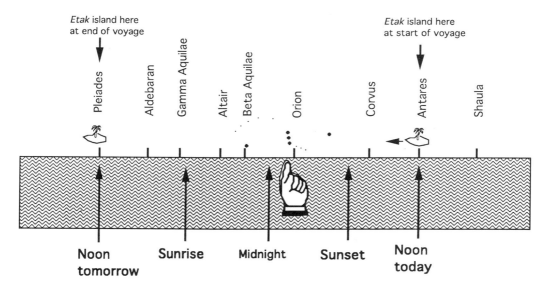

Figure 2.15 Just before midnight the navigator points to the *etak* island. All he needs to do is point to the location of the current time on the time scale that is superimposed on the spatial landmarks provided by the star points.

the time of day and refer to the image of the reference island moving along under the horizon. By pointing to the position on the horizon that represents the present time of day, the navigator has pointed directly at the reference island (figure 2.15).

The assumption that *etak* segments are units of distance led Gladwin to three related apparent inconsistencies: the supposedly confusing effect of having *etak* segments be of different lengths, the conflicting boundaries of *etak* segments defined by using more than one *etak* island at once, and the conflicting boundaries of *etak* segments at the beginning and end of a voyage (caused by using the *etak* of birds and the *etak* of sighting in addition to the star-bearing-defined *etak* segments). Gladwin found these conceptions "completely inconsistent with the theory as described above" (189).

In my model, there is no need to assume that the *etak* segments are units of distance. We dispense with the notion that the numbers of *etak* segments enter into a numerical computation of the proportion of the voyage completed or remaining. The inequality of their lengths is not an awkward conceptual problem; it simply means that on a typical voyage the navigator will have more conceptual landmarks defined by star bearings in the middle of the voyage than at the ends. In fact, if we listen to the navigators, we find that they are not talking about the spatial duration (length) of the *etak* segments, but of their temporal duration. As Gladwin (1970: 187) notes, "They start out being rather long ('slow') and then as the canoe passes close by, they become shorter ('fast') as the reference island swings under one star after another, and then at the end they are long again, a confusing effect." The concern of the navigator is not how far he travels in a particular etak segment, but how long he will travel before asserting that the reference island has moved back under the next star bearing.

When the concept of the *etak* segment is freed from the notion of a unit of distance, the apparent problem of using more than one *etak* island at once, and the apparent problem of overlapping the star-bearing-determined etak segments with those determined by the range of birds and the range of sighting disappear. Using one *etak* island to each side of a voyage gives the navigator more conceptual landmarks on his voyage. There is no reason for it to be a problem to the navigator. If two reference islands were on the same side of the voyage, however, the navigator would have two complete but non-coextensive sets of time-bearing correspondences superimposed on a single horizon, and that probably would be a source of confusion. But Sarfert (1911: 134) was quite clear on this issue; he said that when two *etak* islands are used, they are chosen "specifically in such a way that one lies to the left and the other to the right of the direction of travel." The confusion that Gladwin imagined with one reference island to each side does not arise, since the *etak* segments are mapped not onto the course line but onto the imagery on the horizon in front of the reference islands (figure 2.16).

The strategy of including the *etak* of sighting and the *etak* of birds is entirely consistent with the notion of the star-bearing-defined *etak* division as a conceptual landmark. The star-bearing-defined *etak* segments are conceptual landmarks derived in a particular way, and the *etak* of sighting is a conceptual landmark determined in another way. Once established, they function for the navigator in the same way. They do not enter into a numerical computation; rather, they give the navigator a more direct representation of where he is (or, actually, where land is). In addition, since the star-bearing etak segments are slow in passing near the beginning and near the end of the voyage, it may be helpful to the navigator to have the other conceptual landmarks at those points.

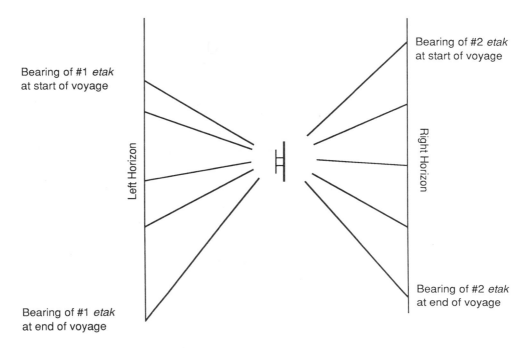

Figure 2.16 The effect of using two *etak* islands, one on each side of the course. The star bearings of the two *etak* islands do not interfere with each other, because they are mapped onto separate images constructed on the horizons on opposite sides of the course.

What of the phantom *etak* islands that correspond to no known bathymetric features? If the conception of *etak* presented here is correct, there is no need for there to ever be an island present at the *etak* point. One need only decide, for any particular voyage, that one is going to model the progress of the voyage as the movement of an unseen point that starts out under a star bearing ahead of and to the side of the course and ends up under a star bearing behind and to the same side of the course. Such a phantom construct does all the conceptual work required of the *etak*. Neisser has remarked that the error of assuming that *etak* islands must be safety islands to which one sails in case of danger is "an overly concrete interpretation of the navigators abstract idea" (Neisser 1976, cited in Frake 1985).

This conception and this technique make computing the location of land trivial when conditions are favorable. Suppose, however, that a voyage must be made under conditions which differ from those expected at the outset of the voyage. How could the navigator update his image of the movement of the reference island to reflect what is happening to his rate of travel? The key to this problem lies in the judgement of speed and in the way that this judgement is expressed. Any experienced Western yachtsman can make fairly accurate judgements of his boat's speed through the water without the aid of instruments. By attending to the feel of the boat as it moves through the water, the accelerations developed as it moves over waves, the feel of the apparent wind, the appearance and sound of the wake (it sizzles at speeds in excess of about 5 knots), the response of the helm, and many other sensations, the small-boat sailor can make judgements that he normally expresses as a number of units—usually knots. The knot is a good choice for the yachtsman; as one nautical mile per hour, it is convenient for subsequent numerical calculations. One might have expressed the speed as furlongs per fortnight, or on a scale of how thrilling it is, but neither of these fits especially well with useful subsequent calculations. The same must be true for the Caroline Island navigators. There is no doubt that they can make accurate judgements of speed; however, expressing those judgements in terms of knots would not be advantageous at all for them, because that unit is not compatible with any interesting computations on a visual image of the moving reference island.

Clearly what is wanted is an expression of speed that bears a compatible relationship to the imagery. Consider the following hypothetical scheme. At some point in the voyage (and it could be any point, including the very beginning) the speed of the canoe changes. The navigator reconstructs his image of the movement of the reference island with the time landmarks placed in accordance with the previous speed. If the change occurs at the very beginning of the voyage, the usual or default speed will be taken as the previous speed. Let the segment of the horizon from the present position of the reference island to any convenient future time landmark represent the previous speed (see the segment labeled "old rate" in figure 2.17). This represents the expected movement of the reference island at the previous speed during the period between the present time and the temporal landmark chosen. The problem is to determine the movement of the reference island during the same time period at the new speed. If the new speed is greater than the old speed, then the reference island will move further along the horizon in the same period; if the speed is less, the movement will be less. Using the old rate as a scale, imagine another segment

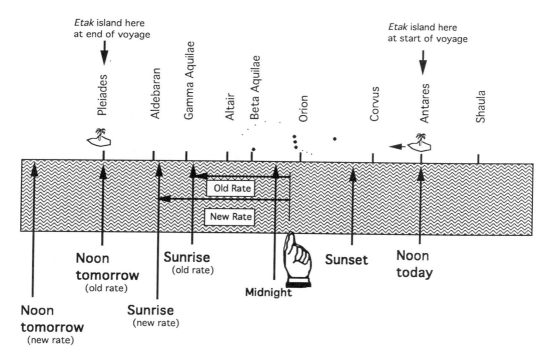

Figure 2.17 Reconstructing the *etak* imagery to reflect a change of speed.

("new rate" in figure 2.17), starting at the present position of the reference island and extending in the direction of the apparent movement of the reference island. This segment represents a judgement of the magnitude of the new speed relative to the old speed. Now simply move the time landmark from the end of the old-rate segment to the end of the new-rate segment. The new-rate segment now defines the new time scale for the new speed. The other time landmarks for subsequent portions of the voyage can be moved accordingly, as in the figure, and a complete new set of expectations for the times at which the *etak* reference island will assume future positions is achieved. This procedure can, of course, be applied anytime there is a noticeable change in the rate of travel of the canoe through the water. Thus the navigator can always keep an updated set of time-bearing correspondences for the *etak* reference island which allows him to gauge how much of his voyage has been completed and how much remains.

The notion of the changing bearing of the reference island can be accommodated by our usual way of thinking, in which the canoe is in motion while the islands remain fixed. Why, then, would

Micronesian navigators insist on what they know to be a fiction and imagine that the canoe is stationary, with the islands in motion about it?

All navigation computations make use of frames of reference. The most prominent aspect of the Micronesian conception is the apparent motion of the *etak* island against the fixed backdrop of the star points defined by the sidereal compass. Here there are three elements to be related to one another: the vessel, the islands, and the directional frame. In order to preserve the observed relationships of motion parallax, one can have the vessel and the direction frame move while the islands stay stationary (the Western solution) or one can have the vessel and the directional frame stationary while the islands move (the Micronesian solution). In the Western case, the directional frame is a compass, or a gyrocompass, and it is carried with the ship. In the Micronesian case, the directional frame is defined by the star points of the sidereal compass, and the star points are fixed. Each of these schemes makes some things easy to compute and others difficult.

The islands move for the Micronesian navigator, because it is computationally less expensive to update their positions with respect to the frame defined by the navigator and the star points than it is to update the positions of both the navigator and the star points with respect to the positions of the islands (Hutchins and Hinton 1984).

Summary

The position-displacement constraint is represented locally in the Micronesian system in every inter-island course. Sailing a constant heading from a known location implicitly represents a line of position. A second line of position is established by the imagined bearing to the *etak* island. The position of the canoe is established as simultaneously satisfying these two one-dimensional constraints, although the two representations are not superimposed directly on each other, as they are on the Western navigator's chart. The line of position representing the track of the canoe is implicit in the steered course of the canoe. The concepts of the *etak* of birds and the *etak* of sighting provide a circle of position constraint. Depth contours are also used, and the Micronesian navigators practice a form of guyot hopping on some voyages by sailing from seamount to seamount. Even though they do not encounter land, they are able to determine their position by the discoloration in the water caused by the presence of the submerged seamount. The distance-rate-time constraint is explicitly represented in the superimposition of temporal landmarks on the spatial landmarks defined by the star bearings of the *etak* island. In this system there are no universal units of direction, position, distance, or rate, no analog-to-digital conversions, and no digital computations. Instead, there are many special-purpose units and an elegant way of "seeing" the world in which internal structure is superimposed on external structure to compose a computational image device. By constructing this image, the Micronesian navigator performs navigation computations in his "mind's eye."

Pre-Modern Western Navigation

The practice of modern navigation is of more recent origin than many of us probably imagine. Before the introduction of the magnetic compass (around 1100 A.D.), navigation in European waters looked a good deal like a rather unsophisticated version of Micronesian navigation. We do not know the extent to which the similarities between the two systems are due to independent invention or how much they share from a common origin. Some scholars have attempted to find a common Arab origin for some of the features (Lewis 1976), but the evidence of such a connection is scanty at best. Whatever the reasons for their existence, consider the following parallels.

Before the discovery of the magnetic compass needle, the sun and the stars were the guides for Western navigation. In the *Odyssey*, Homer has Odysseus come home from the west by keeping the bear (the Big Dipper) on his left and sailing toward the rising of the Pleiades and Arcturus. The Pleiades and Arcturus have similar declensions (they rise out of the same point in the eastern horizon) and are 11 hours different in right ascension (they are on opposite sides of the night sky), so one or the other would be in the sky on any night regardless of season (Taylor 1971). This is clearly a linear constellation construct, although having only two stars in the constellation is of limited utility (since the navigator will not always have one of the stars near enough the horizon to be useful for course setting).

In ancient Greece, very short distances were given in *stadia* (a *stade* is about a tenth of a mile), but longer distances in early voyages were given in terms of a day's sail. This was the distance a "normal ship would accomplish during a twenty-four-hour run with a fresh following wind" (Taylor 1971: 51). The units in which the distances between islands are given in the Micronesian system are based on exactly the same concept, the only difference being that Micronesians are interested in a day's sail of a canoe (Riesenberg 1972). This still requires the navigator to recognize the conditions under which a "day's sail" will be accomplished in a day. Making this judgement is probably the sort of skill that no practitioner can describe in detail—"But ever since sailing began, masters and pilots have always prided themselves on knowing the 'feel' of their ship and how much way she was making" (Taylor 1971: 52).

The *kenning*, "a unit of distance used by early mariners, equivalent to the distance at which the shore could first be seen from the offing when making landfall" (Cotter 1983b: 260), appears to be a European version of the *etak* of sighting—although, since the decks of European ships are generally higher than the decks of Micronesian canoes, it is a greater distance. This is a salient concept for mariners of all kinds. In the Western system it became the basis of a unit of distance. Once determined, it was used as a unit of distance in sailing directions that give "the kennings between headlands and ports" (Cotter 1983b: 255).

The sighting of birds has been important in the Western tradition since biblical days. Fuson (1987) reports the following entries in the log of Christopher Columbus on his first voyage to the New World:

Later in the day I saw another tern that came from the WNW and flew to the SE. This is a sure sign that land lies to the WNW because these birds sleep ashore and go to sea in the morning in search of food, and they do not fly sixty miles. (65)

I know that most of the islands discovered by the Portuguese have been found because of birds. (71)

The first quote shows that Columbus was not only using the behavior of birds to find land, he was also making the same sort of inferences as are made by the Micronesian navigators. The second quotation gives an indication of Columbus's estimation of the importance of this technique. Since in the century before his voyage no European nation had discovered more islands than Portugal, this is a strong endorsement of the technique.

When Europeans first ventured into the open ocean, they could roughly determine latitude by measuring the altitude of the North Star, or of the sun as it passed the local meridian. Yet they had no way to determine their longitude with any accuracy. To find an island known to be at a particular latitude and longitude, a European navigator would attempt to arrive at the target latitude well upwind of the target longitude; he could then simply sail downwind, maintaining the specified latitude until the island was sighted. This technique of "latitude sailing" was probably practiced by traditional Pacific navigators too, although because of the nature of the traditional practices the evidence is simply lacking. It is interesting to note, however, that a young Hawaiian navigator, Nainoa Thompson, who apprenticed himself to an experienced Caroline Island navigator, has invented or discovered a technique for determining the latitudes of specific islands at sea, and has used this technique to support the latitude-sailing strategy in long-distance voyages between Hawaii and Tahiti without the aid of instruments. The technique relies on the observation of pairs of stars rising out of or setting into the horizon. At a particular latitude, if one can find two stars that rise out of the eastern horizon at the same instant, then the more northerly of the two will rise before the other when the observer is north of that latitude, and the more southerly of the two will rise before the other when the observer is south of that latitude. By identifying a few pairs of stars for each target island, it is possible to use the latitude-sailing strategy with great accuracy.

The Divergence of Traditions

The similarities between early European navigation and Micronesian navigation are based on regularities in the world that are just too useful to miss. The differences between the two traditions are many and appear to have increased in number over time. The divergence of the traditions can be traced through three closely related trends in the development of Western navigation: the increasing crystallization of knowledge and practice in the physical structure of artifacts, in addition to in mental structure; the development of measurement as analog-to-digital conversion, and the concomitant reliance on technologies of arithmetic computation;

and the emergence of the chart as the fundamental model of the world and the plotted course as the principal computational metaphor for the voyage.

The Crystallization of Knowledge and Practice in the Physical Structure of Artifacts

The Micronesian navigator holds all the knowledge required for the voyage in his head. Diagrams are sometimes constructed in the sand for pedagogical purposes, but these (of course) are only temporary and are not taken on voyages. In the Western tradition, physical artifacts became repositories of knowledge, and they were constructed in durable media so that a single artifact might come to represent more than any individual could know. Furthermore, through the combination and superimposition of task-relevant structure, artifacts came to embody kinds of knowledge that would be exceedingly difficult to represent mentally (Latour 1986). Many of the instruments of Western navigation are based on the principle of building computational constraints of the task into the physical structure of the artifact. I will illustrate this pervasive strategy with just a few examples.

THE ASTROLABE
The astrolabe (figure 2.18), a portable mechanical model of the movements of the heavens, was invented in Greece around 200 B.C. Preserved during the Dark Ages by the Byzantines, it was not much modified by the Arabs, via whom it returned to the West around 1000 A.D.

An astrolabe is a memory for the structure of the heavens. As we saw in the discussion of Micronesian navigation, it is possible for an individual navigator to learn an internal image of the heavens so rich that he can recognize arrangements of stars, and even imagine the locations of stars that are obscured by cloud or the horizon. However, it is not possible with such mental representations to control all those spatial relationships with the sort of precision that is possible in a durable external representation. In an external representation, structure can be built up gradually—a distribution of cognitive effort over time—so that the final product may be something that no individual could represent all at once internally. Furthermore, the astrolabe encodes a kind of knowledge that cannot be represented internally. In this respect, it is a physical

Figure 2.18 An astrolabe, which superimposes several kinds of structure to create a celestial computer.

residuum of generations of astronomical practice. It is a sedimentation of representations of cosmic regularities.

The astrolabe also enables its user to predict the positions and movements of the sun and the stars:

Because the astrolabe can be set to show the positions of these heavenly bodies at different times of day or night, on different dates and or different latitudes, the instrument is also a computer, serving to solve problems concerning the positions of the Sun and stars at any given time. (National Maritime Museum 1976)

Any map of the heavens can capture the relationships among the stars. The astrolabe goes further. The physical structure of the moving parts of the instrument captures regularities in the movements of the heavens and the effects of latitude and time on the observations of the heavens. Thus, the astrolabe is not just a memory for the structure of the sky; it is also an analog computer.

The major components of an astrolabe are the *mater*, the *limb*, the *plate*, and the *rete*. The mater is the framework that holds the other pieces together. The limb is a circular scale around the perimeter of the mater. The limb is inscribed with a 360° scale and/or a 24-hour scale. In either case, the limb is a representation of the structure of sidereal time. Each astrolabe is really a kit that can be assembled differently according to the circumstances of its use:

As the configuration of the celestial coordinates changes according to the latitude of the observer, a set of removable plates—sometimes as many as six, engraved on both sides—is usually supplied, fitting into the hollow of the mater, so that the user can select the plate most appropriate to his own latitude. (National Maritime Museum 1976: 14)

The interchangeable plates capture regularities in the effects of observer latitude on the relations of the celestial coordinates to the local horizon. Of course, it is not possible to provide a plate for every observer latitude, since latitudes are infinite in number. The plates provide a coarse discrete representation of the effects of latitude. Even with a large number of plates, the representation of observer latitude will be approximate most of the time. The rete captures the locational relationships of the stars to one another and that of the sun to the stars.

The assembled astrolabe brings these three kinds of structure (and much more) into coordination just the right way so that the interactions of these variables can be controlled in the manipulation of the physical parts of the instrument. An astrolabe can be made of durable materials because the regularities it captures change only very slowly. The variables that do change, observer latitude and time of observation, are represented in the physical structure of the astrolabe either by changeable parts (plates for each latitude) or by changeable relations among parts (the rotation of the rete about the axis with respect to the plate and the limb). The constraints of the represented world are thus built into the physical structure of the device. The astrolabe is a manipulable model of the heavens—a simulator of the effects of time and latitude on the relationships of the heavens to the horizon. The astrolabe is an early example of a general trend toward the representation and solution of computational problems via physical manipulations of carefully constructed artifacts.

THE COMPASS ROSE AND RECKONING THE TIDES
Frake (1985) provides an especially interesting example of the ways in which a variety of kinds of structure are combined in a single artifact to create a computational system. Frake is interested in what Northern European sailors knew about the tides and how they went about knowing what they know. Although he is interested in the tides, his account begins with the so-called wind rose:

The schema of directions ... resulted from a successive division of the quadrants of a horizon circle formed by north-south and east-west lines into 8, 16, and finally 32 named (not numbered) points.... Similar schemata for segmenting the circle of the horizon with invariant directional axes characterize all known early seafaring traditions: those of the Pacific, the China Sea, the Indian Ocean and Europe. In the various traditions, compass directions could be thought of as, and named for, star paths (as in the Pacific and the Indian Ocean) or wind directions (as in island southeast Asia and Europe). In all cases, the compass rose provided an invariant representation of directions which were, in fact, determined at sea by a variety of means: the sun, stars, winds, swells, landmarks, seamarks, sea life and, in later times, the magnetic needle. (Frake 1985: 262)

The wind rose is an ancient schema that, for most of its history and in most places, had nothing in particular to do with representing knowledge of the tides. In the Mediterranean, for example, the tides vary so little that mariners can safely disregard them. In Northern Europe, by contrast, tidal variations are large, and the ability to predict the tides is of great value to mariners. The use of the medieval compass rose in the prediction of tides is a fine example of the empirical construction of an artifact in the absence of a theory of the phenomenon it permits navigators to predict.

The compass rose as a schema for the expression of directions was appropriated as a schema for the representation of time as well (see figure 2.19):

In whatever manner time was determined at some moment, it was thought of and expressed as a compass bearing. The sun bears

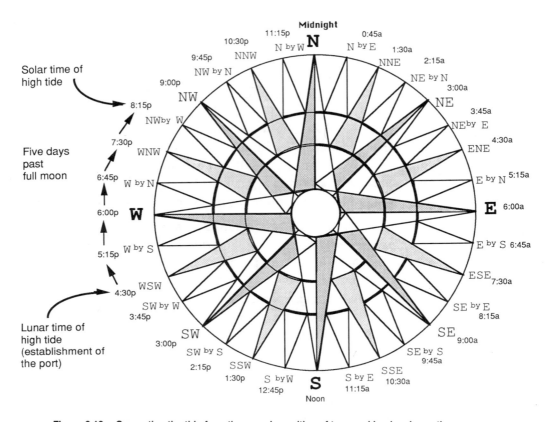

Figure 2.19 Computing the tide from the superimposition of temporal landmarks on the compass rose.

south at noon. It was therefore thought of as bearing north at midnight, east at 6 a.m. and west at 6 p.m. Only the first of these bearings is of practical daily use in northern Europe for determining time. The other bearings were ways of expressing time. (Frake 1985: 264)

Here we have the superposition of two kinds of structure: the temporal structure of the 24-hour solar day on the 32-point compass rose. This yields a set of correspondences between direction and solar time.

If the bearing of the sun is an expression of solar time, the bearing of the moon can likewise be seen as an expression of lunar time. The tides result from the gravitational pulls of the moon and the sun. The effects of the moon predominate. Although the tide does not simply follow the moon in any obvious manner, the phase of the tide at any particular place is always the same when the moon is at any given bearing. That is, for any particular location, the high tide always comes at a particular lunar time. Medieval mariners noticed this fact:

Medieval sailing directions, and presumably the memories of sailors before written directions, specify the tidal regime of a given place by stating the lunar time, named as a compass bearing, of a given state of the tide, usually high. (Frake 1985: 265)

With both solar and lunar time superposed on the compass rose, the relationships between solar time and lunar time can be expressed as directional relationships. A sailor who knows the lunar time of high tide for a given location can use the superposed lunar and solar time representations to compute the solar time of high tide. For example, if it is known that at a given location the high tide will occur when the moon bears WSW,

the sailor has to determine the solar time corresponding to "WSW moon" on a given date and also calculate the state of the tide at any other solar time. It is in the solution of this problem that the compass rose as cognitive schema shows its merits. (Frake 1985: 265)

The simplest case occurs when the phase of the moon is new. In that case, solar time and lunar time are the same, and the time of high tide will be when the moon (and therefore the sun as well) bears WSW. That is, high tide will come at 4:30 p.m. If the phase of the moon is other than full or new, the sailor will have to first determine the relation of solar time to lunar time in order to compute the time of the high tide. It just so happens that dividing the 24-hour day into 32 equal intervals yields intervals of 45 minutes each:

Each day, lunar time, and the tide following it, lags behind the sun by about 48 minutes. Our compass points divide time into 45-minute intervals, close enough to 48 for tidal calculation. (Frake 1985: 265)

Suppose a sailor finds himself approaching this harbor five days past the full moon. Since the moon and the tide lag 48 minutes behind the sun each day, "we can count five points of the compass past WSW to NW by W, a point which marks the solar time of 8:15" (Frake 1985: 265). In this way, the sailor can compute the solar time of the high tide (and therefore the other tides as well) by knowing the phase of the moon and the establishment of the port (figure 2.19).

The tidiness of the compass rose as a representation of these relationships is an entirely fortuitous property of the mapping of the 24-hour day onto the 32 points of the compass rose. The segmentation of the compass rose into 32 points and the segmentation of the day into 24 hours arose independently. Their relationship just happens to map approximately onto the 48-minute daily lag of the moon behind the sun that results from the relation of the 29.5-day lunar cycle to the 24-hour day.

The superposition of the scheme for the 24-hour day on the scheme for the 32-point wind rose yields a system of temporal and spatial landmarks on which the correspondences of the states of the tide and time can be imagined and represented. This is reminiscent of the superposition of temporal and directional landmarks that the Micronesian navigators use to compute their progress on a voyage. Frake noted the abstract similarities of the two systems:

It is the relationship between determining direction and determining time that makes the use of a single schema, the compass rose, appropriate for representing both direction and time. But the compass rose is not a time-finding instrument. It is a very abstract model, a cognitive schema, of the relations of direction to time, of solar time to lunar time, and of time to tide. It is an etak of medieval navigation. (Frake 1985: 266)

Frake's comparison of the compass rose used to compute tides to the Micronesian concept of *etak* is based in the abstract properties of both as organizing schemata. I believe that the links are even stronger in that both systems achieve their computational power by superimposing several kinds of representational structure on a single framework.

Both of these devices—the astrolabe and the compass rose as tide computer—involve the creation of physical artifacts whose structures capture regularities in the world of phenomena in such a way that computations can be performed by manipulating the physical devices. It should be noted, however, that the use of the compass rose as a tide computer is a bit more like the Micronesian navigation case, in that an important part of the structure is not explicitly represented in the artifact itself but is instead supplied by the situated looking of the navigator.

Measurement and Technologies of Digital Computation

A second clear difference between the Micronesian and Western navigation traditions is the reliance of the latter on measurement and digital computation. This difference is apparent in the history of the *chip log*.

THE CHIP LOG

The spread of the use of the chip log in about 1600 marks an important turning point in the history of Western navigation. Before this, European navigation was based primarily on analog computations. The log gave rise to a computational process that begins with analog-to-digital conversion, which is followed by digital computation, then either digital-to-analog conversion for interpretation or digital-to-analog conversion followed by analog computation. Western navigators have been practicing this style of navigation for less than 400 years.

The chip log is a simple analog-to-digital converter that converts the rate of travel of a ship through water into a number by making a direct measurement of the distance the ship moves in a given unit of time. A panel of wood, called the *chip*, is tied to a line and thrown over the side of the ship (figure 2.20). It remains stationary

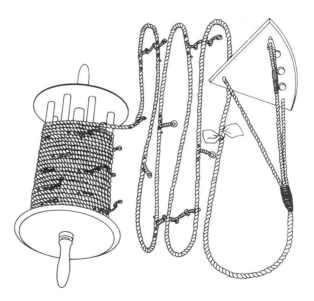

Figure 2.20 A chip log. (From Maloney 1985.)

in the water while the ship sails away from it. The line attached to the chip is allowed to pay out, and the amount of line that pays out in a given period of time is the distance the ship has traveled in that same period. Since speed is distance per unit time, this distance is, by definition, directly proportional to the speed of the ship. In the early days of the use of the chip log, the interval of time was measured by the duration of a spoken prayer. Later, to increase accuracy, a sand glass was used instead. To measure the distance covered, one could reel the line back in and then measure the amount that had paid out during the given interval.

It would be exceedingly difficult for a single person to perform this procedure with accuracy. I have witnessed the use of a traditional chip log aboard the restored late-nineteenth-century Swedish cargo schooner Westkust. The procedure requires three people working in close coordination. One manages the chip and the line, throwing the chip overboard, letting the line run through his fingers, and calling out when the end of the "stray line" has passed his hand. A second person inverts a sand glass when the first indicates that the measured portion of the line is now streaming out, and calls out when the sand has run out. When the time is up, the first person grips the line and stops paying out the line. This stopping is assisted by a third person, who has been, up to this point, holding the spool on which the line is wound so that it can flow out smoothly. The line is dressed with tassels hanging from the knots so that the number of each knot can be discerned at a glance. The number of the knot nearest to hand is noted, and the line is pulled in and wound onto the spool.

Columbus did not mention the use of a chip log, although his logbooks do contain entries recording speeds. It is assumed that he either estimated his speed by eye or used a precursor of the chip log that involved "dropping a piece of wood into the water and timing the passage from bow to stern" (Fuson 1987: 44). As with the early chip logs, the interval of time was measured by the recitation of a chant or a prayer. The first certain use of the chip log was on Magellan's voyage in 1521.

The use of the log or any other technique based on the distance covered by the ship requires both a consistent unit of distance and a means of reliably measuring distance in that unit. This was accomplished by preparing the log line in a special way:

By [1633] it had become the general practice to mark the log line so as to facilitate the calculation of speed. This was done in the following way. If a half minute glass was used then the length of line necessary to indicate a speed of one mile (of 5000 feet) per hour was (30 × 5000 ft)/(60 × 60) or $41\frac{2}{3}$ feet. In other words, at one mile per hour the ship would advance, and the line would run out $41\frac{2}{3}$ feet in 30 seconds. The line was then divided as follows: From 10 to 20 fathoms, depending on the size of the ship, were allowed as "stray line" next to the log chip, to ensure it being clear of the effect of the wake. The end of this stray line was marked either by a knot or a piece of red or white rag, and then from there the line was divided into sections of $41\frac{2}{3}$ feet or 42 feet, each section being marked by a knot in the line. Thus came into being the term known as the measure of a ship's speed in nautical miles per hour. (Hewson 1983: 160)

Even with these refinements, the chip log was not a very accurate instrument. Many things could induce errors in the readings. The friction of the spool, shrinkage of the rope, the surge of the ship working in steep seas, the effects of currents, and the yawing of the ship with a swell on the quarter were among the many things that could cause significant errors. For a navigator relying on a log, there is no choice but to expect error and attempt to allow for it. Just as a carpenter would rather err on the long side in cutting a piece of wood (so that any error can be corrected with minimal waste of material) a navigator prefers to overestimate the distance sailed in order to avoid an unexpected landfall. If an error is made, it is better to have overestimated the distance sailed, so that the problem can be corrected without losing the ship.

Log lines can shrink with use, so it is important to check the length of the segments between the knots. This "was facilitated in most ships by having permanent marks of nails driven into the deck" (Hewson 1983: 166). Decks don't stretch and shrink as ropes do. Putting the calibrating nails into the deck is a way of creating a memory for the lengths between knots in the log line in a medium that has physical properties that match the computational needs of the task. In this case, the marks on the deck are a memory for distance.

In the late eighteenth century many attempts were made to develop more accurate ways to measure speed or distance run through the water. These included the *taff-rail* and *paddle-wheel* logs (Hewson 1983). Although the details of their implementation varied, these were all simple analog-to-digital converters that stood in the same relation computationally to other navigation tools that the chip log had.

The importance of the chip log is that it changed the way navigation was done. Rather than knowing a journey should take some number of days and counting days until the required number had elapsed, a navigator using a chip log used the concept of distance between points and the integration of speed over time to determine the distance covered by the ship. Having created a digital representation of speed, the chip log created a need for a method of calculation that could operate on that representation to tell the navigator what he needed to know.

The chip log and its descendants are among the many measuring instruments that entered the navigation tool kit during the European expansion. Others include a succession of instruments for measuring the altitudes of stars (astrolabe, quadrant, cross-staff, sextant), range-measuring instruments, instruments to measure bearings, azimuths, and courses, and instruments to measure depths. All of these are analog-to-digital converters. All of them create representations that are subsequently processed using a special arithmetic technology in order to produce information that is of use to the navigator.

Consider the enormous importance of common logarithms. With a table of logarithms, one can transform multiplication and division into addition and subtraction. That is, when numerical values are expressed as logarithms, the complex typographic operations required for multiplication and division (the algorithms of place-value arithmetic) can be replaced by a simpler set of typographic operations that implement addition and subtraction. Speaking of Edmund Gunter (1581–1626), Cotter (1983a: 242) says:

He introduced the first tables of logarithmic trigonometrical functions, without which a seaman would find almost insurmountable difficulty in solving astronomical problems. It was Gunter's Tables, published in 1620, that paved the way to the new phase of "arithmetic navigation." Armed with the new logarithmic canon, a navigator who memorized the necessary rules could solve nautical astronomical problems with relative ease.

But the seamen of the time found even the simplified calculations daunting, so Gunter designed a ruler with a number of scales:

Among these are a logarithmic scale of natural numbers, logarithmic scales of sines, tangents and versines; ... and a "meridian line" to facilitate the construction of sea charts on Wright's projection.... With the advent of "arithmetical navigation," in which Gunter played the dominant role, the common log for measuring a ship's speed became commonplace. To the careful seaman using a Gunter scale the proportional problem of finding speed was mechanical and, therefore, trivial. (ibid.)

The predecessor of the slide rule is apparent here. In fact, it appears that two of Gunter's scales were sometimes "laid down on rulers to slide by each other" (*Oxford English Dictionary*, 1971). Again we have an artifact on which computations are performed by physical manipulation. However, there is an important difference between the astrolabe and Gunter's scale in this regard. In both cases the constraints of a represented world are built into the physical structure of the device, but in the case of Gunter's scale the represented world is not literally the world of experience. Instead it is a symbolic world: the world of logarithmic representations of numbers. The regularities of relations among entities in this world are built into the structure of the artifact, but this time the regularities are the syntax of the symbolic world of numbers rather than the physics of a literal world of earth and stars. The representation of symbolic worlds in physical artifacts, and especially the representation of the syntax of such a world in the physical constraints of the artifact itself, is an enormously powerful principle. The chip log and Gunter's scale are representative elements of a cognitive ecology based on measurement and digital computation.

The Chart as a Model of the World

The navigation chart—perhaps the best available example of the crystallization of practice in a physical artifact—is intimately involved in the prototypical cycle of measurement, computation, and interpretation that characterizes so much of Western navigation. These characteristics of the chart will be developed in much more detail in the coming chapters. At this point it is useful to examine another contribution of the chart that marks one of the most important elements of the Western conception of navigation. The chart, by virtue of its interpretation as a model of an expanse of actual space, encourages a conception of a voyage as sequence of locations on the chart.

Descriptive sailing directions were the principal navigation aids up until the end of the eighteenth century. These documents describe to the sailor how to proceed with the voyage and what he can expect to see. Then, with the continued improvement of survey techniques and the increasing range of areas accurately surveyed, sailing directions were supplanted by the pictorial chart. This marks an important change in perspective. Where the sailing directions presented the world from the perspective of the deck of the ship, the coastal chart presented the world from above—from a virtual perspective (a "bird's-eye view") that navigators would never actually experience. Modern navigators may take to the air and adopt something very like a bird's-eye view, but this is not in fact the perspective presented by the navigation chart. The navigation chart presents the world in a perspective that can never be achieved from any actual viewing point.

A chart must be more than an accumulation of observations. The structure of the chart is crucial (Cotter 1983b). The importance of the compass in the actual practice of navigation was paralleled by its contribution to the quality of chart production. The compass made it practical to make accurate charts. It was possible before (by means of the stars) to get directions for bearings and courses, but not nearly so conveniently. Even when a compass was used, serious problems in chart construction remained. For example, early charts of the Mediterranean showed a pronounced upward tilt in the eastern end. This tilt was produced by the difference in magnetic variation between the western and eastern reaches of the Mediterranean Sea. If the cartographer uses a magnetic compass to make the chart, and the navigator uses a magnetic compass to determine courses, and if both compasses show the same errors in the same places, why would anyone care and how could anyone ever notice that the charts put the land in the wrong places?

TAKING THE MEASURE OF THE EARTH
The distortions in charts produced by changes in magnetic variation became an issue when the chart became a point of articulation between the measure of the earth and celestial observations. In or-

der for the effects of distance covered on the face of the globe to be reconciled with the attendant, and also measurable, changes in latitude (a relation to the celestial sphere), the unit of measure for distance had to be grounded in the measure of the earth itself. That is, a degree of arc on the earth's surface is a particular distance, and navigators wanted to be able to combine and interrelate measurements made in terms of distance traveled with measurements of latitude. For example, if I am currently 2° south of my home port, sailing north, how far, in units of distance on the surface of the ocean, must I sail to arrive at the latitude of my home? The question is: How much linear distance on the surface of the earth corresponds to a degree of arc on the same surface? As we saw in the discussion of the historical changes in the length of the nautical mile, establishing a standard that permitted the chart to be a point of articulation between the measure of the earth and the measure of the heavens was no simple task:

The north-up convention is clearly related to the concept of defining position in terms of latitude and longitude. For coastal navigation this concept is of no consequence: a coastal navigator is interested in defining his ship's position not in terms of these spherical coordinates, but in terms of bearings and distances from prominent landmarks of hazards such as rocks and shoals. Early coastal charts, therefore, (and with good reason) were orientated relative to the run of the coast rather than to the compass. (Cotter 1983b: 256)

The modern chart incorporates the global convention of north-up depiction of a plane surface having a discrete address in terms of latitude and longitude for every location. This global framework permits the combination of any number of observations from any number of locations. With this scheme it is possible to compute the relationship between any two locations on earth even though that relationship has never been measured.

The virtual perspective created in the chart does not privilege any actual perspective. A navigation chart is a representation that is equally useful (or not useful) from any actual perspective. It attempts neutrality with respect to the perspectives from which the world will be seen by navigators. Since in the Western tradition nearly all navigable space is represented from this virtual perspective, it is from this virtual perspective that voyages come to be conceived. We imagine the voyage as the movement of our ship over a stretch of water. There is the ship, and there we are, like tiny imagined specks on the tiny imagined ship that is moving in our mind's eye across the expanse of paper that represents the water between origin and destination.

Yet there are moments in which this perspective does not serve the needs of the navigator, as when one attempts to determine what the land depicted should look like from the perspectives that are actually achieved in ships. Here coastal profiles may be included. There is a problem at the moment in which one moves conceptually from being "on the chart" to being "in the world." The *coastal profile* is a concession to this problem. The first coastal profiles appeared in 1541, in Pierre Garcie's book *Le grand routier*. Coastal profiles are representations that privilege particular perspectives that the chart makers anticipate will be encountered often by users of the chart.

The common framework of locations also permits the superposition of a wide variety of structures. In addition to the obvious boundaries of bodies of water and land, the locations of cultural features and of geographical features (both above and below water) are depicted. This superposition of these structures, which underlies much of the computational power of the chart, is so obvious as to go unnoticed by virtually all the users of the chart. Soundings were first shown reduced to a standard half-tide datum in 1584, in Janzsoon Waghenaer's *Speighel der Zeevaert*.

SOCIAL PROBLEMS OF CHART CONSTRUCTION

The birth of astronomical navigation was much less a scientific problem than a question of organization. Jean II of Portugal had the great merit to have known—before any other head of state—to organize the technical exploitation of the theoretical knowledge of his epoch.—Beaujouan, Science Livresque et Art Nautique au XV[e] Siecle; *cited in Waters 1976: 28 (translation by E.H.)*

There is a great deal of knowledge embodied in any navigation chart. To add a new feature to a chart, one must determine its relationship to at least two other features. Since a chart implicitly represents a spatial relationship between the members of every pair of features depicted, any the new feature acquires relationships to all the other features on the chart—not just the ones that were used to establish its location. If the number of relationships depicted is a measure of the knowledge in a chart, there may be more knowledge in a chart than was put into the chart. In fact, most of the relationships depicted on any chart have never actually been measured. Even so, a great many observations are required in order to construct a useable navigation chart. A navigation chart represents the accumulation of more observations than any one person could make in a lifetime. It is an artifact that embodies generations of experience and measurement. No navigator has ever had, nor will one ever have, all the knowledge that is in the chart. The really difficult technical problem in the production of charts is the collection of reliable information. (See Latour 1987 on centers of calculation.)

Compare the problem faced by the Portuguese during their expansion with that faced by the Micronesians. Every Micronesian navigator knows the courses and distances between all the islands in his sailing range—including, as we have seen, courses between islands that have not been visited for many generations. How could a Micronesian navigator come to have this knowledge? Clearly, it is acquired over generations, and what any navigator knows is much more than could be learned by direct observation. The knowledge is a compilation of the experiences of many navigators—some of whom, one must assume, set out on voyages of discovery, knowing which way they were sailing, and how to get home, but not what they would find. Over the years the knowledge accumulated, expressed in the framework of star courses and *etak* images. Today the knowledge of a Micronesian navigator exceeds what could be acquired by direct observation, but it does not exceed what could be remembered by one individual.

The world of the Portuguese fleet in the early fifteenth century was much larger than one group of islands. The total knowledge of the world not only exceeded what could be observed by any individual, it exceeded what could be known by any individual. Like the Micronesians, the Portuguese needed a consistent set of techniques for making observations and a representational framework in which all observations could be expressed. They also needed to train a large number of observers in these techniques so that the experiences of all of them could accumulate in a common store. This was the creation of an enormous system for gathering and processing information—a cognitive system of many

parts that operated over many years to create a collection of representations of the spatial organization of the surface of our planet
(Law 1987).

The Computational Ecology of Navigation Tools

The mutual dependencies among the various instruments and
techniques is clearly visible in the history of navigation. Even
though the chip log was available for use in the sixteenth century,
for example, it was not generally adopted until the middle of the
seventeenth. Why weren't sailors using the log more widely? Because they had no convenient way to carry out the computations
required to turn the readings gained from the log into useful information about the ship's position.

Why was there, before 1767, no nautical almanac giving the
positions of the stellar sphere, the sun, the moon and the planets?
Astronomy was certainly advanced enough to provide these data.
The answer is that these data are useless for marine navigation in
the absence of an accurate way to determine time at sea. The need
was well known, and in 1714 the English Parliament passed an act
"providing a Publick Reward for such person or persons as shall
discover the Longitude at Sea." The reward went unclaimed until
1762, when Harrison constructed a chronometer that would work
reliably at sea (Taylor 1971: 261). The nautical almanac soon
followed.

Before seagoing chronometers were perfected, there was little
incentive to develop better sextants. At the equator, an error of one
minute in time produces an error of 15 miles in east-west position.
Since the earth turns on its axis one degree of arc in 4 minutes of
time, there is no utility in having an instrument that can measure
celestial angles even to the nearest degree unless it is coupled with
a chronometer that is accurate to within 2 minutes. Thus, both the
development of the sextant and the development of accurate navigation tables were arrested by the lack of the chronometer. Both
were technological possibilities before the development of the
chronometer, but there was no use for them until time could be
reckoned accurately.

Similar dependencies can also be seen in the history of the chart
and the plotting tools. Charts were in wide use by the thirteenth
century, but the most basic of plotting tools—the parallel rule—
was not invented until the late sixteenth century (Waters 1976).

Why? Because a straight line has no special meaning on an early chart. Not until the Mercator projection did a straight line have a computationally useful meaning. But the earliest Mercator chart came with no explanation. It is unlikely to have been used at sea (Waters 1976). Navigators needed instruction in the use of exotic technologies. (Note: For some time, the Mercator projection was known to the English-speaking world by the name of the man who published an English version of it in 1599: Edward Wright.)

The early astrolabes and quadrants were university equipment. Ordinary seamen couldn't use them. The tools had to be simplified, and there had to be instructions in their use:

By themselves these instruments (quadrant and astrolabe) were, of course, powerless. The mere fact of sighting a heavenly body through pinholes of an alidade had nothing per se to do with navigation. That sighting, or the reading that corresponded to it, had to undergo a number of complex transformations before it could be converted into a latitude. The construction of a network of artifacts and skills for converting the stars from irrelevant points of light in the night sky into formidable allies in the struggle to master the Atlantic is a good example of heterogeneous engineering. (Law 1987: 124)

Sometimes, as the nature of the practice has changed, the role of particular instruments has changed. For example, the astrolabe was originally used both to measure the altitudes of celestial bodies and to predict the altitude and azimuth of a star. The observation-making duties were subsequently taken over by the quadrant, then by the cross staff, and finally by the sextant. The function of computing the expected altitudes and azimuths of stars was taken over by a complex set of tables. Even though the quadrant and the cross staff were eventually replaced by the sextant (which is much easier to use), their ancestor, the astrolabe, survives as the modern *star finder*. It is now usually made of plastic instead of brass, but it is easily recognizable. A star finder is not considered accurate enough for the purposes of computing expected altitudes, but it is used to set the sextant before making the observation. It is used to get the setting of the precision instrument into the right neighborhood. It has been moved to a new job in the navigation process.

In attempting to understand the history of navigation from a cognitive perspective, it is important to consider the whole suite of instruments that are used together in doing the task. The tools of navigation share with one another a rich network of mutual computational and representational dependencies. Each plays a role in the computational environments of the others, providing the raw materials of computation or consuming the products of it. In the ecology of tools, based on the flow of computational products, each tool creates the environment for others. This is easy to see in the history of the physical tools, but the same is certainly true of the mental tools that navigators bring to their tasks. Frake's compass rose is there for all to see, but it becomes a tide computer only in interaction with the establishment of the port and with a particular way of seeing the circle of directions as a representation of the temporal relationships of the periodic cycles of the sun and the moon.

Every argument showing why a particular tool is easy to use is also an argument showing why both internal and external tools are part of the very same cognitive ecology. It is a truism that we cannot know what the task is until we know what the tools are. Not only is this true of both internal and external tools, it is also true of the relationships among them.

The Transparency of Cultural Representations

How We Fail to See Culture (Ours and Theirs)

I have presented this comparative and historical treatment to remind us all that the ways we have of doing things, the ways that seem to us to be natural and inevitable or simply the consequences of the interaction of human nature with the demands of a given task, are in fact historically contingent. As Benedict (1946: 14) notes,

The lenses through which any nation looks at life are not the ones another nation uses. It is hard to be conscious of the eyes through which one looks. Any country takes them for granted, and the tricks of focussing and of perspective which give to any people its national view of life seem to that people the god-given arrangement of the landscape. In any matter of spectacles, we do not expect the man who wears them to know the formula for the lenses, and neither can be expect nations to analyze their own outlook upon the world.

Of all the many possible ways of representing position and implementing navigation computations in the Western tradition, the chart is the one in which the meaning of the expression of position and the meaning of the operations that produce that expression are most easily understood. As was noted above, lines of position could be represented as linear equations, and the algorithm applied to find their intersection could be that of simultaneous linear equations. As a physical analog of space, the chart provides an interface to a computational system in which the user's understanding of the form of the symbolic expressions (lines of position) is structurally similar to the user's understanding of the meanings of the expressions (relations among locations in the world) (Hutchins, Hollan, and Norman 1986). In fact, the similarity is so close that many users find the form and the meaning indistinguishable. Navigators not only think they are doing the computations, they also invest the interpretations of events in the domain of the representations with a reality that sometimes seems to eclipse the reality outside the skin of the ship. One navigator jokingly described his faith in the charted position by creating the following mock conversation over the chart: "This little dot right here where these lines cross is where we are! I don't care if the bosun says we just went aground, we are here and there is plenty of water under the ship here." For the navigator, the ship *is* where the lines of position intersect.

It is really astonishing how much is taken for granted in our current practice. The difficulties that were overcome in the creation of all these techniques, and the power they provide relative to their predecessors, are not at all apparent to the modern practitioner. Only when we look at the history can we see just how many problems had to be solved and how many could have been solved differently in the course of the development of the modern practices. A way of thinking comes with these techniques and tools. The advances that were made in navigation were always parts of a surrounding culture. They appeared in other fields as well, so they came to permeate our culture. This is what makes it so difficult to see the nature of our way of doing things and to see how it is that others do what they do. We see in the divergence of these traditions not just the development of the tools of measurement, but a passion for measuring and a penchant for taking the representation more seriously than the thing represented.

While all navigation computations seem to be describable by a small number of abstract principles, there is great variation in the representational systems and concomitant algorithmic procedures that may be employed to organize the computations. The actual devices and processes in which these representations and algorithms are implemented have a complex evolutionary history. In the next chapter we will consider in much greater detail the implementation of the computations of Western navigation.

A Broader Sense of Computation

Having considered the computational nature of the problems of navigation and the representational assumptions on which Western navigation is based, let us now take up the question of how the basic computations of navigation are actually implemented.

In his seminal book *The Sciences of the Artificial* Herbert Simon (1981: 153) said that "solving a problem simply means representing it so as to make the solution transparent." Of course, the meaning of 'transparent' depends on the properties of the processor that must interpret the representation. Simon had theorem proving in mind when he made this point, but it applies very nicely to navigation. The basic procedures of navigation are accomplished by a cycle of activity, called the fix cycle, in which representations of the spatial relationship of the ship to known landmarks are created, transformed, and combined in such a way that the solution to the problem of position fixing is transparent.

The fix cycle implements a computation. Since some of the structure involved in this computation is internal to the individuals and some external, it is useful to adopt a concept of computation that does not require a change of theory to cross the skin. The fix cycle is accomplished by the *propagation of representational state* across a series of *representational media*. The representations of the position of the ship take different forms in the different media as they make their way from the sighting telescopes of the alidades to the chart. I will refer to a configuration of the elements of a medium that can be interpreted as a representation of something as a *representational state* of the medium. Representational states are propagated from one medium to another by bringing the states of the media into *coordination* with one another.

Simon's prototypical case of problem solving by re-representation was theorem proving in which the computational system is a set of axiomatic propositions and a set of rules for operating on the propositions. The rules describe operations that preserve the truth of the axioms. The system contains many potential conclusions. A "problem" in this world is defined by a proposition about a relationship between terms. The solution to the problem consists of a sequence of rule applications that demonstrate that the target relationship was true in the axioms. The most straightforward way to prove a theorem is to make a sequence of rule applications that derive the target proposition itself from the axioms—that is, to re-represent what the axioms say in such a way that they become the target proposition. In this way, the problem is represented in a way that makes the solution transparent. David Kirsh (1990) speaks of this process as one of making explicit that which is only implicit in the starting state.

Sequential symbol processing of the sort exemplified by theorem proving can certainly be described in terms of coordination of structure. Rule application is the means of coordination between the rule and the state to which it is applied. The consequence of rule application is a transformed system state. Still, there are many interesting types of coordination of information-bearing structure that are poorly described as explicit symbol processing. This is not to say that they could not be implemented as symbol-processing routines; it is simply to say that, when they are implemented that way, their essential character is lost in the details of the implementation. I propose a broader notion of cognition because I want to preserve a concept of cognition as computation, and I want the sort of computation that cognition is to be as applicable to events that involve the interaction of humans with artifacts and with other humans as it is to events that are entirely internal to individual persons. As we shall soon see, the actual implementation of many interesting computations is achieved by other than symbolic means. For our purposes, 'computation' will be taken, in a broad sense, to refer to the propagation of representational state across representational media. This definition encompasses what we think of as prototypical computations (such as arithmetic operations), as well as a range of other phenomena which I contend are fundamentally computational but which are not covered by a narrow view of computation.

The Fix Cycle as an Implementation of the Computation

The navigation system captures several one-dimensional constraints in the world, then represents them and re-represents them until they arrive at the chart. The chart is a medium in which the multiple simultaneous one-dimensional constraints can be combined to form the solution. At the computational level, we say that the inputs to the system are two or more lines of position and the output is a position fix. The representation utilized is a two-dimensional model of space, and the algorithm defined in that representation for combining lines of position is to find the intersection of the graphical depictions of the lines in two-dimensional space. As we have seen, there are many ways to implement this algorithm on this representation. The algorithm is implemented by manipulating the devices described in chapter 1 in such a way that particular physical states that can be taken to represent the spatial relationship of the ship to its surroundings are propagated from one device or medium to another until they arrive at the chart.

Mappings across Representations

What lies between the problem and its solution? Between the relation of the ship to its environment and the position plotted on the chart lie a number of representational media across which the representations of the spatial relationship of the ship to the world are propagated. Some of the representations through which the information about the ship's relation to the world passes are easily observable. We begin our discussion of the nature of the navigation computation with a consideration of the propagation of representational state across these easily observable media.

THE WORLD

Imagine a ship in a harbor. The ship has a spatial relationship to every object in the surrounding world. Each of these relationships is specifiable as a direction and a distance.

THE ALIDADE

The navigation process begins when a spatial relationship between the ship and a fixed landmark is transformed into a state of the alidade-gyrocompass system. (See figure 3.1 for this and the points to follow.) This is accomplished by aiming the alidade at the landmark so that the hairline in the alidade sight is superimposed on the target. The alidade now has a particular rotational orientation on its base. To be useful, this rotational orientation must be

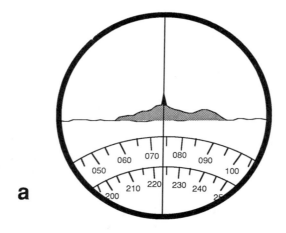

a

	Tower	Hotel	Pier	Depth
13:25		008		23
13:28		006	148	27
13:31		006	146	32
13:34		005	143	29
13:37	205	004	139	30
13:40	211	004	135	35
13:43	218	003	130	24
13:46	224	003	122	26

b

Figure 3.1 The cascade of representations in piloting. A representation of the ship's relationship to the land-mark is propagated from the alidade (a) to the bearing log (b), then to the hoey (c), and finally from the hoey to the chart (d).

expressed as an angle with respect to something. The hairline in the alidade sight also falls over the scale of the gyrocompass card (figure 3.1a). If the gyrocompass repeater is working, the super-imposition of the hairline on the gyrocompass card is an explicit representation of the angle of the line of sight between the ship and the landmark with respect to true north. One end of the hairline provides the coordination of an object in the world with the sight-ing device; the other end provides the coordination of the sighting device with the true-north reference. The whole system hangs by the thread of simultaneous coordination provided by this hairline.

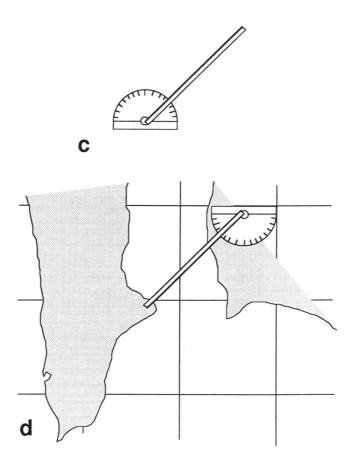

There are three spaces to consider here (see figure 3.2). First, the space in which the ship and the landmark lie is a macrospace. We would like to measure the directional relationship of the ship to the landmark in this space. To do that, we must reproduce that directional relationship in a second space: the microspace of the alidade. When the alidade is aimed and the hairline falls on the image of the landmark in the sight, the directional relationship of the ship to the landmark is reproduced in the directional relationship of the alidade eyepiece to the hairline. The physical structure of the alidade guarantees that the directional relationship of the eyepiece to the hairline will, in turn, be reproduced in the directional relationship of the center of the gyrocompass card to the point on the edge of the gyrocompass card over which the hairline falls. Thus, the directional relationship of the ship to the landmark is reproduced in a third space: the microspace of the gyrocompass card.

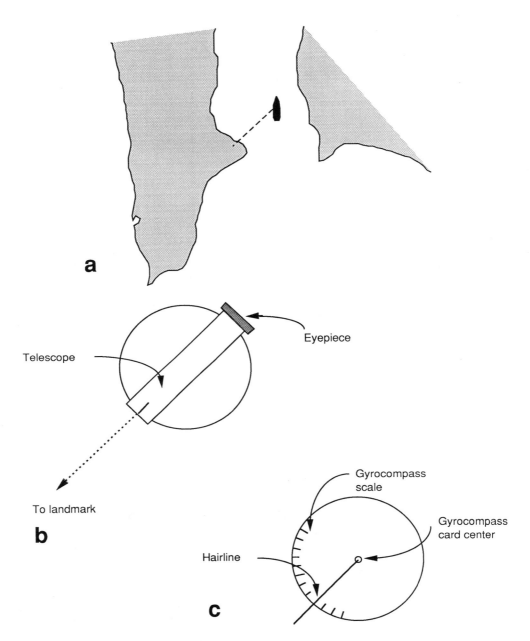

a

Eyepiece

Telescope

To landmark

b

Gyrocompass
scale

Gyrocompass
card center

Hairline

c

Figure 3.2 The three spaces of the bearing sighting. The spatial relationship of the ship to the landmark (a) is reproduced in the physical orientation of the alidade (b), which contains the gyrocompass card (c).

This last space is a thoroughly domesticated space (Goody 1977). It is culturally constructed, measured, and labeled. The locations on the perimeter of the compass card bear labels that are names of directions. When the directional relationship of the ship to the landmark is reproduced in this space, the relationship can be given the name of the point on the perimeter of the compass card that bears the same relationship to the center of the card as the landmark bears to the ship in the world.

Taking the navigation system as our cognitive unit of analysis, we can see the operation of the alidade as an instance of situated seeing implemented in hardware. It is a part of the cognitive system that projects internal structure (the compass rose) and external structure (the landmark) onto a common image space and, in so doing, gives meaning to the thing seen that goes beyond the features of the thing itself. The prism in the alidade that superimposes the image of the gyrocompass card on the image of the landmark is a simple technological device that produces the superposition of internal and external structure.

The printed scale on the gyrocompass card permits the analog angular state of the alidade to be converted to a digital representation. This digital representation may have intermediate external representations, depending on how the task is being done. During Sea and Anchor Detail, for example, the digital representation is spoken over the phone circuit. During Standard Steaming Watch, the single watchstander on duty may mentally rehearse the bearing, or may jot it down on a sheet of paper or even on the palm of his hand while taking other bearings. In any case, this digital representation of the state of the alidade subsequently appears without fail as a written number in the column labeled with the name of the landmark in the bearing record log (figure 3.1b).

The hairline and the telescopic sight add accuracy to the alidade, but they are not essential. Many hand-bearing compasses use a prism or a half-silvered mirror to produce a similar superposition of internal and external structure. The mirror or prism is a simple way to implement the superposition of images that brings the various structural elements into coordination with one another.

THE PHONE CIRCUIT AND BEARING RECORD LOG
The azimuthal orientation of the alidade is an analog representation of the directional relationship between the ship and the

landmark. This analog representation is converted to a digital representation in the act of reading the bearing from the scale of the gyrocompass card. In the previous chapter, it was argued that the analog-to-digital conversions served the application of arithmetic operations. The digital representations produced by reading the gyrocompass scale are not subjected to arithmetic operations before being transformed back into analog form for interpretation. Instead, the analog-to-digital conversion serves another purpose. It provides a representation that is portable and transmissible over a restricted-bandwidth channel. It is easy to imagine a functionally equivalent system in which the result of the sighting with the alidade would be an analog signal. For example, if a two-arm protractor was placed in the alidade and recorded the angle of the observation, this could be used directly to plot the line of position. In that case, though, the protractor would have to be physically transported from the alidade to the chart. This scheme would also require some other technique to support the recording function now served by writing the bearings in the bearing record log. One can imagine the difficulty of storing the history of observations if each one was expressed in an angle on a physical device such as a two-arm protractor. The analog-to-digital conversion employed here creates a representation of the analog angle that is transportable. It can be spoken, and thus the information can move without moving the physical medium in which it is represented. It is also easily recorded, the storage requirements of the digital representation being much less than those required by the analog representation.

The bearing record log is a representational format that is at least 4500 years old in the Western cultural tradition. Sumerian accountants developed similar layouts for recording agricultural transactions as early as 2650 B.C. (Ifrah 1987). The column-and-row format is one of the earliest known devices for superposing representations. Representational structure embodied in the organization of the rows is superposed on representational structure embodied in the organization of the columns to produce a system of coordination between the two structures.

THE HOEY

The digitally represented bearing is subsequently represented as an angle on a one-arm protractor called the *hoey* (figure 3.1c). Here the digital representation of the angular relationship of the ship to the landmark is converted back into an analog form. The angular relationship of the ship to the landmark with respect to true north is now reproduced (with some error) in the angular relationship between the center of the hoey and the point on the hoey scale that bears the name of the bearing. The hoey is another culturally constructed, domesticated space. Again we find labels for directions, the very same labels that are on the gyrocompass card. The direction on the hoey is with respect to some directional referent, which is at this point still unspecified. Ultimately, it must be the same directional referent with respect to which the original measurements were made.

The angle represented in the space of the hoey scale is now reproduced in the space of the hoey arm. The arm is rotated so that its edge (or the hairline index aligned with the edge) is over the point on the hoey scale that represents the bearing of the landmark. This establishes the direction as a physical state of the hoey. This state is protected from inadvertent upset by tightening a friction lock at the center of the hoey.

THE CHART

The hoey, thus configured, is then brought into coordination with the chart (figure 3.1d). In this step, the angle that was measured between the ship and the landmark in the world will at last be reproduced in the space of the chart. There are two essential aspects to this coordination. First, the edge of the arm of the hoey must pass through the symbol on the chart that represents the observed landmark. Whenever this constraint is satisfied, the edge of the hoey arm describes a line of position with respect to the landmark. Second, the base of the hoey must be aligned with the directional frame of the chart. Whenever this constraint is satisfied, the hoey scale represents directions with respect to true north in the space of the chart. When these two constraints are simultaneously satisfied, the edge of the hoey arm describes a line on the chart that is a line of position relative to the landmark with the same angular relationship to true north as the line of sight between the ship and the real landmark in the world.

The latitude-and-longitude grid on the chart plays an essential role in the computation of the fix. The Mercator projection is a computational artifice in which straight lines have special meaning: they are lines of constant direction. The role of the grid in the mechanics of the construction of a line of position (LOP) highlights another important function. It provides a frame of reference that serves as a common anchor for both the locations of the features that are depicted on the chart and the relationship of the ship's position to those depicted features. When the chart was constructed, the locations of the symbols were fixed with respect to the grid. In the course of plotting the LOP, one aligns the base of the plotting device with a line of latitude on the chart. This ties the observation to the reference grid of the chart. Once established by the edge of the arm of the hoey, the line of position can be "saved" by drawing a line on the chart.

Thus one creates the line of position by propagating representational state across a set of structured representational media until it arrives at the chart. The directional relationships of the ship to landmarks in the world are reproduced in a set of spaces: the alidade, the gyrocompass scale, the hoey scale, the hoey arm, and finally the space of the chart. Between the gyrocompass scale and the hoey scale, the direction is represented as a string of digits. The chart is a special medium in which the constraints of several lines of position can be simultaneously represented. The fix is literally a superposition of lines of position. This neatly fits Simon's characterization of problem solving. The ship's situation is represented and re-represented until the answer to the navigator's question is transparent. The ship is where the lines of position intersect. Notice that, although all the information required to fix the position of the ship was present in the bearing log, the ship's position was not apparent in that representation.

The plotted fix position is compared against the position that was projected after the previous fix. Since both of these positions were graphically constructed in the space of the chart, the comparison operation is implemented as a perceptual judgement. This is not to say that it is a simple process. What constitutes a significant difference between the positions? When should a navigator be worried about the process that produces the position fixes? The "seeing" involved in seeing the quality of the fix and its relation to the projected fix is quite complex. If the discrepancy is thought to be significant, it may be used as input to a process that revises the representation of the ship's speed and course.

The ship's future positions are projected from the current fix position. These projected positions have several uses. They are used to ensure that this ship is not standing into danger. They also are used to choose landmarks for the next round of observations. And of course, after the next fix is plotted, it will be compared with the projected position to detect the effects of current or changes in speed.

THE FATHOMETER

Meanwhile, the observed depth of the water under the ship is represented as a mark on the graduated paper of the fathometer. The paper of the fathometer is another domesticated space, arranged with culturally meaningful names for depths. Reading the depth indicated on the paper transforms the position of the pen mark in this domesticated space into a portable digital representation—a number—which is also recorded in the bearing record log. As was explained in chapter 1, the lateral movement of the recording paper under the depth-recording pen converts elapsed time into distance traveled along the ship's track. The movement of the pen from top to bottom of the chart paper turns elapsed time of the signal and echo return into a representation of the depth of the water under the ship in the space of the strip chart. Running the two motions simultaneously and superimposing them on each other creates a representation of the relationship of the ship's track to the depth of the water under the ship. Here is another physical device that superimposes elements of a relatively direct representation of the external world (the distance the pen moves before making contact with the paper) onto elements of a culturally constructed space (the marked paper used to record depth) in order to give meaning to the world. It is another hardware implementation of situated perception. It bears a kinship to the row-and-column format of the bearing record log, except in this case, the organization of rows and columns is dynamically created by the actions of motors and the motion they produce in time.

Like the bearings of landmarks, the depth of water is converted to a digital representation in the act of reading the depth scales on the recording paper. This number is then propagated via the phone circuit to the bearing record log where it appears alongside the bearings of landmarks as a number in a column. The depth of water indicated by a number on the chart at or near the location of the fix is corrected for tidal height and compared with the observed depth. The correction and comparison operations are carried out using arithmetic operations. If the computed fix position consists of a small triangle and the depth of water at the fix point agrees with the measured depth of water, the fix is taken to be correct. If the charted and measured depths disagree, there is reason to believe that one of them is in error. This process of creating and comparing independently generated constraints is a very general procedure for error detection in this domain and in many others.

It is often useful to consider the alternatives to any representational scheme. Before the advent of the echo sounder, the simplest way to measure depths was to lower a heavy weight on a line. Of course, if the water was deep this procedure consumed time and energy. Matthew Maury came up with an ingenious and surprising solution to the problem of measuring great depths. He "made deep sea soundings by securing a cannon shot to a ball of strong twine. The heavy weight caused the twine to run out rapidly, and when the bottom was reached, the twine was cut and the depth deduced from the amount remaining on the ball." (Bowditch 1977) If one knows the length of the line and volume of the ball it is wound onto, one can measure the diameter of the ball and compute what fraction of the volume of the ball, and therefore what fraction of the length, was pulled off by the cannon shot. Alternatively, the ball of twine may be weighed before and after the line has paid out. Knowing the weight of a given length of line one can easily compute how much line was consumed by the sounding.

Stepping Inside the Cognitive System

The basic computations of navigation could be characterized at the computational, representational/algorithmic, and implementational levels entirely in terms of *observable* representations. On this view of cognitive systems, communication among the actors is seen as a process *internal* to the cognitive system. Computational media, such as diagrams and charts, are seen as representations internal to the system, and the computations carried out upon them are more processes internal to the system. Because the cognitive activity is distributed across a social network, many of these internal processes and internal communications are *directly observable*. If a cognitive psychologist could get inside a human mind, he or she would want to look at the nature of the representation of knowledge, the nature and kind of communication among processes, and the organization of the information-processing apparatus. We might imagine, in such a fantasy, that at some level of detail underlying processes (the mechanics of synaptic junctions, for example) would still be obscured. But if we could directly examine the transformations of knowledge representations we might not care about the layers that remain invisible. Any cognitive psychologist would be happy enough to be able to look directly at the content of the cognitive system. With systems of socially distributed cognition we *can* step inside the cognitive system, and while some underlying processes (inside people's heads) remain obscured, a great deal of the internal organization and operation of the system *is* directly observable. On this view, it might be possible to go quite far with a cognitive science that is neither mentalistic (remaining agnostic on the issue of representations "in the head") nor behavioristic (remaining committed to the analysis of information processing and the transformation of representations "inside the cognitive system").

Levels of Analysis and Hierarchy of Task Reduction

As we have seen, the position-fixing task is implemented in the manipulation of external representations and tools. We can follow the trail of representations quite a long way in some cases, but from time to time the stream of representational state disappears inside the individual actors and is lost to direct observation. Thus, while such an analysis may tell us quite a lot about the cognitive properties of the navigation system, it does not, by itself, tell us much about the nature of the processes and representations internal to practitioners of navigation. The problem of individual human cognition is not solved by this analysis, but neither is it simply put off. The description of transformations of representational state in the previous sections is both a description of how the system processes information and a specification of cognitive tasks facing the individual members of the navigation team. It is, in fact, a better cognitive task specification than can be had by simply thinking in terms of procedural descriptions. And the task specification is detailed enough in some cases to put constraints on the kinds of representations and processes that the individuals must be using.

Thus far, I have given a computational description of navigation and have examined the representational foundations for navigation and the algorithms by which the required computations are accomplished. In the last section I began to explore the implementational level of description which specifies the "details of how the algorithm and representation are realized physically" (Marr 1982). The discussion of the propagation of representational state from the alidade to the chart was perhaps the most detailed of these discussions. Here I brought the description down to the level of implementational operations, such as aligning the arm of the hoey with the appropriate point on the hoey scale. Now, this operation is both an implementation of the computation at the system level and a cognitive task facing the individual plotter. As such, one may ask of this computation how its inputs and outputs are represented and what algorithms are used to transform inputs into outputs. One might imagine a story like the following (we will consider this analysis in more detail later): The computation is to align the hoey index with a particular value on the scale. By observing the performance of this task, and especially by noting errors that are made, we may place some constraints on the representations that are used to perform the task. A key component of the task is knowing the direction in which scale values increase. This representational element may be used by an algorithm that finds the target value by doing hill climbing on the values with dynamic gain adjustment. That is, if the index is currently far below the target value it can be moved a large step toward the target. When the index is near the target value, it should be moved in smaller steps. Finally, we might want to say how such representations and algorithms are actually implemented in the minds of the plotters. At this point, however, we overreach the terms of our analysis. The details of these internal processes cannot be directly observed and must remain objects of speculation. Notice that, although some of the representations are internal, they are still all cultural in the sense that they are the residua of a process enacted by a community of practice rather than idiosyncratic inventions of their individual users. In the analysis that follows, I will use culture as a resource in order to more precisely define the nature of the tasks that are actually engaged by the individual members of the navigation team.

A Cognitive Account of a Navigator's Work

The computations of navigation are not platonic ideals; they are real physical activities undertaken by individuals manipulating real physical objects. Even though many of them are symbolic activities and some of the symbols are clearly represented inside the heads of the practitioners, we must never forget that symbols always have some physical realization or that the nature of the physical form of symbols constrains the kinds of operations to which they can be subjected. In the previous section, I described the major computations of the navigation task in terms of the propagation of representational state across a set of physical devices and discussed the physical activities of the members of the navigation team as they manipulate the devices that do the computation. That discussion was both an analysis of the system-level operation of the navigation system and a specification of the tasks facing the individual members of the navigation team. This task specification permits construction of the computational level of description for the individuals. The present section presents the cognitive requirements of performance of the navigation task. What are the people in the setting doing? Here I intend to finally engage what was for a decade the central question of cognitive anthropology: "What do they have to know in order to do what they do?" Or, perhaps a better question, "How do they go about knowing what they know?"

Identifying the directly observable external physical representational media involved in the navigation task was easy. Even the task of describing their internal structures and the mechanisms of coordination among them was relatively straightforward. With respect to structures that are internal to the actors, we are, alas, much more in the dark. It is possible to give functional specifications to the structures that must be present, but we cannot directly observe their internal organization, nor can we specify the mechanisms of coordination by which representational state is propagated. These things are simply beyond the reach of contemporary cognitive science. In what follows, I will attempt to push the theory of computation by the propagation of representational state as far as is possible into the heads of the practitioners of navigation. I will assume that a principal role of the individuals in this setting is providing the internal structures that are required to get the external structures into coordination with one another.

Because cognitive science has historically had difficulty modeling the behaviors of the sensory transducers that connect minds to the "outer environment," much more attention has been paid to "processes that can go on inside the human head without interaction with its environment" (Simon and Kaplan 1989: 39). Furthermore, "deep thinking has proved easier to understand and simulate than hand-eye coordination" (ibid.) Unfortunately, in order to get the cognitive game started in a mind that is profoundly disconnected from its environment, it is necessary to invent internal representations of a good deal of the environment that is outside the head. This requirement is simply not present in a mind that is in constant interaction with its environment. The mainstream thinking of cognitive science in the past thirty years leads us to expect to have to represent the world internally in order to interact with it. This theory of "disembodied cognition" (Norman, 1990) has created systematic distortions in our understandings of the nature of cognition. As we have seen, a good deal of the computation performed by a navigation team is accomplished by processes such as hand-eye coordination (see also Latour 1986). The task of navigation requires internal representation of much less of the environment than traditional cognitive science would have led us to expect.

In the following, I will attempt to posit the minimum internal structure required to get the task done. I choose the minimum because I would go beyond this point with trepidation. In a study of the conduct of science, Bruno Latour (1987) laments the lack of studies of the forms and inscriptions in which scientific and technical knowledge are concentrated. He suggests that one might conclude from this that such studies are not possible. Latour continues:

I draw a different conclusion; almost no one has had the courage to do a careful anthropological study of formalism. The reason for this lack of nerve is quite simple; a priori, before the study has even started, it is towards the mind and its cognitive abilities that one looks for an explanation of forms. Any study of mathematics, calculations, theories, and forms in general should do quite the contrary; first look at how the observers move in space and time, how the mobility, stability and combinability of inscriptions are enhanced, how the networks are extended, how all the informations are tied together in a cascade of re-representation, and if, by some extraordinary chance, there is something still unaccounted for, then, and only then, look for special cognitive abilities. (246–247)

I do not know whether I have fulfilled the terms of Latour's instructions. But although I have described the history, the use, the combination, and the re-representation of the forms, something remains unaccounted for. Perhaps it is not much, but it is something. As we shall see, it is not special cognitive abilities. Indeed, the cognitive abilities that navigation practitioners employ in their use of the forms and inscriptions are very mundane ones—abilities that are found in a thousand other task settings.

The fix cycle is truly a cycle of activity, with no unambiguous beginning or end. Each step depends on a previous step and feeds subsequent steps. Of course, every real navigation performance must have had a first fix cycle, which must have begun somewhere, but where in the cycle the first round begins depends in uninteresting ways on the circumstances of getting the activity going. If the ship has just pulled away from the dock, the fix cycle will begin with an estimated position somewhere in the vicinity of the dock. If the ship has been at sea and has just arrived in coastal waters, the cycle may begin with a set of observations of landmarks. For analytic convenience, we will begin with the symbol that represents the projected position of the ship at the time the fix observations will be made. This is a position plotted on the chart.

Timing the Cycle

The fix cycle repeats at a specified interval. The default interval for Sea and Anchor Detail is 3 minutes. That is, the entire cycle of activity from mark signal to mark signal is 3 minutes. The fix interval may be changed to another value, such as 1, 2, or 6 minutes, on the basis of needs of the ship. If the ship is in circumstances in which it may quickly get into trouble, the interval should be short. As the rate at which the ship can approach danger decreases, the period of the fix cycle can be increased. There are no hard and fast rules for establishing the interval. (The reasons for choosing 3 minutes as the default fix interval will be discussed later in this chapter.)

With a specified fix interval, timing the fix requires reading a timepiece. The implementation at this level is up to the crew. Some procedures specify the ship's clock as the source of the time reference. The bearing recorder aboard the *Palau* used his own wristwatch instead of the ship's clock for two reasons. First, timing the cycle requires knowing the time, computing the next fix time, and vigilance to the clock. By removing his watch and placing it at the top of the bearing record log, the recorder made the time reference much more convenient. This ship's clock was mounted on the bulkhead at the back of the bridge and required the bearing recorder to look away from the chart table to see the time. Second, the bearing recorder's watch had a digital display. Fix times have to be recorded in the bearing record log, and it was easier to read and copy the digital representation of the time than the analog representation presented by the ship's clock. Additional cues that help the bearing recorder remember when to monitor the time reference include the pace of activities. For example, on a 3-minute fix interval, if no problems arise, the plotter will have completed plotting the position of the ship and will have projected future positions before it is necessary to choose the next landmarks and prepare to begin the next cycle. Other cues include the explicit remindings of others. The plotter may say "Isn't it about time for another round?" This illustrates the beginnings of a social distribution of cognitive labor in which remembering is jointly undertaken.

Timing the fix cycle is a cognitive task that cannot be reliably performed by the bearing recorder without the aid of a mechanical timepiece. The task of the bearing recorder is to coordinate his actions with the behavior of the timepiece and so permit the other members of the navigation team to coordinate their actions with his.

Identifying Landmarks

The task of identifying a landmark involves the simultaneous coordination of many elements of structure. In Sea and Anchor Detail, the choice of a landmark is represented to the pelorus operator in the form of a spoken string of words: "Point Loma Light," for example. The pelorus operator must somehow get from this name to both a description of the appearance of the landmark and a sense of where the landmark is in the surrounding space. This must be represented in some sort of memory. Although that memory may not be the sort of storehouse of information that many researchers assume, I think there is no way to dismiss the fact that some internal representation capable of producing a partial description of the landmark from the name of the landmark must exist and must be attributed as a structure internal to the human operator. Furthermore, the appearance of the landmark may depend on the pelorus operator's vantage, so a single description will probably not suffice. The sense of where the landmark is in the environment may guide the search of the surroundings, which in turn changes the contents of the visual field. Ultimately the identification of the landmark must arise from the coordination of the expectation about the appearance of the landmark with the contents of the visual field.

Even though we do not know the mechanisms by which these things are actually implemented in the mind (and I take it to be a virtue of this approach that we do not make any premature commitment to such mechanisms), it is still useful to speak of the propagation of representational state and the superposition of representational state in this description. Perhaps the elements of the description of the appearance of the landmark are represented as images, or perhaps as symbolic structures. Since this question has not yet been satisfactorily settled in the cognitive science community as a whole, we can hardly expect to resolve it here on the basis of observational data. But even without making a commitment to a particular kind of representation and algorithm, we can observe the nature of the task and provide a set of computational-level constraints for theories of cognition that aspire to account for what people do "in the wild."

The identification of the landmark is a highly interactive process, and it is likely that important kinds of learning take place in every performance of this task. Whatever way it is implemented, it may be that all these representations are simultaneously in coordination with one another. That is, the representation of the landmark's name, the expectations about the appearance of the landmark, and the visual scene are all mutually constraining one another when the pelorus operator fixates on the red-and-white tower and declares "There is Point Loma Light." This is another superposition of internal and external structure on a single representational medium. Scanning the currently visible scene may improve the mental map and the representation of the landmark itself and other recognized objects in the scene. The successful visual search may improve the description of the landmark stored in memory and the association of the landmark description to the landmark name.

The task is slightly different when the ship is not in restricted waters and the entire fix cycle is performed by a single watch-stander. In that case, the problem of identifying landmarks may be one of direct reconciliation of the chart and the world. (We will investigate the cognitive consequences of some of these differences in the next chapter.) In some sense, the problem is easier in Standard Steaming Watch because the pelorus operator is also the plotter and the recorder. The navigator thus has access to the chart itself as a representation of the landmark. The chart is a much richer representation both of the appearance of the landmark and of its relation to other objects in the world than is provided by the spoken name of the landmark. Still, the task is not without difficulties.

Consider the following situation. While the *Palau* was steaming eastward, southwest of San Diego Harbor, a quartermaster attempted to identify the Coronado Islands, which lay about 7 miles south of the ship. The three islands were clearly visible out the window of the pilothouse just above the chart table. Of the three islands on the chart, the leftmost island was labeled "North Coronado" and the rightmost one was labeled "South Coronado." Because the quartermaster was looking to the south, however, North Coronado was on the right and South Coronado was on the left in the world (the reverse of their positions on the chart relative to him). By mapping the spatial structure of the chart directly onto the visible world, the quartermaster managed to mistake North and South Coronado for each other. Clearly he had relied on the spurious but well organized spatial correspondences between his perspective on the chart and his view of the world. This example highlights two points. First, human minds are good at finding and projecting structural regularities. Second, since this sort of misidentification is seldom made by an experienced navigator, we must wonder what internal structures are required to do this task correctly.

Aiming the Alidade

Having identified a landmark in the world, the pelorus operator must then aim the alidade at the landmark. This process brings two external structures into coordination with each other. There is no need for an internal representation of the hairline; it is built into the sighting telescope, and the operator has the experience of it in the visual field. Perhaps there is not even a need to maintain an internal representation of the description of the landmark once the landmark is in view, although one suspects that its description and name may remain active during the aiming operation. The coordination between the hairline and the landmark is accomplished by reducing the distance between the hairline and the landmark until they are co-located in the visual field. This procedure might be implemented in many ways.

Reading Bearings

Reading bearings in the alidade may be one of the most complex cognitive skills required of the quartermasters. Even though it is complex, it takes place in a predictable world, and eventually it becomes an overlearned skill. In this subsection I will treat it in what may seem excruciating detail. I do so because activities of this kind are nearly ubiquitous not only in navigation but in many of the everyday activities of inhabitants of the modern world and because, as far as I know, no one has taken seriously the question of just what is required, cognitively, to perform them.

Reading the bearing requires the coordination of at least four elements of structure:

- the experience of the scale and the hairline
- a knowledge of how to read digits
- either a memory for the direction in which scale values increase (clockwise by convention on the circular scale, and to the right as seen through the viewfinder of the alidade), or a procedure for establishing this direction
- a sequence of number names from zero to nine.

There are many ways to bring these elements into coordination with one another in the bearing-reading task. Let us first consider a fairly simple (although not always efficient) method, and then consider other possibilities.

The first two digits of any three-digit bearing can be read directly from the scale itself. These are the first two digits of the name of the nearest labeled major tick to the left of the hairline. This requires the scale and the hairline, the knowledge of how to read digits, and the knowledge of the direction of increasing values.

One must, of course, know how to read the digits in order to make use of the labels. This knowledge is selectively brought into coordination with the labels on the major tick marks at 10° intervals on the scale. Many compasses have only these first two digits of the labels for the major ticks. This saves space on small instruments, and the last digit (which is always 0) may be left off, because it is not required by the procedure used to read the scale. Even though this is an overlearned skill, it sometimes fails. We cannot know from strictly observational data what the actual sources of error are, but we can get some idea of the kinds of considerations involved by looking at the diagnoses of errors applied by other members of the team. During my observations, the following explanations for errors by pelorus operators were offered by the bearing recorder or the plotter:

- The similar appearance of the printed representation of two digits on the face of the gyrocompass card was offered to explain a report of 167 for an actual bearing that was reconstructed as 107. The 6 and the 0 have similar shapes. The confusion of shapes may be facilitated by the blurriness of vision caused by tears in the eyes, which a pelorus operator sometimes gets from working in the wind on the wing bridge.
- An off-by-a-century error, e.g., 324 for 224. This could be produced by a number of cognitive mechanisms, including a data-driven error (Norman 1981) involving increased activation on the second digit. The crewmen offered no specific hypothesis concerning the reason for such an error, but they found it a plausible error to have been made.
- A repetition/substitution error, e.g., 119 for 199. This one is probably due to a shift of activation (Norman 1981).
- A digit transposition, e.g., 235 for 325. Digit transpositions are quite common in environments like this (Wickens and Flach 1988).

The occurrence of these errors, even if they are rare, puts some constraints on the kinds of structures that must be involved in the performance of the task.

Once the first two digits of the bearing have been established, it remains to establish the last. In the simplest case this is done by counting. Counting is the coordination of an internally generated sequence of number tags with a partitioning of perceived unitary objects (Gelman and Gallistel 1978). The knowledge of the direction of increasing values is required in order to know that it is the first two digits of the label to the left rather than the label to the right that will be elements of the bearing name. The importance of the knowledge of the direction of increasing values can be inferred from the occurrence of errors in which a bearing n minor ticks to the left of a labeled tick is reported as being n units larger than the name of the major tick. For example, a bearing of 257 (three ticks to the left of 260) will be reported as 263 if the direction of increasing scale value is inverted. Knowledge of this direction can be remembered, or it may be computed. If computed, the scale increase direction is a representational state that results from the coordination of the experience of the scale with a procedure for finding the direction of increase. The latter may involve a comparison of the magnitudes of the labeled major ticks adjacent to the hairline. The knowledge of the direction of increasing scale values is required in order to orient the partitioning activity. The counting is accomplished by coordinating the shift in attention from one tick to the next (in the proper direction) with the transition from one number label to the next. It is not necessary to remember all the correspondences generated by this process; it is only necessary that the correspondence between the number name and the tick mark nearest the hairline be produced. I believe we can assume that, for the quartermasters, the number sequence runs fairly automatically. No crew member ever attributed a bearing-reporting error to the inability of the pelorus operator to count from one to nine.

The use of the scale requires the abilities to produce the appropriate name (e.g., "1 3 6") for any given tick mark and to locate the appropriate tick mark when given any name between "0 0 1" and "3 6 0." To do this the pelorus operator needs the following:

- a schema for the scale, with ticks (some of which are labeled) in an ordered sequence
- the abstraction of number sequence at least from zero to nine
- the ability to decompose a number representation into a decade (between 01 and 35)
- the ability to use the number sequence locally within a decade to determine the last digit of the bearing
- the ability to reassemble the decade and the last digit into a whole number.

It is not necessary to posit an abstract internal representation of the scale. Instead, the pelorus operator works with the interpreted representation of this scale. This representation is caused by attending to the scale and involves coordination with pre-stored structures that allow the scale to be seen as a scale rather than as something else. What is stored certainly need not be an image of the scale.

If we asked a pelorus operator, while he was not actually using the instrument, to tell us how the scale-reading task is done, he might make use of an imagined internal representation of the scale and imagine the operations performed upon it. This would be a very different task from reading a scale that was present. An internal representation may be acquired through continued interaction with the scale itself. What we know about internal representations of external structures, though, leads me to believe that such a representation would be schematic at best (Nickerson and Adams 1979; Reisberg 1987).

Reporting and Remembering Bearings

Viewing language as one of the structured representations produced and coordinated in the performance of a task highlights language's information-bearing properties. In cognitive science, language is usually thought of primarily as a human computational capacity that must be understood in terms of the processing that individuals must do to produce or interpret it. Looking at the role of language in the operation of a system of socially distributed cognition leads us to wonder about the properties of language as a structured representational medium.

Traditional information theory fails us when we approach spoken language. When a pelorus operator reported the bearing of a landmark, how much information was passed? The number he reported is one of 360 possible full-degree bearings. Does that mean that a bearing report carries $\log_2 360 = 8.492$ bits of information? Or, since there are 1000 numbers that can be constructed of three digits, should we say that each three-digit bearing carries $\log_2 1000 = 9.967$ bits of information? The problem is that the agreement between the sender and the receiver concerning the universe of messages and the ways in which they will be coded is very weakly specified. The information-theoretic measures given above are irrelevant. What counts is what it takes to understand what has been said, and understanding of language is poorly modeled by classical information theory. Even in this highly rationalized and predictable setting, there is no previously agreed upon specifiable universe of possible messages, and the ways of encoding and decoding the messages are themselves negotiable at the time of communication. Rather than attempt to force information theory onto natural language, let us instead look at the problem of language understanding from the perspective of coordination of structured representational media. Utterances themselves are states in structured representational media which we understand by bringing them into coordination with both external and internal structured representational media. Depending on the nature and the modality of the language expression, a great deal of information may be entailed by what looks like the transmission of a trivial message. The message may be garbled and require partial reconstruction by the hearer. The impact of the message on the receiver depends on what the receiver knows. For example, consider a case in which a bearing of 059° is reported. To a novice, this may be only a string of digits that is to be written down in a book. To the experienced navigator, this means a direction that is a little to the east of northeast. When a knowledgeable navigator hears or sees this bearing, he may know which direction he is currently facing and may actually feel the direction indicated by the bearing as a physical sensation. For example, a navigator facing west may hear "059" and experience a sense of the direction to the right of directly behind. This must involve the coordination of the cardinal direction schema with the bodily frame of reference. This is quite similar to what the Micronesian navigator does. The differences in interpretation of such simple verbal strings are easy to observe in the actual interactions among members of the navigation team. At one point, the bearing to Hotel del Coronado was reported as 003 degrees. The bearing recorder simply recorded and relayed the reported bearing as a string of digits, but the plotter, without plotting it, responded: "It better not be. If it is we're pulling into Tijuana right away!" In an interview, this same plotter, a quartermaster chief, once described the ability to feel bearings as directions in the local space defined by bodily orientation as being able to "think like a compass" and said it was something he tried to teach all his men to do. The bearing recorder's willingness to simply record and report the impossible bearing is evidence that he was not "thinking like a compass"—at least, not with respect to that bearing. This bearing meant something more to the plotter than it did to the bearing recorder because the plotter brought it into coordination with a structured representational medium—his sense of directions in local space.

Recording Bearings and Depths

The spoken representations of bearing and depth must be transformed into written representations for entry into the bearing record log. This part of the task is relatively straightforward for competent members of a literate culture. The bearings and depths must be inserted in the appropriate places in the table, and they must be legible. One potential problem here is the ambiguity of symbols. A handwritten 2, for example, may be indistinguishable from a handwritten Z.

Setting the State of the Hoey

Once the plotter has either read or overheard the bearing to a landmark, it must be remembered until it has been represented in the structure of the hoey and the hoey configuration has been locked. The task of locating the position on the hoey scale that corresponds to the name of the bearing is very similar to the task of reading the bearing from the gyrocompass scale. As was noted above, the hoey and the gyrocompass scales are the interfaces between the digital and the analog representations of the bearings. Whereas the gyrocompass scale and the alidade hairline are involved in an analog-to-digital conversion, the hoey's arm and hairline index are used to perform a digital-to-analog conversion.

Plotting and Evaluating the Fix

Once the hoey has been configured with the representation of the bearing, the plotter must remember which landmark is to be associated with the bearing. Sometimes the identity of the landmark is evident from the angle and the expected location of the fix. There is a reconstructive memory process here that may rely on the simultaneous coordination of the memory for the landmarks chosen on the current round, the physical shape of the configured hoey, and the positional constraints provided by the arrangement of symbols on the chart. The functional system that realizes this memory clearly transcends the bounds of the skull and the skin of the individual plotter. If we were to characterize this memory retrieval as a heuristic search, we would have to say that the search (for the appropriate landmark to go with the bearing) is conducted in the space of the chart itself by successive positioning and repositioning of the hoey until a fit between chart, hoey, and projected fix position is found. The navigation system thus remembers which landmark goes with the current bearing, and most of the *structure and process* of the memory function is external to the human actor. The heuristic part of the search lies in the plotter's choices of ways to position the hoey to better satisfy one or another of the spatial constraints of the problem as they are represented in the physical structure of the hoey and the chart. Latour (1986) calls this "thinking with the eyes and hands."

TRANSLATION WITH PRESERVATION OF DIRECTIONAL RELATION
On the Mercator projection, the straight edges of rulers make straight lines which denote sets of locations all bearing the same directional relationship to one another. A frequent component of plotting tasks is the establishment of such a directional relationship with respect to a directional referent and a given location. Thus far I have discussed the use of the hoey, because that was the tool of choice for the plotter aboard the *Palau*. There are, however, several other tools designed to do this same task, and each has slightly different properties. There are two major classes of these tools: those that have directional gradations (a protractor of some sort) built in and need only to be aligned with a directional referent, and those that simply translate direction. The tools in the latter class, parallel rulers and pairs of triangles, rely on a compass rose printed on the chart for the degree gradations. Compass roses appear on some charts with both magnetic and true orientation. On other charts they are printed only with true orientation, and on most non-Mercator-projection charts they do not appear at all (since on most non-Mercator projections directional relationships are not preserved). If a chart is designed for use with the simple direction translating tools that rely on the compass rose and on the translation of direction from the rose to courses, or from relations between points to the roses, several roses are frequently printed so that for any particular operation a compass rose will be nearby on the chart. The farther one has to move a line of direction with parallel ruler or triangles, the greater the probability of error.

Hoey
The hoey is also known as a *one-armed protractor*. Directional reference is established by aligning the base of the protractor with any one of the latitude lines on the chart. The latitude lines provide a true east-west referent for the direction scale of the protractor.

Consider the task of bringing a representational state of the hoey into coordination with the structure of the chart. One has to simultaneously get the edge of the rule lined up with the symbol of the landmark on the chart and also get the base of the hoey lined up with the directional frame of the chart. The task has three degrees of freedom. There are two degrees of freedom in getting the base of the hoey aligned with the directional frame of the chart (one rotational, the other either vertical or horizontal depending on whether the hoey is aligned with a parallel of latitude or a meridian of longitude). The third degree of freedom is in getting the edge of the rule over the landmark symbol. It is difficult to satisfy all of these at once, because one cannot attend to all three at the same time (the hoey base should be far from the landmark symbol in order to present the longest possible line of position), and a change in one tends to change the others. There is a simple mechanical technique for making this coordination easier to do. It reduces the problem from three degrees of freedom to two.

The technique is to place the point of a pencil on the symbol of the landmark on the chart, bring the edge of the rule up against the pencil point, and then, keeping the edge in contact with the pencil point, move the base of the hoey until it is aligned with the directional frame of the chart. This reduces the problem to one with two degrees of freedom, and permits the plotter to attend visually to the rotational and lateral constraints while guaranteeing the satisfaction of the landmark symbol position constraint with gentle pressure on the hoey arm. In producing the coordination between the hoey and the chart, the task performer can transform the task to an easier one by achieving coordination with an internal artifact: the knowledge of this technique. When this skill is well learned it probably becomes an automatic motor skill, and experienced plotters may find it difficult to describe how it is actually performed.

Parallel Ruler

The *parallel ruler* is a pair of straightedges attached to each other by a pair of diagonally mounted bars. While one of the rulers is aligned with the desired direction, the other ruler can be moved away from the first, remaining parallel to it. By alternately holding one ruler down on the chart and moving the other, one can move a direction line anywhere on the chart. Parallel rulers are awkward to use. Not only does their use require physical coordination to walk a line across the chart; sometimes some planning must be done to determine which sequence of walking moves is required to get from the printed compass rose to the desired point on the chart.

PMP

The standard plotting machine or *parallel motion protractor* (PMP) is also known as a drafting machine. When using the PMP it is necessary to tape the charts down to the table, because the directional reference is established via the base of the PMP (which is bolted to the table). If the orientation of the chart with respect to the PMP changed, the directional referent would be lost. Because the direction can be locked into the PMP's arm, which is then free to move in two dimensions while preserving the selected direction, it is easy to use this to pass the given direction line through any selected point. The special technique required to get the hoey into coordination with the chart is not needed with this tool. The arm of the PMP is attached to a platform that has two concentric compass roses. These inner and outer roses can be independently set to establish direction relative to any arbitrary reference. This can be useful if it becomes necessary to plot bearings relative to the ship's head rather than relative to true north.

The hoey is perhaps a bit more difficult to use than the PMP, because the 360° scale is folded over into two scales of 180° each. Efficient use of the hoey requires additional strategies to get the correct line of position. Because a single arm position on the hoey represents both a bearing and its reciprocal, the plotter must be able to determine which bearing is to the landmark and which is from it.

With the straightedge of the plotting tool in the correct position on the chart, the plotter may draw the line of position. Experienced plotters almost never draw a complete line of position extending from the landmark symbol to the position of the ship. Instead they draw a short line segment in the vicinity of the expected fix. The judgement of what constitutes "the vicinity" of the fix may take many factors into account.

Evaluating the Fix

Once three or more lines of position have been drawn, the navigator should evaluate the fix. Is it of good quality? Can it be trusted? Should something different be done in order to improve the quality of future fixes? The primary evidence concerning the quality of the fix is the size of the triangle formed by the three lines of position. If the three lines do not intersect in exactly the same point, the ship's position is uncertain. There are complex arguments about how to place a ship's position relative to various shapes of triangles (Bowditch 1977), but most navigators simply assume that the ship is in the center of the triangle and place a dot there as the fix point.

The displacement between the ship's projected position for the fix time and the actual fix position is a source of information about the quality of the information used in constructing the previous dead-reckoning position. If the ship has not traveled as far as was projected during the fix interval, it must not be traveling as fast as expected. The change in speed may be due to a change in the speed of the ship through the water or to a change in the current through which the ship is moving. Any information of this sort derived from the comparison of the fix position and the projected position must be remembered in order to contribute to future projections.

Extending the Dead Reckoning Track

After the fix has been plotted and evaluated, the dead-reckoning (DR) track of the ship should be projected into the future for at least two fix intervals. This requires the plotter to determine the ship's heading and construct a track line from the current fix position in the direction of the ship's heading. The heading is available in the form of a written number in the deck log. Again the hoey is used to construct a line of position. In this case, it is a line extending from the fix position in the direction of the current heading. Along this line, the plotter now predicts where the ship will be at the end of each of the next two fix intervals. To do this, the plotter must know how fast the ship is traveling.

Mercator-projection navigation charts are not normally printed with distance scales. (This is because the measurement of distance is approximate on the Mercator projection. The amount of error depends on the distance measured and the magnitude of its projection onto the north-south dimension.) Instead they are printed with latitude and longitude scales along the borders. One minute of latitude corresponds to one nautical mile. However, the length on the chart of a minute of latitude increases as one moves away from the equator. A reasonably accurate estimate of distance can be had by using the latitude scale at the mid-latitude of the segment to be measured.

Measurements of distance on the charts are made with dividers. These tools simply span a given extent of space and permit that span to be transferred to another part of space. To measure the distance between two points on a chart, one could span the distance with dividers and move that span to a scale to read its magnitude in the units of the scale. Like the hoey, the dividers are a tool for capturing representational state and moving it to another medium without distortion.

FOUR WAYS TO DO DISTANCE-RATE-TIME PROBLEMS

The way a problem is represented can change what is required of the problem solver. Suppose the plotter has just plotted a fix and needs to compute the ship's speed in nautical miles per hour on the basis of the distance the ship has moved in the interval of time that elapsed between the current fix and the previous one. In particular, suppose the two fix positions are 1500 yards apart and that 3 minutes have elapsed between the fix observations. There are at least four different ways to represent this problem. Each representational condition requires a different organization of cognitive processes.

Condition 1   The task performer has the following resources: paper and pencil, knowledge of algebra, knowledge of arithmetic, knowledge that there are 2000 yards in a nautical mile and 60 minutes in an hour, and knowledge that distance equals rate multiplied by time ($D=RT$).

Condition 2   The task performer has the same resources as in condition 1, except that instead of a paper and pencil the task performer has a four-function pocket calculator.

Condition 3   The task performer has either a three-scale nomogram of the sort shown in figure 3.3 or a nautical slide rule of the sort shown in figure 3.4, and the knowledge required to operate whichever tool is present.

Condition 4   The task performer has no material implements at all, but knows how to use what navigators call the "three-minute rule."

It is impossible to specify in advance exactly how any particular person will actually do this task under any of these conditions, but if the person uses the resources in the ways they are intended to be used it is not difficult to determine what is likely to be involved.

In condition 1, the task performer will first have to use the knowledge of algebra to manipulate the formula $D=RT$ to the form

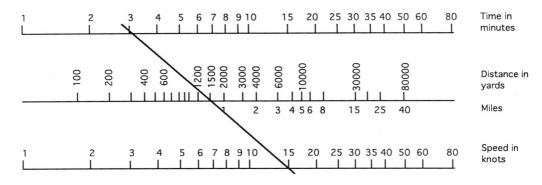

Figure 3.3 A three-scale nomogram.

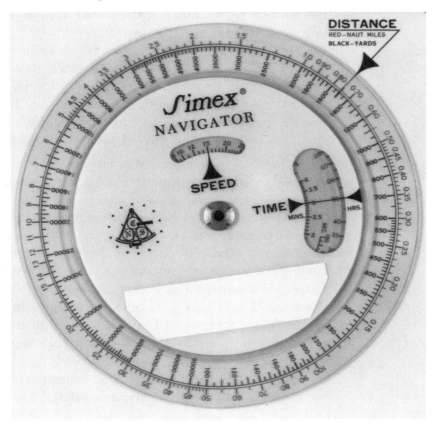

Figure 3.4 A nautical slide rule.

$R = D/T$ so that rate can be solved for directly from the given values of D and T. Then, the distance in yards will have to be converted to the equivalent number of miles using the knowledge of the number of yards in a mile and the knowledge of arithmetic. The time in minutes will have to be converted to the equivalent number of hours using the knowledge of the number of minutes in an hour and, again, arithmetic. The distance measure must be divided by the time measure (arithmetic again) to get the rate. Of course, these things can be done in a different order (for example, the division could come before either of the unit conversions, or between them), but in any case all these things must be done at some point in order to solve the problem.

The reader may want to try this as an exercise just to get a feel for the sort of work that is involved. I believe that this problem would tax the abilities of many navigation practitioners in the Navy, not because the arithmetic is difficult but because the applications of the arithmetic operations must be planned so that the elements of the solution fit together to produce the desired solution. One may be perfectly capable of doing every one of the component subtasks in this problem but fail completely for lack of ability to organize and coordinate the various parts of the solution.

In the calculator version, the procedures for doing the arithmetic operations of division and multiplication are restructured so that, instead of constructing a pattern of symbols on a piece of paper and decomposing the problem to a set of operations on single digit arithmetic arguments, one keys values into a calculator and pushes operator buttons. Also, depending on the order in which the steps are taken, it may be necessary to remember a previous result and enter it into a later operation after other operations have intervened. I think this version of the task would also tax the abilities of many navigation practitioners. The calculator makes the easy part of the problem easier to do. The difficult part is deciding how to coordinate the arithmetic operations with each other, and the calculator provides no support for that part of the task.

The paper-and-pencil condition and the calculator condition are alike in that they utilize completely general computational routines. The knowledge of the equation for distance, rate, and time and the knowledge of the constants required for the unit conversions are specific to the task, but they provide little help in structuring the actions of the task performer. Because of this, the procedures for doing the computation are complex. When we write them out at even the shallow level of detail given above, we find that they contain many steps. If we actually got down to counting each symbol written on the paper or each key-press on the calculator as a step (not an unusually detailed level for a cognitive analysis), we would find that they each contain many tens of steps.

Now consider the cognition required of the task performer in condition 3. To use the nomogram, one finds the value of the time on the time scale and makes a mark there. One finds the value of the distance on the distance scale and makes a mark there. Then one draws a line through those two marks with a straightedge and reads the value of speed, in the desired units, where the drawn line intersects the speed scale. The fact that these scales are already constructed in terms of the units set by the problem clearly gives this condition a substantial advantage over the first two conditions. This is a very common problem, and the nomogram is designed specifically to make its solution easy. The use of the nautical slide rule is very similar to the use of the nomogram. It, like the nomogram, is a medium in which multiplication and division are represented as alignments of logarithmic scales. One aligns the distance index with the desired distance on the distance scale (this could be yards or miles; both are represented, side by side) and aligns the elapsed-time index with the desired time on the time scale (either minutes or hours; both are present, side by side); the speed index will then point to the speed in knots on the speed scale.

Having the scales in the units set by the problem eliminates the need to convert one kind of unit into another. More important, knowledge of algebra is not required for this condition of the task. The nomogram and the slide rule transform the task from one of computational planning (figuring out what to divide by what) to one of simple manipulation of external devices. In the first two conditions, all that stands between the task performer and the nonsensical expressions "$R=DT$" and "$R=T/D$" is a knowledge of the syntax of algebraic transformations. When one is using the nomogram or the slide rule, the structure of the artifacts themselves obviate or lock out such relations among the terms. The relations $D=RT$, $R=D/T$, and $T=D/R$ are *built into* the structure of the nomogram and slide rule. The task performer has no need to know anything about these relations, either implicitly or explicitly. The correct relationships are built into the tool; the task performer simply aligns any two scales to constrain the value of the third. Even more important, the incorrect relations are "built out"—it is not possible to produce those relations with these tools.

On the nomogram, the time and speed scales flank the distance scale. A line drawn between any point on the speed scale and any point on the time scale intersects the distance scale at a point that is the averaged sum of the logarithm of the time and the logarithm of the speed. Since sums of logarithms are products, the physical construction of the nomogram constrains the relationships among the terms to be of the correct type. Similarly, the slide rule is constructed so that the distance reading is the angular sum of the logarithm of the speed and the logarithm of the time.

The task performer still needs to know something, but the knowledge that is invoked to solve the problem with these tools is less complicated and less general than the knowledge required with the paper-and-pencil or the calculator version. A good deal of what needs to be done can be inferred from the structure of the artifacts, which constrain the organization of action of the task performer by completely eliminating the possibility of certain syntactically incorrect relationships among the terms of the computation. One may be more reluctant to say that the answer was actually computed by the task performer in condition 3 than in condition 1 or condition 2. It seems that much of the computation was done by the tool, or by its designer. The person somehow could succeed while doing less because the tool did more. But before we go that far, let us consider the task in condition 4.

Where condition 3 utilized specialized external artifacts, condition 4 utilizes a specialized internal artifact. Since 3 minutes is 1/20 of an hour and 100 yards is 1/20 of a mile, the number of hundreds of yards (twentieths of a mile) a ship travels in 3 minutes (1/20 of an hour) *is* its speed in nautical miles per hour. Thus, a ship that travels 1500 yards in 3 minutes has a speed of 15 nautical miles per hour. In order to "see" the answer to the problem posed, the navigator need only imagine the number that represents the distance traveled in yards, 1500, with the last two digits removed: 15. The distance between the fix positions in the chart is spanned with the dividers and transferred to the yard scale. There, with one tip of the divider on 0, the other falls on the scale at a tick mark labeled 1500. The representation in which the answer is obvious is simply one in which the navigator looks at the yard-scale label and ignores the two trailing zeros. A complex computation is realized by a simple strategy of situated seeing in a carefully constructed environment.

Experienced navigators actually apply this rule in an even more compressed form. The three-minute rule changes the distance itself into speed. The distance I span with the dividers can be interpreted directly as a speed rather than as a distance, and the "yard" scale on the chart (marked in hundreds of yards) is now not a site of distance measurement that is converted to speed; rather, the conversion has worked its way upstream computationally, and a structure that is sometimes read as the "yard" scale is now read as a speed scale. An experienced navigator has no need to imagine the distance in yards in order to use the three-minute rule to compute speed. The extent of space spanned by the dividers may be a representation of a distance as it comes off the chart, but this same extent of space becomes a representation of speed as the dividers approach the scale (which is now being read as a speed scale). When the dividers touch down on the scale, the space they span represents what the scale represents, and the scale represents speed in knots.

When used in this way, the three-minute rule utilizes the same interpretation of space as speed that we saw in the use of the chip log line. If the conditions of measurement can be constructed in the right way, a distance traveled in a fixed period of time can be read directly as a speed. This seems to be a re-evolution of a conceptual solution in a new technical medium. That is, when charts and compasses became accurate enough to measure and plot positions, the careful juggling of units of distance, time and speed to get simple solutions was re-created. In the case of the chip log, the unit of distance between the knots in the rope was constructed ($41\frac{2}{3}$ feet) to yield a speed reading of that distance for a given unit (30 seconds) of time. In the case of the three-minute rule, the time span was manipulated to fit the distance-speed relationship. This is a nice example of the evolution of representations in the ecology of ideas.

The application of the three-minute rule is very neat, but it will not be very useful if the conditions under which it can be applied occur only infrequently. In fact, this is not an unusual problem for a navigator. In the above discussion of the task of setting the fix interval, it was noted that 3 minutes is the default fix interval for Sea and Anchor Detail. Three minutes is the default precisely because this rule is so easy to use. The navigation team is capable of performing the fix cycle on 2-minute, or even 1-minute intervals. Three minutes is by far the most common interval, not because it meets the needs of the ship better than the other intervals, but because it meets them well enough, and it makes this computation so easy to do.

The nautical slide rule and the nomogram are normally used only when the ship is away from land and the fix intervals are much longer than 3 minutes. When the cycle is performed on intervals of 1 or 2 minutes, speed is normally computed by conversion to the 3-minute standard. For example, if the ship travels 800 yards in 2 minutes, it would travel 1200 yards in 3 minutes, so its speed is 12 knots. And regardless of the speed of the ship, as long as both the speed and the fix interval are constant there is no need to actually recompute the ship's speed to project its position for the next fix. The distance traveled during the next interval will be the same as that covered in the last interval, so it can simply be spanned with dividers and laid on the projected track line, without the distance or the rate ever represented as a number.

All the methods for computing speed from distance and time have the same description at the computational level. Each of them, however, represents the inputs in different ways and applies different algorithms to those representations in order to produce the output. Each of them implements the algorithms in operations applied to physical entities. All involve the coordination of representational structure that is inside and outside the task performer, but each calls on a particular collection of internal structures to be coordinated with external structure in a particular way.

What we see here is a set of functional systems, each of which is capable of making the mapping from inputs to outputs but each of which organizes a different set of representational media in relation to one another.

These are low-level functional systems. We will see later how they are embedded in larger functional systems to construct the activity of the navigation team.

What are these tools contributing to the computations? It has now become commonplace to speak of technology, especially information processing technology, as an amplifier of cognitive abilities. Cole and Griffin (1980) show, however, that the appearance of amplification is an artifact of a commonly assumed but mistaken perspective. When we concentrate on the *product* of the cognitive work, cultural technologies, from writing and mathematics to the tools we have considered here, appear to amplify the cognitive powers of their users. Using these tools, people can certainly do things they could not do without them. When we shift our focus to the *process* by which cognitive work is accomplished, however, we see something quite different. Every complex cognitive performance requires the application of a number of component cognitive abilities. Computing speed from distance and time with a calculator involves many component subtasks: remembering a symbolic expression, transforming the expression, determining which quantities correspond to which terms of the expression, mapping the expression to operations on the calculator, finding particular calculator keys, pressing the keys, and so on. The application of these abilities must be "organized" in the sense that the work done by each component ability must be coordinated with that done by others. If we now consider doing the same task with the nomogram or with the three-minute rule, we see that a different set of abilities is enlisted in the task. None of the component cognitive abilities has been amplified by the use of any of the tools. Rather, each tool presents the task to the user as a different sort of cognitive problem requiring a different set of cognitive abilities or a different organization of the same set of abilities.

The tools provide two things simultaneously. First and most apparent, they are representational media in which the computation is achieved by the propagation of representational state. Second, they provide constraints on the organization of action. This is most apparent in the way that the nautical slide rule precludes the execution of operations that violate the syntax of the computational description. The physical structure of the slide rule is not only the medium of computation. By constraining the representational states that can be produced to ones that are syntactically correct, it provides the user with guidance as to the composition of the functional system in which it will participate. In this sense, these mediating technologies do not stand between the user and the task. Rather, they stand with the user as resources used in the regulation of behavior in such a way that the propagation of representational state that implements the computation can take place.

There are two important things to notice about the computational technology of the piloting task. First, these tools and techniques permit the task performer to avoid algebraic reasoning and arithmetic. Those activities are replaced by aligning indices with numbers on scales, or imagining numerical representations and making simple transformations of them. Rather than *amplify* the cognitive abilities of the task performers or act as intelligent agents in interaction with them, these tools *transform* the task the person has to do by representing it in a domain where the answer or the path to the solution is apparent. Second, the existence of such a wide variety of specialized tools and techniques is evidence of a good deal of cultural elaboration directed toward avoiding algebraic reasoning and arithmetic. In fact, there are more methods than I have presented here. The problem could also have been solved by looking up the speed in a table of distances, rates, and times. The kinds of cognitive tasks that people face in the wild cannot be inferred from the computational requirements alone. The specific implementations of the tasks determine the kinds of cognitive processes that the performer will have to organize in order to do the task. The implementations are, in turn, part of a cultural process that tends to collect representations that permit tasks to be performed by means of simple cognitive processes.

Perhaps this should also give us a new meaning for the term "expert system." Clearly, a good deal of the expertise in the system is in the artifacts (both the external implements and the internal strategies)—not in the sense that the artifacts are themselves intelligent or expert agents, or because the act of getting into coordination with the artifacts constitutes an expert performance by the person; rather, the system of person-in-interaction-with-technology exhibits expertise. These tools permit the people using them to do the tasks that need to be done while doing the kinds of things the people are good at: recognizing patterns, modeling simple dynamics of the world, and manipulating objects in the environment (Rumelhart, Smolensky, McClelland, and Hinton 1986). At this end of the technological spectrum, at least, the computational power of the system composed of person and technology is not determined primarily by the information-processing capacity that is internal to the technological device, but by the role the technology plays in the composition of a cognitive functional system.

Choosing Landmarks

The choice of landmarks to shoot for a fix is a complex judgement that may take into account many constraints. It is desirable to have an even angular dispersion among the landmarks. Three landmarks equally spaced at 120° intervals would be ideal. However, rarely are three such landmarks available from the position of the ship at the time of the fix. It is essential to avoid landmarks that are too nearly in the same or opposite direction from the ship. A constant error in one of two lines of position that intersect at a 30° angle will produce a position error twice as great as the same error will produce in lines that intersect at 90°. It is useful to get one bearing nearly ahead or astern, because that will produce the best information about the relation of the ship to its desired track. Similarly, a bearing near the beam provides information about the position of the ship along its track and is sometimes called a "speed line." Additional constraints are imposed by the physical layout of the ship. The port pelorus operator cannot see any landmark located at an angle of less than 10° off the bow, because a large mirror blocks the view. All these constraints may contribute to the choice of landmarks to shoot.

Navigators often use their arms or fingers to assess the relationships among provisional lines of position in the space of the chart or in the surrounding space. I have seen a plotter stand on the bridge and extend each arm toward a landmark, assessing the angle of intersection of his arms. More frequently, the potential lines of position are constructed in gestures over the surface of the chart. A plotter may point on the chart to the symbol depicting the location of a prospective landmark and then sweep his finger across the chart to the projected location of the ship at the time of the next fix. By constructing several such provisional lines of position in the air, a suitable set is chosen. The plotter must be remembering or re-imagining the earlier lines as others are added for consideration, since the judgement cannot be based on the properties of any line alone but must be based on the relations among them. I suspect that the gestures help to create and maintain these representations through time. The memory of the trajectory of the finger decays with time, but it seems to endure long enough that several of these can be superimposed on one another and on the perceptual experience of the chart. Such a composite image permits the navigators to envision the directional relationships among the provisional lines of position. The provisional lines of position are not drawn on the chart, of course, because they would add a great deal of potentially confusing and possibly dangerous clutter to the chart. A different representational technology might permit the temporary construction and evaluation of provisional lines of position.

Pipelining Activities

Humans are opportunistic information processors. An account of the pelorus operator's activity that says "read the number and then report it" is shaped by a powerful pedagogical simplification. It is a very understandable account, but not a very accurate one. In fact, the activities of aiming the alidade, reading the bearing, and reporting the bearing are often interleaved. Standing on the wing, one can sometimes see the pelorus operator swing the alidade to the approximate direction of the landmark, report the first two digits of the bearing, and then, with a slight pause in the report, turn the alidade a bit more and pronounce the last digit of the bearing. In extreme cases even the locating of the landmark may be interleaved with the subsequent activities. Thus, one might observe a report punctuated by short pauses in which non-report work is being done: "Hotel del (short pause to swing alidade), 0 4 (short pause to count to last digit) 3." In such a case many representational structures may be simultaneously in coordination.

If the unit of analysis is defined by the media that are actually in coordination, we should change the unit of analysis as different aspects of the task are considered. When the pelorus operator reads the bearing, the visual scene outside the pelorus is no longer a salient part of the coordination, and the mental structures that encode the description of the landmark are no longer needed. The coordination event that accomplishes the reading of the bearing spans a different set of structures; a different set of media are brought into coordination. Again, the normally assumed boundaries of the individual are not the boundaries of the unit described by steep gradients in the density of interaction among media. Now the unit includes the degree scale, the hairline, and perhaps the structures required to read the digits printed on the scale and count the tick marks lying between the labeled tick mark and the hairline. The bearing taker is still the task performer, but now different aspects of the bearing taker's knowledge and different structures in the environment are brought into coordination. The active functional system thus changes as the task changes. A sequence of tasks will involve a sequence of functional systems, each composed of a set of representational media.

Sometimes the reading is co-articulated with reporting and recording the bearing. The bearing recorder may have already recorded the first digits of the bearing before the bearing taker has read the last digit. In that case, the unit of coordination includes the activities of two persons. The two actors could be said to be in coordination with one another in a profound sense (more on this later). The representational state of the pelorus is propagated onto the representational state of the bearing log by the coordinated actions of two people. But what is in coordination is more than the two people or the knowledge structures of the two people. The functional system includes these components and the artifacts themselves at the same time. When the bearing is recorded as it is being observed, the chain of coordination may include the name of the landmark, partial descriptions of the landmark, the visual experience of the landmark, the hairline of the alidade, the gyrocompass scale, the knowledge and skills involved in reading the bearing, the spoken sounds on the phone circuit, the knowledge and skills involved in interpreting the spoken bearing, and the digits written in the bearing record log.

It is tempting to offer the sequential account as the nominal account and then explore instances in which the subsequences overlap. Doing this makes the exposition clearer, but it does violence to the phenomena. In fact, the maximally co-articulated case is typical. The elements can be strung out sequentially only by a deliberate process that involves other structures. If reporting and recording are co-articulated with the reading of the bearing, for example, neither the bearing taker nor the recorder need remember the bearing. If this same task is strung out serially—read, report, record—then the memories of both must be brought into play. The serial sequential account is the one that appears in the written procedures that describe the task. These rationalized versions are easier to think about, understand, and promulgate than a description of how the system actually works, but it would be both difficult and inefficient to do the job the way it is described in the written procedures.

When we turn to the coordination events and see all the media that are simultaneously in coordination (some inside the actor, some outside), we get a different sense of the units in the system. When a bearing taker sights a landmark, we can imagine that there is coordination between the landmark name and the memory for landmark descriptions that assumes a state of description of the desired landmark, and then that is coordinated with some aspects of the visual scene containing the landmark itself, and then the hairline of the pelorus is superimposed upon that. All these things are in coordination with one another at once. This coordination produces the representational state in the pelorus that is then read in the indicated bearing. Here we have a coordination of two external structures (visual scene and hairline) with an internal structure (landmark description) that is the result of the coordination of two internal structures (landmark name and memory for landmark descriptions).

Constructing the Task Setting

The activities described in the previous section take place in a carefully organized task setting. One cannot performed the computations without constructing the setting; thus, in some sense, constructing the setting is part of the computation. In the most straightforward sense, the setting is constructed by means of preparation procedures that are performed before navigation is begun. The Watch Standing Procedures specify the following steps in preparation for Sea and Anchor Detail:

8.   Preparations for Sea and Anchor Detail. Prior to Sea and Anchor Detail, the Assistant to the Navigator will ensure that:
   a.   All approach and Harbor charts are laid out with:
       (1)   Track with courses and distances labeled
       (2)   Turn bearings taking into account the tactical characteristics of the ship (utilize 15 degrees rudder and 10 knots of speed)
       (3)   Danger bearings/ranges where ever necessary, especially if the ship must head straight at a shoal
       (4)   Outline in bright indelible marker all hazards to navigation and all soundings of thirty feet (5 fathoms) or less
       (5)   A convenient yard scale for quick use
       (6)   If anchoring, lay out the anchorage as recommended in the Officer of the Deck's Manual
   b.   All pertinent publications are corrected, and marked, the information reviewed by the Navigator, and plotter.
   c.   Tides and currents graphed and posted.
   d.   If possible, the gyro error is determined within one hour of stationing the detail.
   e.   Qualified personnel are assigned to each position.

Getting the Right Charts onto the Table in the Right Order

While a ship is entering a harbor, several charts may be required. The change from one chart to another must be accomplished quickly. It is important to get a new fix on the new chart as soon as possible. It would not do to be digging in the chart collection looking for the right chart when navigation needed to be done. A typical warship carries more than 5000 charts, so the search could be very time consuming. Furthermore, the charts are stored forward, near the auxiliary conning space. Therefore, all the charts that will be needed for a particular detail are assembled ahead of time and arranged on the chart table, one over the other, in the order in which they will be needed. This makes it possible to change charts quickly by simply pulling the top chart off and exposing the next chart. Extra copies are stored in the chart table so that they can be brought up quickly if the charts in use are inadvertently destroyed or are collected as evidence in the case of an incident.

Computation of Entry (Exit) Track

The task of navigating a ship into a harbor can be greatly simplified by planning the ship's track ahead of time. This consists of plotting on the chart the courses to be steered, the lengths of the legs, the locations of turns, the identification of turn bearings, and the landmarks to be used to determine turn bearings. Of course, constructing this track requires considerable effort. It also requires the determination of the tactical characteristics of the ship. Recall that ships do not turn on a dime. After the rudder is put over, a ship will move forward and to the side some distance before it reaches its new desired heading. The amount it moves forward is called *advance*; the amount it moves to the side is called *transfer*. It is possible to compute these values, but it is much simpler to look them up in an advance and transfer table (figure 3.5). These tables change the nature of the computations involved in preplotting the track, which in turn changes the nature of the computations done during Sea and Anchor Detail. The advance and transfer tables make it easier to plot the projected track, and the projected track makes it easier to provide support to the officer of the deck. We can say more than that these tasks have been made easier. By specifying the changes in the cognitive requirements of the tasks that must be performed, we can say how they have been made easier. The structure of these artifacts is such that the required computations can be achieved by simpler cognitive processes in interaction with these artifacts than by the method they replace.

These features of the planned route of the ship do not change from one entry of the harbor to another, so they are often plotted on the chart in ink. They thus become permanent features of the chart. Since the exit track is different from the entry track (ships keep to the right of a channel), a chart is usually made up for entry and another for exit, at least for the home harbor. Yard scales showing distances prior to the turns are plotted directly on the ship's projected track. All this could be done while the ship is entering port, but doing it ahead of time changes the cognitive requirements of the tasks that are to be done. One of the most important tasks of the navigation team is to provide advice to the OOD on the progress of the ship. Having the chart properly made up ahead of time makes this task much easier. For example, if the desired track has been plotted already, displacement left or right of track can be measured directly. The information regarding the next course is ready at hand and need only be read off the chart after the position has been plotted. On a chart made up in this way, the number of yards to the next turn need not be measured; it is available by simple inspection.

Further customizations to the chart include drawing in the critical depth contours (areas of water that are shallower than the draft of the ship), plotting bearings of landmarks that will keep the ship out of dangerous areas, and laying out the approaches to an anchorage. As with the projected tracks, these modifications to the structure of the chart are specific to the ship and support computations that could otherwise be done on-line, but only at the cost of greater cognitive demands during the actual performance of the main task.

Updating the Chart

Charts must be kept updated. Channels silt in, sandbars move, new buildings are constructed, and lighthouses may be demolished and rebuilt. Since it is expensive to publish a new edition of a chart, periodic notices of changes are published and distributed. These changes should be incorporated in a ship's existing charts. Furthermore, the crew may choose to add landmarks to a chart that are not yet on it or on a published change notice. The crew of the *Palau* added a new tower to their chart by establishing bearings to the tower from several position fixes acquired while exiting the harbor. Doing this meant adding workload to one performance of the task in order to make future performances less effortful or more flexible.

Charts are thus customized in ways that transform the nature of the work that can be done with them and change the cognitive requirements of doing that work. The customizations to the chart

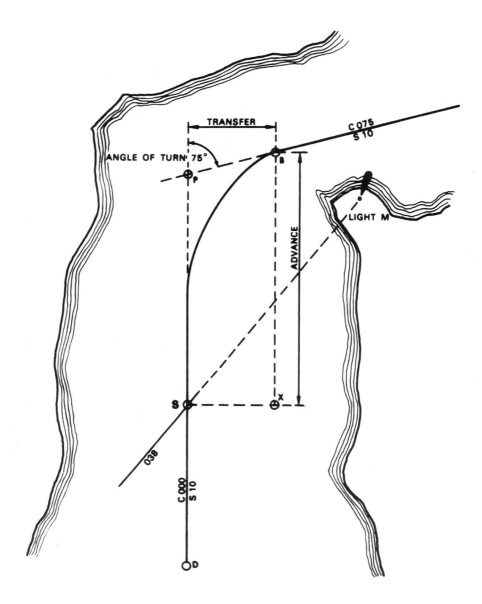

Standard Tactical Diameter, 15000 Yards — Standard Rudder 15°					
Angle of Turn	Advance	Transfer	Angle of Turn	Advance	Transfer
15°	500	38	105°	993	853
30°	680	100	120°	933	1013
45°	827	207	135°	827	1140
60°	940	347	150°	687	1247
75°	1007	513	165°	533	1413
90°	1020	687	180°	867	1500

are bits of structure that will become components of cognitive functional systems that operate during the performance of the navigation task. The computations are distributed in time, and these customizations to the chart are examples of moving computation out of the high tempo activities of Sea and Anchor Detail by doing the computation ahead of time.

Computation of the Compass Deviation Table

Although the magnetic compass is not normally used as a primary navigation instrument, when it is called into service it becomes very important. Every magnetic compass has small errors that are a consequence of the electromagnetic environment of the compass. These are corrected when possible. Often some minor errors remain. In order to remove these errors, a deviation table is constructed. The error of the compass on headings at 10° intervals is observed empirically and entered into a table. The entries in this table can be used later to compensate for errors in compass readings. The deviation table must be constructed ahead of time when a reliable directional referent is available.

The Compilation and Posting of the Tide and Current Graphs

As each fix is plotted, the navigation team must verify that the depth of water observed under the ship corresponds to the depth of water shown on the chart for the location of the fix. This comparison would be trivial if there was no tidal variation. The actions of the tide cause the water to be shallower at some times and deeper at others. In some places tidal ranges of 15 feet are common. Depths reported on the chart are given with respect to the *tidal datum* of the chart, a reference with respect to which tidal heights are also reported. If the reported tide is 0 feet, then the depths reported on the chart should be accurate. If the reported tide is +4 feet, then the water will be 4 feet deeper than the depths shown on the chart. Predictions of tidal movement are provided in tables.

The tides are one of the messier aspects of navigation. In the open ocean, tidal fluctuations are relatively regular. Where tides

Figure 3.5 A table of advance and transfer. These descriptions of a ship's handling characteristics are determined empirically and are used to plan turning maneuvers in restricted waters. (From Maloney 1985.)

interact with land (and especially in harbors, where they interact with complex basin shapes), the regularities become quite complex. When planning maneuvers in a harbor, one must compute a general tidal amplitude and phase for the tidal movement. This may be a good description of the tidal movement at one point; however, as the tide surges into and out of the harbor, the peak tide occurs at different times and with different amplitudes at different points in the harbor. The navigator must be able to compute the times and heights of the tides at all points along the planned route. Additional tables are published showing the corrections of phase and amplitude at selected points in the harbor. Figuring the tides on a basin with a complex shape, such as San Francisco Bay, can be a real nightmare. In preparing to enter or exit a harbor, the navigation team will construct a set of graphs of the height of the tide at a sample point (or several sample points) in the harbor along the planned track. These graphs provide corrections to the calculations of the expected depth of water under the ship for comparison to the depth observed by the fathometer operator.

The crew also produces a current graph showing the direction and velocity of the tidal current at selected locations. These currents can be quite strong in bays and harbors. They affect the speed made good over the ground (a standard nautical term), and this can be a very important consideration affecting rate calculations and steering commands.

Cashing In the Precomputation

Precomputations Redistribute Cognitive Workload across Time

Many of the elements of the preparation for Sea and Anchor Detail involve the performance of the parts of the anticipation computations. It is easy to see that one of the effects of doing as much as possible ahead of time is a reduction in the amount of work that has to be done in the high-tempo phases of the Sea and Anchor Detail. Because the task is event driven, and since the quartermasters do not have the option of quitting or starting over, this is an important strategy for keeping the workload within the capacity of the navigation team. Stacking the charts on the table in the order in which they will be needed is an example of this sort of redistribution of effort across time.

Precomputations Transform the Tasks Performed

Many of the elements of the preparation do more than simply move some the computational activity out of the time-limited performance of the main task. They create new structures that change the cognitive nature of the tasks that must be done in the time-limited performance of the main task. The pre-plotted entry track transforms the task of generating advice for the officer to the deck. The "convenient yard scale for quick use," in concert with a pair of dividers and the three-minute rule, becomes an element in a functional system that performs distance-rate-time calculations via perceptual inferences. Tide graphs, turn bearings, and danger ranges have similar roles to play in the on-line computations. The activity of the fix cycle collects all these constraints together in a medium where their combined effects interact. The precomputations are saved representational structures that transform the nature of the task performance. They aren't just doing part of the task ahead of time, they are doing things ahead of time that make the task easier to do. Thus, in the distribution of cognitive effort across time, the integral of effort over time is not the same in the case of doing part of the task ahead of time as it is in doing a restructuring precomputation ahead of time. In the latter case, the total effort may actually be less.

Of course, the construction of the chart itself could also be described in exactly this way. It is a structure that is constructed ahead of time and changes the nature of the computation that is to be done in the period of high-tempo activity. The Micronesian navigator's imagery of the voyage is very much like a chart in that it is a precomputed structure onto which observations can be mapped so that the answer to the pressing question is literally staring the navigator in the face. A great deal of prior experience is distilled in the structure of the chart and in the Micronesian navigator's knowledge of the stars and seas. In both cases, the structure that is the centerpiece of the computational functional system is not something that could have been created by the navigator alone. In both cases, there is a general framework onto which specific observations that are local in time and space are projected.

Precomputations Capture Task-Invariant Properties on Multiple Time Scales

Each of these precomputations is a way of building local invariants into the structure of the tools that are used in the performance of the navigation task. The invariants are temporally local in the sense that none of them lasts forever. They are local with respect to the persistence of the invariant they encode. Structure, both in the world and in representations of the world, endures over variable periods of time. In general, where structure in the world is invariant, the computation can be made more efficient by building representations of the invariants into the representations of the world. The chart, as published, encodes invariants of the navigation environment. These are relatively long-lasting, and so is the chart when properly cared for. The publication of notices to mariners and the updating of the chart in accordance with them are concessions to the fact that the invariants of the chart may be longer-lived than those of the world it represents. Many of the customizations to the chart are based on the physical characteristics and handling properties of the ship—the locations of turn bearings and the danger depth contours, for example. These are invariants that could not be encoded on the chart as published, since the chart must serve the needs of many ships. These items are, however, invariant so long as the chart is used aboard *this* ship, so the crew adds them indelibly to the chart. Shorter-lived invariants, such as those pertaining to any particular transit of the waters depicted on the chart, are marked in pencil or some other erasable medium. Some ships even add an acetate overlay over the track lines on frequently used charts so that accumulated erasures do not destroy the underlying features. Invariants that are specific to a particular fix are captured in the structure of malleable media such as the hoey, in which state is preserved only as long as the locking screw is twisted down tight.

Different tools may permit different sorts of invariants to be captured. Consider the difference between the parallel motion protractor (PMP) and the hoey in the plotting of magnetic bearings. With the PMP, one can add magnetic variation into the structure of the device itself by rotating and locking the outer compass rose. With the PMP so configured, magnetic bearings can be plotted and "automatically" corrected for magnetic variation. This is useful because magnetic variation is an approximate invariant over local space (within tens of miles) and local time (within tens of years). The cost of capturing this invariant with the PMP is that it depends on maintaining the orientation of the charts with respect to the base of the instrument. The charts must therefore be taped to the chart table. It is not possible to build the invariant of magnetic variation into the structure of the hoey. Plotting magnetic bearings with the hoey requires additional arithmetic operations to correct each line of position, because the hoey captures only the more local invariant of the bearing itself. The lock on either the hoey or the PMP provides a way to "write" or "save" the current value in the structure of the device.

All these precomputational activities are instances of a wider class of computational phenomena called *modularity*. They are modular in the sense that they remove from local computations any aspects that are invariant across the spatial and temporal extent of the computation. Thus, in addition to redistributing computation in time and transforming the character of computations, these precomputational elements eliminate redundant computation. One must know the relationship of the observed fix position to the desired position, but one does not reconstruct the projected track at every fix or even on every transit of the waters depicted. Since the desired track is invariant across all entries of this particular harbor, it need be constructed only once if it is constructed in a medium that endures. The relationship of charts to plotting procedures thus implies a particular modularity of the task. This will become clearer in the consideration of the adaptation of the system to change in chapter 8.

The chart table and its environs are preconstructed by the crew to serve the purposes of the task. The prepared chart is a layered set of representations, each of the layers matching the temporal or spatial extent of invariants that it represents. This permits the final computation to be performed by adding a final layer of short-lived representations to a representational medium in which many layers of longer-lived invariants have already been superposed upon one another. With three quick strokes of a pencil, the plotter places the lines of position in coordination with one another and in coordination with a deeply layered representation of the world and the ship's relationship to it. There, instantly, is the position of the ship in relation to the land, to the previous positions, to the desired track, to possible future positions, to the depth of the water, to the next turn, to the latitude and longitude grid, and more.

Precomputations Are a Window on a Cultural Process

The computation of the present fix relies on the most recent setting of the hoey, which was done a few seconds ago. The present computation also involves the projection of the dead-reckoning position, a piece of work that was done just a few tens of seconds ago; on the tide graphs that were constructed a few hours ago; on the changes to the chart that were plotted a few days ago; on the projected track and the turning bearings, which were laid down when this chart was "dressed" a few weeks ago; on the placement of the symbols on this chart, which was done upon the publication of the new chart issue a few years ago; on the nature of the plotting tools, which were designed a few decades ago; on the mathematics of the projection of the chart, which was worked out a few centuries ago; and on the organization of the sexagesimal number system, which was developed a few millenia ago. It may seem silly to tie this moment's navigation activity to a number system developed by the Babylonians. Notice, however, that when we get down to looking at the details of the practice we see that the most mundane facts about the representations chosen have consequences for the sorts of things that are easy to do and those that are difficult to do. This was one of the lessons of the comparison with Micronesian navigation. These details present certain opportunities for error while precluding others. This system is part of a cognitive ecology in which the various representational technologies constitute one another's functional environments. Since the presence of any one technology may change the computational potentials of the others, it is not possible, in principle, to exclude any contributing element from the list of precomputations simply on the basis of its antiquity.

Given that each of these elements makes as large a contribution to the computation as any other, we may wonder where we should bound the computation in time. It will not do to say that the current computation is bounded by this second, for clearly it spans many seconds. Perhaps we should use the navigators' partitioning of the world into meaningful pieces and say that the current computation is the fix and is temporally bounded by the fix interval. That too is a fiction, because the fixes are elements of a fix cycle and any starting point is as arbitrary as any other. We may attempt to put temporal bounds on the computation that we observe now, today, in any way we like, but we will not understand that computation until we follow its history back and see how structure has been accumulated over centuries in the organization of the material and ideational means in which the computation is actually implemented.

This is a truly cultural effect. This collection through time of partial solutions to frequently encountered problems is what culture does for us. Simon (1981) offered a parable as a way of emphasizing the importance of the environment for cognition. He argued that, as we watch the complicated movements of an ant on a beach, we may be tempted to attribute to the ant some complicated program for constructing the path taken. In fact, Simon says, that trajectory tells us more about the beach than about the ant. I would like to extend the parable to a beach with a community of ants and a history. Rather than watch a single ant for a few minutes, as psychologists are wont to do, let us be anthropologists and move in and watch a community of ants over weeks and months. Let us assume that we arrive just after a storm, when the beach is a tabula rasa for the ants. Generations of ants comb the beach. They leave behind them short-lived chemical trails, and where they go they inadvertently move grains of sand as they pass. Over months, paths to likely food sources develop as they are visited again and again by ants following first the short-lived chemical trails of their fellows and later the longer-lived roads produced by a history of heavy ant traffic. After months of watching, we decide to follow a particular ant on an outing. We may be impressed by how cleverly it visits every high-likelihood food location. This ant seems to work so much more efficiently than did its ancestors of weeks ago. Is this a smart ant? Is it perhaps smarter than its ancestors? No, it is just the same dumb sort of ant, reacting to its environment in the same ways its ancestors did. But the environment is not the same. It is a cultural environment. Generations of ants have left their marks on the beach, and now a dumb ant has been made to appear smart through its simple interaction with the residua of the history of its ancestor's actions.

Simon was obviously right: in watching the ant, we learn more about the beach than about what is inside the ant. And in watching people thinking in the wild, we may be learning more about their environment for thinking than about what is inside them. Having realized this, we should not pack up and leave the beach, concluding that we cannot learn about cognition here. The environments of human thinking are not "natural" environments. They are artificial through and through. Humans create their cognitive powers by creating the environments in which they exercise those powers. At present, so few of us have taken the time to study these environments seriously as organizers of cognitive activity that we have little sense of their role in the construction of thought.

Where Is the Computation?

Relating Mental Activity to Computation

Ship navigation involves lots of numbers. Numbers have to be processed in order to find out where the ship is and especially to determine where it will be. It is easy to assume that navigators must be good at arithmetic. When I looked closely at the practice of navigation, however, I found the navigators engaged in very few arithmetic tasks. How can that be?

It must be evident by now that the computations performed by the navigation system are not equivalent to the cognitive tasks facing the individual members of the navigation team. It is possible to describe the computations performed by the navigation team without recourse to the cognitive abilities or activities of the individual members of the team. I have done so above in the description of the propagation of representational state across a set of structured representational media. The navigation system combines one-dimensional constraints to fix a ship's position. The members of the navigation team read scales and translate spoken representations into written ones. The navigation system computes distance from rate and time, while the members of the team imagine four-digit numbers as two-digit numbers. The computations that are performed by the navigation system are a side effect of the cognitive activity of the members of the navigation team. The tools of the trade both define the tasks that are faced by the navigators and, in their operation, actually carry out the computations. As we have seen, the very same computation can be implemented many ways, each implementation placing vastly different cognitive demands on the task performer.

I argued above that the naive notion of these tools as amplifiers of cognitive activity was mistaken. Is a written procedure an amplifier of memory? Not if the task performer never knew the procedure. Then, and always, the functional system that performs the task is a constellation of structured representational media that are brought into coordination with one another. These tools permit us to transform difficult tasks into ones that can be done by pattern matching, by the manipulation of simple physical systems, or by mental simulations of manipulations of simple physical systems. These tools are useful precisely *because* the cognitive processes required to manipulate them are not the computational processes accomplished by their manipulation. The computational constraints of the problem have been built into the physical structure of the tools.

The slide rule is one of the best examples of this principle. Logarithms map multiplication and division onto addition and subtraction. The logarithmic scale maps logarithmic magnitudes onto physical space. The slide rule spatially juxtaposes logarithmic scales and implements addition and subtraction of stretches of space that represent logarithmic magnitudes. In this way, multiplication and division are implemented as simple additions and subtractions of spatial displacements. The tasks facing the tool user are in the domain of scale-alignment operations, but the computations achieved are in the domain of mathematics. The chart is a slightly subtler example of the same principle. Consider the preplotting of danger bearings. Once this has been done, the determination of whether the ship is standing into danger is made by simply seeing on which side of the line the position of the ship lies. In this case, a conceptual judgement is implemented as a simple perceptual inference.

These tools thus implement computation as simple manipulation of physical objects and implement conceptual judgements as perceptual inferences. But perhaps this refinement will be lacking from the next generation of tools. By failing to understand the source of the computational power in our interactions with simple "unintelligent" physical devices, we position ourselves well to squander opportunities with so-called intelligent computers. The synergy of psychology and artificial intelligence may lead us to attempt to create more and more intelligent artificial agents rather than more powerful task-transforming representations.

In thinking about the slide rule, one may also reflect on doing multiplication by mental arithmetic. There are many ways to do mental multiplication. In Western culture a person faced with the need for mental arithmetic typically does some version of imagining place-value arithmetic. The person applying the algorithms of place-value arithmetic to mental images of numbers is using an internal rather than an external artifact. These internal artifacts are cultural programs (D'Andrade 1981, 1989). Internalizing the artifactual structure imposes new cognitive tasks, to be sure, and the properties of the individual processors put limits on the sorts of artifactual structures that can be successfully manipulated internally. Faced with a mental multiplication problem, even those who are familiar with the operation of a slide rule don't try to imagine how they would manipulate a slide rule to solve the problem. This is because what makes the slide rule work is the precision of the placement of the tick marks that represent numbers. The medium of mental imagery is poorly suited for preserving such precise spatial relationships, especially when one set of them must be moved relative to another.

What was said above about the difference between the processes realized by the manipulation of the artifact system and the cognitive processes required to perform the manipulation is as true for internalized representations as it is of external ones. Internal representations are capable of transforming tasks too. And we should expect that they would be. If the cognitive system acquires new capabilities by combining representations in new functional constellations, then it is just as likely that an internal representation will give rise to a a new constellation as it is that an external one will. Doing mental place-value arithmetic imposes a particular set of requirements on the task performer. Doing the same problems with some other system—the Trachtenberg system of speed arithmetic (Cutler and McShane 1975), for example; or the Chinese base-17 system (Taylor 1984), which uses no carry bits—imposes different requirements. In each case, the task is accomplished by the operation of a functional system composed of a number of representations that are brought into coordination.

We are all cognitive bricoleurs—opportunistic assemblers of functional systems composed of internal and external structures. In developing this argument I have been careful not to define a class, such as cognitive artifacts, of designed external tools for thinking. The problem with that view is that it makes it difficult to see the role of internal artifacts, and difficult to see the power of the sort of situated seeing that is present in the Micronesian navigator's images of the stars. The stars are not artifacts. They are a natural rather than a human-made phenomenon, yet they do have a structure which, in interaction with the right kinds of internal artifacts (strategies for "seeing"), becomes one of the most important structured representational media of the Micronesian system. The more or less random sprinkling of stars in the heavens is an important component of the Micronesian system. In a sky with an absolutely uniform distribution of stars, navigation by the stars would be impossible: information is difference, and there would be no differences to be seen as informative.

If we ascribe to individual minds in isolation the properties of systems that are actually composed of individuals manipulating systems of cultural artifacts, then we have attributed to individual minds a process that they do not necessarily have, and we have failed to ask about the processes they actually must have in order to manipulate the artifacts. This sort of attribution is a serious but frequently committed error.

Knowing Why Things Work

A well-known student of navigation laments the effects of this accumulation of structure as follows:

Even today, of course, since the ultimate sources of time-keeping and position-finding are the heavenly bodies, the sailor must look up at the sky. But so long and so far has the chain of experts— professional astronomers, mathematicians, almanac-makers, instrument-makers and so forth—separated the ordinary man from the first-hand observation that he has ceased to think beyond the actual clock, time-signal, map calendar, or whatever it may be that "tells" him what he wishes to know. (Taylor 1971)

Frake (1985: 268) makes a similar point about modern knowledge of the tides:

[Modern tidal theory] is far beyond the reach of the modern navigator. Sailors today have no need to understand tidal theory at any level. They merely consult their tide tables anew for each voyage.

The Mercator-projection chart is a specialized analog computer, and the properties of the chart that make its use possible are profoundly mathematical in nature. But those parts of the computation were performed by cartographers and need not be a direct concern of the chart's users. The cartographer has already done part of the computation for every navigator who uses his chart. The computation has been distributed over time as well as across social space. The navigator doesn't have to know how the chart was made and doesn't need to know about the properties of the Mercator projection that give special computational meaning to straight lines. The device is actually more powerful if the user does not have to know how or why it works, because it is thereby available to a much larger community of users. The computational abilities of the mind of the navigator penetrate only the shallows of the computational problems of navigation. In the day-to-day practice of navigation, the deeper problems are either transformed by some representational artifice into shallow ones or not addressed at all.

Having presented an account of the performance of the component tasks of the fix cycle in chapter 3, here I will address the ways in which those component tasks can be coordinated to form a larger computational system. In Sea and Anchor Detail, this requires getting the activities of a number of team members into coordination. Thus, in this chapter I consider not only how the tools are used but also how the members of the navigation team use the tools together. The unit of cognitive analysis in this chapter will be the navigation team rather than the individual watchstander.

In anthropology there is scarcely a more important concept than the division of labor. In terms of the energy budget of a human group and the efficiency with which a group exploits its physical environment, social organizational factors often produce group properties that differ considerably from the properties of individuals. For example, Karl Wittfogel (1957, cited in Roberts 1964), writing about the advent of hydraulic farming and Oriental despotism, says:

A large quantity of water can be channeled and kept within bounds only by the use of mass labor; and this mass labor must be coordinated, disciplined, and led. Thus a number of farmers eager to conquer arid lowlands and plains are forced to invoke the organizational devices which—on the basis of premachine technology—offer the one chance of success; they must work in cooperation with their fellows and subordinate themselves to a directing authority.

Thus, a particular kind of social organization permits individuals to combine their efforts in ways that produce results (in this case a technological system called hydraulic farming), that could not be produced by any individual farmer working alone. This kind of effect is ubiquitous in modern life, but it is largely invisible. The skeptical reader may wish to look around right now and see whether there is anything in the current environment that was not either produced or delivered to its present location by the cooperative efforts of individuals working in socially organized groups.

The only thing I can find in my environment that meets this test is a striped pebble that I found at the beach and carried home to decorate my desk. Of course, the very idea of bringing home a pretty pebble to decorate a desk is itself a cultural rather than a personal invention. Every other thing I can see from my chair not only is the product of coordinated group rather than individual activity, but is *necessarily* the product of group rather than individual activity.

All divisions of labor, whether the labor is physical or cognitive in nature, require distributed cognition in order to coordinate the activities of the participants. Even a simple system of two men driving a spike with hammers requires some cognition on the part of each to coordinate his own activities with those of the other. When the labor that is distributed is cognitive labor, the system involves the distribution of two kinds of cognitive labor: the cognition that is the task and the cognition that governs the coordination of the elements of the task. In such a case, the group performing the cognitive task may have cognitive properties that differ from the cognitive properties of any individual.

In view of the importance of social organization and the division of labor as transformers of human capacities, it is something of a surprise that the division of *cognitive* labor has played such a very minor role in cognitive anthropology. There have been few investigations of the many ways in which the cognitive properties of human groups may depend on the social organization of individual cognitive capabilities. Over the years there has been some interest in the way that the knowledge of a society is distributed across its members. Schwartz's (1978) "distributional model of culture" was one of the best worked out of such approaches. In recent years there has been increasing interest in intracultural variability, the question of the distribution of knowledge within a society (Romney, Weller, and Batchelder 1986; Boster 1985, 1990). For the most part, this recent work has addressed the question of the reliability and representativeness of individual anthropological informants and has not been oriented toward the question of the properties of the group that result from one or another distribution of knowledge among its members.

The notion that a culture or a society, as a group, might have some cognitive properties differing from those of the individual members of the culture has been around since the turn of the century, most conspicuously in the writings of the French sociologist Emile Durkheim and his followers and largely in the form of programmatic assertions that it is true. This is an interesting general assertion, but can it be demonstrated that any particular sort of cognitive property could be manifested differently at the individual and group levels? Making a move in that direction, Roberts (1964) suggested that a cultural group can be seen as a kind of widely distributed memory. Such a memory is clearly more robust than the memory of any individual and undoubtedly has a much greater capacity than any individual memory has. Roberts even speculated on how retrieval from the cultural memory might be different from individual memory retrieval and how a variety of social organizational devices might be required for the continued support of memory retrieval functions in increasingly complex cultures. Roberts explored these issues in a comparison of four American Indian tribes, holding that information retrieval (what Roberts called *scanning*) at the tribal level among the Mandan was more efficient than among the Chiricahua because "the small geographical area occupied by the tribe, the concentrated settlement pattern, the frequent visiting, the ceremonial linkages, made even informal mechanisms (of retrieval) more efficient" (ibid.: 448). Roberts also noted that the tribal-level information-retrieval processes of the Cheyenne had properties that were different from those of the Mandan or Chiricahua. He linked the properties to particular features of social organization: "If the membership of a council represents kin and other interest groups in the tribe, each member makes available to the council as a whole the informational resources of the groups he represents.... Councils have usually been viewed as decision-making bodies without proper emphasis on their function as information retrieval units." (ibid.: 449)

In the sentences cited above, Roberts attributes the differences in retrieval efficiency at the group level to the size of the group, the pattern of interactions among individuals, the pattern of interaction through time, and the distribution of knowledge. Thus, it seems important to come to an understanding of the ways in which the cognitive properties of groups may differ from those of individuals. In the comparison of the physical accomplishments of pre- and post-hydraulic agriculture societies it is obvious that the differences in physical accomplishment are due to differences in the social organization of physical labor rather than to differences in the physical strength of the members of the two societies. Similarly, if groups can have cognitive properties that are significantly different from those of the individuals in them, then differences in the cognitive accomplishments of any two groups might depend entirely on differences in the social organization of distributed cognition and not at all on differences in the cognitive properties of individuals in the two groups. This theme is the topic of the next two chapters.

Sea and Anchor Detail

What role does social organization play in the cognition of the navigation team during Sea and Anchor Detail? In chapter 1 we saw that the ship's documents specify a normative division of labor for this task. The specified roles were listed as follows:

3. The Sea and Anchor Piloting Detail will consist of:
   a. The Navigator
   b. The Assistant to the Navigator
   c. Navigation Plotter
   d. Navigation Bearing Recorder/Timer
   e. Starboard Pelorus Operator
   f. Port Pelorus Operator
   g. Restricted Maneuvering Helmsman
   h. Quartermaster of the Watch
   i. Restricted Maneuvering Helmsman in After Steering
   j. Fathometer Operator
   (When sufficient Quartermasters are available, each of the positions except Navigator, will be filled by a Quartermaster.)

The procedures to be followed and the duties of each member of the navigation team are also given in the watch standing manual. In considering these procedures and the division of labor they imply, it will become apparent that the written procedures are not used by the members of the navigation team as structuring resources during the performance of the task, nor do they describe the actual tasks performed. Furthermore, if a system was actually constructed to perform as specified in the procedures as written, it would not work. Still, the normative procedures are a good starting point and provide a stable framework within which the properties of the system can be described. In the following paragraphs, the elements of the task as specified in the Watch Standing Procedures are interspersed with text discussing the roles of the procedural elements in the constitution of the navigation team as a cognitive system.

4. While operating in Restricted Waters, the following procedures will be adhered to:
   a. Fixes will be taken at least every three minutes (Periodicity may be increased by the Navigator)

The default fix interval is 3 minutes because this permits the simplification of certain computations. This interval can be made shorter by the navigator if more resolution is required. The fix interval is a parameter that controls the rate of sampling the environment.

b. A fix will be obtained immediately following each turn

Because of the nature of the position-fixing and position-projecting computations, a ship's course will be made to approximate a series of straight segments punctuated by turns. This is entirely a consequence of the way courses are steered and positions are computed. With a different computational technology (the satellite-based Global Positioning System, for example), it would be possible to have ship's track consist of smooth curves. There are two problems with fixes taken while the ship is turning. The first is that it is difficult to make accurate observations from a turning platform. Even though the true bearing of the landmark may change little while the pelorus operator is aiming at it, if the ship is turning then the relative bearing of the landmark will be changing at whatever the rate of turn is. This may leave the pelorus operator "chasing" the landmark with the telescopic sight of the alidade. The second problem with fixes taken while the ship is turning is that even if they can be made accurately, they are a poor basis for the projection of the ship's position in the future. It is impossible to know the exact shape of the ship's track while the ship is making the turn, so a position fix in a turn does not permit an accurate projection of where the ship will be at the next fix time. For these reasons, fixes are not normally taken in turns. As soon as the ship steadies on a new course, however, it is desirable to take a fix from which future positions on the new course leg can be projected as straight lines.

c. Each set of bearings and/or ranges will be accompanied by a sounding, which will be compared against plotted position

This element of the procedure establishes a cross-check among the representations generated in the fix cycle. The role of comparison of representations in error detection will be discussed in chapter 6.

d. The Fathometer Log will be maintained by the Fathometer operator

The quartermaster of the watch (QMOW) normally keeps all the logs. In Sea and Anchor Detail, however, the fathometer log is kept by the fathometer operator. This is one of many shifts in the distribution of cognitive labor brought about by Sea and Anchor Detail.

> e.   The Magnetic Compass Checkbook will be secured on stationing the Sea and Anchor Detail. Checking headings for each course will be entered in the Deck Log by the QMOW
> f.   The Ship's Position Log will be secured on stationing the Sea and Anchor Detail, with annotation to that effect

The magnetic compass checkbook is used in Standard Steaming Watch to keep track of the behavior of the magnetic compasses. This and the ship's position log are secured (put away) during Sea and Anchor Detail because the information that would normally go into them is being generated in much more detail and recorded elsewhere (in the bearing log and the deck log).

> g.   If sufficient Quartermasters are available, the Assistant to the Navigator will not tie himself down to the plot. He will instead supervise the entire team with emphasis on the plot, the recorder, and the bearing takers.

The Assistant to the Navigator, the Quartermaster Chief, would like to be able to supervise all the activities of the navigation team. When I first went aboard the *Palau*, the team was operating in this configuration. Unfortunately, the quartermasters were not well enough trained to keep up with the workload, and the chief had to step into the role of plotter. It was not even always possible to fill all the positions with quartermasters. During some of my observation periods at sea, sailors of the signalman rating served as pelorus operators and fathometer operators. The effects of personnel availability on this aspect of team composition is one of the differences that was observed between ships. During Colleen Seifert's observations aboard another ship, for example, the Assistant to the Navigator had a completely supervisory role and evaluated the fixes as they were produced. This element of the procedure concerns the distribution of access to information in the navigation team and can be seen as a specification of one aspect of the computational architecture of the navigation team.

> h.   Periodically, every third or fourth fix, the information passed from secondary plot in CIC will be plotted on the Primary plot for comparison purposes.

There is a clear tradeoff here between the costs of constructing the redundant plot and the benefits of increased error detection that it provides. In view of the nature of the representations used, the information from Combat Information Center (CIC) cannot be passed to the bridge in the form of plotted positions. Rather, it is passed in a format that requires additional processing by the bridge team. The information could be passed as raw data (bearings and/or ranges of landmarks), as latitude and longitude coordinates, or in terms that locate the ship relative to the precomputed track. The latter format is most frequently observed. "Combat holds us 30 yards right of track, 600 yards to the turn" is a typical CIC status report. Given such a report, the plotter might "eyeball" the position and say, "I'll buy that." This apparently offhand comment represents the outcome of a computation. The coordinates passed by CIC fit the structure that is available to the plotter on the chart. Remember that the distances to the turns are marked in hundreds of yards. Locating a point on the chart that represents a position 30 yards right of the planned track and 600 yards prior to the next turn is therefore relatively easy. Economical encoding of position in relation to the planned track is possible only if both the bridge navigation team and the Combat Information Center have the *same* track plotted on their charts. The report is about the position of the ship, but it assumes shared representations of the framework with respect to which the position is reported.

This redundant processing by the plotter provides another opportunity for the detection of error through the comparison of independently computed representations. The navigation process generates many representations from sources of data that are reasonably independent. The positions plotted in the CIC, for example, are based on radar returns rather than on visual bearings. The comparison of such representations is a very general theme in the practice of navigation. The measures listed here are simply specifications for Sea and Anchor Detail of procedural strategies that are followed in all navigation. In Standard Steaming Watch for example, the following instruction holds:

> h. During prolonged periods in which no nav aids are available (1 hour or more), both the DRAI [Dead Reckoning Analyzer Instrument] and Nav Sat DRs will be recorded in the Ship's Position Log, and plotted as estimated positions for comparison against the hand DR. If unexplainable differences develop, the Assistant to the Navigator will be called immediately.

We see here again the emphasis on the comparison and correlation of representations from different sources. The chart is the "common ground" on which all of these representations can be compared.

> i. The Navigator will act as overall coordinator of the Bridge Party during Sea and Anchor Detail.

This is another element in the organization of the computational architecture of the navigation team. The navigator is given the authority to reconfigure the navigation team as he sees fit.

> j. If the ship goes into a condition of Reduced Visibility during Sea and Anchor Detail, the senior Quartermaster will man the LN-66 Radar on a time sharing basis with the OOD.

The ship never went into a condition of reduced visibility while I was aboard. As reported in chapter 1, the assistant to the navigator claimed that he would not abide by the procedural specification of the relationship between the CIC and the bridge in reduced-visibility situations. It must be remembered that there is a surface-search radar unit on the bridge that can be used for observing radar bearings and ranges of landmarks (the LN-66 mentioned above). The Assistant to the Navigator should attempt to generate his own navigation data using that device. However, the competition for the use of the radar between the navigation team and the officer of the deck is likely to be intense in such a setting. In reduced-visibility situations, it might be impossible to even see past the edge of the flight deck. The officer of the deck will want to adjust the radar to be most effective in detecting and tracking other ships. The quartermaster using the radar will want to adjust it to measure the bearings and ranges of landmarks. These two uses conflict with each other.

The procedures given above describe the procedures and the division of labor mandated for Sea and Anchor Detail. These have a variety of cognitive consequences at the system level, including changes in the organization of the perceptual apparatus of the system to meet anticipated changes in environmental conditions, robust error-detection procedures grounded in the comparisons of multiple representations of the same situation, increase in work capacity provided by distributing cognitive labor across social space, and self-reflection provided by supervisory functions.

The duties of the individual members of the Sea and Anchor Detail team are further specified as follows:

5. The Navigation Plotter will:
   a. Plot each fix.
   b. Plot periodic fixes from CIC
   c. Maintain a constant DR ahead for a minimum of two fix intervals.
   d. Provide the following information to the Navigator/OOD
      (1) Present position with respect to track
      (2) Present SOG (Speed over the ground.)
      (3) Distance to the next turn, and time at present SOG

(4) Turn Bearing for the next turn
(5) Set and Drift when determined (approximately every third fix)
(6) Nearest shoal water forward of the beam
(7) If anchoring, distance and bearing to the drop point, slow point, stop point, or back point, whichever is next.

The first three duties of the restricted-maneuvering plotter are straightforward. The items of information listed in paragraph d above are not actually reported on every fix, or even on the stated intervals where specified. Rather, they are provided when they are thought to be of use to the OOD. This requires the plotter to know something about the nature of the work being done by the OOD, so that he can anticipate the OOD's information needs and provide the right information at the right time. As noted in chapter 3, the determination of the relation of the ship to the intended track is greatly simplified by the precomputation of the track.

The ship's speed over the ground may be very different from its speed through the water because the water itself may be moving. The speed over the ground is of concern to the officer of the deck, because it is the rate at which the ship is moving relative to land. The motion of the ship over the ground is the vector sum of the motion of the ship through the water and the motion of the water with respect to land. In harbors, tidal effects may produce very strong currents that can augment or diminish the speed of the ship over the ground. (Racing yacht tacticians on San Francisco Bay sometimes joke that the anchor is the fastest piece of equipment on the boat. In truly adverse current conditions, a boat at anchor with zero speed over the ground may be doing better than a boat sailing fast against a current so strong that its speed over the ground is negative or in the wrong direction.) The direction of the movement of the water over the ground is called the *set*, and the speed of the water over the ground is called the *drift*. This is useful information for the officer of the deck because it affects both the speed over the ground and the handling characteristics of the ship.

6. The navigation Recorder/Timer will:
    a. Time each fix to three minutes, or the Navigator's instructions
    b. Keep the Bearing Record Book in accordance with the instructions posted therein
    c. Inform the Pelorus Operators of nav aids to be used
    d. Speak out continuous bearings when ordered to do so
    e. Obtain soundings from the Fathometer Operator
    f. Record data for at least three LOPs

The navigation recorder/timer provides temporal and informational coordination among the other elements of the navigation team. His timing signals and instructions on the navigation aids to be used control the behavior of the pelorus operators. His entries in the bearing record log are the system's first permanent representation of its relationship to a landmark. The structure of the bearing record log in standard form (OpNav Form 3530/2) is a resource for the organization of action. Its columns and rows are preprinted with labels. Entries must be made in ink, and no erasures are permitted: "If an error is made, the recorder must draw a line through the entry that is in error and enter the correct information leaving both entries legible." (Maloney 1985)

7. The Restricted Maneuvering Fathometer Operator will:
   a. Take soundings and send them to the bridge on request.
   b. Record the time and sounding every time a sounding is sent to the bridge.

The fathometer operator makes a redundant recording of the soundings in the sounding log.

8. The Bridge Wing Pelorus Operators shall:
   a. Acquaint themselves with all available information on the nav aids to be utilized prior to the Sea and Anchor Detail
   b. Clothe themselves for comfort.
   c. Checkout the operation of their Alidade as soon as they reach the Bridge, reporting any discrepancy immediately to the Leading Quartermaster.
   d. Maintain sound powered phone communications with the Recorder.
   e. Take and report bearings to the objects ordered by the Recorder and when ordered by the Recorder.

The pelorus operators must acquaint themselves with the navigation aids so that they will be able to find them when directed to shoot bearings to them. Aboard some ships, the aids are given letter identifiers and are referred to over the phones in that way. This lettering scheme is an example of a feature that benefits one part of the organization while putting costs elsewhere (Grudin 1988). On an entry to an unfamiliar harbor, the landmarks may be labeled in alphabetical order from the harbor entrance to the pier. This simplifies the work at the plotting table because it imposes a coherent ordering on the landmarks. It makes the work of the pelorus operators much more difficult, however, because they must master a set of arbitrary names for the landmarks. Some quartermasters have remarked that this can be a real problem going into a foreign port.

Once on duty, the pelorus operators are expected to stay at their posts for the duration of Sea and Anchor Detail. Since the peloruses are located outside the skin of the ship, it is important that pelorus operators dress appropriately from the beginning so that they do not become uncomfortable while exposed to the elements. These prescriptions for the pelorus operators cover several aspects of their contribution to the piloting system. They are required to pre-pare to do the job, avoid an anticipated failure due to discomfort, test sensors with enough time to make repairs, maintain connection to the rest of the system, and operate as instructed.

9. The QMOW shall:
   a. Maintain the deck log
   b. Maintain the Gyro Behavior Log
   c. Maintain a copy of the Pac Fleet Organization Manual
   d. Maintain a copy of the Rules of the Road for immediate reference.

This is a contraction of the normal duties of the QMOW. The deck log and the gyro behavior log are repositories of memories.

Paragraphs 5–9 of the Watch Standing Procedures lay out the allocation of jobs to the members of the team and the interlocking system of functions they perform. Since the work of the team is a computation, we can treat this as a computational system and treat the social organization of the team as a computational architecture.

Social Organization as Computational Architecture

In a paper titled "Natural and Social System Metaphors for Distributed Problem Solving," Chandresekaran (1981) discussed properties of distributed problem-solving systems. Chandresekaran took social systems as a base domain for the metaphorical organization of distributed computer systems. Of course, the computational properties of the computer systems that are built on the social metaphors may also be computational properties of the social systems themselves. Thus, although it is not customary to speak of the computational properties of social institutions, the navigation team in Sea and Anchor Detail can be seen as a computational machine. In this section I explore this metaphor, looking at the ways in which aspects of the behavior of the system can be interpreted in a computational framework. This seems to me a much more solidly grounded application of the computational metaphor to a cognitive system than the application of this metaphor to the workings of an individual mind. See chapters 7 and 9 for further discussion.

When computational tasks are socially distributed, there are two layers of organization to the activity: the computational organization, as defined by the computational dependencies among the various parts of the computation, and the social organization, which structures the interactions among the participants to the computation.

Activity Score

In order to examine the properties of the performance of the navigation team, it is useful to have a representation of the activity that makes clear the relations among the activities of the various members of the team.

Figure 4.1 is an activity score for a typical position fix. The purpose of the activity score is to show the temporal pattern of activity across the representational media that are involved in the fix cycle. Along the left axis of the figure are the names of the media, the sensors at the bottom and the "higher-level" processing media (such as the chart) at the top. Across the bottom is a time scale marked off in 2-second intervals. Each fill pattern in the score denotes the activities that involve the coordination of representations of a single landmark bearing. The first event shown, at the extreme left of the diagram, is the "stand by to mark" signal that brought the bearing recorder and the two pelorus operators into coordination.

As indicated in the Watch Standing Procedures, the pelorus operators should aim their alidades at their landmarks when they receive the "stand by to mark" signal from the recorder. This is indicated in the activity score by the regions that show simultaneous coordination of each pelorus operator with his alidade and an element of the world of landmarks (beginning at time 59). In this case, the starboard pelorus operator had the landmark called Dive Tower and the port pelorus operator had Point Loma. Immediately before giving the "mark" signal, the recorder and the plotter were discussing which landmarks to use on this fix. This caused the recorder to be late giving the "stand by to mark" signal. The interval between the "stand by to mark" and "mark" signals was less than 3 seconds, rather than the usual 10 seconds. The team is on a 2-minute fix interval at this point. This is one of the reasons that the recorder rushed the mark signal. The fix is accompanied by a sounding that is provided by the fathometer operator via the phone circuit just after the "mark" signal. The fathometer operator, who expects to have a 10-second window between the "stand by to mark" and "mark" signals in which to report the depth, began to read the depth while the recorder was giving the "mark" signal. He

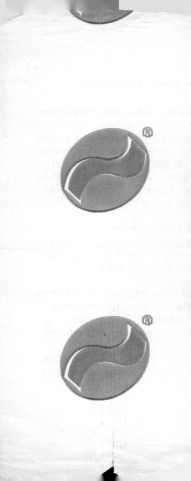

ID: 858357153792114

Thank you for your entry in the $100,000 GiveAway. We will be in contact if you have won a prize or if you are eligible for another great gift such as a Carnival Cruise, Las Vegas Vacation, a new home theatre system, or even a free trip to Hawaii.

Be sure to check www.entertowin.net/winners weekly to see if you may have won a weekly prize.

For more information including details, pictures, video, and winner lists, please visit www.entertowin.net

save this receipt as your proof of entry

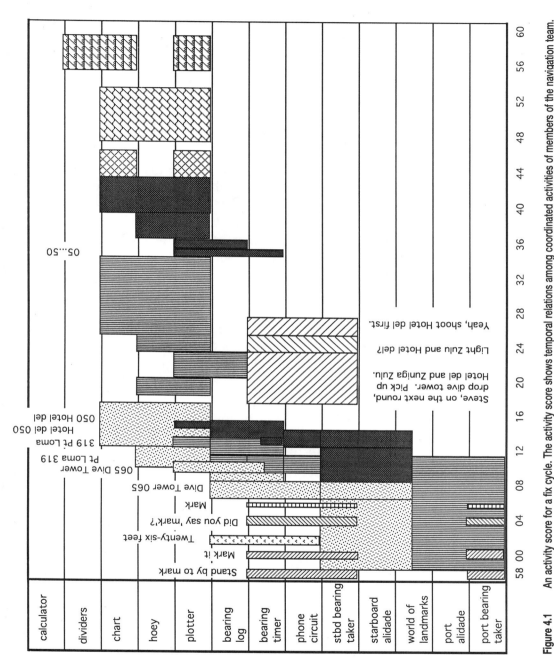

Figure 4.1 An activity score for a fix cycle. The activity score shows temporal relations among coordinated activities of members of the navigation team.

deferred to the recorder and then repeated the depth report immediately after the mark signal.

The "mark" signal also seemed to take the pelorus operators by surprise. They were probably still locating their landmarks and aiming their alidades when it arrived. About $3\frac{1}{2}$ seconds after the "mark" signal, the starboard pelorus operator asked "Did you say 'mark'?" The recorder answered by simply repeating the "mark" signal (at time 06). Any additional explanation offered by the recorder at this point would only have delayed the fix even more. The starboard pelorus operator read the bearing of the Dive Tower and reported it (at time 08).

While recording the bearing in the log, the bearing recorder read the bearing aloud for the plotter to hear (at time 10). Meanwhile, the port pelorus operator aligned Point Loma in the sights of his alidade and reported the bearing of Point Loma just as the bearing recorder was reading the Dive Tower bearing to the plotter (at time 11).

Upon hearing the bearing from the recorder, the plotter said "OK" and aligned the scale of the hoey to reproduce the bearing (at time 11–13). He then aligned the hoey with the chart and plotted the line of position for Dive Tower (time 13–18).

Just after the plotter applied the hoey to the chart to plot the LOP for Dive Tower, the recorder read aloud the bearing to Point Loma. Since the plotter had already aligned and locked the hoey, he was no longer dealing with the bearing to Dive Tower as a number. Hearing the spoken bearing to Point Loma probably interfered little with the task of getting the aligned hoey into coordination with the directional frame of the chart. If the plotter had still been aligning the hoey scale when the new bearing was spoken, we might have expected some destructive interference between the two tasks.

While the bearing recorder was repeating the bearing to Point Loma, the starboard pelorus operator reported the bearing to Hotel del Coronado ("Hotel del"). Again, the overlap between the speaking and listening tasks did not cause destructive interference. The pelorus operator pronounced the name of the new landmark while the recorder was speaking the name of the previous landmark. The numbers did not overlap.

When the plotter had finished plotting the LOP for Dive Tower, he began scaling the hoey for Point Loma. He may have been able to attend at least partially to the spoken report of the bearing while he was placing the hoey on the chart a few seconds earlier. However, after fiddling with the hoey for 2 seconds he looked into the bearing log and read the bearing of Point Loma (time 21–24). He then returned to the scaling task (time 24–26) and then applied the hoey to the chart and plotted the LOP (time 26–35).

Meanwhile, the bearing recorder was instructing the starboard pelorus operator on a change of landmark that the recorder and plotter had decided upon in the seconds leading up to the current fix.

The bearing recorder completed his instructions to the starboard pelorus operator while the plotter was still plotting the Point Loma LOP. When the recorder saw that the plotter had finished plotting Point Loma, he read the bearing of Hotel del aloud from the bearing log (time 35). The plotter had already turned to the log and read the bearing there (time 36) before setting the bearing into the state of the hoey (time 37–40) and plotting the LOP (time 40–44).

After plotting the third LOP, the plotter marked and labeled the fix (time 44–47). He then went on to extend the dead reckoning positions (time 48–60).

This example illustrates a number of interesting properties of the team performance of the fix cycle.

Parallel Activities

Perhaps the most obvious property is that the activities of the members of the team take place in parallel. For example, at time 11 the port pelorus operator was reporting the bearing of Point Loma to the recorder, who was at that moment reporting the bearing of the Dive Tower to the plotter. At the same moment, the starboard bearing taker was aiming his alidade at the Hotel del landmark.

This is a clear example of the simultaneous coordination of many media in a functional system that transcends the boundaries of the individual actors. In chapter 3, identifying the landmark, aiming the alidade, reading the bearing, and reporting and remembering the bearing were each described as processes in which a set of mutually constraining media are placed in coordination by the pelorus operator. In chapter 3 we also saw how recording the bearings involved the construction of a complex functional system by the bearing recorder. Now we see that these two functional systems were assembled into a larger functional system in the coordination of the activities of the two crew members. Here two team members, the pelorus operator and the recorder, worked together on a single problem.

This example also demonstrates simultaneous activity within a single individual. The bearing recorder was reading one bearing and listening to another at the same time. The overlap of activity is such that there is no destructive interference between the two tasks, although if the timing was even a few tenths of a second different there could be. The recorder's words and the port wing bearing taker's words overlap like this:

Recorder: 0 6 5 Dive Tower
Port Wing: Point Loma 3 1 9.

Bottom-Up and Top-Down Processes

The propagation of the bearings from the alidades to the chart is a "bottom-up" information process. The representation of the relationship of the ship to the world is transformed into symbolic form and moved across a set of media until it arrives at the chart. In an idealization of the fix cycle, information flows bottom-up, from sensors to central representation, in the first part of the cycle; it flows top-down, from the central decision makers to the sensors, in the latter part of the cycle, when the pelorus operators are instructed to shoot particular landmarks. The general trend is apparent in figure 4.1 in the form of the upward slope of activity regions from left to right. The top-down activities in the fix cycle are more diverse. As soon as the bearings had been reported, the recorder instructed the starboard pelorus operator to shift to a new landmark.

The "stand by to mark" and "mark" signals are also top-down messages. This example illustrates some of the potential complexities of the flow of information in the system. Because of a disruption of the recorder's activities, the expected mark signal came at an unexpected time.

Other top-down messages guide the sensors to targets in the world. For example, the recorder instructed the pelorus operator: "Shoot the end part that is away from you." On another occasion, the plotter asked the recorder: "Give me a quick line ahead, then back to the Aero Beacon."

Some top-down messages request information about sensor capability. Before a fix, the recorder asked a pelorus operator "Can you still see Bravo pier?" During a fix, when a pelorus operator failed to report, the recorder asked: "Are you still there? What happened, man?"

Top-down messages also give the sensors feedback on their performance. When the LOPs yielded a tight triangle on the chart, the recorder told the pelorus operators "Excellent fix, guys." When the bearing reports were coming in too slowly, he chided "Let's pick up the marking, man." The top-down signals observed in the operation of the navigation team in Sea and Anchor Detail also included recalibrations of the senses. The plotter instructed the recorder as follows: "The fixes are getting open; tell them to mark their heads." To mark heads means to have the two pelorus operators simultaneously report the true heading of the ship with respect to the gyroscope. Any difference between the reported "heads" is an indication of a failure of the gyro-repeater system. This comment from the plotter is simultaneously a complaint about the quality of the information received, an indication of a hypothesis concerning the source of the degradation of the data (that the repeaters are not aligned), and an instruction to perform a procedure that will provide a test of the hypothesis.

Human Interfaces

The creation of human and organizational interfaces to tasks is ubiquitous. Roy D'Andrade (personal communication) has pointed out that in the academic world we appoint discussion leaders to act as interfaces for the rest of us to some particular reading. The discussion leader in the meeting has a rank, a responsibility, and certain privileges that are bestowed by the rest of the group. Aboard a ship, the quartermaster chief has the authority to make one of his men an interface to a particular task. From a functional perspective, the navigation team is the conning officer's interface to the navigation problem. The team provides mediation of such a complex form that it is barely recognizable as mediation.

DAEMONS

A commonly created sort of interface to a task is what in computer science is called a *daemon*. A daemon is an agent that monitors a world waiting for certain specified conditions. When the trigger conditions exist, the daemon takes a specified action.

Setting a depth threshold detector

During an approach to an antenna-calibration buoy near the shore, Chief Richards assigned Smith to the fathometer with instructions to report when the depth of water under the ship shoaled to less than 20 fathoms. This is an example of the social construction of an information-processing mechanism. In this case, the chief had reconfigured the navigation team to create within it a daemon to detect a particular condition. The reconfiguration involved the construction of a short strand of representational state. Smith was stationed at the fathometer, concentrating on the relationship of the marks indicating the depth of water to the labeled 20-fathom line on the echo-sounder graph paper. His job was to detect a certain analog relationship (depth indication above the 20-fathom line) and transform that to a symbolic signal to the plotter.

Continuous bearings

Continuous bearing reporting is a nice case of setting up a somewhat more complicated information-processing structure that detects a single very specific condition. On the open sea, turns are made at specified times or when the ship is reckoned to have reached a specified position. In restricted waters more precision is required. For this purpose, turn bearings are constructed (see chapter 3).

When the ship is approaching the turn bearing, the plotter will ask the recorder to have the pelorus operator on the appropriate side observe the landmark on which the turn bearing is based and give continuous readings of its bearing. These are not recorded in the bearing record log, but are relayed verbally to the plotter. By aligning the plotting tool with the landmark and the spoken bearings, the plotter can move the represented position of the ship along the course line in a relatively continuous fashion. Since the track is marked in 100-yard increments, it is then easy for the plotter to determine and call out the distance to the next turn.

An excerpt from the transcript of the moments leading up to a turn looks as follows. (The turn bearing is 192° on North Island Tower. The CIC COMM is a phone talker who relays information between the chart table and the plotting table in CIC. See figure 4.2 for the position of the ship during this event.)

Plotter: OK. What course is he on? OK, how about continuous bearings . . .

Recorder: Continuous bearings on North Island Tower.

Plotter: . . . on the Tower.

Recorder: 2 2 9 . . . 2 2 8 . . . 2 2 7 . . . 2 2 6 . . . 2 2 5 . . . 2 2 4 . . .

Plotter: Five hundred yards to the turn. Next course will be 2 5 1.

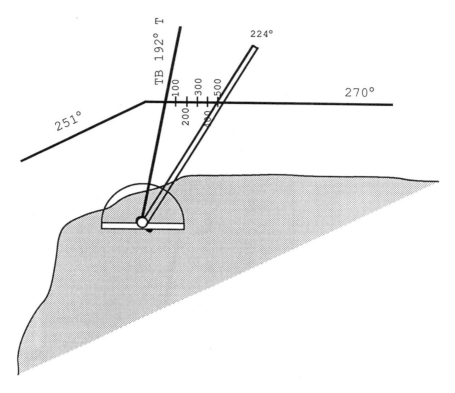

Figure 4.2 Moving the hoey arm in coordination with continuous bearing reports. The turn bearing for this turn is 192° to North Island Tower. The plotter, having aligned the hoey with the chart, holds the base steady and moves the arm of the hoey to each of the bearings as it is reported. This permits him to read the distance to the turn directly off the chart.

CIC Comm: Navigation holds 500 yards to the turn.

OOD: Very well.

Plotter: Ah ... see if I try 8 knots, 8 and a half maybe.

CIC Comm: Combat holds 420 yards to the turn.

Recorder: 2 2 1 ... 2 2 0 ... 2 1 9 ... 2 1 8 ... 2 1 7 ... 2 1 6 ... 2 1 5 ... 2 1 4 ...

Plotter: Three hundred yards to the turn. Next course 2 5 1.

Recorder: 213

CIC Comm: Navigation holds 300 yards.

Recorder: 2 1 2 ... 2 1 1 ... 2 1 0 ... 2 0 9 ... 2 0 8 ...

Plotter: Two hundred yards to the turn.

Recorder: 2 0 7 ... 2 0 6 ... 2 0 5 ... 2 0 4 ... 2 0 3 ... 2 0 2 ... 2 0 1

Plotter: One hundred yards to the turn.

CIC Comm: Navigation holds 100 yards to the turn.

Recorder: 2 0 0 . . .

Plotter: One hundred yards to the turn.

Recorder: 1 9 9 . . . 1 9 8 . . . 1 9 7 . . . 1 9 6 . . . 1 9 5 . . . 1 9 4 . . . 1 9 3

Plotter: Recommend coming left 2 5 1.

Recorder: 1 9 2 . . .

OOD: Left 15 degrees rudder. Steer course 2 5 1.

CIC Comm: Left 15 degrees rudder, change course 2 5 1.

Helm: Change course 2 5 1, aye sir. Left 15 degrees. Course 2 5 1.

OOD: Very well.

The recorder also had access to the chart and knew which land-mark the bearings would be taken on before the plotter had finished telling him to begin continuous bearings. Every bearing spoken out by the recorder was spoken out just the instant before by the pelorus operator. The trajectory of representational state in this case flows without interruption from the relationship between the ship and the world to the state of the pelorus to the bearing spoken by the pelorus operator to the bearing spoken by the recorder to the state of the hoey on the chart to the advice announced by the plot-ter for the OOD to begin the turn. In making a turn in Sea and Anchor Detail, the system hooks up four people and a suite of technology into a tightly coupled functional system. It is a tempo-rary structure that brings media and processes into coordination in order to track the ship's relationship to its environment on a finer time scale than in normal operations. This entire functional system is organized around the detection of a single condition: the arrival of the ship at the turn point.

BUFFERS

The bearing recorder and bearing record log are information buff-ers. They enable the pelorus operators, whose job is to make the observations as nearly simultaneously as is possible, and the plot-ter, whose job is to get the lines of position onto the chart, to oper-ate asynchronously. There is a great deal of variation in the pace of the work done by the members of the navigation team. The buffer-ing activity of the bearing recorder introduces slack into the system so that the temporal constraints of the pelorus operators do not in-terfere with the temporal constraints of the plotter. The bearing record log is also a special kind of filter that passes the bearings without passing the temporal characteristics of their production. In this way, it inhibits the propagation of some kinds of representational state. Without this buffering, the reports of the pelorus operators might interfere with the plotting activity of the plotter, or data might be lost because both sender and recipient were unable to attend to a message at the same time.

The bridge team is connected to other parts of the ship by sound-powered phone circuits like the one used by the pelorus operators and the bearing recorder. These lines provide the bridge team with communication links to the foc'sle, to after-steering, to the combat information center, to the signal bridge (where lookouts are posted), and to other locations on the ship. There is a person called a *phone talker* posted at each end of each of these phone lines. The numerous phone talkers around the ship are also information buffers. Each pair of them permits communication to take place when the sender and the receiver are not overloaded. For example, rather than simply blurt out whatever message has arrived, a bridge phone talker can wait for a pause in the OOD's work to pass a message to him. The phone talker can hold the message until an opportunity to insert it into the activity on the bridge has arrived. Someone sending a message to the bridge from another part of the ship cannot know when would be an appropriate moment to interject the message. The phone talker is a sophisticated buffer who uses his knowledge of conversational turn taking to decide when to forward a message.

Buffering contributes to what Perrow (1984) has called "loose coupling" of the system. The buffering prevents the uncontrolled propagation of effects from one part of the system to another. Buffering provides protection against destructive interference between processes running in parallel.

Communication and Memory

In any implementation of the fix cycle, representational state needs to propagate physically from the pelorus to the bearing record log and then to the chart. In Standard Steaming Watch, the states are propagated from the pelorus to the memory of the watchstander and then transported from the pelorus to the bearing record log. In Sea and Anchor Detail, the state is also propagated from the pelorus to the mind of the pelorus operator, but it is then propagated by way of communications technology to the mind of the bearing recorder. It is then propagated to the bearing record log. Thus, the work that is done by individual memory in the solo condition is replaced in the group condition by interpersonal communication. Perhaps this should come as no surprise. If we think of individual memory as communication with the self over time (Lantz and Stefflre 1964), then the replacement of intrapersonal communication by interpersonal communication is an expected consequence of the move from individual to team performance of a task.

For example, the quartermaster in Standard Steaming Watch will have to remember which landmarks have been chosen while moving from the chart table to the peloruses on the wings. More challenging, the quartermaster will have to remember or record the observations as they are made, so that they can be recalled and recorded in the bearing log. The chart and the bearing log are located in the pilothouse, while the peloruses are located on the wings. Between the time when the first observation is made and the time when the bearings are recorded in the bearing record log, the quartermaster will have to make two other observations and then return to the chart table. Some watchstanders rely on spoken rehearsals of the bearings to remember them. In this case only the numbers are usually rehearsed, not the numbers and the names. The assignment of names to the numbers can be made at the chart, and the position of the lines on the chart can help the quartermaster remember which landmark has the bearing being plotted. The problems with this are that the subsequent bearings may interfere with the earlier ones; that the talk in the pilothouse itself often is filled with unrelated numbers, so it too may interfere; and that if the chart is being used to disambiguate the assignment of landmarks to remembered bearing numbers, the power of error checking at the chart is sharply diminished. Other quartermasters jot the bearings down on a sheet of paper or on one hand as each is observed. If the landmarks are off to the port side of the ship and the weather is cold, the quartermaster may have to walk aft to gain access to the port pelorus via the passageway at the back of the island because the captain will not permit the door behind his chair to be opened. This means that the bearing will have to be remembered longer, which introduces additional cognitive requirements. This is an example of the way that the cognitive requirements of real-world task performance may be driven by unexpected factors.

Task Allocation and Equipment Layout

The arrangement of equipment in a workplace might seem to be a topic for traditional, noncognitive ergonomics. However, it has an interpretation in terms of the construction of systems of socially distributed cognition. The interaction of the properties of the senses with the physical layout of the task environment defines possibilities for the distribution of access to information. For example, the location of the fathometer in the charthouse, away from the bridge, makes a distribution of labor necessary in order to meet the time requirements of Sea and Anchor Detail. It is simply not possible for a single watchstander to make the required observations in the allotted time, given the physical locations of the equipment. In fact, the computational consequences of the locations of equipment may interact in unexpected ways with other aspects of the ship's operation. In Standard Steaming Watch a single quartermaster may be responsible for all navigation activities. While making the bearing observations for the fix, the QMOW must go out on the wings. The starboard pelorus is within 10 feet of the chart table, and it is easily accessed through a nearby door. The port pelorus is about 30 feet from the chart table, just outside a door on the port side of the bridge. On this particular ship, however, if the captain is on the bridge, taking a bearing with the port pelorus can involve an absence from the chart table of up to a minute. The reason is that, as was mentioned above, the captain likes to keep the door immediately behind his chair closed while he is on the bridge. In order to get to the port pelorus, the QM must go aft to a doorway at the back of the port wing and walk forward on the wing to reach the pelorus. Upon returning to the pilothouse, the QM should then go to the helm and leehelm stations to see if any changes in course or speed have been ordered in his absence.

Chief Richards says it would be nice to have instrument repeaters at the chart table. A speed log repeater would be especially useful. In Sea and Anchor Detail, the QMOW should be able to keep track of speed and heading changes by attending to the commands issued by the conning officer to the helmsman and the leehelmsman. In practice, however, it is not always possible to do this. Speed and heading are also available to the QMOW on instruments, but the instruments are not conveniently located. Their placement requires the QMOW to leave the vicinity of the chart table to acquire this information. The master gyrocompass is located in the steering binacle, and the speed display is forward on the port side of the bridge, in front of the captain's chair. These facts have nontrivial consequences for the information-processing properties of the navigation team.

Sequential Control of Action

Russian legend has it that Prince Potemkin once organized a band in which each musician had a horn, but each horn could only sound one note. To play a piece, "the players had to be extremely skillful in order to preserve the synchronic performance of all the instruments and weave their own note into the melody at the right time" (Kann 1978: 52). Playing in Potemkin's horn band was apparently an enormously difficult coordination task. Sequential control was achieved by having every musician know the plan of the entire piece and also know the place of every instance of his own note within the piece.

A procedure is *sequentially unconstrained* if the execution of any enabled operation will never disable any other enabled but as yet unexecuted operation. A task that has no sequential constraints can be accomplished by a "swarm of ants" strategy. In such a scheme, there is no communication between the active agents other than their effects on a shared environment. Each agent simply mills about taking actions only when he encounters situations on which he can act.

A procedure is *sequentially constrained* if the execution of any enabled operation will disable any other enabled but as yet un-executed operation. Where there are sequential constraints, it is necessary to have some control over the sequence of actions.

The performance of a sequentially constrained procedure may require planning or backtracking. For example, getting dressed is sequentially constrained because at the moment in which one has neither shoes nor socks on, putting on shoes disables the operation of putting on socks. The sequence of operations for orthodox dressing contains a sequential constraint on the donning of socks and shoes.

Whether a task is sequentially constrained may depend on the representation of the task as well as on the formal properties of the task. Zhang (1992) has recently shown that it is possible to change the sequential constraints of isomorphs of the Tower of Hanoi problem by embodying some of the sequence-constraining "rules" in the physical instantiation of the problem. For example, in one version of the puzzle, placing a smaller disk on a larger disk is a violation of a sequence-constraining rule. In Zhang's coffee cup isomorph, this same move would be executed by placing a small coffee cup in a larger one—an act that causes coffee to spill. These are ways to build the sequential constraints into the behavior of the game tokens and thereby reduce the requirement for memory of sequence-constraining rules in support of planning and backtracking.

One general technique for turning sequentially constrained tasks into sequentially unconstrained tasks is to manipulate the enablement conditions of various operations. A simple rule is "suppress the enablement of any operation that could disable another already enabled operation." This can be done through interlocks. In many automobiles, for example, the starter motor will not turn unless the transmission is in park or neutral. This is the mechanical enforcement of a sequential constraint on the engine-starting procedure.

THE NAVIGATION TEAM AS A PRODUCTION SYSTEM

Sequentially unconstrained procedures are easily distributed or can be solved by very loosely interconnected systems. Tasks that have sequential constraints require some coordination among the actions to be taken. There are many ways to achieve this coordination. Specifying the overall pattern of behavior in a script, a score, or an overall plan is an obvious solution to the sequencing problem. Since there are many sequential constraints among the actions of the fix cycle, one might assume that the fix cycle unfolds according to a stored plan or description of the sequence of actions involved.

In fact, it is possible for the team to organize its behavior in an appropriate sequence without there being a global script or plan anywhere in the system. Each crew member only needs to know what to do when certain conditions are produced in the environment. An examination of the descriptions of the duties of the members of the navigation team shows that many of the specified duties are given in the form "Do X when Y." Here are some examples from the procedures:

a. Take soundings and send them to the bridge on request.
b. Record the time and sounding every time a sounding is sent to the bridge.
e. Take and report bearings to the objects ordered by the Recorder and when ordered by the Recorder.

These and other instructions suggest that the navigation team could be modeled by a set of agents, each of whom can perceive the environment and can act on the environment when certain triggering conditions appear there. An interlocking set of partial procedures can produce the overall observed pattern without there being a representation of that overall pattern anywhere in the system.

Each participant knows how to coordinate his activities with the technologies and persons he interacts with. The pelorus operators know to negotiate the order of report with each other and to take and report bearings when given the "mark" signal. The recorder knows to say "Stand by to mark" before the mark, then to say "Mark," and then to attend to and record the bearings. The plotter knows to plot the recorded bearings to get a position, and then to project the dead-reckoning positions and choose new landmarks. The plotter's duties may cover a longer procedural stretch than those of any other member of the group, but even they do not come close to completing the cycle. The whole cycle is something that emerges from the interactions of the individuals with one another and with the tools of the space. The structure of the activities of the group is determined by a set of local computations rather than by the implementation of a global plan. In the distributed situation, a set of concurrent socio-computational dependencies is set up. These dependencies shape the pattern of behavior of the group. The existence of the plotter waiting for bearings is how the system remembers what to do with the recorded bearings. These concurrent dependencies are not present in the solo performance case.

When the nature of the problem is seen as coordination among persons and devices, much of the organization of behavior is removed from the performer and is given over to the structure of the object or system with which one is coordinating. This is what it means to coordinate: to set oneself up in such a way that constraints on one's behavior are given by some other system. This is easy to see in the use of the recorder's wristwatch. Perhaps through some complicated toe tapping or counting the recorder could provide a regular meter for the performance of the rounds of fixes and dead-reckoning projections, but that is unlikely. The only way humans have found to get such tasks done well is to introduce machines that can provide a temporal meter and then coordinate the behavior of the system with that meter. The system's coordination with the meter of the watch is provided by the recorder's coordinating with the watch and the others' coordinating with the recorder. The recorder's coordinating with the watch requires him to maintain (1) vigilance to the watch and (2) a test of when it is time to take another round. For the second of these, he must have (1) a procedure for determining (or a memory of) when the next round should fall and (2) a way of determining when that time has been reached. Both parts of this task require some cognition, to be sure, but no sophisticated reasoning.

It should be noted, however, that the members of the team may engage in considerably more cognitive activity than the minimum required. The various actors may have ideas about what a particular task requires, and they may anticipate particular sorts of failures on the basis of these ideas. In the case of the recorder's maintaining coordination with the watch, lack of vigilance due to the appropriation of attention by other tasks may cause the recorder to miss a mark. The plotter, who shares the physical environment of the recorder, apparently sometimes participates in that task redundantly and has been observed to comment "Isn't it about time for a round?"

The coordination problem is more difficult for the quartermaster standing watch alone in the Standard Steaming Watch configuration. In that case, the task performer must not only provide coordination with each of the devices, but must coordinate those activities with other activities. In Sea and Anchor Detail, this latter sort of higher-level coordination is accomplished via the social coordination of the distributed situation. It is still ultimately provided by the human participants, but the cognitive load is not only distributed; it is also lessened by distribution. Here is how: Consider the relation between the pelorus operator and the recorder. The recorder coordinates his activities with the behavior of his wristwatch. That is to say, he has delegated some aspect of the control of his own behavior to this external device. Now, the pelorus operator coordinates his activity with the (timing) behavior of the recorder. He waits for the "mark" signal to read his bearing. He has delegated some aspect of the control of his own behavior to the recorder. He has also delegated some other aspects of his behavior to the device with which he interacts. His behavior is nicely and comfortably constrained by the two coordination activities. He gets the "mark" signal and invokes the coordination with the alidade—which, in its relation to the world, is coordinating him (and, through him, the whole system) with a particular aspect of the setting of the ship in the surrounding world. He reads the bearing. When he does so, the recorder coordinates his (recording) behavior with the pelorus operator. His other activities are on hold while he attends to and (perhaps simultaneously) records the bearing.

The problems of coordination in the solo performance concern the control of the change in roles and the meta-coordination required to move through the sequence of steps required. It is in the consideration of solo performances that the apparent importance of executive function emerges. This is to be expected because, from the point of view of the individual, the task in the solo performance is sequentially constrained in a way that the modular tasks faced by the individual team members in the distributed performance are not. There are certainly still sequential constraints in the distributed form, but each individual is responsible for satisfying fewer of these constraints than in Standard Steaming Watch. In the place of an executive we find a continual collision of interest and negotiation of coordination status.

The quartermasters align themselves as a coordinating structure that passes information from one transforming device to another. The people are the glue that sticks the hardware of the system together. What is the relationship between the position of the ship in the world and the location of the fix on the chart? The formal relationship is one of spatial correspondence. The causal relationship is a tissue of human relationships in which individual watchstanders consent to have their behavior constrained by others, who are themselves constrained by the meaningful states of representational technologies. The sequential constraints of the procedure, which are in part determined by the representation of the problem, constrain the universe of social arrangements in which the procedure can be performed. That is, they specify a coordination task that must be solved by the social organization of work.

SOCIAL STRUCTURE AND GOAL STRUCTURE

The distribution of labor in Sea and Anchor Detail creates a distribution of attention to goals such that the system is unlikely to halt before completing a task. Imagine a problem described by the goal tree shown in figure 4.3a. Individuals engaged in problems with deep goal trees sometimes lose sight of higher-level goals and halt after satisfying a lower-level goal. This is the sort of problem faced by the solo watchstander in Standard Steaming Watch: Having shot a bearing, what should I do next? Now, suppose that rather than a single watchstander we have a team, and we give each

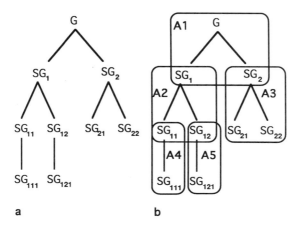

Figure 4.3 Goal hierarchy and distribution of responsibility for goal satisfaction. Responsibility for the satisfaction of the goals shown in panel a can be allocated to agents (the enclosed shapes in panel b) in such a way that social dependencies provide control structure.

member of the team responsibility for a main goal and for the subgoals required to achieve the main goal. The areas of responsibility of the members of the team are superimposed on the goal tree in figure 4.3b. Let the social contract between the agents be such that a subordinate can halt only when his superior determines that the responsibilities of the subordinate have been met. Agent A2, for example, can halt only when agent A1 judges subgoal SG$_1$ to be satisfied. Each agent is responsible only for a shallow section of the goal hierarchy, so goal stack depth is not a problem for individual processors. Such a setup results in computational control through a network of social relationships. When a problem has a deeply nested goal structure, a social hierarchy can provide a mechanism for distributing the attention to various parts of the goal structure.

Social structure and problem representation both interact with goal structure in the implementations of solutions to the problem of sequential control of action. These things constrain the computational properties of systems of socially distributed cognition and cannot be excluded from an understanding of human cognition as it is manifested in such systems.

The fit between the computational dependencies and the social organization is an important property of the system. We might imagine a situation in which those of higher rank provide input to a lower-ranking individual, who integrates the information and makes decisions. That would be a very strange relationship between the social organization and the computational dependencies. Gathering and providing information for the support of a decision are low-status jobs. Integrating information and making decisions are high-status jobs. There are, of course, exceptions, and some such relationships are more workable than others. In general, however, the goals are in the hands of higher status individuals—those who control the goals are, by cultural definition, of higher status.

Beam Bearings in Sea and Anchor Detail

The members of the navigation team normally take for granted the accomplishment of sequential ordering of their own actions in coordination with one another. The fact that the sequential ordering of action is no simple accomplishment, especially when it is not built into the social or material structures of the task, is highlighted in the case of beam bearings. The *beam* of the ship is those directions that are perpendicular to the keel of the ship. Thus, the bearings of landmarks that are off to either side of the ship, rather than ahead or astern, are called *beam bearings*. The navigation team must both decide which landmarks to observe and determine an order in which to observe them. To produce a high-quality fix, they must make their observations of the landmarks as nearly simultaneously as is possible. The undesirable effects of delays between the observations can be minimized by shooting first the landmarks with which the angular relationship (bearing) is changing most quickly and shooting last the landmarks whose bearings are changing least rapidly.

Why Some Bearings Change More Rapidly Than Others

The rate of change of a bearing depends two things: (1) the component $\mathbf{v}$ of the relative velocity vector that is perpendicular to the line joining the objects and (2) the distance between them, $\mathbf{d}$. Thus, $dB/dt = \mathbf{v}/\mathbf{d}$. For objects of equal distance from the ship, the bearings of those objects off to the side of the ship, rather than those that are ahead and astern, will be changing most rapidly, because nearly all of the relative velocity of the object with respect to the ship will be perpendicular to the line joining the object and the ship. This is not the only consideration, however, since for any given relative bearing objects that are nearer will change in bearing faster than objects that are farther away. Distance and relative bearing affect the rate of change of bearings, and the total time between observations affects the magnitude of the errors in the observations. The quartermasters must therefore shoot the bearings quickly and in the correct order.

Example of Effects of Beam Bearings

A ship with a speed over the ground of 10 knots will cover 1000 yards in 3 minutes. Suppose a bearing 1000 yards out on the beam of the ship is taken 10 seconds late. What effect will this have on the plotted position? The ship will have moved 55 yards in those 10 seconds, so the line of position defined by that landmark's bearing will be 55 yards further down track than it should have been (figure 4.4). All of the forward motion of the ship is captured in the observation of a beam bearing; for this reason beam bearings are also called *speed lines*. Now consider a bearing ahead or astern of the ship. The ship moves the same 55 yards in those 10 seconds, but the direction from the ship to landmarks ahead and astern

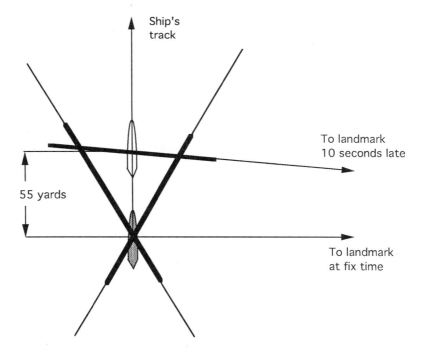

Figure 4.4   The effects of a late beam bearing. Heavy lines indicate the portions of the bearing lines that are actually drawn on the chart to plot the fix. The darkened shape depicts the location of the ship at fix time. The light shape depicts the location of the ship 10 seconds after the fix time.

changes little. The component of relative motion between the objects that is perpendicular to the line connecting the objects is small, so the rate of change of the bearing is small, and the magnitude of any error caused by delayed observations will also be small.

The Rule of Thumb

The requirement of this geometry is captured in the rule "Shoot the beam bearings first." This rule ignores the distance of the landmark from the ship. In principle distance could be an important factor, but in practice it is not. This procedure is most critical when the ship is in a channel, and in that case bearings on the beam tend not to differ greatly in distance from the ship. Furthermore, the measurements and calculations required to assess the effects of differing distances of objects could be a more serious disruption of the fix procedure than the errors caused by ignoring those effects. Thus, to shoot the beam bearings first is a good rule of thumb to use in sequencing the observations.

Configuring the Team

The application of the "shoot the beam bearing first" rule to the Standard Steaming Watch situation is straightforward. The bearings must be observed sequentially, and the beamiest bearing should be observed first. In Sea and Anchor Detail, two pelorus operators work in parallel while shooting the three bearings. One of the pelorus operators will have two bearings to shoot; the other will have just one bearing. How should the pelorus operators sequence their actions in order to produce the best fix?

Finding a procedure for performing this sequentially constrained task turns out to be a nontrivial problem for the crew. It must be kept in mind that the port pelorus operator may not be able to see the landmarks assigned to the starboard pelorus operator and vice versa. Any bearing on the beam of one side of the ship will not be visible to the pelorus operator on the opposite side, so neither pelorus operator can see enough to decide who has the beamiest bearing. The directional relationship between the bearings is easier to imagine at the chart table, but determining the shooting sequence there would impose an additional burden on an already busy bearing recorder. Before we examine what the crew actually does with this problem, it may be useful to indicate the form of the

correct solution. The sequencing of observations could have adverse consequences if the order in which the elements of the procedure were executed delayed the observation of a landmark. The
bearing recorder is a limiting resource in this procedure because he
can attend to only one bearing report at a time. Imagine that the
starboard pelorus operator has one landmark to shoot, and that it is
on the beam. The port pelorus operator has the other two landmarks, but they are not so beamy as the one to starboard. Figure 4.5
depicts this situation.

If the pelorus operator with the beamiest bearing goes first, and
going first is understood to mean both shooting and reporting, then
the sequence of actions shown in figure 4.5a will result. (This figure
is intended only to show relative times of completion.) The solution shown in figure 4.5.a mimics the structure of the performance
when it is done by a single watchstander. It fails to take advantage
of the parallelism of activity that is possible with two pelorus
operators.

Both of the pelorus operators could observe a bearing immediately upon hearing the "mark" signal. If each pelorus operator
observes the "beamiest" of the assigned bearings immediately, and
they still report the beam bearing first, the sequence shown in figure 4.5b will result. The port pelorus operator will have to wait
while the starboard pelorus operator reports the bearing of the
landmark on the beam because the bearing recorder can only attend
to one report at a time. This is an improvement over the previous
solution because it packs the same number of actions into a smaller
period of time, thus reducing the magnitude of the errors in position caused by delays in making the observations. In particular, the
first bearing observed by the port pelorus operator is shot at the
mark signal, rather than after the starboard pelorus operator has
shot and reported a bearing, and the second bearing observed by
the port pelorus operator now comes one action cycle earlier. This
implementation takes advantage of some of the parallelism of activity that is possible with two pelorus operators.

A further gain can be achieved by realizing that the observation
of the bearing and the report of the bearing can be procedurally
separated from one another. The computational constraint is on the
sequence and times of the observations. The beam bearings must be
shot before less beamy bearings, and the three observations must be
made as near in time to the mark signal as is possible. *There is no
similar constraint on the reporting of the observations.* As far as the

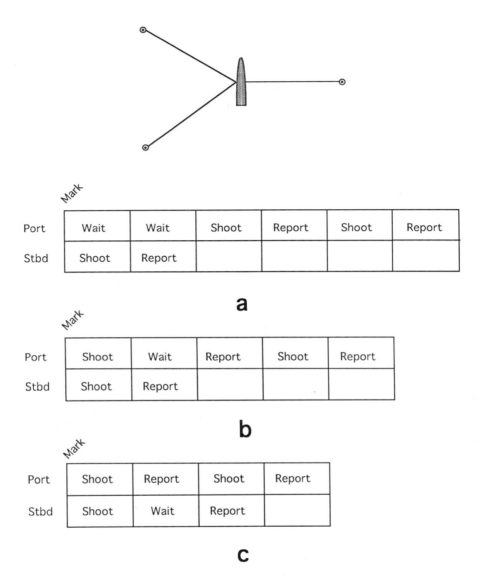

Mark						
Port	Wait	Wait	Shoot	Report	Shoot	Report
Stbd	Shoot	Report				

a

Mark					
Port	Shoot	Wait	Report	Shoot	Report
Stbd	Shoot	Report			

b

Mark				
Port	Shoot	Report	Shoot	Report
Stbd	Shoot	Wait	Report	

c

Figure 4.5   Coordinating the actions of the pelorus operators. With two landmarks to port and one to starboard, the pelorus operators can organize their actions in several possible sequences. (a) No overlap of activity; shoot and report actions linked; beamiest bearing reported first. (b) Overlapping observations (beam bearing shot at mark); beamiest bearing reported first. (c) Overlapping observations (beam bearing shot at mark); pelorus operator with two landmarks reports first.

quality of the fix goes, as long as the three bearings are accurate, they may be reported in any order—beam first, beam second, or beam last. In order to take full advantage of the parallelism of action that is possible in the team configuration, two rules are required: (1) Each pelorus operator should shoot the beamiest of the landmarks assigned to him immediately at the mark signal, and (2) the pelorus operator who has two bearings to shoot and report should report first. The application of these two rules results in the pattern shown in figure 4.5c.

Instructions Concerning Beam Bearings

When explained with diagrams like those shown in figure 4.5, the appropriate patterns of activity are fairly obvious. When the members of the navigation team attempt to organize their efforts in the performance of the task, however, the application to the group condition of the "rule of thumb" that serves so well in the solo task performance case is problematic at best. All of the members of the team seem eventually to "know" and understand the rule, but their attempts to use the rule to coordinate their actions in time repeatedly fail. To see why, consider the instructions that are passed among the members of the team concerning the need to take beam bearings first. In the simplest case, the sequencing instruction may come from the people working at the chart table.

EXAMPLE 1
The landmarks are Hotel del, Dive Tower, and Point Loma. The ship is outbound from the harbor, west of the 1SD channel marker. The ship's course is 270°, so 360° and 180° are the beam bearings. The starboard pelorus operator's name happens to be Mark. Here is the beginning of the round:

Recorder: Stand by to mark, Point Loma, Hotel del, and Dive Tower.
Plotter: Tell him to take Point Loma first. It's on his beam.
Recorder: Take Point Loma first, Mark. Beam bearing first, mark it.
SW: Point Loma 3 5 9.

In this example, an invocation of the rule is embedded in the instructions from the bearing recorder to the pelorus operator concerning the order in which the observations should made. The example is unproblematic, but there is an opportunity here for the

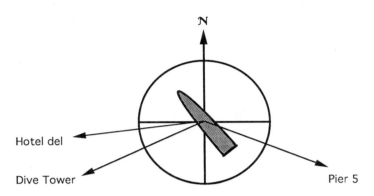

Figure 4.6 The situation of example 2.

pelorus operator to see that Point Loma is an example of a beam bearing and perhaps add to his knowledge of the meaning of the expression. This is thus also an example of language socialization.

EXAMPLE 2

Example 2 is a case in which the recorder chose two landmarks near the beam on the same side of the ship. As a consequence, the lines of position did not converge on a tight fix triangle. The plotter tried to explain the spread of the lines to the recorder. Ship's course: 324°. Beam bearings: 054 and 234. Landmarks: Pier 5 122°, Dive Tower 244°, Hotel del 267°. (See figure 4.6.)

Plotter: See, the reason is ... you get the spread, ah, is that these (Hotel del and Dive Tower) are both close to the beam.

Recorder: Yeah.

Plotter: Right. They are both close to the beam. They're gonna sp ... I mean, unless he can get 'em really, really fast, he's gonna split it even at 10 knots, you know. Ten knots, he is progressing along in between the time he reads those.

Recorder: Yeah.

Plotter: 'Cause they're both so, both so close to the beam.

Recorder: Yeah.

Plotter: That's the reason.

There are two potential problems with what the recorder has done. The plotter explains one of them at length. Since both bearings for the port pelorus operator are near the beam, no matter which one the pelorus operator shoots first, the other will change while he is shooting the first. The second problem is that two bearings within

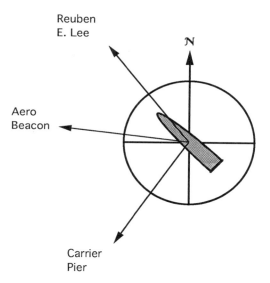

Figure 4.7 The situation of example 3.

$30°$ of each other intersect at a shallow angle, so small errors in the observation move the point of intersection a long ways.

EXAMPLE 3

A beam bearing (to the carrier pier) was the last bearing observed. The plotter and the recorder have discussed the effects of shooting beam bearings last, and the recorder tells the pelorus operators to remember to shoot the beam bearing first. Course: $309°$. Beam bearings: 039 and 219. Landmarks: Reuben E. Lee $328°$, Aero Beacon $281°$, Carrier Pier $210°$. (See figure 4.7.)

Recorder (to plotter): That was a late bearing.

Plotter: Yeah, see, he's gotta remember that. These late bearings on beam are doing, is why you get these big open fixes. Your beam bearing's gotta shoot first. Tell those guys to watch what the hell they are doing.

Recorder: That's what I've been tellin' 'em.

Plotter: Yeah, but tell him, OK, over there he's got to go to the beam one first.

Recorder: OK.

Plotter: Because that is the one that is changing on him real fast.

Recorder (to pelorus operators): OK guys. Remember to shoot the beam bearings first.

Notice that much less is communicated to the pelorus operators in the recorder's last turn than what passes between the plotter and the recorder. The plotter and the recorder share the chart as well, and it is a rich communicative resource. When the plotter refers to "these big open fixes" he is pointing to the fix triangles on the chart. The pelorus operators are separated from this scene by the phone circuit. The instruction to them contains only an admonition to shoot beam bearings first.

The next example raises the possibility that the pelorus operators do not know how to make sense of what they are being told, and there is nothing here to help the pelorus operators determine how to put the advice into practice.

EXAMPLE 4

Example 4 is the most complete and complex interaction concerning the strategies for sequencing the activities of the pelorus operators. Because of the size and complexity of this example, I will break it into segments punctuated with commentary. It begins with a question from the starboard pelorus operator (SW).

SW: I got two points. You want the fartherest first, and then the closest?

Recorder: Oh, OK.

SW: I got two points, right?

Recorder: Whatever is closer to the beam. Shoot the beam first. The one closer to sidewise. You got two points, um.

SW: So I shoot the fartherest one first, then the closest.

Recorder: If you got three, you shoot the one in the middle, then forward, then aft. If you got two, forward and aft.

SW: If you got ... (interrupted by port wing pelorus operator)

Recorder: OK, just a reminder. You always shoot the beam bearings first. If you got three of them, you best shoot the ones ... (port pelorus operator talking)

Recorder: If you got two of 'em, only shoot the ones up forward and back.

Plotter: Huh?

Recorder: I was just trying to explain which ones to shoot first. Beam bearings first.

Plotter: Beam, then forward and aft.

Recorder: Forward and aft. If he's got two, he's got to shoot forward first and then aft. (Recorder talks to port pelorus operator on headset.)

The origins of the starboard pelorus operator's ideas about shooting the most distant landmarks first is unknown. The instruction from the recorder, "If you got two, (shoot) forward and (then) aft," will lead to the wrong sequence if the aft bearing is closer to the beam than the forward one. The difficulty here is interpreting the meaning of the rule of thumb across a wide range of possible configurations of landmarks. After hearing this exchange, the plotter went out to the starboard wing to talk to the starboard pelorus operator. (In the conversation that followed, REFTRA refers to an upcoming inspection in which the crew's performance will be observed by an evaluation team.)

Plotter: Remember, one of the things you guys wanna do, the guys on the wings. Them REFTRA guys'll watch for it no matter who's out on the wings, and supposedly you're all inter . . . any of you can be there. If the guy that sees . . . When a round is comin' up and he knows, he says, see, you know, pretty clo . . . you know about, you can tell. The guy who knows he's going to have a beam bearing. He gets through saying "OK on the next round I want you to have . . ." and that guy can see he's gonna have it on the beam, tell the other guy "I've got the beam bearing." OK, so that . . .

SW: Beam? Where is the beam? Right here?

Plotter: Right here (demonstrates with his arms). The beam is between here and here. The bearing that's chas . . . changing fastest. Right along side of the ship. Even if it's out there, it's the bearing . . .

SW: Uh huh

Plotter: . . . that's changing the fastest. OK. That's your speed line. That's the one that should come first, and then the other guy can go ahead and shoot forward or, or, you know, he can go and shoot. But always the beam first. And if the guy that's got the beam bearing, see, the other guy can't see what you can see. Just like you can't see his. If you got the beam bearing, say "Hey, mine is the beam bearing." That way, he'll shut up . . .

SW: You'll never have . . .

Plotter: . . . and let you give your beam.

SW: Comin' into a channel though, you could both have a bearing on the beam.

Plotter: True, you could, you could.

SW: You could, yeah, but not . . .

Plotter: But not very often, 'cause he don't give things that are right across from one another.

In this conversation it becomes evident that the pelorus operator was not at all clear on the meaning of "beam bearing." The plotter describes it to him, but also includes additional features of the beam bearings (e.g., "changing fastest" and "speed line") which are conceptually salient to the plotter but are probably meaningless to the pelorus operator, who is just trying to figure out how to identify the beam bearing. Notice also that the plotter links the observation of the bearing to the report of the bearing in his description of how the pelorus operators should negotiate the sequence of their activities. This is important because observation and report must be uncoupled in order to produce a more efficient procedure.

EXAMPLE 5

Later in the same entry, the ship was inbound. Course: 345°. Beam bearings: 075° and 255°. Landmarks: port, Point Loma 335; starboard, Dive Tower 045 and Hotel del 032. (See figure 4.8.) It is unclear what either participant takes "go first" to mean in the following exchange.

SW: When I got two points and he's only got one, shouldn't he let me go first?

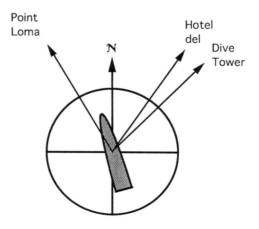

Figure 4.8   The situation of example 5.

Recorder: Nah, it doesn't matter really right now.

SW: Doesn't matter?

(S in conversation with CIC seems to have no time to pursue question from SW)

The answer to the starboard pelorus operator's question should have been an unequivocal "Yes." The recorder's response probably leaves the starboard pelorus operator in some confusion. Saying that it doesn't matter is a way for the recorder to indicate that he does not wish or does not have time to intervene in the negotiation between bearing takers at this moment. Unfortunately, this conversational move also has a substantive interpretation: that the number of landmarks one has is irrelevant to the order in which the bearings are reported. In this case, the starboard pelorus operator should observe Dive Tower first (before observing Hotel del, because Dive Tower is beamier) and should report first (that is, before the port pelorus operator reports, because the port pelorus operator has only one bearing to report). The two senses of "first" are different, as are the reasons for the two relative orderings. In either case, however, the starboard pelorus operator should have gone first.

EXAMPLE 6

Course: 35°. Beam bearings 083° and 263°. Landmarks: port, Point Loma 327; starboard, Dive Tower 058, Hotel del 044. (See figure 4.9.) In this sequence the recorder encourages the linkage of shooting and reporting.

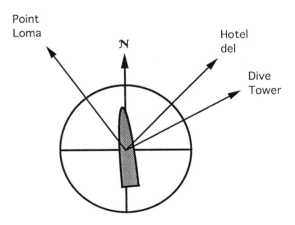

Figure 4.9 The situation of example 6.

SW: John?

Recorder: Yo!

SW: Is the Dive Tower right on our beam?

Recorder: Say again?

SW: Dive Tower. Isn't it just about on our beam?

Recorder: Yeah, just about. (2 seconds) OK, Shades?

PW: What?

Recorder: Steve's gonna be shooting the Dive Tower first, so let him say, uh, let him say the bearing first.

PW: You want Point Loma last, then?

Recorder: Yeah, that's fine.

In this example, the starboard pelorus operator's question about the beam status of the Dive Tower is interpreted by the recorder as also being an indirect request to shoot and report that bearing first, perhaps in accordance with their previous discussion. The recorder takes up the role of negotiating the sequence and seems to expect the port pelorus operator to share this interpretation of the starboard pelorus operator's request. Once again, the recorder's instructions explicitly combine shooting with reporting.

EXAMPLE 7

Time: 6 minutes later. Course 353°. Beam bearings: 083° and 263°. Landmarks: port, Point Loma 275°; starboard, Hotel del 066°, Light Zulu 049°. (See figure 4.10.)

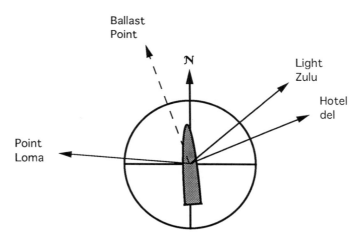

Figure 4.10   The situation of example 7.

Plotter: What did you take a bunch of beam bearings for? Why ain't you shooting up there (ahead) some place. Look what you did. You shot three beam bearings. You shot three beam bearings. You better tell 'em to shoot from up ahead some place.

Recorder: OK. Drop Point Loma and pick up Ballast Point, John.

PW: OK.

Failure to Uncouple Shoot and Report Actions

The rule "shoot the beam bearing first" works fine in solo watch-standing. Yet the attempts of the navigation team to use that rule to coordinate their actions through time fail repeatedly. Why is the application of this simple rule so difficult? Why is the team unable to use this rule to organize its performance? The above examples of instructions concerning the taking of beam bearings provide some clues.

When the rule is invoked in Standard Steaming Watch by a single quartermaster standing watch alone, the beam bearing refers to the bearing in the set of three that is nearest the beam of the ship, and the sequence specifier "first" is established with respect to the entire set of three bearings. In the group version of the task, a pelorus operator cannot always determine whether any bearing he has been assigned is nearer the beam than any bearing assigned to the other pelorus operator. A pelorus operator stationed on one wing of the ship cannot give either of these words the meaning it has for a solo watchstander. It is as though other words were missing from the simple statement of the rule. A more explicit version of the rule in the solo watchstanding case would be *"Of the set of three bearings*, shoot the beam bearing first." It is not necessary to say these words in the solo watchstanding context, because the entire set of three bearings is the watchstander's responsibility. Their presence in that context is not needed, and their absence when the context has changed is not noticed. If these words had been present, the problems of giving the rule to the individual members of the team may have been more apparent. The statement of the rule implies or assumes a perspective that takes in all three bearings at once. That is the meaning of 'beamiest' that we get from looking at the diagrams, it is the meaning exchanged by the recorder and the plotter when they are looking at the chart, and it is the meaning that the plotter brings out onto the wing when he explains to the pelorus operator how to apply the rule. But the perspective on which this meaning rests is not available to the pelorus operators. Neither pelorus operator can see the entire set, and neither can really know the relation of the bearings on his side to those on the other. The pelorus operators need a meaning of 'beamiest' that they can apply on the basis of what they can see, and they cannot see all three bearings at once. Transporting knowledge from the solo performance context to the group performance context is very problematic. It may require changes in the meanings of words.

There is also considerable difficulty in interpreting the meaning of the rule across a wide range of possible configurations of bearings. The pelorus operators have never stood watch alone, and may not even know what the beam is. This highlights the fact that the group performance requires a particular distribution of knowledge.

Both the plotter and the recorder link the observation of the bearing to the act of reporting the bearing in their descriptions of how the pelorus operators should negotiate the sequence of their actions. This has multiple causes. First, observing and recording are a unit in the solo version of the task (which is the source of the rule). Second, an explicit vocabulary is required to sort out observing from reporting. It is not easy, in the absence of a diagram, to describe what the order of actions should be. It is still more difficult to negotiate this sequence without a prior agreement about how observing can be decoupled from reporting. What is needed is a language for the two aspects of the rule: The operator who has two bearings should report before the operator who has only one, and he who has two bearings should always shoot the beamier of the bearings before the other. The rule that comes from solo performance has no such terms.

Here is an aspect of the organization of team activity that is problematic for the team. The members perceive it as being a problem, and they apply themselves to it, but they come to no satisfactory solution. Transporting the simple rule of thumb from the solo watchstanding configuration to the group configuration presents unexpected difficulties. The words of the rule themselves seem to change meanings when the rule is moved to a new context, and new words seem necessary to make distinctions in the new context that were not needed and not made in the old context. The conceptual linkage between observing and reporting prevents the team from exploiting possibilities of the socially distributed system for manipulating the temporal relations among actions. It is difficult to reason about a system as complex as this from a position within it. Quartermasters are not trained in the sorts of reflection on organization that are required to solve problems like this.

Going Beyond the Job Description

One important aspect of the social distribution of this task is that the knowledge required to carry out the coordinating actions is not discretely contained inside the various individuals. Rather, much of the knowledge is intersubjectively shared among the members of the navigation team. This permits the human component of the system to act as a malleable and adaptable coordinating tissue, the job of which is to see to it that the proper coordinating activities are carried out. In their communication and in their joint actions, the members of the navigation team superimpose themselves on the network of material computational media. They provide the connecting tissue that moves representational state across the tools of the trade. In addition, they dynamically reconfigure their activities in response to changes in the task demands. This amounts to a restructuring of functional systems that transcends the individual team members. The individual team members do their jobs by constructing local functional systems that bring media in their immediate environment into coordination. They also must coordinate their activities of helping one another achieve coordination. The computation is implemented in the coordination of representational states, and the human participants coordinate their coordinating actions with one another.

Shared Task Performances

Sometimes the coordination of actions occurs at a very fine grain. One day during Standard Steaming Watch, Silver and Smith were working the chart table together. They needed to use the hoey determine the direction of a line between two points. Smith placed the tip of his pen on the one of points. Silver put the point of his pencil down on the second point and pushed the edge of the hoey arm up against the pencil and pen points. Then, while Silver held the hoey arm in place, Smith rotated the base of the protractor to align it with a latitude line and read the bearing from the hoey scale. This *ad hoc* division of labor was based on a shared understanding of the microstructure of the task. There was no verbal negotiation of the parts of the task to be done by each man; they simply created this coordination in the doing of the task. The social skills required to enter into shared task-performance relationships probably develop fairly early in life.

Distributed Memory

Task-relevant information is present in many representations in this system. Some of these representations are in the minds of the participants. During an exit from a harbor, the plotter expected a 1000-yard interval between fixes. Instead he measured only 700 yards. This indicated that the ship had slowed from 10 to about 7 knots. This is troubling, because it indicates a discrepancy between the information used to project the dead-reckoned position and the actual observations. To resolve the discrepancy, the plotter began by talking to himself, but quickly addressed a question to the keeper of the deck log.

Plotter: This is not showing no, a no goddamn ... they show a two-thirds, still got a two-thirds bell, right?

Deck log: One-third bell.

Plotter: Why?

CIC talker: Got the pilot off.

Plotter: Oh, that's why. OK, he's [the pilot] getting off right now, isn't he?

CIC talker: Yeah. He [the OOD] went back to 5 knots.

Plotter: That's what messed me up. They have this goddamn 7-knot goddamn thing in here and I'm trying to figure out why.

In this exchange, both the CIC talker and the keeper of the deck log provide the plotter with task-relevant representational state. The plotter could have gotten the information about the one-third bell (ahead one-third on the engine-order telegraph) from the deck log itself, or from the engine-order telegraph, or from the leehelmsman as well as from the keeper of the deck log. This bit of system state is redundantly represented in the memories of several participants, and in written records. The information about the departure of the harbor pilot was probably not present in any record at this time, because as far as the bridge crew knew the pilot was still on board.

Still, the CIC talker knew about this and was able to judge that it would be of use to the plotter at this time.

In another instance, while simultaneously watching a fishing boat that crossed close under the bow of the ship and discussing the watch bill for the remainder of the day, the plotter and recorder missed a fix time. This problem was caught by the keeper of the deck log about 2 minutes late.

Deck log: Chief, you're going to have another call. Missed at 3. Your round at 3.

Plotter: I'll get one here in a minute.

Recorder: Stand by to mark.

Plotter: Time is 5, yeah 5; we'll just kind of space this one out.

Even though timing the fixes is not part of the keeper of the deck log's job, he is a participant at the chart table and in this case, happens to have noticed that a scheduled fix was missed. This sort of overlapping knowledge distribution is characteristic of cooperative work and is an important source of the robustness of such systems in the face of error and interruption.

Recorder Cuing the Plotter

With only two landmarks visible, the team substituted a radar range on one of the visible landmarks for the third line of position. After advising the pelorus operators to stand by for a round, the recorder turned to the plotter and said: "Get a range, Chief? (2 seconds) Mark it." The plotter had apparently forgotten that he was required to take the radar range of the landmark as part of the position fixing operation. In this case, an element of the sequential organization of the plotter's activity was provided by the recorder. This is not strictly in accordance with the normal division of labor. The plotter was supposed to remember that the "stand by to mark" signal was his cue to take the radar range. He and the recorder had come to an agreement about a nonstandard division of labor to meet the needs of an unusual situation. We may speculate that the recorder's memory for the plotter's role was in part cued by the fact that he had labeled a column in the bearing record log as "Range Pt. Loma." The need to fill the cell in the bearing log at the intersection of this labeled column with the row representing the current time acts as a memory for the decision to take the radar range and may remind the recorder of the plan for getting the range.

Landmark Descriptions

Since the ideal manning requirements are seldom met, it is often the case that the pelorus operators are not entirely familiar with the landmarks they will be required to observe. When pelorus operators fail to locate a landmark, the plotter and recorder may attempt to help them out by providing verbal descriptions. In the following example, the port pelorus operator is unable to find a landmark. (This one, the Dive Tower, is frequently a problem.) Notice also that the plotter interjects additional sequencing advice at the beginning of the fix cycle. (The starboard pelorus operator's name is Mark). Those portions of the recorder's talk that are transmitted over the phone circuit appear in boldface.

Recorder: **Stand by to mark, Point Loma, Hotel del, and Dive Tower.**

Plotter: Tell him to take Point Loma first. It's on his beam.

Recorder: **Take Point Loma first, Mark. Beam bearing first. Mark it.**

SW: Point Loma, 3 5 9.

Recorder: 3 5 9 Point Loma.

Nav: Ten knots good speed?

Plotter: Yes. Anything you want. We're clear now. Wherever you want to go.

PW: Hotel del 0 3 8.

Recorder: 0 3 8 Hotel del.

PW: I can't find the Dive Tower.

Recorder: **Can't find the Dive Tower.**

Plotter: Tell him it is about 8 degrees, 9 degrees to the right of Hotel del (plotting)

Recorder: Nine degrees?

Plotter: Yeah.

Recorder: **It's about 9 degrees to the right of Hotel del. It's about 0 4 6.**

The clue provided by the plotter in this case is not a description of the landmark, but a location relative to a previously reported landmark toward which the pelorus operator should look. This is evidence of how strong the expectations of the position of the landmark are. Also notice that the recorder transforms the description even further, converting it by mental arithmetic to a bearing at which the pelorus operator should look for the landmark.

In this example we see something of the relationship of social structure and computational structure. Given a computational procedure and a social organization, there are better and worse ways to distribute the computation across the social network. One way in which the distribution of tasks can be better or worse concerns the relation between the amount of information that must be passed between computational segments and the capacity of the medium of communication between the participants responsible for those segments. That is a computational argument for a particular decomposition of the task. The observed decomposition works well in many respects but is frustrating for certain classes of problems.

Recorder Setting Up Plotting Tool for Plotter

In another instance, the plotter was called away from the chart table just as the bearings of the landmarks were reported. After recording the bearings in the bearing record log, the recorder reached across the chart and set the hoey arm to the value of the first bearing. When the plotter returned to the chart table, he looked in the log for the bearing. When he looked at the hoey, he noticed that it had already been set to the proper bearing. He then simply aligned it with the chart and plotted the line of position. Setting the hoey was not in the recorder's job description, but it was a way of pushing the representational state a little further toward its end point.

Flexibility and Robustness

These examples also illustrate the robustness of the system of distributed knowledge. If one human component fails for lack of knowledge, the whole system does not grind to a halt. If the task becomes difficult or communications break down, the navigation team does not have the option of stopping work. The task is driven by events and must be performed as long as the ship is underway. In response to a breakdown, the system adapts by changing the nominal division of labor. It is the bearing taker's job to find the landmarks, for example, but if he is unable to do so, some other member of the team will contribute whatever is required to ensure that the landmarks are found and their bearings observed. This robustness is made possible by the redundant distribution of knowledge among the members of the team, the access of members to one another's activities, and the fact that the individual workloads are light enough to permit mutual monitoring and occasional assistance. Both the knowledge required to do the task and the responsibility for keeping the system working are distributed across the members of the navigation team. We can think of the team as a sort of flexible organic tissue that keeps the information moving across the tools of the task. When one part of this tissue is unable to move the required information, another part is recruited to do it.

Performance as a Language of Social Interaction

The division of labor mandated in Sea and Anchor Detail distributes the elements of the fix cycle across social space. Wherever computations are distributed across social organization, computational dependencies are also social dependencies. Performance is embedded in real human relationships. Every action is not only a piece of the computation, a bit of the task completed; it is also a social message. Building and maintaining good social relationships becomes an important motive for competent performance. In order to do the computation, the members of the team must interact. They depend on one another. More precisely, the portion of the computation for which each is responsible may depend on the portions for which the others are responsible. In order to plot the next line of position, the plotter needs the bearing, which means he needs to communicate with and secure the cooperation of the pelorus operator.

An important aspect of these interrelated social and computational structures is that both of them provide constraints on the behavior of the participants. One can embed a novice who has social skills but lacks computational skills in such a network and get useful behavior out of that novice and the system. The reason is that the social structure (and the structure of the tools) of the task may provide enough constraints to determine what turns out to be a well-organized computational behavior even though the behavior was not motivated by any understanding of the computation. The task world is constructed in such a way that the socially and conversationally appropriate thing to do given the tools at hand is also the computationally correct thing to do. That is, one can be functioning well before one knows what one is doing, and one can discover what one is doing in the course of doing it.

The social structure is not only the framework on which the communication is based, it is also the mechanism that is in place prior to the interactions to ensure that they take place as required. Why should the pelorus operator cooperate? Because adequate performance is the currency of social interaction. The novice quartermaster is institutionally located in such a way that his actions can be taken both as contributions to the process and as claims to or justifications of membership in the social world of the other quartermasters. And, since this is the military, a novice who does not perform adequately can be harshly sanctioned.

How to Say Things with Actions

My initial assumption about work in military settings was that behaviors are explicitly described and that people act more or less as automatons. It should be apparent by now that this is far from the case. I also naively assumed that most communication on the job would be part of the job and nothing more. As I worked with the data, something that Roy D'Andrade once said kept coming back to me. A student was making a point about what people do at work, saying that in an auto factory people mostly make cars. Roy said something like: "How do you know what they are doing? Maybe what they are making is social relationships and the cars are a side effect."

It is clear that when quartermasters report bearings, assign landmarks, or ask for data, they are not just constructing position fixes; they are also constructing social relationships. And the fact that their respective responsibilities are so well specified does not eliminate the possibility of loading social messages into the communication acts that make up the work. In fact, the well-formed expectations about what constitutes competent verbal behavior in this setting may give the participants an especially subtle means of communicating social messages. Doing the absolute bare minimum required when others know that one has the time and resources to do more is a clear statement.

Computational Properties of the Navigation Team

Local functional systems are established in the individual jobs. Each member of the navigation team is responsible for the construction of a number of local functional systems. These are the processes of bringing media into coordination as described in chapter 3.

These local functional systems are coordinated in the interaction of the members of the team. In their interactions, the team members assemble the component functional systems into a larger functional system.

The larger system has cognitive properties very different from those of any individual. In fact the cognitive properties of the navigation team are at least twice removed from the cognitive properties of the individual members of the team. The first remove is a result of the transforming effects of the interactions with the tools of the trade (chapter 3); the second remove is a consequence of the social organization of distributed cognition.

In Sea and Anchor Detail the navigation team implements a distributed problem-solving system in which various elements of the computation are embodied in the operations of functional systems constructed by the members of the team. Among the advantages of distributed processing discussed by Chandresekaran (1981) are the following:

The decomposition of processing is a strategy for controlling the complexity of computation. By breaking the problem down into pieces, the team can have several workers operating in parallel. This decomposition of the task also permits each member of the team to attend closely to only a limited set of data. As Chandresekaran points out, the complexity of computation is often an exponential function of the size of the input space. If the problem can be divided up, each person can deal with a tractable problem. For example, each pelorus operator needs to deal with the landmarks on only one side of the ship's track. It is possible to learn the landmarks for the starboard side without knowing the landmarks for the port side. There are also filtering processes applied that prevent the growth of input space. Thus, the recorder does not normally have to deal with the complexity of the visual scene outside the ship. His experience of the bearings is pre-processed by the pelorus operators and takes the form of strings of spoken digits. An important advantage of social distribution of computing is that novices can be embedded in social arrangements such that much of the structure required for them to organize their activity is available in the social relations. Even though the skills have mainly social significance to the novices, they can learn a great many skills that have computational significance to the system.

A second property noted by Chandresekaran is that distributed computing "increases the prospects for graceful degradation" of system performance when components fail. This is apparent in the response of the navigation team to local failures such as the inability of a pelorus operator to locate a landmark. Because the members of the team have overlapping knowledge, it is possible for them to reconfigure dynamically in response to a problem. The individuals are a sort of flexible tissue that moves to ensure the propagation of task-relevant representational state. Because their competences overlap and they have access to one another's activities, they are able to aid one another and fill in for one another in the event of a local failure.

Adaptation to change may be easier in distributed than in centralized systems. Chandresekaran says that "as the external environment changes, distributed information processing makes adaptation to change easier, since again, as long as the rate of change is not large, changes to the system can be mostly local." I will discuss an example that illustrates this in some detail in chapter 8.

Having the pelorus operators negotiate the shooting sequence among themselves is an example of the uses of modularity. Notice that this modularity was violated when the starboard pelorus operator asked the bearing recorder to settle the shooting and reporting order.

One of the costs of distribution is the filtering performed by the sensors. The pelorus operators are expected to pass only the results of their computations to the bearing recorder. All information about the process that went into achieving that result is lost in the report of the bearing as a single number. This reduces the bandwidth required for communication (the phone circuit is adequate for this), and it also reduces the processing demands on the central processor (plotter). However, this kind of filtering makes it more difficult to diagnose the causes of errors committed by the pelorus operators, since nothing of the process is normally communicated.

Representing the bearings symbolically also introduces new possibilities for error. For example, the landmarks light 2 and light zulu are very different from each other in location and appearance. It is unlikely that one would ever be mistaken for the other. Their symbolic representations, "light 2" and "light Z," however, are very similar and might easily be confused. This potential was recognized by the plotter, and he instructed the recorder to put a slash through the Z.

Another potential cost of distribution is the potential disruption of one processor by another. The buffers are a way to overcome this sort of temporal discoordination. The phone circuit has different properties from the bearing log because one endures in time while the other does not.

The problem of the design of the distribution of labor remains. As we saw with the case of beam bearings, the mapping from individual performance to the group configuration is a nontrivial one. Opportunities exist in the distributed version of the task that are simply not present in the solo-performance case. Finding and exploiting these opportunities may require reflection on explicit representations of the work itself, and the members of the navigation team are ill equipped to do such reflection.

The theme of this chapter is that organized groups may have cognitive properties that differ from those of the individuals who constitute the group. These differences arise from both the effects of interactions with technology and the effects of a social distribution of cognitive labor. The system formed by the navigation team can be thought of as a computational machine in which social organization is computational architecture. The members of the team are able to compensate for local breakdowns by going beyond the normative procedures to make sure that representational states propagate when and where they should. The difficulty in mapping a rule of thumb developed for solo watchstanding into the group configuration highlights the differences between these modes of operation and provides insights into the limits on the team's abilities to explicitly plan the coordination of their actions.

Communication and Task Decompositions

In chapter 4 I argued that the bandwidth of communication available to the members of the navigation team would affect the computational properties of the team as a cognitive system. I will report some computer simulation results that support this claim later in this chapter. However, casting the phenomenon in terms of a single quantitative measure, such as bandwidth, obscures important properties that should be discussed.

The fact that the navigation team distributes computational procedures across a social organization raises the possibility that there may be better and worse ways to arrange the distribution. One way in which the distribution of computational procedures can be better or worse concerns the relation between the kinds of structure that can be passed between computational elements and the kinds of structure with which the passed structures must be coordinated in the performance of the task.

Consider again the task of the reconciliation of the chart to the world as it occurs in Sea and Anchor Detail. One person can see the chart and another can see the world. They communicate with one another on a telephone line. Achieving a reconciliation between chart and world is a very difficult task, and sometimes verbal communication alone is not sufficient. It would be easy to say that the telephone circuit provides only a low bandwidth of communication and that more information must be transmitted if the pelorus operator is to locate the correct landmark in the world. The problem with that account is that it commits us to a measure of quantity of information that may be both practically and theoretically impossible. On what grounds could it be claimed that the recorder's going to the wing and pointing to the landmark in the presence of the pelorus operator has a greater bandwidth than a lengthy verbal description? The process of assigning landmarks is performed under time constraints, but it does not appear that efforts to communicate the location of a landmark are ever given up just because time runs out. These efforts are abandoned because of a perceived qualitative rather than quantitative deficiency. Verbal descriptions typically fail not because they don't provide enough structure but because they provide the wrong kind of structure. The difference between the right and the wrong kinds of structure is determined by both the nature of the task and the other structural resources that are available.

The theory of computation by propagation of representational state poses the question differently. It asks instead what kinds of structure the pelorus operator must bring into coordination with the communicated structure in order to perform the task. As described in chapter 3, when the landmark description is spoken on the telephone, the pelorus operator must coordinate the spoken description of the landmark with knowledge of the landmark's appearance, which must be coordinated with the visual field. The problem for the pelorus operator involves searching the available visual field to find a scene that can be construed as a match with the target description. Pointing isn't more information than a detailed verbal description: it is a different kind of information that can be put to work in a different way.

Language Behavior as a Determinant of the Cognitive Properties of Groups

Consider the following example in which the structure of the lexicon constrains the cognitive properties of the group: One evening, a Marine commander on board the *Palau*, Major Rock, telephoned the charthouse. Quartermaster Second Class Smith answered the phone. Major Rock asked Smith what the phase of the moon would be that night. Smith asked Chief Richards, who was sitting nearby. Richards immediately replied "Gibbous waning." Smith relayed the answer to Rock. Rock apparently did not understand the answer, and he and Smith talked past each other for several conversational turns. Finally, Smith put his hand over the mouthpiece and said "Chief, he says it's got to be one of, 'new', 'first', 'full', and 'last'." Chief Richards said "It's last." Smith told Rock, and Rock hung up. Chief Richards had a rich vocabulary for phases of the moon. Rock's vocabulary was impoverished. Giving Rock the mapping in terms of the richer vocabulary did no good because he could not connect it to his simplified notions. Rock eventually provided both the question and the possible answers to it, the latter in the form of the four categories he recognized. Once the chief knew what Rock was looking for—knew the look of the map Rock was trying to articulate with the moon phases—he could settle on 'last' as the nearest match to 'gibbous waning'. After Smith hung up the phone, Chief Richards said: "Rock is a great big guy with a brain about this big (making a circle with the tip of his index finger touching the first joint of his thumb). He must never have taken an amphib mission onto a beach at night. He might get by on a crescent moon, but on a gibbous moon he'll be dead."

This example raises two points. First, the amount of information that is conveyed by a given utterance is not a simple function of the volume of structure in the utterance. Information and coding theory define the minimum bandwidth required to encode a given set of alternative messages. From the perspective of information theory, natural language is not an efficient code. Suppose X bits are required to represent the name of the present phase of the moon. The amount of information in the message depends on how many other phases of the moon can be named, not on how many bits it took to represent the name of the phase of the moon. Second, the expressiveness of the code may determine the cognitive properties of the larger system. Whether a team of planners can mount a successful amphibious landing may depend on the range of distinctions that can be made in the language spoken by the mission planners.

Because so much of the communication within this system is verbal communication, the properties of language become important determinants of the nature of the computation that is accomplished. The properties of language change with the register of the speech and with the medium in which the utterances are carried. The mandated language on the intercom is almost telegraphic. This is adequate when the desired communications have been anticipated—when the possible messages have been spelled out and agreed upon in advance. However, it is difficult to negotiate a novel understanding of the nature of a problem or to jointly interpret a complex world on such a low-bandwidth channel.

Viewing language as one of the structured representations produced and coordinated in the performance of the task highlights the information-bearing properties of language. In cognitive science, language is usually thought of primarily as a human computational capacity that should be understood in terms of the processing that individuals must do to produce or interpret it. Shifting attention from the cognitive properties of an individual to those of a system of socially distributed cognition casts language in a new light. The properties of the language itself interact with the properties of the communications technology in ways that affect the computational properties of the larger cognitive system.

Linguistic determinism is the idea that the structure of one's native language determines properties of individual thought. This is not an appropriate place to review that literature, but the answer to the question "Does the structure of language determine the structure of thought?" seems to be "Sometimes and sometimes not." When so-called noncognitive tasks are organized in such a way that subjects can use the structure of their language as a mediating resource in organizing task performance, then language structures thought. When the structure of language is not useful as a mediating resource in task performance, then task performance does not seem to be affected by the structure of language. When cognitive activities are distributed across social space, the language or languages used by task performers to communicate are almost certain to serve as structuring resources, and the structure of language will affect the cognitive properties of the group even if they do not affect the cognitive properties of individuals in the group.

Communication in a Shared World

Communication between persons who are copresent in a shared physical environment differs in many ways from communication across a restricted bandwidth medium. The Officer of the Deck tends to trust the navigation plot maintained on the bridge better than he trusts the plot generated in the Combat Information Center. This is because the OOD can come to the chart table, look at what the navigation team is doing, and talk to the quartermasters. In this relatively rich face-to-face interaction, an understanding can be negotiated. The work that went into the recommendation can be displayed and discussed. Such negotiation of meaning is difficult when one is dealing with CIC via the phone talkers. For example, at one point CIC advised the bridge that the ship could continue on its present course and speed for 4 hours before reaching the boundary of the operations area. The navigator had the conn and doubted this. He went to the chart table and consulted with Quartermaster Third Class Charles, who had just computed a time of 75 minutes to the boundary of the operations area on present course and speed. By looking at the charted track and talking with Charles, the navigator convinced himself that the position shown there was correct. He told the phone talker to tell CIC that they were off by 3 hours.

In another example, the weapons officer was unhappy to have been assigned a general quarters (GQ) station on the signal bridge rather than on the navigation bridge. He wanted to have his duty station changed to the navigation bridge because he felt it would be easier to communicate a complex set of options to the commanding officer (CO) in face-to-face interaction than over the intercom. He was also worried that the CO would find the arguments of the department heads who were co-present with him more compelling than those that came to him over the intercom.

The previous two examples concern intentional communication in a shared world. A good deal of our behavior has communicative function without communicative intent. Segal (1990) points out the importance of crew-station layout for the unintended communication among members of aircraft flight crews. The following example illustrates this and other features of communication in a shared world.

Recorder: Mark it.

SW: Pier 5, 1 1 7.

Recorder: 1 1 7, Pier 5.

[The recorder's echoing the bearing as reported is (1) an acknowledgement that it has been received, (2) a readback with content to permit checking by the sender, and (3) the communication of the bearing to the plotter. Thus, it is part of two conversations at once. The plotter, at this point, is waiting for the first bearing so he can begin work. The plotter begins plotting the pier 5 line of position with bearing 117.]

PW: Diving Tower, 2 5 0.

Recorder: 2 5 0, Diving Tower.

(At this point, the chief is still plotting the first LOP bearing 117. He may be simultaneously plotting 1 1 7 and subvocally rehearsing the second bearing, 2 5 0.)

Helm: Steady 3 0 8, Sir. Checking 2 9 2.

CICComm: Steady course 3 0 8.

(There are other numbers being spoken in the environment. In order to prevent interference from these, the bearings are frequently subvocally rehearsed.)

(The plotter is setting up the hoey to plot Diving Tower with a bearing of 2 5 7, rather than the correct 2 5 0. This may be a data-driven error due to the interference of 117's being plotted while 250 was heard and possibly rehearsed.)

PW: Stanchion 18, 2 9 7 point 5.

Recorder: For 18, 2 9 7 point 5.

(The plotter aligns the hoey with charted symbol of Dive Tower with 257 bearing. The LOP is not near the expected position. The plotter leans toward the recorder, then looks at the hoey to read the value he has already aligned on it.)

Plotter: 2 5 7?

Recorder: 2 9 7.

(The plotter leans further toward the recorder, looks in the bearing record log, and points to the Dive Tower column heading.)

Plotter: Hm, um, no.

Recorder: 2 5 0.

(The plotter stands upright and moves the hoey arm.)

Plotter: OK, I might believe that.

CON: Engine ahead two-thirds.

Leehelm: Engine ahead two-thirds, aye.

(The QMOW has his hand on the chart in the way of the plotting tool. The plotter whacks it with the hoey while aligning it for the LOP.)

QMOW: It hurts, Chief.

(The plotter plots the LOP for Diving Tower.)

Plotter: Get your hand out of the way.

QMOW: Yes, sir.

Plotter: And what?

Recorder: 2 9 7 point 5.

(The plotter aligns the hoey and plots the last LOP.)

In this example the bearings are propagated bottom-up from the alidades to the chart. Spoken representations of the bearings 297.5 and 117 are in the environment of the hearing of 250 and seem to interfere with its processing; 250 turns into 257 in this environment. It is not possible to know which, if either, of these other signals interfered, but the transformation was made. The momentary breakdown in communication is, in part, a consequence of the property of the spoken medium. Since speech is ephemeral, one must attend to it as it is being produced. The lack of a way to buffer this input imposes a need for temporal coordination between the plotting activity and the delivery of bearing information. Since the plotter is still engaged in plotting the previous line of position, his attention to the spoken bearing is incomplete. Whatever the cause of the transformation of the form of the bearing for Dive Tower, when propagated to the chart it does not "work." The line of position does not fall where expected.

The plotter asks for confirmation of the bearing. Was it indeed 257? In asking this question, the plotter refers to the hoey scale, constructing part of his query by reading the bearing he has plotted. The recorder attempts to match the request to what he knows to have been the previous communications. This is a negotiation of the meaning of the question. The recorder must determine which LOP is being asked about.

The recorder responds "297." He has matched the plotter's query to one of the reported bearings (297.5) and, in the process, has rounded off the reported bearing. The plotter leans over to look in the log and rejects the 297 bearing. He may know it is not correct because it is even bigger than 257, and 257 was already too big to work. The properties of the media are involved here again. The written record endures, so the plotter directs his attention there to answer his own question. Before the plotter is even finished rejecting the 297 bearing, the recorder has realized that the plotter wants the bearing to the Dive Tower, not the bearing to stanchion 18. The plotter has also gestured toward the column in the bearing record log labeled Dive Tower. This gesture may be involved in two activities here. First, it is part of the plotter's procedure for looking up the bearing. It is a bit of structure that the plotter creates in his world to guide his looking in the bearing record log. It is a way to control the allocation of his own visual attention. Second, it is simultaneously a clue for the recorder about which bearing it is that the plotter is looking for. The communicative function of the gesture is opportunistic. It does not seem to be intended. The recorder now says "250." The plotter makes a quick adjustment to the hoey and sees that a 250 bearing works well. The plotter closes this negotiation by saying "OK, I might believe that."

The fix itself is completed when in response to the plotter's asking "And what?" the recorder responds with the last of the three bearings, 297.5. It is interesting that it is not now rounded off, as it was in response to the question of 257. Then it was tailored to fit the query; now that the confusion has been resolved, it is reported as it was recorded. The utterance "And what?" is interpretable only in the context of an understanding of the task being performed and the place of the plotter in the execution of the task. The recorder is able to determine that the plotter intends to plot the last bearing. He responds in a way that assumes that "And what?" refers to the one bearing that remains to be plotted. The plotter's continued plotting activity—arriving at a satisfactory fix—is evidence that the recorder's interpretation and response were correct.

The plotter's use of his finger in locating the bearing in the bearing record log is very interesting. Because the bearing log is a memory for the observed bearings in this distributed cognitive system, the plotter's action is part of a memory-retrieval event that is internal to the system but directly observable. From the perspective of the individual, the technology in use here externalizes certain cognitive processes. This permits some aspects of those processes to be observed by other members of the team. Because of this, the chief's pointing can be both a part of his private cognitive processing and an element of communication to the recorder about the sort of thing the chief is trying to accomplish. Some kinds of media support this sort of externalization of function better than others. The existence of a gesture that has both private and public functions suggests that other communicative features may also have these two roles. I suspect that prosody might have a similar dual role in the production of verbal representations, helping the speaker to shape the allocation of his own attention while simultaneously providing the listener with structure that can be used to determine what the speaker is trying to accomplish.

The above example shows clearly that the normative description of information flow in the fix cycle, which maintains that information flows bottom-up from the alidades to the chart, is wrong. Far from being a simple one-way trajectory for information, the communication is in fact the bringing together of many kinds of constraints in both bottom-up and top-down directions. The meanings of statements and questions are not given in the statements themselves but are negotiated by the participants in the context of their understandings of the activities underway. The participants use guesses about one another's tasks to resolve ambiguities in communication. Particular meaningful interpretations for statements are simultaneously proposed and presupposed by the courses of action that follow them. The evidence that each participant has of successful communication is the flow of joint activity itself.

The Negotiation of Meaning in Interaction

The following exchange, which is full of breakdowns and repairs, illustrates the negotiation of meaning in interactions.

Recorder: Stand by to mark. Time 0 ... 0 1 2.

CIC Talker: Combat holds 3100 yards to the turn. Holds 50 yards left of track.

Recorder: 26 feet under the keel. Mark it.

(After a 13 second pause, the plotter watches the recorder write down the first bearing, sets the hoey, and aligns it with the chart.)

Plotter: What's at 2 7 7? (plotting)

Recorder: 2 7 1.

(The recorder's correction may be based on a re-reading of the log entry or on memory of the actual bearing reported. Notice the properties of the medium in which the bearing is represented—there is a greater potential confusion of 1 and 7 in written form than "one" and "seven" in spoken form.)

Plotter: What is it?

(The plotter uses the positions of landmarks on the chart, the projected position of the ship, and the angle on the hoey in evaluating the bearing. This one does not fit any of the landmarks he expects.)

Recorder: Um, carrier tower.

Plotter: Oh, I don't want that thing. It's OK, go ahead.

(The chief does not want this landmark because its position is not yet established. It is a back-plot. Once they have established several of their positions with known landmarks, they can back-plot the position of the tower and make it a usable landmark in the future.)

Recorder: The aero beacon is 2 9 2. 10th Avenue Terminal is 1 0 5. (then speaking into the phone circuit) Give me the last bearing you took.

Plotter: 1 0 5. (The plotter is reading this from the bearing record log.)

Plotter: Is that 10th Avenue Terminal that is 1 0 5? Or that little pier?

Recorder: 0 5 9 is that little pier. This one is 0 5 9 (pointing to the depiction of the pier on the chart).

(The referent of "this one" in the recorder's statement is determined indexically by his orientation to the symbols on the chart.)

Plotter: OK. What's at 1 0 5?

Recorder: 10th Avenue is at 0 5, 1 0 5.

Plotter: Still outside here.

Recorder: Still outside?

Plotter: What's the other one?

(The notion of "the other one" relies on the knowledge that three lines of position are required for the fix. The recorder seems to have a problem with the back-plot in the procedure.)

Recorder: 2 7 1.

Plotter: No, no, that's back-plot.

Recorder: Carrier tower.

Recorder: 2 9 2.

Plotter: Yeah, yeah. What's that?

Recorder: Aero beacon, OK, 1 0 5.

Plotter: What's that?

Recorder: That's 10th Avenue.

Plotter: Oh, it is huh.... is he use ... He must be using the tip of it. (8 seconds) Well, it's almost ... actually nothing.

In this passage, the recorder and the plotter attempt to communicate a set of landmark-to-bearing correspondences. The meanings of utterances are established through reference to the chart itself, the structure of the task, the relation of the structure of the hoey to the structure of the chart, and previous elements of the exchange. That is, all these structures are brought into coordination at once in the performance of the task.

Meanings can only even be imagined to be in the messages when the environment about which communication is performed is very stable and there are very strong constraints on the expectations. In many endeavors, creating and maintaining the illusion that meanings reside in messages requires that a great deal of effort be put into controlling the environment in which communication takes place. Meanings seem to be in the messages only when the structures with which the message must be brought into coordination are already reliably in place and taken for granted. The illusion of meaning in the message is a hard-won social and cultural accomplishment.

Confirmation Bias in Individuals and Groups

I have argued above that the cognitive properties of a group may depend as much on the system of communication between individuals as on the cognitive properties of the individuals themselves. It is one thing to assert such an effect and another to demonstrate it. Though I find the examples from actual interactions compelling, events in the real world are almost always complicated by unwanted interactions. Fortunately, a different kind of demonstration is also possible. In the following pages I will describe a computer simulation that explores the role of communication in the production of the cognitive properties of a group.

To test the notion that the cognitive properties of groups may differ from those of the individuals who constitute the group, it is necessary to focus on some particular cognitive property that is generally agreed to be a property of individual cognition and then develop some way to show that whether that property is manifested by a group depends on the social organization of the group. For the purposes of this study, I will use the phenomenon known as *confirmation bias*.

Confirmation Bias in Formation of Interpretations

Confirmation bias is a propensity to affirm prior interpretations and to discount, ignore, or reinterpret evidence that runs counter to an already-formed interpretation. It is a bias to confirm an already-held hypothesis about the nature of the world. This is a commonsense notion. We talk about the difficulty of changing someone's mind once it is "made up." The importance of "first impressions" is an obvious corollary of our folk belief in this principle. There is also compelling scientific evidence of the generality of confirmation bias across such areas as attribution, personality traits (Hastie and Kumar 1979), logical inference tasks (Wason 1968; Wason and Johnson-Laird 1972), beliefs about important social issues (Lord et al. 1979), and scientific reasoning (Fleck 1979; Tweney et al. 1981).

To the extent that this propensity to stick with prior interpretations and discount disconfirming evidence often leads us to maintain faulty interpretations of the nature of the world, it seems maladaptive. After all, knowing what is going on in the environment is an important ability for any creature, and, in general, the more complex the creature, the more complex is that creature's sense of what is in the environment. A property of cognitive processing that prevents us complex creatures from finding better interpretations once we have a good one seems very maladaptive indeed. Why, then, would such a property survive? Clearly there must be a tradeoff here between the ability to move from one interpretation to a better one and the need to have an interpretation—*any* interpretation—in order to coordinate with events in the environment. A system that maintains a coherent but suboptimal interpretation may be better able to adapt than a system that tears its interpretations apart as fast as it builds them.

This propensity is widely accepted as a general feature of *individual* cognition. If it represents a sometimes infelicitous tradeoff between keeping a poor interpretation and having no interpretation at all, one wonders if it might not be possible for a group of individuals, each of whom has this propensity, to make a different sort of trade-off. That is, might a group be organized in such a way that it is more likely than any individual alone to arrive at the best of several possible interpretations, or to reject a coherent interpretation when a better one is present? The plan of the remainder of this chapter is to accept confirmation bias as a property of individual cognition and then to ask what properties it might produce in systems of socially distributed cognition. What I hope to show is that the consequences of this property of individual cognition for the cognitive capabilities of groups of humans depends almost entirely upon how the group distributes the tasks of cognition among its members. That is, some ways of organizing people around thinking tasks will lead to an exacerbation of the maladaptive aspects of this property of mental systems, whereas other forms of organization will actually make an adaptive virtue on the group level of what appears to be an individual vice.

Interpretation Formation as Constraint Satisfaction

Many important human activities are conducted by systems in which multiple actors attempt to form coherent interpretations of some set of phenomena. Some of these systems are small, composed of only a few individuals, while others are very large indeed.

The operation of a complex system is often accomplished by a team. A shift of operators at a nuclear power plant, an aircraft flight crew, or the bridge team on a large ship is a small system in which multiple individuals strive to maintain an interpretation of the situation at hand. The complexity of a system may make it impossible for a single individual to integrate all the required information, or the several members of the group may be present because of other task demands but may be involved in distributed interpretation formation. Management teams in business and government are also systems of distributed interpretation formation, as are juries in the court system. A community of scientists may be the best example of a very-large-scale system in which a group strives to construct a coherent interpretation of phenomena.

Forming an interpretation is an instance of what computer scientists call a *constraint-satisfaction problem*. Any coherent interpretation consists of a number of parts; call them *hypotheses*. Some of the parts go together with others or support one another; others exclude or inhibit one another. These relationships among the parts of the interpretation are called *constraints*. Consider the following incident taken from Perrow's book *Normal Accidents* (1984):

On a beautiful night in October 1978, in the Chesapeake Bay, two vessels sighted one another visually and on radar. On one of them, the Coast Guard cutter training vessel Cuyahoga, *the captain (a chief warrant officer) saw the other ship up ahead as a small object on the radar, and visually he saw two lights, indicating that it was proceeding in the same direction as his own ship. He thought it possibly was a fishing vessel. The first mate saw the lights, but saw three, and estimated (correctly) that it was a ship proceeding toward them. He had no responsibility to inform the captain, nor did he think he needed to. Since the two ships drew together so rapidly, the captain decided that it must be a very slow fishing boat that he was about to overtake. This reinforced his incorrect interpretation. The lookout knew the captain was aware of the ship, so did not comment further as it got quite close and seemed to be nearly on a collision course. Since both ships were traveling full speed, the closing came fast. The other ship, a large cargo ship did not establish any bridge-to-bridge communication, because the passing was routine. But at the last moment, the captain of the* Cuyahoga *realized that in overtaking the supposed fishing boat, which he assumed was on a near parallel course, he would cut off that boat's ability to turn as both of them approached the Potomac River. So he ordered a turn to the port.*

The two ships collided, killing 11 sailors on the Coast Guard vessel. The captain's interpretation contained a number of hypotheses (that the other ship was small, that it was slow, and that it was traveling in the same direction as his own ship). These hypotheses were linked to a set of observations (the ship presented a small image on the radar; it appeared to the captain to show two lights; the distance between the ships was closing rapidly) to form a coherent interpretation in which the hypotheses were consistent with one another and with the observations. Several of the hypotheses of the mate's interpretation were in direct conflict with some of the hypotheses in the captain's interpretation. For example, the hypothesis that the ships were meeting head on and the hypothesis that one was overtaking the other were mutually exclusive.

A good interpretation is one that is both internally consistent and in agreement with the available data. Evidence from the world makes some of the hypotheses of the interpretation more or less likely. These hypotheses that are directly driven by evidence have constraining relations to other hypotheses for which there is, perhaps, no direct evidence. For example, in the ship collision described above, there is no direct evidence concerning the speed of the other vessel. That hypothesis is derived from the hypothesis that the Coast Guard ship is overtaking the other ship and the observation that the distance between the ships is closing rapidly. If those two things are true, then the other ship must be moving slowly. The job of forming an interpretation can thus be seen as attempting to assign likelihoods to the various hypotheses in such a way that the constraints among the hypotheses and between the hypotheses and the evidence in the world are as well satisfied as is possible.

The project at hand is to develop a framework for describing these situations and the factors that control the cognitive properties of these socially distributed systems. What is needed is an abstraction that is pertinent to the phenomena and that captures the similarities among a number of classes of distributed interpretation formation in spite of the diversity of details out of which they are composed. The desired account should explicitly address the issue of the formation of interpretations and the ways in which interpretations can be influenced by evidence from the environment as well as by evidence communicated by other actors in the setting. It should allow us to look at what is going on inside individuals and also what is going on among them. It should allow us to characterize both the properties of individuals and the properties of systems composed of several individuals.

All these goals can be met by a computer simulation. And while a simulation can permit us to explore effects of communication in aworld that is free of unwanted interactions with uncontrolled surrounding events, it has limitations that must be acknowledged in advance. The principal shortcoming of all simulations is that they are, of necessity, extreme simplifications of the phenomena they are intended to model. In the present case, many of the important facts about real communication in human systems are not represented at all. Questions of indexicality of reference and of negotiation of meaning are much too complex to be modeled by simple simulations and thus are not represented in the simulation presented here. In spite of these limitations, I believe that the simulation model does make clear a number of issues that might otherwise be obscured.

Constraint-Satisfaction Networks

A particular kind of connectionist network called a *constraint-satisfaction network* provides a rough model of individual interpretation formation. Rumelhart et al. (1986) define a constraint-satisfaction network as follows:

a network in which each unit represents a hypothesis of some sort (e.g., that a certain semantic feature, visual feature, or acoustic feature is present in the input) and in which each connection represents constraints among the hypotheses. Thus, for example, if feature B is expected to be present whenever feature A is, there should be a positive connection from the unit corresponding to the hypothesis that A is present to the unit representing the hypothesis that B is present. Similarly, if there is a constraint that whenever A is present B is expected not *to be present, there should be a negative connection from A to B. If the constraints are weak, the weights should be small. If the constraints are strong, the then the weights should be large. Similarly, the inputs to such a network can also be thought of as constraints. A positive input to a particular unit means that there is evidence from the outside that the relevant*

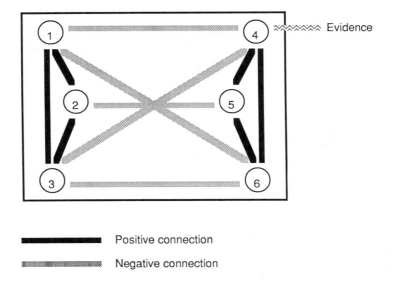

Positive connection

Negative connection

Figure 5.1   A simple constraint-satisfaction network composed of six units. Each unit represents a hypothesis, and the connections among units represent supportive or competitive relations among the hypotheses represented by the units. In this network, units 1, 2, and 3 support one another and units 4, 5, and 6 support one another. The units in each of these clusters inhibit the units in the other cluster. The network has two coherent interpretations: one in which units 1-3 are active while units 4-6 are inactive and one in which units 4-6 are active and units 1-3 are inactive. This figure does not show the pattern of activation across the units. Evidence in the environment that supports a particular hypothesis is implemented as the addition of activation to the unit that represents that hypothesis. This network receives evidence that supports the hypothesis represented by unit 4.

feature is present. A negative input means that there is evidence from the outside that the feature is not present.

With each unit adjusting its activation (likelihood of being true) on the basis of the activations of its neighbors and the strengths of the connections to those neighbors, such a network will eventually settle into a state in which as many of the constraints as is possible will be satisfied.

Imagine a network in which there are two clusters of units (figure 5.1). Among the units within each cluster there are positive connections. Thus, each cluster of units represents a set of hypotheses that are consistent with one another. All the connections that go from a unit in one cluster to a unit in the other cluster are negative. This means that the hypotheses represented by the units of one cluster are inconsistent with the hypotheses represented by the units of the other cluster. When such a network tries to satisfy as many constraints as it can among the hypotheses, it will end up with all the units in one cluster highly active and all the units in the other cluster inactive. That is, it will arrive at an interpretation in which one set of hypotheses is considered true and the other is considered false. Once it has arrived at such a state, the network will be very insensitive to evidence that contradicts the interpretation already formed. Notice that there are two kinds of patterns here: the pattern of interconnections among the units and the pattern of activation across the units. An interpretation of an event is a particular pattern of activation across the units—for example, the state in which all the units in the left cluster are active and all the units in the right cluster are inactive. The stable interpretations of the network are determined by the pattern of interconnectivity of the units. In this case the connection strengths have been carefully arranged so that there will be just two stable interpretations.

In the collision scenario presented above, the captain and the mate share the schema for interpreting the motion of other ships on the water. Because of the conventions for lighting ships at night, seeing two lights supports the hypothesis that one is viewing the stern of the other ship whereas seeing three supports the hypothesis that one is meeting it head on. If it is an overtaking situation, a rapid closing of the distance to the other ship supports the hypothesis that it is going slowly. The mate would doubtless endorse these constraints among hypotheses. But he reached a different interpretation because he "saw" different evidence than the captain saw. In the model, sharing the schema is sharing the pattern of connections among the units. Sharing the interpretation is having the same pattern of activation across the units.

For the individual whose constraint-satisfaction network is represented in figure 5.1, an interpretation is a pattern of activation across the six units of the network. The space of possible interpretations for this network is thus a six-dimensional space. The locations of the two good interpretations in this space are known to be {111000} (left cluster active, right cluster not) and {000111} (right cluster active, left cluster not). Unfortunately, it is very difficult to think about events in six dimensions. Fortunately, this six-dimensional space can be mapped into two-dimensional space. Since it is possible to compute the Euclidean distance of any pattern of activation from the patterns of activation of the two good interpretations, it is possible to build a new, two-dimensional space in which the two dimensions are distance from interpretation 1 and distance from interpretation 2. Thus, the location of any pattern of activation can be plotted in this interpretation space in terms of its

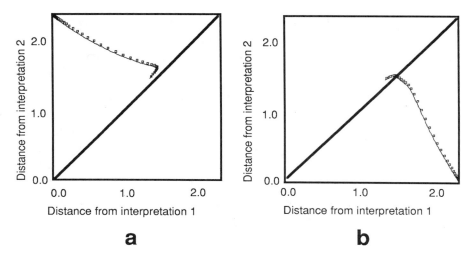

Figure 5.2   The trajectories of a single network in interpretation space. Here the interpretation space is plotted in two dimensions. The *x* axis shows the distance of the current interpretation from interpretation 1: The *y* axis indicates the distance of the current interpretation from interpretation 2. Thus, for example, the lower right corner is as close to interpretation 2 as is possible and as far from interpretation 1 as is possible. It therefore represents the location of interpretation 2. The diagonal line is everywhere equidistant between the two interpretations. The track of the network is shown in time. Its position is plotted at equal time intervals, so the distances between the plotted positions is proportional to the speed at which the network's interpretation is changing. The network shown in panel a began slightly nearer to interpretation 1 than to interpretation 2. It began moving slowly at first away from both interpretations, then it turned toward interpretation 1 and picked up speed. Finally, it made a slow approach to interpretation 1. The same network is shown in panel b, but this time it has evidence from the environment in favor of interpretation 2. Even though it began slightly predisposed to interpretation 1, it was swayed by the evidence from the environment and went to interpretation 2.

nearness to the two good interpretations. For example, the pattern of activation {0.5 0.5 0.5 0.5 0.5 0.5} in which every unit is neither active nor inactive, is equally distant from the two good interpretations. The plotting of positions in interpretation space is of no computational consequence; it simply makes the motion of the networks visible. Note also that not all locations in the space are possible and that the fact that two networks are at the same location in the space does not mean that they have the same pattern of activation. Figure 5.2a shows the trajectory in interpretation space of an individual who starts out about halfway between the two interpretations. In this individual all the units have approximately equal levels of activation. This network is not strongly committed to either of the interpretations. When it begins passing activation among its units, it moves toward one interpretation and away from the other.

Constraint networks can also receive input from the environment. This corresponds to direct evidence for one of the hypotheses. Input from the environment is implemented as the addition or subtraction of activation to a single unit (figure 5.1). Thus, if the individual represented in figure 5.2a is taken back to its starting point and given evidence that one of the hypotheses consistent with interpretation 2 is true, it will follow the trajectory shown in figure 5.2b. This simply demonstrates that a network that has not yet formed a strong interpretation can be influenced by evidence from the environment. If, however, the network had already arrived at interpretation 1, evidence for interpretation 2 would have little effect on the individual.

Three variables determine the behavior of the isolated individual. The first is the pattern of interconnectivity of its units. This is the network's schema of the phenomena about which the interpretation is formed. The second is the initial pattern of activation across its units. This consists of the network's preconceptions about the state of affairs in the world, and t can be seen in the trajectories of networks in interpretation space as the point at which a network starts. The third variable consists of the external inputs to particular units of the network; it represents the evidence directly in favor of or against particular hypotheses that are parts of the interpretations. The trajectories shown in figure 5.2 demonstrate the effects of these variables.

COMMUNITIES OF NETWORKS

The behavior of a single constraint-satisfaction network mimics, in a rough way, the phenomenon of confirmation bias as it is observed in individual human actors. Even more complicated versions of these networks could provide more accurate models of confirmation bias. The simple networks presented here are close enough to serve our present purpose, which is to find a simulation that allows us to explore the relationships among properties of individuals and properties of groups. In order to make such an exploration, I have created and examined the behavior of communities of networks. This may not seem to be the most obvious strategy to pursue. Since the processing in connectionist networks is distributed across units in a network, and the processing in a system of socially distributed cognition is distributed across a number of people, there is a strong temptation to adopt a superficial mapping between the two domains in which units in a network are seen as corresponding to individuals and the connections among units are seen to correspond to the communication links among individuals. In this way, a single network would be taken as a model of a community. There are many problems with this mapping. Let me simply issue the warning that this most obvious mapping is quite likely a dead end, and suggest instead that the real value of connectionism for understanding the social distribution of cognition will come from a more complicated analogy in which individuals are modeled by whole networks or assemblies of networks, and in which systems of socially distributed cognition are modeled by communities of networks. The latter approach is the one taken here.

PARAMETERS OF THE MODELS

What happens in a system in which there are two or more constraint-satisfaction networks, each trying to form an interpretation? A system composed of two or more networks has at least seven parameters that are not present in a single network. Three of these parameters have to do with the distribution of structure and state across the individual members of a community of networks. The other four concern the communication among the networks in the community. Table 5.1 lists the natures of these parameters and the features of real communities to which, for the purposes of the model, they are intended to correspond.

Table 5.1   The principal parameters of the simulation models and the features of individual and group processing they are intended to represent.

IN THE MODEL	IN A REAL HUMAN SYSTEM
Distributions of properties of individual nets	
Pattern of interconnectivity among units in the net	Schemata for phenomena
External inputs to particular units in the net	Access to environmental evidence
Initial pattern of activation across units in the net	Predispositions, current beliefs
Parameters that characterize communication among nets	
Pattern of interconnections among the nets in the community	Who talks to whom
Pattern of interconnectivity among the units of communicating nets	What they talk about
Strengths of connections between nets that communicate	How persuasive they are
Time course of communication	When they communicate

Distributions of Individual Properties

The pattern of connectivity among the units within a network defines the *schema* for the event to be interpreted. Thus, the first additional consideration is the *distribution of event schemata* across the members of the community. Clearly a system in which all the networks have a consensus about the underlying structure of the domain of interpretation is different from one in which different networks have different patterns of constraint among the hypotheses. As a simplifying assumption, I have assumed that all the networks have the same underlying constraint structure. This is simply an implementation of the ethnographer's fantasy that all the individuals in a culture have the same schemata for the events to be interpreted (Boster 1990). In the ship-collision situation it appears that the Captain and the mate shared the schemata for interpreting the motion of other ships. Both understood that seeing two lights was evidence that one was viewing the stern of the other ship and that seeing three lights indicated that one was meeting it head on. But the mate thought he saw three lights and the captain thought he saw two. Thus, consensus on schemata is not the same thing as consensus about the interpretations of events. Two individuals could have the same schema for some phenomenon and still reach different interpretations of events if their assessment of the evidence led them to instantiate the schemata in different ways.

The networks may receive inputs directly from an environment. The *distribution of access to environmental evidence* is an important structural property of a community of networks. If all networks in the community have the same underlying patterns of constraints among hypotheses and all receive input from the same features of the environment, then all networks in the community will arrive at the same interpretation. If different networks have access to different inputs from the environment, then they may move to very different interpretations of the world. It turns out that in the ship-collision situation the captain had some difficulty with his eyesight.

At any moment, the pattern of activity across the units in a particular network represents the current state of belief of that network. A coherent interpretation is a pattern of activation that satisfies the constraints of the connections among units. When a community of networks is created, it may be created such that different networks have different patterns of activation. Thus, the third parameter concerns the *distribution of predispositions* across the networks in the community. The initial activations in these simulations are always low; that is, the individuals do not start with strong beliefs about the truth of any of the hypotheses.

Communication Parameters

In such a system, at least four additional parameters that describe the the communication between the networks must be considered. For the sake of simplicity I have modeled the communication between networks as external inputs applied directly to the units in each network. (This simplification ignores the fact that communication is always mediated by artifactual structure. In Hutchins 1991 I modeled this explicitly in another community of networks with a different network architecture. If a particular node in one network is, say, highly active, then some fraction of that activity may be applied as an external input to the corresponding node in some other network. Thus, in this model, communication between individual networks is represented by direct communication of the activation levels of units in one network to units in another network (figure 5.3). This is based on the assumption that real communication about belief in a hypothesis from one individual to another should have the effect of making the activation level of the hypothesis in the listener more like the activation level of the hypothesis in the speaker. This is the most problematic simplification in the system.

A fourth parameter describes the *pattern of interconnections among the networks* in the community. This corresponds to the patterns of communication links in a community. Each particular network in the community may communicate with some subset of the other networks in the community.

Each network that communicates with another does so by passing activation from some of its own units to the corresponding units in the other network. The *pattern of interconnectivity among the units of communicating networks* determines which of the units of each network pass activation to their corresponding numbers in the other networks. This corresponds to a determination of what the networks can talk to one another about. It could be thought of as a limitation on vocabulary that permits the networks to exchange information about only some of the hypotheses that participate in the interpretations.

Recall that a network passes only a fraction of the activity of its unit to the corresponding unit in another network. This fraction of

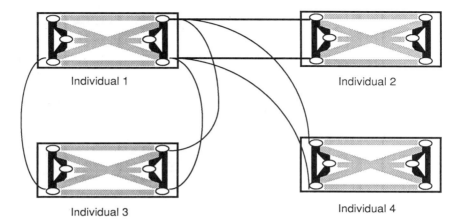

Figure 5.3 Communication among the individual networks. This figure illustrates three of the four communication parameters. In terms of the pattern of interconnections among the networks (who talks to whom), individual 1 talks to all the other individuals: individual 2 talks only with individual 1: individual 3 and individual 4 talk with each other and with individual 1. In terms of the pattern of interconnectivity among the units of communicating nets (what they talk about), individual 1 and individual 2 talk about the most (about hypotheses 2, 4, and 6): individual 3 and individual 4 talk only about hypothesis 4; and individual 2 and individual 4 don't talk about anything. In terms of the strengths of connections between nets that communicate (how persuasive they are), individual 1 and individual 2 find each other's arguments about hypotheses 4 and 6 very persuasive. The last communication parameter, the time course of communication (when they communicate), is not represented in this figure. The combination of parameters shown in this figure is intended only to illustrate the range of possible communicative patterns within a group. Subsequent simulation experiments explore the cognitive consequences of a variety of patterns.

the activity of a unit in one network that is applied as an external input to the corresponding unit in the other network may be called the *persuasiveness* of the source. It determines how important it is for a unit to agree with its corresponding unit in the other network relative to the importance of satisfying the constraints imposed by other units in its own network.

The final community-level parameter is the *time course of communication*. This refers to the temporal pattern of the exchange of external inputs between the networks. This can vary from continual exchange of external inputs to no communication at all. In between these extremes are an infinite number of patterns of connection and disconnection. Again, it would be possible to have a different time course of communication for every connection between the networks, and even to have the persuasiveness of each connection be a function of time; for simplicity, however, this too will be a global parameter, with all connections either on or off at whatever strength they have been assigned at any point in time.

Social Organization and the Cognitive Properties of Groups

With these simulation pieces, an exploration of the relationships among the properties of the individuals and of the group with respect to confirmation bias can be made.

THE COMMONSENSE ARCHITECTURE OF GROUP INTELLIGENCE
It is often assumed that the best way to improve the performance of a group is to improve the communication among the members of the group, or, conversely, that what is lacking in groups is communication. In his 1982 novel *Foundation's Edge*, Isaac Asimov describes a world, Gaia, that is a thinly disguised Earth in the distant future. Whereas James Lovelock's original concept of Gaia referred only to the notion that Earth's entire biosphere could be taken to be a single self-regulating organism, Asimov extended the concept to the cognitive realm. On Asimov's Gaia, every conscious being is in continuous high-bandwidth communication with every other. There is but one mind on Gaia. In Asimov's book it is a very powerful mind, one that can do things that are beyond the capabilities of any individual mind. Is this really an advisable way to organize all that cognitive horsepower? Our simulations provide us with a means to answer this question. They indicate that more communication is not always *in principle* better than less. Under some conditions, increasing the richness of communication may result in undesirable properties at the group level.

Consider a simulation experiment in which only the persuasiveness of the communication among networks is varied. (Recall that this is implemented by changing the strength of the connections between units in one network and corresponding units in other networks.) In the initial community of networks, all the networks have the same underlying constraint structure, and all have the same access to environmental evidence, but each has a slightly different initial pattern of activation than any of the others. Furthermore, all the networks communicate with one another, all the units in each network are connected to all the units in the other networks, and the communication is continuous. This can be regarded as a model of mass mental telepathy. Under these conditions, when the communication connection strength (persuasiveness) is zero, the networks do not communicate at all, and each settles into an interpretation that is determined by its initial predispositions (figure 5.4a). If the community is started again, this time with a nonzero persuasiveness, each individual network

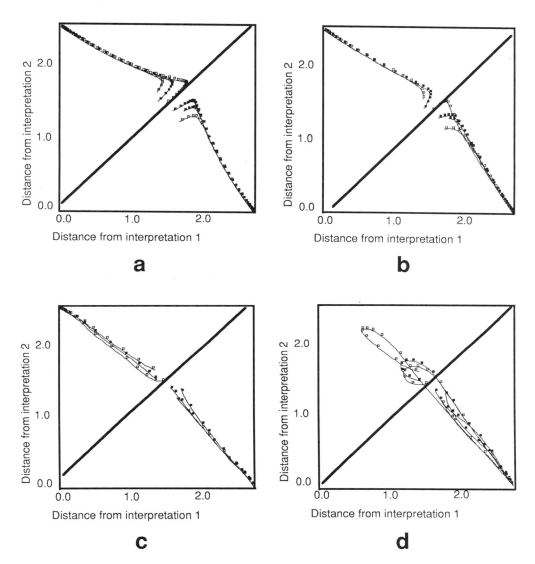

Figure 5.4 The trajectories of six individuals in interpretation space. Each panel in this figure represents the same six individuals starting in the same locations. The persuasiveness of the communication among them is manipulated; all other parameters are held constant. In panel a, the persuasiveness is 0. The individuals are not communicating with one another, and each goes to the interpretation that is nearest its initial position in interpretation space. In panel b, with some communication among the individuals, the individual who started most nearly equidistant from the two interpretations has been influenced by the three individuals who favor interpretation 2 and has followed them to that interpretation. In panel c, at a higher level of communication, the unsure individual has been captured by the two individuals who favor interpretation 1 and has followed them there. In panel d, with the persuasiveness set even higher, those individuals who start nearer to interpretation 1 begin to move toward that interpretation, but as those moving toward interpretation 2 become surer of their own interpretations the persuasive communication with the others draws them also towards interpretation 2. Under conditions of high persuasiveness the system shows a confirmation bias similar to that of the individual.

moves toward the interpretation that it had moved to in the absence of communication, but now it does so more quickly. If the community is restarted again and again, with the persuasiveness increased each time, the velocity of the networks in conceptual space increases even more. They hurry in groups to the available interpretations (some to one, some to the other), and once there, they respond only a little to additional evidence from the environment. Figure 5.4b illustrates such a state in which one of the networks has changed the interpretation it arrives at as a consequence of the influence of the other networks on it. As the inter-network connection strength is increased even more, the undecided individual is drawn back to its original interpretation (figure 5.4c). With the persuasiveness turned up even more, the networks that started out toward interpretation 1 are drawn back by the emerging consensus, and all of them rush to the same interpretation. Having arrived at that interpretation, they remain there, absolutely unmoved by any amount of evidence from the environment (figure 5.4d). At high levels of persuasiveness, this system thus manifests a much more extreme form of confirmation bias than any individual alone. In retrospect, it is easy to see why. When the level of communication is high enough, a community of such networks that receive similar inputs from the world and that start near one another in the interpretation space behave as one large network. Wherever the networks go in interpretation space, they go hand in hand and stay close together. Because they are in continual communication, there is no opportunity for any of them to form an interpretation that differs much from that of the others. Once in consensus, they stay in consensus even if they have had to change their minds in order to reach consensus. When the strengths of the connections between networks is increased to a point where it far outweighs the strengths of the connections within networks, the networks all move to a shared interpretation that is incoherent. In this condition, the importance of sharing an interpretation with others outweighs the importance of reaching a coherent interpretation.

It is clear that a megamind such as that described by Asimov would be more prone to confirmation bias than any individual mind. It might be a mind that would rush into interpretations and that, once it had lodged in an interpretation, would manifest an absolutely incorrigible confirmation bias. Is it possible for communication to ever be rich enough in a real human community to lead to this sort of group pathology? Perhaps. Even in individual networks, as a coherent interpretation forms, units representing hypotheses that have no direct support in the world receive activation from neighboring units and a whole coherent schema is filled in. This well-known effect in individual cognition seems even more powerful in some group settings. Buckhout (1982) asked groups to produce composite descriptions of a suspect in a crime that all had witnessed and reported that "the group descriptions were more complete than the individual reports but gave rise to significantly more errors of commission: an assortment of incorrect and stereotyped details." This looks like a case in which the members of the group settle into an even more coherent interpretation than they would do acting alone. That is just what happened to the networks in the simulation.

Of course, this extremely tight coupling is very unusual. The next section considers cases where there is some interesting distribution of access to evidence, where the communication connection strengths are moderate, where the pattern of interconnectivity is partial (that is, where the individuals don't talk about everything they know, only about some of the important things), and where the communication is not continuous.

PRODUCING A DIVERSITY OF INTERPRETATIONS

The problem with confirmation bias is that it prevents an organism from exploring a wider range of possible interpretations. Although the first interpretation encountered may well be the best, a search of the interpretation space may reveal another one that better fits the available evidence. How can this search be accomplished? I have already shown that in the absence of communication the interpretations formed by the individual networks—as each exhibits its own confirmation bias—depend on the three parameters that characterize the individual networks: the underlying constraint structure, the access to environmental evidence, and the initial pattern of activation. If a community is composed of individuals that differ from one another in terms of any of these parameters, then various members of the community are likely to arrive at different interpretations. Thus, diversity of interpretations is fairly easy to produce as long as the communication among the members of the community is not too rich.

Organizational Solutions to the Problem of Reaching a Decision

Some institutions cannot easily tolerate situations in which the group does not reach a consensus about which interpretation shall be taken as a representation of reality. In some settings it is essential that all members of the group behave as though some things are true and others are false, even if some of the members have reservations about the solution decided upon. The members of an aircraft crew, for example, must coordinate their actions with one another and with a single interpretation of the state of the environment even if some of them doubt the validity of the interpretation on which they are acting. Such institutions may face the problem of guaranteeing that a shared interpretation is adopted in some reasonable amount of time.

HIERARCHY

A common solution to the problem of reaching a decision is to grant to a particular individual the authority to declare the nature of reality. This is especially easy to see in settings where the relevant reality is socially defined—such as the law, where an important state of affairs (guilt or innocence) exists only because some authority (a judge) says it exists. But this solution is also adopted with respect to physical realities where time pressures or other factors require a commitment to a particular interpretation. This second case comes in two versions: one in which the other members of the community may present evidence to the authority, and one in which the authority acts autonomously. Here are two simulation experiments on this theme:

Hierarchy without Communication

Suppose all members of a group attempt to form an interpretation, but one network has the authority to decide the nature of reality for all the members. The cognitive labor of interpreting the situation may be socially distributed in a way that permits an exploration of more alternatives in the interpretation space than would be explored by a single individual with confirmation bias; however, if the alternative interpretations never encounter one another, the wider search might as well have never happened. The decision reached by the group is simply the decision of an individual. One might imagine this as a sort of "king" or "dictator" model, but lack of communication can also bring it about in situations that are not supposed to have this property. The ship collision discussed earlier is an example of a case in which the correct interpretation of a situation arose within a group but somehow never reached the individual who had the authority to decide which model of reality the group must organize its behavior around.

Hierarchy with Communication

This situation is modeled in the simulation by changing the communication pattern so that one of the networks (the one in the position of authority) receives input from all the others, but the others do not receive external inputs from one another. In the simulation under these conditions, the network that is the authority will follow the weight of the evidence presented to it by the other networks (figure 5.5). As the other networks move in interpretation space, the center of gravity of the weight of evidence presented by the other networks also moves. Depending on the persuasiveness with which the other networks communicate with the authority, it may be pulled to one interpretation or another, or even change its mind about which is the better interpretation (figure 5.5c). The authority thus becomes a special kind of cognitive apparatus; one that tracks the center of gravity of the entire community in conceptual space at each point in time. At very high levels of persuasiveness, this authority network may find the evidence for both interpretations compelling and be drawn to a state in which it has high activations for the units representing all the hypotheses in both interpretations (figure 5.5d).

CONSENSUS

Quaker Decision Rule—Unanimity or Nothing

Imagine a world in which each network can attend to only one aspect of the environment at a time, but all networks communicate with one another about the interpretations they form on the basis of what they are attending to. Suppose further that there is more information in the environment consistent with one interpretation (call it the *best interpretation*) than with another. Then, any single individual acting alone will reach the best interpretation only when it happens to be attending to some aspect of the environment that is associated with that interpretation or when it happens to be predisposed to that interpretation. If there are many networks and the aspect of the environment each attends to is chosen at random, then on average more of them will be attending to evidence supporting the best interpretation than to evidence supporting any other interpretation, since by definition the best interpretation is the one for which there is most support. If the networks in such a group are in high-bandwidth communication with one another from the outset, they will behave as the Gaia system did, rushing as a group to the interpretation that is closest to the center of gravity of

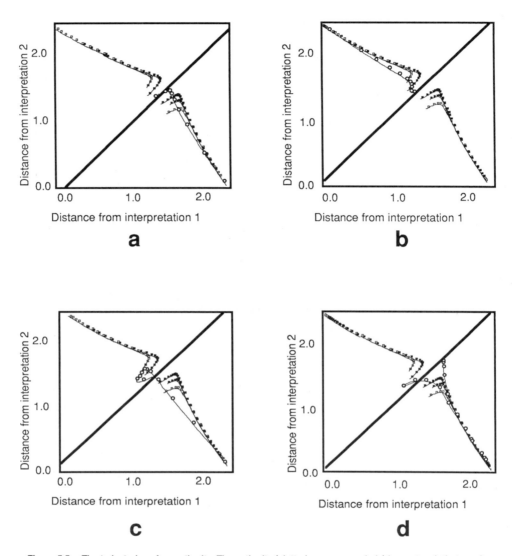

Figure 5.5 The trajectories of an authority. The authority (plotted as an open circle) is a network that receives input from the other networks. The other networks do not communicate among themselves. The authority follows the center of gravity of the interpretations of the group. In panel a, with low persuasiveness by subordinates, it follows the three who go to interpretation 2. With more persuasiveness, as in panel b, it follows the two who move more quickly toward interpretation 1. With still more persuasiveness, it starts toward interpretation 1 but is eventually drawn to interpretation 2. Panel d shows what happens with very high values of persuasiveness. The authority is drawn first to interpretation 2. But the two networks that have arrived at interpretation 1 make it impossible to ignore the elements of that interpretation and the authority is driven to a state in which there is high activation for the units representing all of the hypotheses of both interpretations.

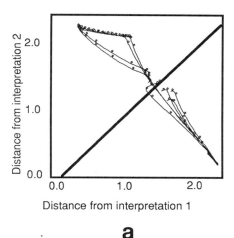
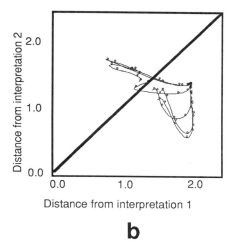

a　　　　　　　　**b**

Figure 5.6　Generation of diversity followed by consensus. In this simulation, the networks start out not communicating. As time goes on, the persuasiveness with which they communicate increases rapidly. Panel a shows some individuals nearly reaching interpretation 1 before being compelled by the others to move to interpretation 2. A diversity of opinion is resolved into a consensus. In panel b, the networks again begin exploring the interpretation space, this time with a more rapid rate of increase in persuasiveness of communication. The networks achieve a consensus, but the interpretation on which consensus is reached does not fit either of the coherent interpretations.

their predispositions regardless of the evidence. If, however, they are allowed to go their own ways for a while, attending to both the available evidence and their predispositions, and then to communicate with one another, they will first sample the information in the environment and then go (as a group) to the interpretation that is best supported. Figure 5.6a shows the group exploring the space first (two networks almost reach interpretation 1) and then, with increasing persuasiveness of communication, reaching consensus on interpretation 2. Not only is the behavior of each individual different in the group setting than it would have been in isolation; the behavior of the group as a whole is different from that of any individual, because the group, as a cognitive system, has considered many kinds of evidence while each individual considered only one.

The simulations indicate two shortcomings of this mode of resolving the diversity of interpretations. First, if some individuals arrive at very well-formed interpretations that are in conflict with one another before communication begins, there may be no resolution at all. They may simply stay with the interpretations they have already formed. Sometimes such "hard cases" can be dislodged by changing the distribution of access to evidence in the community by giving stubborn networks direct access to evidence that contradicts their present interpretation. However, this may only drive the network to a state in which it has no coherent interpretation of the situation (figure 5.6b).

Demographics of Conceptual Space: Voting

Another set of methods for establishing an interpretation to be acted upon by a group relies on measuring the demographics of the community in conceptual space. In the initial state the members of the group are sprinkled around in the conceptual space. The starting location of each is defined by the preconceptions it has about the situation. Some may begin closer to one interpretation, some closer to another. As each one tries to satisfy the constraints of its internal schemata and the available external evidence, it moves in conceptual space. This movement is usually toward one of the coherent interpretations defined by the underlying schemata. As was shown above, if the members of the community are in communication with one another, they may influence one another's motion in conceptual space. A mechanism for deciding which interpretation shall be taken as a representation of reality may be based on the locations of the members of the community in conceptual space. If a majority are at or close to a particular interpretation, that interpretation may be selected as the group's decision. This is, of course, a voting scheme.

A majority-rule voting scheme is often taken to be a way of producing the same result that would be produced by continued negotiation, but short-cutting the communication. In these simulations, voting does not always produce the same results that would be achieved by further communication. That this is so can easily be deduced from the fact that the result of a voting procedure for a given state of the community is always the same, whereas a given state of the community may lead in the future to many different outcomes at the group level (depending on the time course and the bandwidth of subsequent communication).

A Fundamental Tradeoff for Organizations

Many real institutions seem to embody one or another of these methods for first generating and then dealing with diversity of interpretation. Obviously, real social institutions come to be organized as they are for many reasons. For example, the political consequences of various schemes for distributing the authority to make interpretations real are important aspects of the actual implementation of any institution. I do not claim that institutions are the way they are because they produce particular kinds of cognitive results. The point is rather that social organization, however it may have been produced, does have cognitive consequences that can be described. By producing the observed structures of organizations—largely ones in which there are explicit mechanisms for resolving diversity of interpretations—social evolution may be telling us that, in some environments, chronic indecision may be much less adaptive than some level of erroneous commitment. This may be the *fundamental* tradeoff in cognitive ecology. The social organization, or more precisely the distribution of power to define situations as real, determines the location of a cognitive system in the tradeoff space. Where the power to define the reality of situations is widely distributed in a "horizontal" structure, there is more potential for diversity of interpretation and more potential for indecision. Where that power is collected in the top of a "vertical" structure, there is less potential for diversity of interpretation, but also more likelihood that some interpretation will find a great deal of confirmation and that disconfirming evidence will be disregarded.

Where there is a need for both exploration of an interpretation space and consensus of interpretation, a system typically has two modes of operation. One mode trades off the ability to reach a decision in favor of diversity of interpretation. The participants in the system proceed in relative isolation and in parallel. Each may be subject to confirmation bias, but because they proceed independently, the system as a whole does not manifest confirmation bias. The second mode breaks the isolation of the participants and exposes the interpretations to disconfirming evidence, the goal being to avoid erroneous perseverence on an interpretation when a better one is available. This mode trades off diversity in favor of the commitment to a single interpretation that will stand as the new reality of the situation. Often the two modes are separated in time and marked by different social structural arrangements.

Summary

In this chapter I have tried to take some tentative steps toward a framework for thinking about cognitive phenomena at the level of groups. The simulation models are both a kind of notation system that forces one to be explicit about the theoretical constructs that are claimed to participate in the production of the phenomena of interest and a dynamical tool for investigating a universe of possibilities. The simulations show that, even while holding the cognitive properties of individuals constant, groups may display quite different cognitive properties, depending on how communication is organized within the group and over time. Groups can be better at generating a diversity of interpretations than any individual is; however, having generated a useful diversity, they then face the problem of resolving it. From the perspective presented here, several well-recognized kinds of social organization appear to provide solutions to the problems of exploring a space of interpretations and discovering the best available alternative.

All the strategies that overcome confirmation bias work by breaking up continuous high-bandwidth communication. This is true whether the strategies are implemented in social organization, in the interaction of an individual with an external artifact, or through the use of an internal mediating structure.

In the simulations presented in this chapter, the effects of group-level cognitive properties are not produced solely by structure internal to the individuals, nor are they produced solely by structure external to the individuals. Rather, the cognitive properties of groups are produced by interaction between structures internal to individuals and structures external to individuals. All human societies face cognitive tasks that are beyond the capabilities of any individual member. Even the simplest culture contains more information than could be learned by any individual in a lifetime (Roberts 1964; D'Andrade 1981), so the tasks of learning, remembering, and transmitting cultural knowledge are inevitably distributed. The performance of cognitive tasks that exceed individual abilities is always shaped by a social organization of distributed cognition. Doing without a social organization of distributed cognition is not an option. The social organization that is actually used may be appropriate to the task or not. It may produce desirable properties or pathologies. It may be well defined and stable, or it may shift moment by moment; but there will be one whenever cognitive labor is distributed, and whatever one there is will play a role in determining the cognitive properties of the system that performs the task.

The primary function of a peacetime military is what is called "the maintenance of readiness." The military establishment is a big institution, full of terrifying weapons systems and other artifacts. The glue that holds the artifacts together—that makes the separate ships and planes and missiles and bombs into something more than a collection of hardware—is human activity. But there are high rates of personnel turnover in the military. The human parts keep passing through the system. Thus, even though the system is ready to make war one day, it will not be ready the next day unless the expertise of the people departing is continually replaced by the newly acquired skills of those who have recently entered. This high turnover of personnel and the resulting need for the continual reproduction of expertise makes the military a fertile ground for research into the nature of learning in cultural context.

The Developmental Trajectory of the Quartermaster

It takes about a year to learn the basics of the quartermaster's job. For a young person learning to be a quartermaster, there are many sources of information about the work to be done. Some quartermasters go to specialized schools before they join a ship. There they are exposed to basic terminology and concepts, but little more. They are "trained" in a sense, but they have no experience. In fact, the two quartermaster chiefs with whom I worked most closely said they preferred to get as trainees able-bodied seamen without any prior training in the rate. They said this saved them the trouble of having to break the trainees of bad habits acquired in school. Most quartermasters learn what to do and how to do it while on the job. Nonetheless, some of a trainee's experience aboard ship is a bit like school, with workbooks and exercises. In order to advance to higher ranks, the novice must work through a set of formal assignments that cover the full spectrum of navigation practice; these must be reviewed and approved by a supervisor before the student can progress to the next rank in the rating.

Sea and Anchor Detail

In the world of navigation, as in many other systems, novices begin by doing the simplest parts of a collaborative-work task. Long before they are ready to stand watch under instruction in Standard Steaming Watch, novice quartermasters begin to work as fathometer operators and pelorus operators in Sea and Anchor Detail. As they become more skilled they move on to more complex duties, making way for less skilled individuals behind them. The procedural decomposition of the task in this work configuration permits unskilled persons to participate in complex activities. The jobs in Sea and Anchor Detail are, in order of increasing complexity, the following:

- monitoring the fathometer
- taking bearings
- keeping the deck log
- timing and recording bearings
- plotting fixes and projecting the dead reckoned track.

This list of jobs defines a career trajectory for individuals through the roles of the work group. Interestingly, it also follows the path of information through the system in the team's most basic computation, position fixing. The simplest jobs involve gathering sensed data, and the more complex jobs involve processing those data. The fact that the quartermasters follow the same trajectory through the system as does sensed information, albeit on a different time scale, has an important consequence for the larger system's ability to detect, diagnose, and correct error. To see why this is so, however, we need to consider the distribution of knowledge that results from this pattern of development of quartermasters.

System Properties

The Distribution of Knowledge

Analysts often assume that in cooperative tasks knowledge is partitioned among individuals in an exhaustive and mutually exclusive manner such that the sum of the individuals' knowledge is equal to the total required, with little or no overlap. Consider the knowledge required to perform just the input portion of the basic fix cycle. This requires the knowledge of the pelorus operators, the

Figure 6.1 A nonoverlapping distribution of knowledge among the members of the navigation team.

bearing recorder, and the plotter. We could imagine designing an experiment along these lines by training a different person to perform each of these roles and then putting the individuals in interaction with each other. This assumes no history for the participants except that each is trained to do his job. This would result in a nonoverlapping distribution of knowledge, as shown in figure 6.1. It is certainly possible to organize a working system along these lines, but in fact, outside of experimental settings, this is a very rare knowledge-distribution pattern. More commonly there is substantial sharing of knowledge between individuals, with the task knowledge of more expert workers completely subsuming the knowledge of those who are less experienced. At the other end of the knowledge-distribution spectrum, one can imagine a system in which everyone knows everything about the task. This too is a rare pattern, because it is costly to maintain such a system.

In many human systems, as individuals become more skilled they move on to other roles in the task-performance group, making way for less skilled individuals behind them and replacing the more expert individuals before them who advance or leave the system. This is what we observe in the case of the development of navigation skills among quartermasters. A competent pelorus operator knows how to do his job, but because of his interaction with the bearing recorder he also knows something about what the recorder needs to do (figure 6.2a). The bearing recorder knows how to do his job, but he also knows all about being a pelorus operator, because he used to be one. Furthermore, he knows a good deal about the activities of the plotter, because he shares the chart table with the plotter and may have done plotting under instruction in

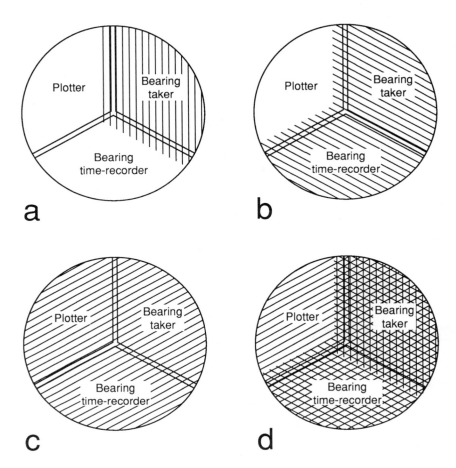

Figure 6.2 Overlapping distributions of knowledge among the members of the navigation team. (a) What the bearing taker knows. (b) What the bearing recorder knows. (c) What the plotter knows. (d) The distribution of redundant coverage in the system as a whole.

Standard Steaming Watch. What the bearing recorder knows is shown in figure 6.2b. Finally, a competent plotter knows how to plot, but he also knows everything the bearing recorder and the pelorus operators must know in order to do their jobs, because he has done both of those jobs before advancing to plotting. What the plotter knows is shown in figure 6.2c, and the distribution of knowledge that is the sum of these individual expertises is shown in figure 6.2d. Thus, this movement of individuals through the system with increasing expertise results in a pattern of overlapping expertise. Knowledge of the entry-level tasks is represented most redundantly, and knowledge of the expert-level tasks is represented least redundantly.

The Decompositions of Tasks

The structure of the distributed task provides many constraints on the learning environment. The way a task is partitioned across a set of task performers has consequences for both the efficiency of task performance and the efficiency of knowledge acquisition. For example, if the decomposition into subtasks cuts lines of high-bandwidth communication (that is, if two processes that need to share information often in order to reach completion are distributed across different task performers), the task performance may suffer from the effects of a bottleneck in interpersonal communication. What parts of the process need to communicate with which other parts and what sorts of structures can be represented in the available communications media are important determinants of optimal task partitioning. In chapter 4 the situation in which inexperienced pelorus operators attempt to find landmarks in the world was presented as a way to explore the computational consequences for the larger system of various means of communication. This chapter considers the implications of this same phenomenon for learning by individual members of the team.

If the pelorus operator already knows how to find the landmark in question, then little information needs to be passed. The name of the landmark may be all that is required. If the pelorus operator is unsure of the location or appearance of the landmark, more information may be required. For example, in the following exchange, the starboard pelorus operator needed additional information to resolve an ambiguity concerning the identity of a landmark. (In this exchange, SW is the starboard wing pelorus operator and S is a qualified watchstander working as bearing recorder. They were communicating via the sound-powered phone circuit.)

SW: The one on the left or the one on the right?

S: The one on the left, OK?

SW: Yeah, I got it.

When the confusion or lack of knowledge is more profound, it is simply impossible to communicate enough information, or the right kind of information, over the phone circuit; someone has to go to the wing to show the pelorus operator where to find the landmark. A little later during the same exit from port, the starboard pelorus operator was unable to find the north end of the 10th Avenue terminal. The plotter C, who is also the most-qualified and highest-ranking member of the team, went onto the wing to point it out to him. On the wing, C put his arm over SW's shoulders and aimed his body in the right direction.

C: The north one, all the way up.

SW: OK.

C: If you can't see the light, just shoot the tangent right on the tit of the, the last end of the pier there.

SW: OK, that pier, where those two . . .

C: Yeah, all the way at the end.

SW: All right.

C: There should be a light out there, but if you can't see the light out there at the end of the pier just shoot the end of the pier.

In this example, verbal and gestural interaction provides the additional identifying information. Furthermore, the instructions include expectations about what will be visible at the time of the next observation and instructions as to what the pelorus operator should do if he is unable to see the light on the pier.

The Horizon of Observation

Lines of communication and limits on observation of the activities of others have consequences for the process of acquiring knowledge, because they determine the portion of the task environment that is available as a learning context to each task performer. The outer boundary of the portion of the task that can be seen or heard by each team member is that person's *horizon of observation*.

OPEN INTERACTIONS

During an early at-sea period, L, the keeper of the deck log, had served as bearing recorder, but his performance in that job was less than satisfactory. That was the job that was next in line for him, though, and he was eager to acquire the skills required to perform it. One of the most important aspects of the bearing recorder's job is knowing when particular landmarks will be visible to the pelorus operators on the wings. One complication of this judgement is the fact that a large convex mirror is mounted outside the windows of the pilothouse just in front of the port wing pelorus operator's station. The mirror is there so that the commanding officer, who sits inside the pilothouse, can see all of the flight deck. Unfortunately, the mirror obstructs the port pelorus operator's view forward, and the bearing recorder must be able to judge from his position at the chart table whether the port wing pelorus operator's view of a chosen landmark will be blocked by the mirror.

L was standing at the chart table with C (the plotter) and S (the bearing recorder). The ship had just entered the mouth of the harbor, and the team was running the fix cycle on 2-minute intervals. The previous fix, taken at 36 minutes after the hour ("time 36"), was complete, and C had just finished plotting the dead-reckoned track out through times 38 and 40. S indirectly solicited C's assistance in deciding which landmarks should be shot for the next round of bearings. L stood by, watching what S and C were doing. All the pointing they did in this interchange was at the chart.

1. S: Last set still good? OK Ballast Point, light Zulu.

2. C: Here's (time) 3 8 (pointing to the DR position on the chart).

3. S: So it would be that (pointing to light Zulu), that (pointing to Bravo Pier) . . .

4. C: One, two, three. Same three. Ballast Point, Bravo. And the next one . . .

5. S: (Time) 4 0 should be, Ballast Point . . .

6. C: Front Range, Bravo.

7. S: And Balla . . .

8. L: He may not be able to see Front Range.

9. S: Yeah.

10. C: Yeah, he can. Once we get up here (pointing to the ship's projected position for the next fix).

11. S: Yeah. Up there. OK.

12. C: Down here (pointing to ships current position) he can't. It's back of the mirror, but as you come in it gets enough so that you can see it.

Because the actions of S and C are within L's horizon of observation, L has a chance to see how the landmarks are chosen. Furthermore, the fact that the decision about which landmarks to shoot is made in an interaction opens the process to him in a way that would not be the case if a single person were making the decision alone. In utterance 8, L raises the possibility that the port wing pelorus operator may not be able to see the landmark. Three days earlier, on another Sea and Anchor Detail, L had made the same suggestion about the mirror blocking the port wing pelorus operator's view and C had agreed with him. In the present circumstances, however, L's caveat is inappropriate. S and C have already anticipated the problem raised by L, and they jointly counter L's objection, each building on what the other has said. Clearly, if L did not share the work space with S and C or if there was a strict division of labor such that individuals did not monitor and participate in the actions of their fellows, this opportunity for L to have even peripheral involvement in a task that will someday be his would be lost. Furthermore, L's horizon of observation is extended because the decision making about landmarks is conducted as an interaction between S and C.

OPEN TOOLS

Simply being in the presence of others who are working does not always provide a context for learning from their actions. In the example above, the fact that the work was done in an interaction between the plotter and the bearing recorder opened it to other members of the team. In a similar way, the design of tools can affect their suitability for joint use or for demonstration and may thereby constrain the possibilities for knowledge acquisition. The interaction of a task performer with a tool may or may not be open to others, depending upon the nature of the tool itself. The design of a tool may change the horizon of observation of those in the vicinity of the tool. For example, because the navigation chart is an explicit graphical depiction of position and motion, it is easy to "see" certain aspects of solutions. The chart representation presents the relevant information in a form such that much of the work can be done on the basis of perceptual inferences. Because the work done with a chart is performed on its surface—all of the work is at the device's interface, as it were—watching someone work with a chart is much more revealing of what is done to perform the task than watching someone work with a calculator or a computer.

The openness of a tool can also affect its use as an instrument of instruction. When the bearing recorder chooses a set of landmarks that result in lines of position with shallow intersections, it is easy to show him, on the chart, the consequences of his actions and the nature of the remedy required. Figure 6.3 shows a fix that resulted from landmark assignments made by the bearing recorder. Bearings off to the side of the ship rather than ahead or astern are called "beam" bearings. When the plotter plotted this fix and saw how it came out, he scolded the bearing recorder:

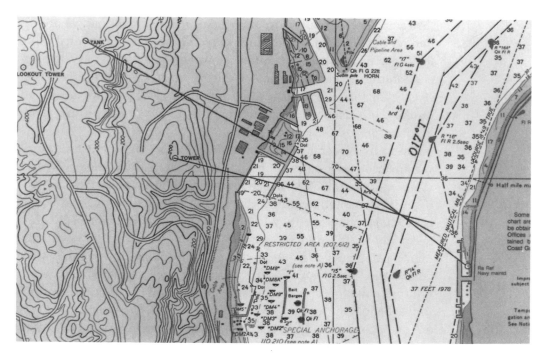

Figure 6.3 A fix constructed with beam bearings. Because of the open graphical properties of the chart as a shared workspace, it is easy for the plotter to show the bearing recorder both that the fix includes beam bearings and why the beam bearings make a poor fix.

C: What did you take a bunch of beam bearings for? Why ain't you shooting up there (points out the front window of the bridge) someplace? Look what you did! (points to the chart) You shot three beam bearings. You shot three beam bearings. You better tell 'em to shoot from up ahead someplace.

Once the fix was plotted, of course, it was easy for the bearing recorder to see the nature of his error. Imagine how much more difficult it would be to explain the inadequacy of the landmark assignment if the lines of position were represented as equations to be punched into a calculator rather than as lines drawn on the chart.

Learning from Error

Most studies of error focus on its reduction or elimination. Clearly, there are many steps that can be taken to avoid or prevent error. Yet error is inevitable in human systems. This is commonly attributed to the fact that we humans can become tired, or confused, or distracted, or inattentive to our work, or to the idea that we are inherently fallible in some other way. These are real contributing factors in many errors, of course. However, in the case of systems of cooperative work in the real world there is a more fundamental reason for the inevitability of error: Such systems always rely on on-the-job learning, and where there is the need for learning there is room for error.

Naturally situated systems of cooperative work must produce whatever it is they produce and must reproduce themselves at the same time. They change over time. Sometimes they are reorganized. Sometimes they change the things they do, and sometimes the technology they have to do the job with changes. Even if tasks and tools could be somehow frozen, the mortality of the human participants guarantees changes in personnel over time. Most commonly, relatively expert personnel are gradually lost while relatively inexpert personnel are added. Even if the skills required to do the job are learned off the job, in school, the interactions that are characteristic of cooperative work can generally only be learned on the job.

Designing for Error

Norman (1983, 1986, 1987) argues that because error is inevitable it is important to "design for error." Designers, he says, can "inadvertently ... make it easy to err and difficult or impossible to discover error or to recover from it" (1987, chapter 5: 24). Norman suggests that designers should design to minimize the causes of error, make it possible to "undo" errors, and make it easier to discover and correct errors. Each of these suggestions is aimed at protecting the current task performance, yet in the broader perspective of production and reproduction in cooperative work it would be useful if the response to error in the current task could also in some way protect future task performance. That is, another aspect of designing for error might be designing systems that can more easily learn from their errors.

That would give us three major classes of design goals with respect to errors: to eliminate, avoid, or prevent errors wherever possible; to facilitate the recovery of the system from any errors that do occur; and to facilitate learning from any errors that do occur so that future errors become less likely. There is something of an equilibrium to be maintained here. As career trajectories take experienced members out of the work group and expertise is lost from the system, the likelihood of error may increase. This increase in likelihood of error must be offset by the decrease in likelihood of error that comes from learning by the remaining and new members of the cooperative work group.

Controlling the Effects of Error

ERROR DETECTION

Error detection may require extensive resources. Observations of the conditions under which errors are detected indicate that the following elements are necessary:

Access   In order to detect an error, the detector must have access to the behavior that is in error or some indication of it.

Knowledge or expectation   The detector must have knowledge of the process being performed or some expectation about its correct outcome with respect to which the observed process or outcome can be judged to be in error.

Attention   Whoever detects the error must attend to the error and monitor it in terms of expectation.

Perspective   Some perspectives are better than others at bringing interested attention relevant expectations to bear on the evaluation of behavior.

Access

The structure of the task and the extent to which the behaviors of the participants are available to the other participants have consequences for error detection. In the following example, the team had shot Front Range, Silvergate, and Light 2 on the previous round. S began to make a shift that would drop Front Range on the port side and pick up North Island tower on the starboard side. After instructing PW to drop Front Range, he then discovered that SW couldn't yet see North Island tower. Only a request for clarification from another sailor making a redundant plot in the combat information center (CIC) made it clear that S had decided not to shift landmarks at all and that PW had misunderstood the situation.

S: (to PW) OK, shift to Silvergate, John.

PW: Drop Front Range.

S: Drop Front Range. (to SW) Steve, pick up (3 seconds) ah, just stick with number 2.

PW: All right.

CIC: (to S) OK, John, you're gonna shoot Light 2, Silvergate, and the Front Range, right?

S: Yeah, Light 2, Silvergate and Front Range.

CIC: OK.

PW: I thought we dropped Front Range.

S: No, picked that up because he couldn't see the tower on this side here (starboard).

PW: The Front Range and Silvergate, right?

S: Yeah.

The point of this example is that the density of error correction possible depends on the horizons of observation of the team members. Here PW is on the phone circuit with CIC and S. In this case, this problem would surely not have been detected had the communication between S and CIC not been available to PW.

Knowledge

The importance of the distribution of knowledge produced by the overlapping careers of a set of quartermasters following a career trajectory that coincides with the flow of sensed information can now be stated: As a consequence of the alignment of one's career trajectory with the path of information through the system, if one has access to an error, then one also has knowledge of the processes that may have generated it, because one has already, at an earlier career stage, performed all the operations to which the data have been subjected before arriving at one's current position. The overlap of access and knowledge that results from the alignment of career path and data path is not a necessary feature of these systems, nor is it apparently an intentional one here, but it does give rise to especially favorable conditions for the detection and diagnosis of error.

Attention

The attention required to detect error may be facilitated or even forced by the nature of coordinated tasks. If errors in the upward propagation of sensed data are not caught at the lower levels, they are likely to be noticed at the chart table by the plotter—in part because the plotting procedure itself is designed to detect error. Any two lines of position define the location of the ship, but a position "fix" always consists of three lines of position. The value of the third line of position in the fix is that, if an error is present, it is likely to show up as an enlarged fix triangle, which will be detected by the plotter. It is, of course, possible for independent errors to conspire to produce a nice tight fix triangle that is actually in the wrong place, but such an event is quite unlikely. The nature of the plotter's task makes errors in the bearings evident.

Many errors are detected by team members who are simply monitoring the actions of those around them. Competition may develop among peers doing similar tasks. Feedback can be provided in attempts to show competence, as in the following example, where PW faults SW's reporting sequence.

S: Stand by to mark time 1 4.

F: Fifteen fathoms.

SW: Dive tower 0 3 4.

PW: He didn't say "mark."

S: Mark it. (2 seconds) I've got the dive tower, Steve, go ahead.

PW: Point Loma 3 3 9.

Here SW was supposed to wait for the "mark" signal, but he blurted out the bearing of Dive Tower when he heard the "stand by to mark" signal. PW jumped on him. S then gave the "mark" signal and waited for reports, but the earlier confusion seemed to have disrupted the coordination of the reports, and no one said anything for 2 seconds. The work of getting bearings must continue uninterrupted. Stopping to repair the situation would ruin the fix because the near simultaneity of the observations would be violated. S minimized the damage by acknowledging the early report on Dive Tower and asking PW to report.

Not only is each member of the team responsible for his own job; each seems also to take responsibility for all parts of the process to which he can contribute. Since detection depends on access, however, the extent to which the activities of the team members are conducted where they can be observed (or overheard) by others may affect the rate of error detection. Error detection also requires attention, which may be a scarce resource. The consequences of a high workload may include both an increase in the rate of error itself (due to the effects of stress) and a reduction in the rate of error detection (due to the reduction of resources available for monitoring the actions of others).

Perspective

The way the plotter thinks about the bearings and uses them in his task is different from the way the bearing observers think about the bearings. For the bearing observer, the bearing may be no more than a string of three digits read from a scale in a telescopic sight. It is not necessary for the bearing observer to think of the directional meaning of the number. In contrast, the plotter's job is to recover the directional meaning of the reported bearing and combine the meanings of three bearings to fix the position of the ship. Different jobs in the team require attention to different aspects of the computational objects, so different kinds of errors are likely to be detected (or missed) by different members of the team.

On some ships the job of making a global assessment of the quality of the work of the navigation team is institutionalized in the role of the *evaluator*. This evaluator is a qualified navigation practitioner who is not engaged in doing the navigation computations themselves, but instead monitors the process by which the computation is performed and the quality of the product. There is a tradeoff here between using the evaluator's processing power to do the computations themselves (and possibly achieving lower error rates but certainly risking lower error-detection rates) and having less processing power in the task itself (and possibly generating more errors but certainly detecting more of the errors that are committed).

The important structural property of the evaluator's role is that the evaluator has access to and knowledge of the performance of the task but does not participate in the performance. Instead, the evaluator *attends* to the way the task is done and specifically monitors the performance for error. The social role of the evaluator is a way of building into the system attention to an aspect of the system's behavior that would not otherwise be reliably present.

RECOVERY FROM ERROR

Not every recovery from error is instructional in intent or in consequence. Some are simply what is required to get the job done. There may be no need to diagnose the cause of the error in order to know how to recover from it.

Other error-recovery strategies involve diagnosis of the source of the error and perhaps explicit demonstration of the correct solution, where the demonstration may also be the performance that is required. Diagnosis may require modeling the reasoning of the person who committed the error. The distribution of knowledge in which access to an error and knowledge of its causes are aligned ensures that most errors that are detected will be detected by individuals who already have experience with the operations that led to the error. This gives each task performer a much better basis for diagnosing the possible causes of any observed errors than he would have in a system with discrete knowledge representation. When a bad bearing is reported, the plotter can examine it and may develop hypotheses about, for example, whether the pelorus operator misread the gyrocompass scale or whether the bearing recorder mistranscribed it into the bearing log. These hypotheses are based on the plotter's experience in each of these roles.

Furthermore, the time, the processing resources, and the communication channels required for the composition and delivery of appropriate instruction must be available to the person providing correction at or near the time that the error is committed. In navigation teams, error feedback is sometimes reduced to a contentless complaint or an exhortation to do better. Such limited feedback may be of little use to the person who has committed the error, but it may be all that the error detector can do under the circumstances of the task.

LEARNING FROM ERROR
A system can learn from its errors in many ways.

Learning by Detecting and Correcting
As a consequence of having engaged in the activities of detecting and/or diagnosing the cause of an error, the person doing the detecting may come to a new insight about the nature of the operation of the system. This is true whether the error was committed by that person or by someone else. It may be particularly important for novices who detect the errors of others. Getting confirmation of a detection could also be important. Furthermore, every instance of correction presents an opportunity to develop error-detection skills which may save the system from the consequences of a future error.

Learning from the Correction of One's Own Mistakes
This is the most obvious case, the one that comes first to mind when one asks how response to error could improve future performance. Even feedback that lacks instructional content can contribute to refinement of understanding of the task requirements that may not be apparent from correct performance alone. Such

corrections may help the learner induce the principles that define correct performance. This can be especially important with concepts that must be inferred from cases rather than explicitly stated. Where there is a solution space to be explored, errors are a form of exploration of that space, and the response to an error can guide the discovery of the concept underlying the solution.

Contentful corrections can help a novice learn recovery strategies that can be applied even when errors are self-detected. For example, S and L were plotting together in Standard Steaming Watch. Just after plotting a fix at 0745, L spanned the distance ($7\frac{1}{2}$ miles) that the ship would cover in the coming 30 minutes and plotted the dead-reckoning fix. However, he incorrectly labeled the fix 0800 rather than 0815. S noticed the error, and he and L constructed the correction interactively. This is a nice example of monitoring, error detection, and correction in a jointly performed task:

S: Isn't that (pointing to the distance along the track) half an hour?

J: No, it's (the time interval) 15 minutes.

S: Sure, 0745 to 0800 is 15 minutes, but we don't go that far (distance along track).

J: Huh?

S: This (time label of DR point) must be 0815. Otherwise we are going 30 knots.

Learning from the Correction of the Mistakes of Others
When an error is detected and corrected in the context of collaborative work, many participants may witness and benefit from the response. Depending again on who has access to what aspects of the behavior of others, an error and its correction may provide a learning context for many of the participants. For example, a fathometer operator who has not yet worked as a pelorus operator can learn a good deal about the task by sharing the phone circuit with the pelorus operators and witnessing their mistakes and the corrections to them. In a system populated by novices and experts, many errors are likely to occur; but since there are many sources of error correction, most errors are likely to be detected. Witnessing such a correction may be of value to those who are already competent in the task in which the error occurred, if they will subsequently be in a position to detect and correct such errors. They can learn about how to provide useful feedback by watching the corrections of others. This could lead to an improvement of sub-

sequent learning for others in the system. Thus, the value of a response to error for future performances may depend on the horizons of observation of the various members of the team. This observation leads to the somewhat paradoxical conclusion that some nonzero amount of error may actually be functional on the whole. A low level of error that is almost certain to be detected will not, in ordinary circumstances, harm performance, yet every error-correction event is a learning context not just for the person who commits the error but for all who witness it.

Tradeoffs in Error Management

Widening the horizon of observation may lead to more error detection, but it may also cause distractions that lead to the commission of more errors. At present I know of no way to quantify these tradeoffs, but recognizing their nature is surely a useful first step.

The costs of error include the undesirable effects of undetected errors in the performance of the current task. Even when errors are intercepted, there are costs of detecting and recovering from error. Under some conditions, these costs can be offset to some extent by benefits derived from the process of detecting, diagnosing, and correcting errors. Achieving these benefits is not automatic. There are ways to organize systems that are more and less likely than others to detect errors, to recover from them adequately, and to learn from them.

The Social Formation of Competence in Navigation

Standard Steaming Watch

As was described in chapter 1, when the ship is far from land, where the requirements of navigation are relatively light and the time pressures are relaxed, navigation is conducted in a configuration called Standard Steaming Watch. In this condition, a novice may stand watch "under instruction" with someone who is qualified to stand watch alone. Depending on his level of experience, the novice may be asked to perform all the duties of the quartermaster of the watch. While he is under instruction, his activities are closely monitored by the more experienced watchstander, who is always on hand and who can help out or take over if the novice is unable to satisfy the ship's navigation requirements. However, even with the help of a more experienced colleague, standing watch under instruction requires a significant amount of knowledge, so novices do not do this until they have several month's experience.

The task for the novice is to learn to organize his behavior so that it produces a competent performance. In chapter 4 and the earlier parts of this chapter, I tried to show how a novice who lacks specific knowledge can contribute to a competent performance if the missing knowledge is provided by other members of the Sea and Anchor Detail. This makes learning a doubly cultural process. It is cultural first and foremost because what is learned is a set of culturally prescribed behaviors, but it is also cultural to the extent that the participants in the system have expectations about who needs what kinds of help in learning the job. The scaffolding provided to the novice by the other members of the team is constructed on cultural understandings about what is hard and what is easy to learn. In this sense, what individuals don't do for one another may be as revealing as what they do.

In the following example, a novice quartermaster, Seaman D, was standing watch under instruction by C. The tasks were to fill out routine position-report and compass-report forms. The position report requires the current latitude and longitude of the ship. D was unsure how to proceed, so C asked him to measure the latitude and longitude of the ship's current position on the chart and dictate the values to C, who then recorded them on the position-report sheet. Here, the labeled blank spaces on the printed form provided some of the structure of the task. Filling the blanks in order, from the top to the bottom of the form, provided a sequence for the elements of the task. That sequential structure was presented explicitly to D by C, who assigned the subtasks.

In this case, the functional unit of analysis is defined by the requirements of the computation involved in getting the numbers into the position-report form. The functional system that accomplishes this task transcends the boundaries of the individual participants in the task. Mediating structure is required to organize the sequence of actions that will produce the desired (culturally specified) results. The questions are: Where does the mediating structure reside? How does it get into coordination with other bits of structure to produce the observed actions?

The chief uses the organization of the form as a resource in organizing his behavior. He employs a simple strategy of taking items in order from top to bottom on the form. The novice coordinates his actions with those of the chief by responding in order to the tasks presented by the chief. The whole ensemble, consisting of the printed form, the chief (with his internal structures—the ability to read, etc.), and the novice (with his own skills—his understanding of English and his knowledge of how to measure latitude and longitude on the chart), is the functional system that accomplishes this element of the culturally defined activity of navigation.

The chief's use of the form is both a way to organize his own behavior and an example to the novice of a way to use such a resource to organize behavior. Given the form, the novice might now be able to reproduce the chief's use of the form to organize his own behavior without the chief's being present. The performance of the task also provides the novice with the experience of the task and the sequence of actions that can accomplish it. We might imagine that, with additional experience, the novice would be able to remember the words of the chief's queries, remember the meanings of the words, and remember physical actions that went into the satisfaction of those queries. In such a case, we would have a different functional system accomplishing the same task in the navigation system. Suppose the written form was not present, but the watchstander wanted to extract the information required by the form and write it on the form later. In such a case the functional system would produce the specified products by using different sorts of mediating structures (several kinds of memory internal to the watchstander). In the next chapter I will describe learning itself in terms of these rearrangements of functional systems with experience.

Later, while working on the compass report, D was again unsure what to do. The task is to make sure the gyrocompass and the magnetic compass are in agreement. This is done by taking simultaneous readings from the two compasses and then applying corrections to the magnetic-compass reading and seeing whether the corrected magnetic heading is the same as the observed gyrocompass heading. The magnetic-compass reading is called the *checking head*, and the corrections to the magnetic compass include a quantity called *deviation*. As C filled in the form, he and D had the following conversation:

C: What's our checking head?

D: 0 9 0 and 0 7 4 (reading the gyrocompass and magnetic compasses at the helm station)

C: What's the table deviation for 0 7 4?

D: One east (reading from the deviation card posted on the binnacle).

In asking D these questions, C was not only getting him to practice the subtasks of reading headings from the compasses and finding the deviation in a table; he was also guiding D through the higher-level task structure. D knew how to do the component tasks, but he didn't know how to organize his actions to get the task done. Some aspect of the organization of action required is present in the labeled blank spaces on the compass report form, but D was, by himself, unable to make use of that structure. C interpreted that structure for D by asking the questions that are implied by the spaces. With C (himself in coordination with the form) providing the task organization, D became part of a competent performance. As D becomes more competent, he will do both the part of this task that he did in this instance and the organizing part that was done in this instance by C. The next time D confronts this task, he may use the structure of the form to organize his actions. When D becomes a fully competent quartermaster, he will not need the form for its organizing properties; he will be able to say what the form requires without consulting it, and will use the form only as a convenient place to compute corrections.

The structure required a the novice to organize his behavior in a competent performance in Standard Steaming Watch is sometimes provided by the supervising watchstander. Similarly, when the quartermasters work as a team in Sea and Anchor Detail, each provides the others, and the others provide each, with constraints on the organization of their activities. A good deal of the structure that a novice will have to acquire in order to stand watch alone in Standard Steaming Watch is present in the organization of the relations among the members of the team in Sea and Anchor Detail. The computational dependencies among the steps of the procedure for the individual watchstander are present as interpersonal dependencies among the members of the team. To the extent that the novice participant comes to understand the work of the team and the ways various members of the team depend on each other, perhaps especially the ways he depends on others and others depend on him, he is learning about the computation itself and the ways its various parts depend on one another. Long before he knows how to choose appropriate landmarks to shoot, the pelorus operator learns that landmarks must be chosen carefully and assigned prior to making observations.

There are at least two important implications of the fact that computational dependencies are social dependencies in this system. First, the novices' understandings of the social relations of the workplace are a partial model of the computational dependencies of the task itself. If it is true that human minds evolved to process social relations, then packaging a task in a social organization may facilitate understanding it. Levinson (1990) argues that this may be related to the commonplace strategy of explaining mechanical and other systems in terms of social relations among anthropomorphized components. Second, the communicative acts of the members of the navigation team are not just about the computation; they *are* the computation. When this is the case, the playing out of computational processes and the playing out of social processes are inextricably intertwined. Social moves have computational as well as social consequences. Computational moves have social as well as computational consequences.

The first of these points is closely related to Lev Vygotsky's notion of the social origins of higher mental functions:

Any higher mental function necessarily goes through an external stage in its development because it is initially a social function. This is the center of the whole problem of internal and external behavior... When we speak of a process, "external" means "social." Any higher mental function was external because it was social at some point before becoming an internal, truly mental function. It was first a social relation between two people. (Vygotsky 1981: 162, quoted in Wertsch 1985)

Vygotsky was, of course, aware that internalized processes were not simple copies of external processes: "it goes without saying that internalization transforms the process itself and changes its structure and functions" (Wertsch 1981: 163). For the sake of clear explication, no doubt, and perhaps because the primary concern has been with the development of young children, many of the examples provided in the literature of activity theory present cases in which the structure of the external activity is evident and the required transformations are fairly simple. What happens if we consider adults learning more complicated thinking strategies in more complex social settings where the primary goal of the activity is successful task performance rather than education?

If social processes are to be internalized, then the kinds of transformations that internalization must make will be in part determined by the differences between the information-processing properties of individual minds and those of systems of socially distributed cognition. Let us consider two such differences that were raised in chapter 4 in the discussion of the navigation activity in its individual and socially distributed forms.

First, socially distributed cognition can have a degree of parallelism of activity that is not possible in individuals. While current research tells us that much of individual cognition is carried out by the parallel activity of many parts of the brain, still, at the scale of more molar activities, individuals have difficulty simultaneously performing more than one complex task or maintaining more than one rich hypothesis. These are things that are easily done in socially distributed cognitive systems. Ultimately, no matter how much parallelism there may be within a mind, there is the potential for more in a system composed of many minds.

Second, communication among individuals in a socially distributed system is always conducted in terms of a set of mediating artifacts (linguistic or other), and this places severe limits on the bandwidth of communication among parts of the socially distributed system. Systems composed of interacting individuals have a pattern of connectivity that is characterized by dense interconnection within minds and sparser interconnection between them. A cognitive process that is distributed across a network of people has to deal with the limitations on the communication between people.

Because society has a different architecture and different communication properties than the individual mind, it is possible that there are interpsychological functions that can never be internalized by any individual. The distribution of knowledge described above is a property of the navigation team, and there are processes that are enabled by that distribution that can never be internalized by a single individual. The interpsychological level has properties of its own, some of which may not be the properties of any of the individuals who make it up. This, of course, is no challenge to Vygotsky's position. He didn't say that every interpsychological process would be internalized, only that all the higher mental functions that did appear would get there by being internalizations of social processes.

That leads one to wonder whether there might be intrapsychological processes that could not be transformations of processes that occurred in social interaction. Finding such a process would be a challenge to Vygotsky's position, but unless there are constraints on the possible transformations there is no way to identify such a process.

Clearly there are higher mental processes that could never have been realized in their current form as interpsychological processes simply because they exploit the rich communication possible within a mind in a way that is not possible between minds. Here is an example we have already encountered: The task of reconciling a map to a surrounding territory has as subparts the parsing of two rich visual scenes (the chart and the world) and then the establishing of a set of correspondences between them on the basis of a complicated set of conventions for the depiction of geographic and cultural features on maps. As performed by an individual, it requires very high bandwidth communication among the representations of the two visual scenes. Very occasionally, this task appears as a socially distributed task when a pelorus operator has no idea how to find a particular landmark. In that case, the restricted bandwidth of communication between the pelorus operator (who can see the world) and the bearing recorder (who can see the chart) makes the task virtually impossible. The spatial relations implied by the locations of symbols on the chart are simply too rich to be communicated verbally in such a way that the pelorus operator can discover the correspondences between those verbally expressed relations and the relations among the objects he can see in the world.

Of course, it may be that the real difficulty here is with the volume of information to be processed, and that the actual technique for reconciling map and territory is an internalization of a social activity in an informationally sparser environment. Without a much more detailed account of the acquisition of this process, it will be impossible to decide this case. For now, one can do no more than raise the question of whether internal processes might exist that are not internalizations of external processes. And doing that seems to throw the spotlight squarely on the nature of the transformations that occur in the internalization process.

Throughout the previous chapters, I have tried to move the boundary of the unit of cognitive analysis out beyond the skin of the individual. Doing this enabled me to describe the cognitive properties of culturally constructed technical and social systems. These systems are simultaneously cognitive systems in their own rights and contexts for the cognition of the people who participate in them. I have intentionally not attempted to discuss the properties of individuals before describing the culturally constituted worlds in which those properties are manifested. To do so is a mistake for two reasons.

First, since cognitive science must content itself for the foreseeable future with models of unobservable processes that are capable of generating observable behavior, it is important to get the right functional specification for the human cognitive system. What sorts of things do people really do? Many behavioral scientists seem to think that they can answer this question by introspection. I believe, on the contrary, that such questions can be answered only by the study of cognition in the wild. The representativeness of contexts for the elicitation of behavior in laboratories is seldom addressed. What cognitive tasks do people really engage in a normal day? What is the distribution of such tasks? What sorts of strategies do people invoke for dealing with the tasks they do encounter? There is now a growing literature based on studies of everyday cognition. This literature is of value to cognitive theory in the same way that the observations of early naturalists were important to the development of a number of theories in biology. A close examination of the context for thinking may change our minds about what counts as a characteristic human cognitive task.

Second, seeing human cognitive activity as an integral part of such a larger system may bring us a different sense of the nature of individual cognition. Any attempt to explain the cognitive properties of such a larger system without reference to the properties of its most active integral parts would be deficient. Similarly, though, any attempt to explain the cognitive properties of the integral parts without reference to the properties of the larger system would also be incomplete.

Human beings are adaptive systems continually producing and exploiting a rich world of cultural structure. In the activities of the navigation team, the reliance on and the production of structure in the environment are clear. This heavy interaction of internal and external structure suggests that the boundary between inside and outside, or between individual and context, should be softened. The apparent necessity of drawing such a boundary is in part a side effect of the attempt to deal with the individual as an isolated unit of cognitive analysis without first locating the individual in a culturally constructed world. With the focus on a person who is actively engaged in a culturally constructed world, let us soften the boundary of the individual and take the individual to be a very plastic kind of adaptive system. Instead of conceiving the relation between person and environment in terms of moving coded information across a boundary, let us look for processes of entrainment, coordination, and resonance among elements of a system that includes a person and the person's surroundings. When we speak of the individual now, we are explicitly drawing the inside/outside boundary back into a picture where it need not be prominent. These boundaries can always be drawn in later, but they should not be the most important thing.

In this chapter I will attempt to partially dissolve the inside/outside boundary and provide a functional description of processes that could account for learning and thinking in the kind of cognitive activity that has been described in the previous chapters. In this and all that follows, internal representations are identified by their functional properties only. I make no commitment to proposed mental mechanisms or computational architectures with which the behaviors of the representations might be modeled. As far as I can tell, it is not possible to distinguish among competing models on the basis of available evidence, and it is certainly not possible to do so on the basis of the sorts of evidence that can be collected in the wild.

Chapter 3 introduced the idea of a complex functional system consisting of many media in simultaneous coordination. The examples given there included the functional system formed by the bearing taker, the bearing recorder, and their technological aids. When the team produces a record of an observed bearing, the chain of coordination may include the name of the landmark, partial descriptions of the landmark, the visual experience of the land-mark, the hairline of the alidade, the gyrocompass scale, the knowledge and skills involved in reading the bearing, the spoken sounds on the phone circuit, the knowledge and skills involved in interpreting the spoken bearing, and the digits written in the bear-ing record log. In chapter 3 I tried to describe the functional prop-erties of some of those internal structures, but I did not address the question of how the internal structures could actually develop as a consequence of particular experiences, or how a watchstander could manage to get the right things into coordination to form use-ful functional systems. I couldn't treat those things there because I had not yet provided a reasonable description of the other (ob-servable) parts of the dynamic system in which "internal" struc-tures form. Dealing with these issues requires an architecture of cognition that transcends the boundaries of the individual.

The proper unit of analysis for talking about cognitive change includes the socio-material environment of thinking. *Learning is adaptive reorganization in a complex system.* It is difficult to resist the temptation to let the unit of analysis collapse to the Western view of the individual bounded by the skin, or to let it collapse even further to the "cognitive" symbol system lying protected from the world somewhere far below the skin. But, as we have seen, the relevant complex system includes a web of coordination among media and processes inside and outside the individual task perfor-mers. The definition of learning given here works well for learning situated in the socio-material world, and it works equally well for private discoveries made in moments of reflective thought. In this chapter I take up the question of the formation of internal struc-tures as a consequence of experience.

The richness of the universe of possible solutions to real-world problems is often taken as a reason not to study in the wild. In ex-perimental design, it is important to ensure that all subjects in a particular condition are doing the task in the same way. If subjects are using many different strategies to solve a problem, it will not be possible to infer the representational bases of the performances by comparing the behaviors of subjects in one condition with those of subjects in another condition. The difficulty is, as Newell (1973) says, that we cannot learn about underlying processes by aggregat-ing across methods. However, the flexibility of the formation of functional systems in response to real-world tasks appears to be an important cognitive phenomenon in its own right. This is a phenomenon that is entirely missed by research paradigms that, for good reasons, intentionally limit the methods subjects may use to perform a task.

The point of this chapter is to examine the process of learning while doing with respect to a sort of learning task that is frequently encountered in the world of navigation. I will attempt to approach this learning problem from the perspective of a softened boundary of the individual and to see the learning that happens inside an individual as simply adaptation of structure in one part of a complex system to organization in other parts. Individual learning is the propagation of some kinds of organization from one part of a complex system to another. Some of the parts that are reorganized are inside the skin. It is not possible to understand how that reorganization takes place without looking at the other kinds of organization that are present in the larger system.

Many tasks in the world of navigation are described by written procedures. When a person uses a written procedure in the performance of a task, the procedure is a mediating artifact. In ordinary usage, a mediating artifact stands between the person and the task. It mediates the relationship between the performer and the task. On closer inspection, however, the situation becomes more complex. The stand-between reading of mediation assumes that the task and the performer can be bounded independently. Rather than focus on the mediating artifact as something that "stands between," I will view it as one of many structural elements that are brought into coordination in the performance of the task. Any of the structures that are brought into coordination in the performance of the task can be seen as a mediating structure. It is difficult in this context to say what stands between what, but they certainly all participate in the organization of behavior. The question of individual learning now becomes the question of how that which is inside a person might change over time as a consequence of repeated interactions with these elements of cultural structure.

The phenomena of mediated performance are ubiquitous. For the purposes of exposition, I have chosen as an example a simple explicit external mediation device: a written procedure. Many tasks in our culture are mediated by written procedures or procedure-like artifacts, but even considering all of them would not begin to approach the full range of mediated performances. Language, cultural knowledge, mental models, arithmetic procedures, and rules of logic are all mediating structures too. So are traffic lights, supermarket layouts, and the contexts we arrange for one another's behavior. Mediating structure can be embodied in artifacts, in ideas, in systems of social interaction, or in all of these at once. I have chosen the written procedure because it is a typical artifact in the world of ship navigation and because it provides a relatively explicit example of mediation for which a relatively simple exposition can be given.

The task of learning a procedure is interesting because it can be mediated by so many different kinds of structures. This is just another way of saying that there are many possible ways of organizing functional systems to perform a task. After discussing the mediation of procedural performance by the written procedure, I will consider other forms of mediation. This wide range of ways to organize the performance of procedures raises the question: What kind of architecture of cognition is required to accommodate the flexible constitution of functional systems of so many kinds?

Putting the question of the flexible constitution of functional systems first means approaching the study of cognition from a different starting point. It requires a different view of cognition, and it demands that our models of cognition be capable of different sorts of computations. This is a consequence of an attempt to build a theory of cognition that comes after, rather than before, a description of the cultural world in which human cognitive behavior is embedded.

Theoretical Perspective for the Construction of a Model

I take the fundamentals of an architecture of cognition and a sense of a unit of analysis from Gregory Bateson, who said that "the elementary cybernetic system with messages in circuit is, in fact, the simplest unit of mind; and the transform of a difference traveling in a circuit is the elementary idea" (1972: 459).

The problem of how to bound a unit of analysis is crisply summed up by Bateson in his well-known example of a blind man with a stick:

Suppose I am a blind man, and I use a stick. I go tap, tap, tap. Where do I start? Is my mental system bounded at the handle of he stick? Is it bounded by my skin? Does it start halfway up the stick? But these are nonsense questions. The stick is a pathway along which transforms of difference are being transmitted. The way to delineate the system is to draw the limiting line in such a way that you do not cut any of these pathways in ways which leave things inexplicable. (ibid.)

The proper unit of analysis is, thus, not bounded by the skin or the skull. It includes the socio-material environment of the person, and the boundaries of the system may shift during the course of activity. Temporal boundaries are important too. As the analysis of the construction of the task environment in chapter 3 showed, arbitrary boundaries on the temporal extent of the unit of analysis also risk cutting pathways in ways that leave things inexplicable. In the present context, many things remain inexplicable until we consider the history of the person in the task environment. This seems especially pertinent to the nature of learning, since learning must be a consequence of interaction with an environment through time.

In a section titled "External Representation and Formal Reasoning," Rumelhart et al. (1986) sketch a proposal for a view of symbolic processing that fits well with what has been proposed here. They describe doing place-value multiplication with paper and pencil as follows:

Each cycle of this operation involves first creating a representation through manipulation of the environment, then a processing of the (actual physical) representation by means of our well-tuned perceptual apparatus leading to further modification of this representation. By doing this we reduce a very abstract conceptual problem to a series of operations that are very concrete and at which we can become very good.... This is real symbol processing and, we are beginning to think, the primary symbol processing that we are able to do.

They account for internal symbol processing as follows:

Not only can we manipulate the physical environment and then process it, we can also learn to internalize the representations we create, "imagine" them, and then process these imagined representations—just as if they were external.

With experience we learn about the regularities of the world of external symbolic tokens and we form mental models of the behaviors of these symbolic tokens that permit us to perform the manipulations and to anticipate the possible manipulations. With even more experience, we can imagine the symbolic world and apply our knowledge, gained from interactions with real physical symbol tokens, to the manipulations of the imagined symbolic worlds. "Indeed," Rumelhart et al. note, "we think that the idea that we reason with mental models is a powerful one precisely because it is about this process of imagining an external representation and operating on that."

These ideas also apply to interactions among individuals. Rumelhart et al. propose that we can also imagine aspects of interactions and then operate on or with the image of external representations:

We can be instructed to behave in a particular way. Responding to instructions in this way can be viewed simply as responding to some environmental event. We can also remember such an instruction and "tell ourselves" what to do. We have, in this way, internalized the instruction. We believe that the process of following instructions is essentially the same whether we have told ourselves or have been told what to do. Thus, even here, we have a kind of internalization of an external representational format (i.e., language).

The practice of navigation includes many instances of this kind of instruction. In an example given at the end of chapter 6, a novice and an expert quartermaster organized their activity around a written form. That example was actually more complex than any considered by Rumelhart et al., but the processes they propose should apply here too. In that example, the novice organized his own actions by coordinating them with the actions of the expert. The development of sequential control of action also concerns the relationship of public and private symbol systems and the processes that link them.

In this chapter I will integrate the functional-systems perspective with Bateson's unit of analysis and Rumelhart's notions of imagining external representations into an account of how internal structures may form as a consequence of experience.

Constructing Action Sequences

There are many ways to construct the sequence of actions that constitutes the fix cycle. Quartermasters who get navigation training in school first encounter the sequence of actions of the fix cycle as a written list of steps to be performed.

Solution procedures for many navigation tasks are presented to students in the form of what are called "strips." A strip is a list of labeled blank spaces which the student is supposed to fill in order. The strip guides the student through a sequence of steps that produces a solution to the problem at hand. One quartermaster chief complained to me that strips don't give the learner any command of conceptual structure. Students who learn to fill in the blanks on a strip have no idea what they have done, and are unable to perform the task in the absence of the strip. In what follows, I will show why strips don't necessarily provide conceptual understanding. I will also show how conceptual knowledge can be added to the sequential knowledge.

The presupposition of much of military education is that memorizing the sequence of elements in a procedure will lead to successful performance. There are, however, many interpretations of what it might mean to say that a watchstander has "remembered the sequence of elements in the procedure." This might be taken to mean that the names of the elements have been remembered such that they could be recited in order. Perhaps when the procedure is well learned the name of each element gives way to the name of the next, around and around the cycle, like the words of the chorus of a familiar song. Another interpretation of the memory for the procedure consists of a sequence of mental images of the elements. Perhaps the watchstander can imagine the actions to be taken and can see the unfolding sequence of elements as if watching a movie in his "mind's eye." Yet another interpretation for the memory of the elements of the task consists of a motor memory for the sequence of actions involved in doing the elements of the task. Perhaps a watchstander who has this sort of memory can simply initiate the task and observe as his hands remember what to do. The differences between these interpretations of the phrase "remembered the sequence of elements in the procedure" are nontrivial. In this chapter I will argue that the correct interpretation might simultaneously include all these sorts of memory and more.

In order for a sequence to be remembered in any form, it must have been experienced in some fashion. This experience may have come in many forms. Chapters 4, 5, and 6 described many aspects of the organization of the learning environment. For the moment, let us consider the relationships among these different sorts of representations of task structure.

Written Procedure as Mediating Structure

Consider a person using a written procedure to organize the performance of a task in a case where it is essential that the actions of the performance be taken in a particular order and that all the actions be taken before the performance is judged complete. Here is a written procedure for the quartermaster in Standard Steaming Watch:

1. Choose a fix interval and a first fix time.
2. Choose a set of landmarks and information sources for the fix.
3. Just prior to the fix time, go to the chart house and record the fathometer reading.
4. At the fix time, observe the bearings of the landmarks. (Observe landmarks near the beam of the ship first.)
5. Record the observed bearings in the bearing record book.
6. Plot the observed bearings on the chart.
7. Compare the fix to the previously projected position for this fix. (determine the effects of current)
8. Compare the fix to the prior fix, measure distance and time difference.
9. Compute the ship's speed.
10. Determine the ship's heading.
11. Project the position of the ship two fixes into the future.
12. Go to step 2 and repeat.

An actor always incurs some cognitive costs in coordinating with a mediating structure. To use the written procedure above, for example, the watchstander must control his attention and deploy his reading skills. But some types of mediated performance may be less costly to achieve than others. The reduction of error or increase in efficiency obtained via the use of the procedure may compensate for the effort required to use it. For the unskilled performer, of course, the task may be impossible without the use of the procedure, so the economy of mediated performance in that case is clear.

In order to use a written procedure as a guide to action, the task performer must coordinate with both the written procedure and the environment in which the actions are to be taken. Achieving coordination with the written procedure requires the actor to invoke mental procedures for the use of the written procedure. These include reading skills and a strategy of sequential execution that permits the task performer to ensure that the steps will be done in the correct order and that each step will be done once and only once (figure 7.1). The fixed linear spatial structure of the written procedure permits the user to accomplish this by simply keeping track of an index that indicates the first unexecuted (or the last executed) item. Written procedures often provide additional

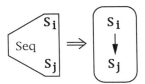

Figure 7.1 Creating a sequential relationship. A strategy of sequential execution in interaction with the physical structure of the written procedure permits the task performer to take the elements of the procedure in a particular sequence. Here and in the rest of the figures in this chapter, items in lightface are processes or structures inside the skin; items in boldface are structures outside the skin. Seq is the sequential execution strategy. S_i and S_j are written steps in the procedure. The arrow indicates that the item on the left constrains the development of the one on the right. The trapezoidish shape to the left indicates a complex coordination process; the rounded rectangle to the right indicates a sequential relationship.

features to aid in the maintenance of this index: boxes to check off when steps are completed, a window that moves across the procedure, etc. The mediating artifact may thus be designed with particular structural features that can be exploited by simple interactive strategies to produce a useful coordination. If the items are written in a list, the sequential relations among them emerge from the interaction of the physical structure of the list and a particular strategy for reading it (from top to bottom, for example). The spatial relations among items on the written list become sequential relations in the interaction. Notice, however, that the sequential relations among the steps of the procedure are *implicit* in the physical structure of the list. They become explicit only in interaction with some sequential strategy. The top-to-bottom strategy produces one set of sequential relations among steps, but another strategy (say, bottom to top) would produce a different ordering from the very same physical structure. It is important to note, however, that some spatial structures afford simple strategies whereas others do not. A written procedure may not be needed if the spatial relations among the things referred to by the procedure permit the imposition of a simple strategy. The walk-around inspection of an airplane provides an example. In the walk-around, the pilot examines various parts of the airplane for flightworthiness. This task is not usually mediated by a written procedure, because the spatial arrangement of the parts of the plane themselves support a simple strategy that produces sequence from space. The pilot adopts a "flow" or trajectory of attention, going around the airplane clockwise starting at the boarding ladder (for example). The items that lie ahead on that trajectory are the things that remain to be inspected; those that lie behind are those that have already been inspected. The pilot's own body acts as the delimiter between the two sets. Every one of these interaction strategies can be seen as metamediation—that is, a mediating artifact that organizes the use of some other mediating artifact.

In finding the next step to do in the written procedure, the actor applies the sequential execution strategy to the written procedure to determine which step is the next one, and perhaps to determine an index of the next step that can be remembered. There are two related issues concerning this index: where it is located and what it contains. The index could be encoded in the memory of the actor, or the actor could take some action on the world (making a mark on the written procedure). If the index is simply a mark on paper, the memory task is only to remember what the mark means. If the steps are numbered, the index can be a number. Thus, in the above example, the quartermaster could remember that all steps up to step 3 had been accomplished. The index can also be the lexical or semantic content of the step's description. The quartermaster could remember that everything up to shooting the bearings had been done. Each of these alternatives requires a different set of coordinating actions to implement the sequential execution strategy. For example, if the content of the step index is the lexical or semantic content of the step itself, then finding the next step (by reading through the steps until you arrive at one that has not yet been done) and establishing the step index (identifying a step that has not been done) are the same action. If the content of the step index is a mark on paper or a number to be recorded or remembered, however, then some action in addition to finding the next step must be undertaken to establish the step index. For example, you would have to find the last mark and move to the step following it, or remember the number, increment it by one, and then find the printed numeral that matches the new step's index number.

Although the primary product of the application of this sequencing strategy is the determination of the next step to be performed, either the written procedure as an object in the environment or the internal procedure that implements the sequential execution strategy may also be changed as a consequence of the actions involved in finding the next step.

Having generated a step index (in whatever form), the actor can bring that index into coordination with the written procedure to focus attention on the current step. Though the goal of using the written procedure as a mediating artifact is to ensure sequential control of the actions taken in the task domain, it is clear that the task of bringing the written procedure into coordination with the domain of action may not itself be linearly sequential. For example, if a user loses track of the step index, in order to determine the next step to be taken he may go back to the beginning of the written procedure and proceed through each step in the procedure, not executing it but asking of the task world whether the expected consequences of the step's execution are present. When a step is reached whose consequences are not present in the task world, one may assume that it has not yet been executed. This is a simple illustration of the potential complexity of the metamediation that may be undertaken in the coordination of a mediating structure with a task world.

It is clear from this discussion that the symbols in figure 7.1 are oversimplified and hide much of the potential complexity of this relatively simple task. The remaining figures in this chapter hide similar complexities. If all these were included, however, it would be impossible to assemble the pieces into a coherent whole.

Once the current step has been identified, the user may coordinate its printed representation with shallow reading skills in order to produce an internal representation of what the step says in words (figure 7.2).

The shallow reading skills here refer to organized (perhaps already automated) internal structures that can create internal representations of words from their external printed counterparts. The representation of what the step says may be in the visual or the auditory modality, or perhaps in both. Whether this internal representation is primarily auditory or visual or something else is not important for the present argument. There is some evidence that meanings are accessed both via direct lexical access (from word to meaning) and via sound codes (from word to sound representation to meaning), even in silent reading (Pollatsek and Rayner 1989).

Figure 7.2 Finding what the step says. S_i is the written representation of the ith step of the procedure; s_i is an internal representation of what that step says; Read is the shallow reading skills of the person. The arrow indicates the propagation of representational state from one medium to another. The complex trapezoid represents a complex coordination process.

The internal representation may even be in a tactile or haptic modality, if the procedure was written in Braille. The important thing is that the representation be capable of permitting the actor to "remember" the lexical content of the step at a later time. It is obvious that this process may proceed concurrently with the process of reading what the step means. However, I have separated shallow and deep readings, primarily because shallow and deep readings produce different sorts of products that can be shown to exist independently. Thus, a user who does not understand the domain of action may know and be able to recall what a step "says" without having any idea of what it "means." The default case for this example will be a written procedure. The external mediation is often provided verbally by another person. In that case, the shallow reading skills are replaced by listening skills.

Most models of reading involve the construction of meaning in the absence of the world described. However, reading a procedure is directed toward understanding a world that is present. Determining the meaning of what a step says requires the coordination of what the step says with the task world via the mediation of a deeper sort of reading (figure 7.3). This deep reading relies on two internal structures: one to provide semantic mappings from linguistic descriptions provided by the procedure to states in the world and another to provide readings of the task world to see what is there. What the words in the step description are thought to mean may depend on the state of the task world that has been produced by prior actions. The arrow goes both ways between the representation of what the step says and what it means because each depends on the other. The words we think we saw or heard may depend on what we think makes sense. Let us assume for the moment that the meanings that appear in this medium are image-like and that they are the same kinds of structures that would result from actual performance of the task.

It is tempting to think that the words and the world are coordinated by language in order to produce the meanings. It is more

Figure 7.3   Discovering what the step means. L is deep language skills; TW is the task world; M_i is the meaning of the ith step.

accurate to say that the meanings, the world, and the words are put in coordination with one another via the mediating structure of language. It is difficult to place the meaning of the step cleanly inside or outside the person, because some component of the meaning may be established by a kind of situated seeing in which the meaning of the step exists only in that active process of superimposing internal structure on the experience of the external world. That is, at some point in the development of the task performer's knowledge the step may not have a meaning in the absence of the world onto which it can be read. Perhaps the meaning of a step can reside cleanly inside a person only when the person has developed an internal image of the external world that includes those aspects onto which the mediating structure can be superimposed. The structure of language may be changed by its use, and what is thought to be in the world may be changed by describing it in a particular way. Each of the structures provides constraints on the others, and all are to some extent malleable. The system composed of a task performer, mediating structures, and the task world settles into a solution that satisfies as many constraints as is possible. The arrow in figure 7.3 goes both ways because there are mutual constraints between these structures. This constraint satisfaction is a computation. We must keep in mind, however, that side effects of the computation may include changes in the constraint structures.

Finally, having determined what the step means, the user of the procedure may take actions on (and in) the world to carry out the step (figure 7.4). The action, like the meaning of the step, may be difficult to locate cleanly inside or outside the actor, because actions taken on the environment involve phenomena inside and outside the actor and because for many mental acts (those based in mental imagery, e.g.) the task world itself may be substantially inside the actor. In any case, the meaning of the step, the action, and the task world are brought into coordination. The arrow between meaning and action goes both ways because the meaning of the

Figure 7.4   Performing the step. Mot is the motor orientation process; A_i is the action that is taken to realize the ith step of the procedure.

step is used to organize the action, and the monitored performance of the action may change the understood meaning of the step. Remember that the meanings we have discussed so far are equivalent to the sensory experiences encountered in the actual performance of the task. Having completed this step, the user of the procedure may find the next step and continue.

In an actual performance of a step of the procedure, all the structures discussed so far may simultaneously be in coordination with one another as is shown in figure 7.5.

Consequences of Mediated Task Performance

While the procedure is being followed, high-level organization of task-related behavior is produced—in part by the physical structure of the written representation of the procedure. The interaction with the procedure produces for the actor a sequence of experiences of step descriptions. Each of these experiences may have several components: what the step says, what the step means, and the actions in the task world that carry out the step. Figures 7.1–7.4 show that many layers of transforming mediating structure may lie between a simple mediating artifact (e.g., a written procedure) and the performance of a task. Now suppose a task performer uses this written procedure to guide many performances of the task. What are the consequences for structures inside the actor of the repeated achievement of the coordinations depicted in figures 7.1–7.4? How might internal structures develop as a consequence of interactions with external structures?

The discussion above introduced three functionally distinct internal media: a lexical medium dedicated to representing what the steps of the written procedure say, a semantic medium dedicated to

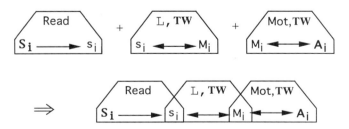

Figure 7.5   Multiple simultaneous coordinations in the performance of a step of a written procedure. Shallow reading, deep reading, and motor orientation mediate the propagation of state from the printed representation of the step (S_i), to its lexical representation (s_i), thence to its semantic representation (M_i), thence to the motor sequences that constitute the performance of the step (A_i).

representing what the steps mean, and a motor medium dedicated to effecting the actions taken in the task world. Each medium holds structure of a particular kind. Now, imagine that each medium has the simple property that it will, as a consequence of being driven through a sequence of states, come to have the capacity to reproduce that sequence of states. That is, when placed in any state in the sequence, the medium can produce the next state of the sequence, and then the next, and so on to the last state in the sequence.

LEARNING THE SEQUENCE OF STEPS DESCRIPTIONS
Consider the lexical medium. As the task performer reads the steps of the procedure, this medium is driven first into a state that represents what the first step says, then into a state that represents what the second step says, and so on through the entire procedure. This sequence of states produced by the shallow reading of the written step descriptions is a mediated sequence. If the lexical medium has the property described above, with repeated exposures to the sequence it will come to be able to reproduce the sequence of states that represents what the steps of the procedure say (figure 7.6). It will be able to do this without the mediation of the sequential interaction strategy applied to the written procedure and the reading skills. The sequential relations among the representations of what the steps say were originally mediated by the sequential relations of the items on the written procedure. With experience, these sequential relationships become unmediated.

This newly created internal representation of the sequence of what the steps say is of the same class of phenomena as our knowledge of the order of the letters of the alphabet or of the names of the lower numbers. Originally constructed through complex mediation processes, it gains some modularity and autonomy as a consequence of experience. The lexical representation of each step

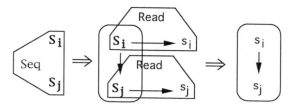

Figure 7.6 Producing an internal sequence of states. Applying the sequential execution strategy to the written procedure produces a sequence of internal states (indicated by the rounded rectangle at right).

of the sequence is explicitly re-represented by a state that this medium is capable of producing, but the sequential relations among the states are implicit in the behavior of the medium.

Loosely speaking, we could say that the lexical medium has internalized the written procedure. We must use the word 'internalize' with caution, however. The process in question here is specifically the development of a medium that, when placed in a state corresponding to the experience of what step N says, will automatically undergo a transition to a state corresponding to the experience of what step $N+1$ says. In a literal sense, nothing has moved from outside to inside. Via the mediation of the shallow reading process, structure in the written representation of the steps of the procedure has given rise to certain internal experiences. Then, as a consequence of repeated experience, a new functional ability has been created out of the entirely internal states of the lexical medium. Careless use of 'internalization' here is dangerous because it glosses over the processes involved and lumps together many kinds of representations that differ from one another in functionally significant ways.

Once the lexical medium has developed the capacity to produce, in order, representations of what the steps say, it may become the controlling structure for subsequent performances. (See figure 7.7.) This amounts to the task performer's having learned what the procedure says, so that instead of reading the next step he can "remember" what the next step says, use that to construct the meaning of the next step, and use that meaning to organize an action. A performance guided by the memory of the words in the procedure is still a mediated task performance, but the mediating structure is now internal rather than external. The lexical medium that encodes

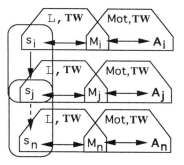

Figure 7.7 The mediation of task performance by the learned sequence of step descriptions. The internal representations of what the steps say can be used to control the sequence of actions.

what the steps of the procedure say provides explicit representations of the steps of the procedure. It can move through a sequence of states, each of which corresponds to the experience of reading what a step of the procedure says. Moving from external to internal mediation also introduces new possibilities for the relations between the actor and the environment, because the environment no longer need contain the mediating structure.

The lexical medium must become an automatized system before it can be used alone to mediate the task performance. This internal mediation system, while having explicit representational content in its states, relies for its controlling behavior on automatized implicit encodings of relations among its states. The issue of what is implicit and what is explicit depends on the question being asked. The internal memory for the procedure consists of states that represent explicit descriptions of the actions to be taken. But the sequential relations among those step descriptions are implicitly encoded in the behavior of the lexical medium, much as the sequential relations among the step descriptions in the external procedure were implicitly encoded in the spatial relations among elements on the written-procedure artifact. Consider briefly another common mediating structure: alphabetical order. It is used in many storage and retrieval schemes in our culture, so we take care to ensure that children learn it. In learning the alphabet song, the child is developing an explicit internal automatized version of the alphabet's structure. The content of the states—the words of the song—are explicit, but the sequential relations among them (which were originally provided by another mediating system, a teacher) are implicit. A child who knows the song can tell you what comes after P (perhaps after singing the names of the first 17 letters), but that same child will have a difficult time saying why Q follows P. There is simply no explicit representation of that in what the child knows.

When a person first performs a task using written instructions, there is an apparent alternation between coordination with the written procedure and coordination with the world. One deals first with the written procedure and then with the world it describes. However, no alternation of attention is necessary once one has developed an internal representation of even the lexical level of the procedure description. Then the coordination with the representation of the procedure (whether lexical, semantic, or motor) and the world in which the procedure is carried out is no longer one of alternation of attention focus; it is one of simultaneous coordination. Understanding a step in the description may depend on understanding the state of the world in which it is to be carried out. The experience of the meanings of the descriptions of the steps contains experience of the task world, and the doing of the actions contains the experience of the meaning of the task steps. The importance of this is that in this mediated performance the actor becomes a special sort of medium that can provide continuous coordination among several structured media. It fact, the alternation of focus of attention when one is using a written procedure is a solution to a problem of competing demands for visual resources that is created by the particular physical instantiation of the written procedure. Alternating the focus of attention is simply a way to time-share a particular scarce perceptual resource.

LEARNING THE SEQUENCE OF STEP MEANINGS

Of course, at the same time that the medium dedicated to the representation of what the steps say is driven through a series of states, the medium dedicated to representing the meanings of the steps is also driven through a series of states. This is shown in figure 7.8. Once this semantic medium has been trained, the actor can remember the meanings of the steps, if necessary without reference to the memory of what the steps say. Since the lexical structure is around, however, and since humans are unrelentingly opportunistic, it is likely that both the memory of the meaning of the step and the meaning derived from interpreting the memory of what the step says will be used in concert to determine the meaning of the step.

Figure 7.8 describes one way to establish the sequential relations among the meanings of the steps of the procedure. There is another way that is mediated by conceptual knowledge about the task. The

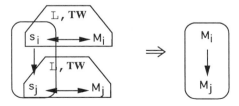

Figure 7.8 Automatization of the step meaning sequence in the semantic medium. Once trained, the semantic medium can produce the succession of states corresponding to the meanings of the steps of the procedure.

meanings of the steps represented in this semantic medium are imagined and observed courses of action. There are other kinds of meanings, however, that concern the conceptual relations among elements of a procedure. The steps of the fix-cycle procedure, for example, are related by a set of computational dependencies. It is not possible to plot a line of position until an observation of a landmark has been made, and it is not possible to make the observation until a landmark has been chosen to observe. These kinds of dependencies constrain the possible orderings of steps in the procedure, and may help the quartermaster remember what comes next. Let M_p be the experience of plotting a line of position, and let $\mathcal{M}_p$ be a representation of the concept "plotting a line of position." Let M_o be the experience of making an observation of a landmark and let $\mathcal{M}_o$ be a representation of the concept "making an observation of a landmark." There is a conceptual and computational dependency between $\mathcal{M}_o$ and $\mathcal{M}_p$, such that $\mathcal{M}_o$ must precede $\mathcal{M}_p$. This relationship explains the experience of the sequential ordering of M_o and M_p (figure 7.9).

The meanings of the steps would have only implicit relations to one another were it not for the potential mediating role of conceptual knowledge in the task domain. If conceptual knowledge is tied to the meanings of the steps, some other medium in the system may assume states that explicitly represent a reason why step $N + 1$ follows step N. However, such a mediating structure need not be learned before the sequence of meanings of the steps is learned. Sometimes we discover *why* we do some task the way we do long after we have learned to do the task itself.

While I was working on a program to improve radar navigation training, I interviewed many navigation instructors. The task involved a complex set of plotting procedures. One of the instructors reported to me that he had spent 3 years at sea doing radar naviga-

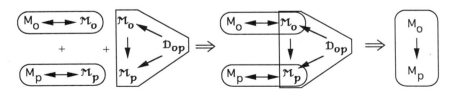

Figure 7.9 The use of conceptual knowledge to establish sequential relationships among meanings of steps in the procedure. The relationships among the meanings of the steps may be mediated by knowledge of the conceptual and computational dependencies among the steps. $\mathcal{D}_{op}$ is the conceptual dependency that holds between $\mathcal{M}_o$ and $\mathcal{M}_p$.

tion procedures before he realized the conceptual relationship between relative and geographic motion. He told me that the insight came to him as he lay in his bunk one night. He got out of bed and rushed down to the combat information center to confirm that his newfound understanding was indeed correct and that it accounted for the organization of the procedures he had been executing for years. This story is more dramatic than most, but the phenomenon is far from rare. I believe that much of our learning consists of filling in conceptual details and relationships in tasks we already know how to do.

Problem solving and planning in the space of conceptual dependencies are two of the means of mediating this task. These kinds of activities have been the mainstay of an important tradition of research in cognitive science and artificial intelligence. In the case of real-world procedures, however, there are so many other sources of structure that it may be relatively rare to find a person working from the conceptual dependencies alone to determine a sequence of action.

LEARNING THE SEQUENCE OF ACTIONS
Whether the task is organized by an external procedure or by an internal representation of it, the mental apparatus involved in the performance of the task is driven through a sequence of states. Because of the nature of the structured interaction of the task performer with the environment, the sequence of states is repeated more or less consistently each time the procedure is followed. The motor medium begins to encode the sequential relations among the successive states (figure 7.10).

Something of the organization of the $(N+1)$th state is in the potential of the medium when the Nth state is present. The capacity of the motor medium to produce the sequence of states that

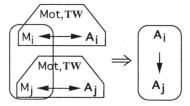

Figure 7.10 The development of sequential relationships in the motor medium. The motor medium can now produce the succession of states that generate the actions taken in the task world. There is no longer a need for any mediation via the meanings of steps.

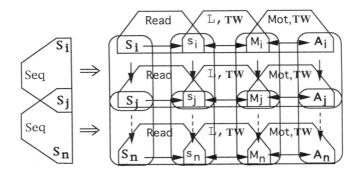

Figure 7.11 The assembled tissue of coordination. In expert performance, the succession of states produced depends on both horizontal and vertical coordination. Every state constrains and is constrained by others. (The conceptual relations among meanings, which also provided constraints, have been omitted from this figure because of the limitation of a two-dimensional diagram.)

is experienced in and that constitutes the performance of the task is no different from the capacity of the other media to produce their respective sequences of states. But unlike the states in the lexical and semantic media, the states of the motor medium are not descriptions of actions. They are not referential; they are not *about* anything. They are the states of the motor medium that constitute the performance of the actions. There is no mediation between the states of the motor medium and the action. When the sequence of these states has been learned, the medium, once placed in state 1, can *do* the task automatically without reference to any explicit representation of the either the steps or their sequential relations.

The mediated performances leading up to this condition could be thought of as training trials for the medium that produces the action. The system has now reached the condition described by figure 7.11. In this condition, for a normal task performance, the motor medium no longer needs the organizing constraints of the meanings of the steps. Once placed in the initial state, the motor medium simply moves through the states that constitute the doing of the task. This is the nature of automatized skill performances—performances that no longer utilize the organizing constraints of complexly mediated structure. Of course, if unusual circumstances arise in the task world, the automatized performance may fail, requiring additional recourse to other mediating structure.

This is a simple model in which a person is situated in a sociomaterial world and learning is adaptive reorganization of part of the system in coordination with organization in other parts of the system. The system operates by the propagation of representational state across media, and the media themselves acquire functional organization as a consequence of the repeated impositions of representational state upon them. The lexical medium, for example, acquires the ability to move sequentially through states that can be read as representations of what the step says. The basic building blocks of the system are the coordinative processes that move representational state (horizontally in figure 7.11) and the functional properties of the representational media that permit them to learn to move through a sequence of states.

I began this section with the question of what it might mean that a watchstander can "remember the elements of a procedure." The answer is clearly not that something is retrieved from memory as a physical structure might be retrieved from a storehouse, or even as a pattern of bits might be retrieved from a magnetic storage medium in a computer. Rather, remembering is a constructive act of establishing coordination among a set of media that have the functional properties such that the states of some can constrain the states of others, or that the state of one at time t can constrain its own state at time $t+1$. The meaning of the next step in a procedure can be partially established by sequencing from the meaning of the current step. It can be constructed from the interpretation of the description of the next step in coordination with the task world. It may be wholly or partially derived from conceptual dependencies between it and the other steps (not shown in figure 7.11). It can be in part derived from monitoring the real or imagined motor sequences that realize it in the world. The multiple representations of each element of the procedure are woven into this tight fabric of relationship and constraint. Remembering is not a retrieval of an identifiable single structure; rather, it is a process of construction via simultaneous superimposition of many kinds of constraints.

If local structures are sufficient to produce unambiguous states in the task-performance media, the other media may not be activated. A very well-learned sequence of actions may run off without conscious intervention. When snags are encountered or when ambiguous states arise, the range of structures that are brought into coordination may expand to include other media. Perhaps when automatic motor processes reach an impasse, the semantic medium can provide a representation of the next step that the motor planning processes can use to construct a new motor plan. That is, one can remember what the step means in order to reconstruct a motor sequence to carry it out. When the relations in the semantic medium are insufficient to produce a new state, the lexical medium can be brought into coordination with the semantic medium to produce a description of what the next step says, and that can be used to produce the meaning of the next step. One can remember what the next step says in order to reconstruct its meaning. And if all that fails, one may construct a functional system that again coordinates with the written procedure to provide representations of the next step. That is, one can reread the step from the written procedure.

While the procedure is being learned, organization propagates from left to right and from top to bottom in figure 7.11, and from outside to inside and then back to outside. As learning proceeds, a wave of organization moves across the media and each medium acquires functional properties that permit it to produce structured behaviors. Just as the individual quartermasters follow the same trajectory in their careers that the data follow through the navigation team, the incremental spread of organization of media that is learning follows the same trajectory that representations follow in the course of a single performance of the task.

The processes by which an individual learns to perform the task can be seen as the propagation of a wave of organization moving across a complex set of media. Organization propagates from external media to internal media and back to external media. The changes that happen inside an individual as a consequence of learning are adaptations in a part of a larger dynamical system to organization or structure that is present in other parts of the system.

WHY WE CAN'T SAY WHAT WE DO

A common observation concerning automatized skill is that skilled performers may have difficulty saying how they do what they do. This analysis provides three explanations for this phenomenon.

First, the automatized motor medium for the procedure is a way of producing in the relation of the person to the environment a sequence of actions that constitute the doing of the steps described by the procedure. Because it encodes a relationship between the person and the environment, the execution of the procedure by the automatized motor medium requires the cooperation of the environment in a way that remembering the procedure does not. For example, the attempt to do a step can be frustrated by the lack in the environment of something required by the step. Yet one may remember a description of a step even though the conditions required to carry it out are absent. In the example above, the actor may be forced by the lack of the required condition to do some other actions in preparation for the previously frustrated step. In giving an account of how to do a task, the performer must assume a world (perhaps more correctly, the report must presuppose a world) in which the described actions make sense. Except where the task in question occurs in a very stable set of environments, the assumed world is certain to differ from many of the actual worlds in which the task is attempted, and the description will therefore fail in many of the actual worlds in which the task is performed.

Second, the reports skilled performers can give are sometimes based on the mediating structures that were used to control their behavior while they were acquiring automatized skill. The accounts that are given, being descriptions of mediating structure, may be just what is needed to communicate the skill from one person to another because the only way to produce the automatized skill in any medium is to have the medium learn it from experience and the only way for a novice to experience it is by getting into coordination with mediating structure. However, if the memory for the mediating structure has atrophied as a result of long disuse during automatized performance, then an expert asked how he does something may simply have no meaningful answer to give. The automated system does what it has been trained to do, but it has no explicit representation of what it is doing. The *representation* of what it is doing exists only in the apparatus that provided the training, that is, the mediating structure which is now atrophied.

A third situation that results in the expert task performer's inability to account for his own task performance arises when the mediating structure is present as constraints in the environment that shape the development of the motor medium directly, without the development of internalizations of explicit mediating representations. This seems to be the case for many motor skills. When asked to describe how the skill is performed, such an expert may describe events in which the skill was manifested. One view of such a response might be that the expert is being uncooperative, but when we understand that the mediating structure was in the environment of the skill acquisition we see that describing events in which the skill was manifested is the best the expert can do to describe the mediating structure under which the skill developed.

With this example I have attempted to highlight the complexity and richness of interaction of mediation structures of different sorts in the performance of what seemed at the outset to be a relatively simple mediated task performance. I don't think this analysis should lead us to change our minds about the relative simplicity of using procedures. On the contrary, I hope it heightens our awareness of the diversity of the kinds of mediating structure that come into play in everyday cognitive activities.

OTHER KINDS OF MEDIATING STRUCTURE

The example presented at the end of chapter 6 involved mediation by both a written artifact (the position report form) and the behavior of another person (the chief petty officer ,who asked the novice a set of questions in sequence). Clearly the source of the step descriptions can be an interaction with another person rather than with a written procedure. If the mediating structure is provided by the activities of another person, the novice who has internalized that structure can then act alone. This echoes Vygotsky's (1978) general genetic law of development in which mediating structure appears twice: first in interpsychological processes and second in intrapsychological processes.

There is much more to "internalization," however, than simply imagining an internal conversation. It is not that some content is copied from the outside world into some internal storage medium. Rather, the process of interaction creates a new process. Notice, for example, that even the lexical medium (closest to the surface of any of the media proposed here) has a sequence of states implicitly encoded in its behavior. The sequential relations among states were not a property of the medium from which the states were learned; rather, they were a property of a particular pattern of interaction with the external medium. Internalization has long connoted some thing moving across some boundary. Both elements of this definition are misleading. What moves is not a thing, and the boundary across which movement takes place is a line that, if drawn too firmly, obscures our understanding of the nature of human cognition. Within this larger unit of analysis, what used to look like internalization now appears as a gradual propagation of organized functional properties across a set of malleable media.

When individual task performance is considered in the context of a larger system, individual learning and mastery of the skills of a job appear as a shift in the location of the mediating structures that constrain the organization of action. In all cases, the mediating structures must exist somewhere in the functional system. In the case of team performance, some of the constraints are in the environment in the form of the behaviors of the other members of the team. If the team is experienced, this means that there will be redundant representation of the constraints on sequence, since they will exist both in the individual actors and in the interactions among them. Furthermore, conceptual dependencies may be learned more or less directly from participation in the team activity. As was noted in chapter 6, the computational dependencies among the steps of the procedure for the individual watchstander are present as interpersonal dependencies among the members of the team. These dependencies need never be stated to be learned. They are enacted in social relations, and they can be learned as patterns of social interaction rather than as words. The processes required to get from words to meaningful representations of such dependencies are probably as complex as the processes required to get from patterns of social interaction to representations of the same dependencies.

WHY WE TALK TO OURSELVES

The next chapter describes activities in which members of the navigation team enter data into a navigation calculator. While pushing the buttons of the calculator, the quartermasters can be heard to recite the names of the keys they press. Why do we do this verbal shadowing? Consider an example from everyday life: I don't seem to be able to open the combination lock on the storage shed in my yard without inwardly speaking the numbers of the combination as I do it. I have had years of experience with the lock. Yet, in spite of my best efforts to suppress the numbers, I still say them inwardly as I spin the lock's dial. Since I usually do this task entirely alone, the speech must be there for its self-regulatory function, not for any communicative function. How could it be self-regulatory? It is interesting to note that I do not verbalize the directions in which the dial should be turned. The dial must be turned clockwise to the first number, then counterclockwise past the first number to the second number, then clockwise again to the last number. I seem to have learned the sequence of directions of turning in the action specification, because I never say the names of the directions. I also turn the dial several times in the clockwise direction as I start without any verbalization. As the index for the dial nears the first number, I find myself saying that number. When I go counterclockwise, however, I not only say the second number of the combination; I also tend to say, "back past 33, 21." The direction of turning may be in the muscles, but the specification of how far to turn is not. I remember the meaning of the numbers by the appearance of the dial itself. For example, I know that 21 is the mark just to the right of the large tick labeled 20 without doing any counting. I just recognize it as being right. Even though I know the directions of turning in the action plan, and I seem to know the appearances of the three target numbers in sequence, I still say the numbers subvocally. The sequence of number names is a very stable structure for me. The reason I recite them subvocally, I believe, is that when I say the numbers aloud I interpret the meanings of the spoken numbers right onto the medium in which I am constructing the memory of the appearances of the numbers. In this way, I add constraints to the process that is the reconstruction of a memory that will drive the action. I superimpose multiple representations of the same action in order to produce the memory of the action. And the memory of the action is in the doing of the action itself. Of course, the action itself is also contributing to the construction of the memory, since I am monitoring the action and seeing what it means. By subvocally shadowing my action, I add a well-organized set of constraints to an already well-constrained problem. As a result, the performance is very robust.

In order to get useful mental work done, of course, the actor must be capable of bringing these structures into coordination. As we saw with the coordination of the procedure with the task world, bringing mediating structures into coordination may require still more (metamediating) structures. The consequences of the lack of this ability are encoded in our folk wisdom about "book learning" versus experience. One may have complete mastery over a major mediating structure for some task without having developed any of the metamediation required to put it to work in a real task environment.

Counting

From the point of view developed here, following a written procedure and counting have important structural similarities. Both involve the coordination of a sequence of tags with a partitioning of objects or events. In the case of counting, a set of sequential transitions through the names for the numbers is coordinated with the movement through the collection of individual objects or events of the partition between those things that have not yet been counted and those things that have already been counted. Similarly, following the procedure consists of coordinating the sequential transitions through the list of steps with the movement through the collection of actions to be taken of the partition between those things that have not yet been accomplished and those things that have already been accomplished.

Why do people count on their fingers? Because it is a strategy that transforms a task by forming a functional system that includes a representational media (the fingers) that permits other media to be coordinated in new ways. Nowadays counting on one's fingers is viewed as a sort of cognitive atavism, but "scarcely more than 400 years ago the use of one finger counting technique was so common among learned Europeans that arithmetic books had to contain detailed explanations of it if there were to be considered complete" (Ifrah 1987: 58). The system Ifrah describes is complex and required some training to master. Still, some of us resort to finger counting for simple problems. Suppose today is Tuesday, December 29. What will the date be on Saturday? I might say to myself "Let's see: Wednesday, Thursday, Friday, Saturday" and extend a finger for each day name spoken. Then I would look at my hand. Next I would coordinate again, this time bringing in the sequence of number names—"30 (um, December has) 31, and 1, 2"—directing my attention to the first raised finger when the first day number is spoken, and moving it to the next raised finger with each successive spoken day number until I arrived at the last finger. The last day number spoken would be the answer to my question. Solving the problem in this way brings the day names and the day numbers into coordination with the movement of attention along the row of fingers. The hand serves as a malleable and handy medium upon which representational states can be imposed and simple operations can be performed. The structure of the hand that results from those operations is a portion of a partial description of the answer to the question. The remainder of the propagation of representational state, from structure of the hand to spoken number, is accomplished either by simple pattern matching or by another simple coordination operation. The task can be done without using the fingers, of course, or even by coordinating the two sequences (day names and day numbers) directly. However, trying to simultaneously manipulate the two sequences internally requires more memory resources than some of us can muster.

Many cognitive scientists would think of this as a silly problem, or as a problem of performance that only highlights the weaknesses of the human mind and does not tell us anything about cognitive architecture. But I believe the real power of human cognition lies in our ability to flexibly construct functional systems that accomplish our goals by bringing bits of structure into coordination. That culturally constituted settings for activity are rich in precisely the kinds of artifactual and social interactional resources that can be appropriated by such functional systems is a central truth about human cognition. The processes that create these settings are as much a part of human cognition as the processes that exploit them, and a proper understanding of human cognition must acknowledge the continual dynamic interconnectivity of functional elements inside with functional elements outside the boundary of the skin.

What you think cognition is and what you believe is part of the architecture of cognition depends on what you imagine to be typical or important cognitive tasks and what you think a person is. In thinking about the use of a written procedure, it is clear that there are many ways to produce the coordination between the physical structure of the procedure and the processes that execute the actions described by the steps of the procedure. Even the simple task of considering steps in order can be solved in many ways at different times, or perhaps can be solved by the confluence of many methods at one time. Given the ubiquity of such performances in modern life, I take this to be the sort of cognitive performance for which we should be able to account. There is also a good deal of this kind of activity in nonliterate societies. Procedures can be encoded in structure other than writing. The arrangement of persons or objects in space (in a queue, for example) can serve as a mediating device for the sequential control of action and may elicit a set of coordinating procedures like those observed in interactions with written procedures.

From this perspective, what we learn and what we know, and what our culture knows for us in the form of the structure of artifacts and social organizations, are these hunks of mediating structure. Thinking consists of bringing these structures into coordination so that they can shape and be shaped by one another. The thinker in this world is a very special medium that can provide coordination among many structured media—some internal, some external, some embodied in artifacts, some in ideas, and some in social relationships.

In this chapter I will raise some questions about the processes by which the organization of work arises. While in the previous chapter I examined learning by individuals, here I will look closely at an incident in which learning takes place in the larger unit of cognitive analysis. Common sense suggests that work is organized in accordance with plans created by designers who reflect on the work setting and manipulate representations of the work process in order to determine new and efficient organizational structures. When "outside" designers are not involved, the reorganization of work is attributed to conscious reflection by members of the work group. Examining the response of the *Palau*'s navigation team to a change in its informational environment, I will argue that several important aspects of a new organization are achieved not by conscious reflection about the work but by local adaptations to the emerging conditions of the work itself. The solution reached is one that we recognize in retrospect as being just the sort of solution we would hope designers could produce, yet it is a product of adaptation rather than of design.

While I was aboard the *Palau* observing the navigation team, the ship's propulsion system failed unexpectedly during an entry into San Diego Harbor. The opening paragraphs of chapter 1 describe the event and the bridge team's response to the difficulties created by the failure of the propulsion plant. Without steam pressure, the crew could neither steer the ship effectively nor bring it to a rapid stop. All thoughts of continuing to the pier were abandoned, and the crew struggled to simply prevent the ship from going aground until it had lost enough speed so that the anchor could safely be dropped. In an impressive exhibition of seamanship, the crew brought the *Palau* to anchor out of the main shipping channel. Tugboats were summoned and the propulsion plant was restarted. The ship later continued to the pier under its own power.

Besides taking away the ability to maneuver, the loss of steam pressure brought a cascade of electrical failures that affected many aspects of the ship's operation. Among the electrical devices that failed was the gyrocompass, which is crucial to navigation. This incident provided me with an opportunity to witness and record the response of a complex organizational system to a very real crisis.

The immediate response of the navigation team to the loss of steam and electrical power was simply to continue with the fix they were in the midst of taking. However, one of the pieces of electrical equipment that lost power was the main (Mark-19) gyrocompass. There are two layers of redundant protection for the gyrocompass function: independent emergency electrical power and a backup gyrocompass. Unfortunately, the emergency power supply for the gyrocompass failed to come on line, and the backup gyrocompass had been secured (taken out of service) earlier because of a maintenance problem. The main gyrocompass did not fail completely when the lights went out, but it does appear to have been mortally wounded. The gyrocompass operates by spinning a disk at very high speed and will operate adequately for a while before it spins down and loses stability. Sixteen minutes after the loss of power, the *Palau*'s speed had dropped to less than 4 knots and the ship was less than half a mile from its intended temporary anchorage when word was passed to the bridge from the forward interior communications (IC) room that the gyrocompass had ceased operation. This was an especially critical period for the navigation team. The chosen anchorage location was out of the navigation channel and near an area where the water shoaled rapidly. Dropping the anchor too soon would leave the ship obstructing traffic in the channel; dropping it too late might allow the ship to swing around and ground upon a shoal. Simply restoring power to a gyrocompass is not sufficient to bring it to a usable state; several hours are usually required for the gyro to "spin up and settle in" so that it will provide reliable readings.

Figure 8.1 shows the relations among the various terms of the computation. With the gyrocompass working, the alidade (telescopic sight) mounted on the pelorus permits the direct measurement of the direction of the bearing of the landmark with respect to true north ("true bearing" in the figure). When the gyrocompass failed, all that could be measured by the bearing takers with the pelorus was the direction of the landmark with respect to the ship's head ("relative bearing"). In order to compute the true bearing of the landmark, once the relative bearing has been determined, it is necessary to determine the direction of the ship's head with respect

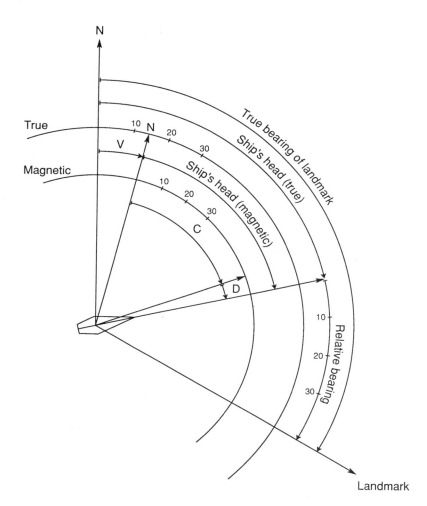

Figure 8.1 The relationships among the terms of the bearing-correction computation. True bearing of landmark from ship equals compass heading (C), plus deviation (D), plus magnetic variation (V), plus relative bearing (RB).

to true north. The magnetic compass, which does not require electrical power, measures the direction of the ship's head with respect to magnetic north (C in the figure). But the compass reading must first be corrected for errors, called *deviation*, that are specific to the compass and dependent upon the heading (D in the figure). Cartographers measure the difference between true north and magnetic north for all mapped regions of the world. This is called the *variation* (V in the figure). The sum of these terms is the true bearing of the landmark, which was directly measured by the gyrocompass when it was working.

There is a mnemonic in the culture of navigation that summarizes the relations among the terms that make up the ship's true head. It is "Can Dead Men Vote Twice?" and it stands for the expression $C+D=M$, $M+V=T$ (compass heading plus deviation equals magnetic heading, magnetic heading plus variation equals true heading). This specifies a meaningful order for the addition of the terms in which every sum is a culturally meaningful object in the world of navigation. Every competent navigation practitioner can recite this mnemonic, and most can give an accurate account of what it means. The knowledge that is embodied in this formula will be an important component of the solution discovered by the navigation team. Notice, however, that this mnemonic says nothing about relative bearings.

The computational structure of the task is well known. As was described above, computing true bearings for landmarks from relative bearings involves adding together the ship's compass heading, the compass deviation for that heading, the magnetic variation appropriate for the geographic location, and the bearing of the landmark relative to the ship's head. The procedure for a single line of position therefore requires three addition operations. If one used this procedure for each line of position, the set of three lines of position that make up a position fix would require nine addition operations. There is a substantial saving of computational effort to be had, however, by modularizing the computation in a particular way. Since all three lines of position in any given fix are observed as nearly simultaneously as is possible, the ship's head for all of them must be the same. Thus, one can compute the ship's true heading (sum of compass heading, deviation, and variation) just once and then add each of the three relative bearings to that intermediate sum. This procedure requires only five addition operations for the entire fix (two for the ship's true head and one for each of the relative bearings), compared to the nine addition operations required by the non-modularized procedure. As we shall see when we consider the details of the actual performance of the team, even a small saving of computational effort can be very helpful in this high-workload environment.

A search of the *Palau*'s operations and training materials revealed many documents that describe in detail the nominal division of labor among the members of the navigation team in the normal crew configurations, and many that describe the computational requirements for deriving a single line of position from compass heading, deviation, variation, and relative bearing. There was, however, no evidence of a procedure that describes how the computational work involved in fixing position by visual observation of relative bearings should be distributed among the members of the navigation team when the gyrocompass has failed. The absence of such a procedure is not surprising. After all, if the ship had a procedure for this situation, it should have procedures for hundreds of other situations that are more likely to occur, and it is simply impracticable to train personnel in a large number of procedures in an organization with a high rate of turnover.

What might a procedure for dealing with the event we are considering be like? Clearly it should take advantage of the benefits of modularizing the computation. Perhaps it should call for the computation of ship's true head, followed by the computation of each of the true bearings in turn. That much seems straightforward, but how should one organize the activities of the separate team members so that they can each do what is necessary and also get the new job done in an efficient way? This is a nontrivial problem because there are so many possibilities for permutations and combinations of distributions of human effort across the many components of the computational task. The design should spread the workload across the members of the team to avoid overloading any individual. It should incorporate sequence-control measures of some kind to avoid discoordinations (in which crew members undo one another's work), collisions (in which two or more team members attempt to use a single resource at the same time), and conflicts (in which members of the team work at cross-purposes). It should exploit the potential of temporally parallel activity among the members of the team, and where possible, it should avoid bottlenecks in the computation. This is quite a complicated design problem, and it looks even more difficult when we examine the relationships between the members of the navigation team and their computational environment. Given the nature of the task they were performing, the navigation team did not have the luxury of engaging in such design activities. They had to keep doing their jobs, and in the minutes between the loss of the gyrocompass and the arrival of the ship at anchor the requirements of the job far exceeded the available resources

The Adaptive Response

Viewing the navigation team as a cognitive system leads us to ask where in the navigation team the additional computational load imposed by the loss of the gyrocompass was taken up and how the new tasks were accomplished. To summarize before examining the performance of the team in detail: The additional computation originally fell to the quartermaster chief, who was acting as plotter. He attempted to do the added computations to correct the relative bearings passed to him using mental arithmetic, but it was more than he could do within the severe time constraints imposed by the need for fixes at one-minute intervals. By trading some accuracy for computational speed he was able to determine when the ship had arrived at its intended anchorage. After the *Palau* came to anchor, the plotter introduced a handheld calculator to relieve the burden of mental arithmetic under stress and recruited the assistance of the recorder in the performance of the computation. There was no explicit plan for the division of the labor involved in this added task between the plotter and the bearing recorder. Each had other duties that were related to this problem. Dropping the anchor did not remove the requirement to fix the position of the ship. A ship at anchor may be blown by the wind or pushed by the tides and swing around its anchor. As it swings, the ship sweeps over a circle the diameter of which is the sum of the length of the ship and the distance from the bow of the ship to the anchor. Even in shallow water, the *Palau* can sweep a circle more than 1500 feet in diameter. Since there was shoal water on one side and a shipping channel on the other, it was important to maintain awareness of the location of the ship.

Since this correction computation has well-defined subparts, we may ask how the subparts of the task were distributed among the participants. But here we find that at the outset there was no consistent pattern. The order in which the various correction terms were added and who did the adding varied from one line of position (LOP) to the next, and even the number of correction terms changed over the course of the 66 LOPs that were shot, corrected, and plotted between the loss of the gyrocompasses and the arrival of the *Palau* at its berth. Gradually, an organized structure emerged out of the initial chaos. The sequence of computational and social-organizational configurations through which the team passed is shown in figure 8.2. After correcting and plotting about 30 LOPs, a consistent pattern of action appeared in which the order of application of the correction terms and the division of labor between the plotter and the bearing recorder stabilized. While the computational structure of this stable configuration seems to have been at least in part intended by the plotter, the social structure (division of

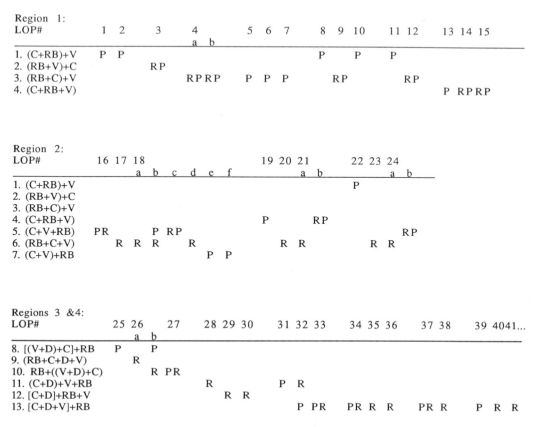

Figure 8.2 Computing a line of position. The structure of the computation is given in the left column. Lines of position are numbered across the top of each section of the figure. P indicates an LOP computation performed entirely by the plotter. R indicates an LOP computation performed entirely by the recorder. RP indicates an LOP computation begun by or structured by the recorder and completed by the plotter. PR indicates a computation begun by or structured by the plotter and completed by the recorder.

labor) seems to have emerged from the interactions among the participants without any explicit planning.

Analysis

The bearing takers out on the wings of the ship were only slightly affected by the loss of the gyrocompass. For them, it meant only that they had to remember to shoot the bearings relative to ship's head—the outer rather than the inner of the two azimuth circles in the alidade viewfinder (figure 1.7). The analysis will therefore focus on the activities of the plotter, Quartermaster Chief Richards, and the bearing recorder, Quartermaster Second Class Silver.

We can consider the behavior of the plotter and the recorder to be a search in a very complex space for a computational structure and a social structure that fit each other and that get the job done. As figure 8.2 shows, these two men explored 13 different computational structures and many social configurations on their way to a stable configuration.

How can we account for this seemingly bizarre search of computational and social space? I will claim that there are four main principles that organize the computation:

- computational structure driven by the availability of data
- the use of a normative description to organize computation
- the computational advantages of modularizing the addition task
- the fit between computational and social organization.

The events that occurred between the failure of the gyrocompass and the end of the task can be partitioned into four temporal regions on the basis of these principles. In the first region, lines of position 1–15, the plotter did all the computation himself and the computational structure was driven primarily by the availability of data. The end of this region is marked by the introduction of an electronic calculator. In the second region, LOPs 16–24, the plotter began to push some of the computational load onto the recorder. While providing the recorder with instruction on how to do the computation, the plotter began to use a normative description to organize the computation. In the third region, LOPs 25–33, the modularity of the computation became a shared resource for the two men through their joint performance of the modular procedure. In the fourth and final region, LOPs 34–66, they discovered a division of labor that fit the computation and they coined a lexical term for the modular sum, thus crystallizing the conceptual discovery in a shared artifact. Now let us look at the details of the work at the chart table, considering the lines of position plotted from the time the gyrocompass failed until the system settled into its new stable configuration. (Refer to figure 8.2.)

REGION 1: COMPUTATIONAL STRUCTURE DRIVEN BY DATA AVAILABILITY

The plotter computed the first 12 lines of position using what would normally be called mental arithmetic. In some cases, this arithmetic was aided by artifacts in the environment. In the very first LOP, for example, he used the scale of the hoey (chart plotting tool) as a medium for addition, aligning up the scale index with 29 (the compass course), sliding it 52 gradations upward (the relative bearing), and sliding it an additional 14 gradations to add the variation. In LOP 2 he used the bearing log as a memory during the computation, tracing out the addition columns with his fingers. LOPs 8 and 9 were computed using paper and pencil in the margins of the chart. The plotter had a good deal of trouble keeping up with the demands of the task; this is shown by the fact that, even though three bearings were observed for each fix, the plotter was able to plot only two LOPs for the first fix, one for the second, and two for the third.

The anchor was dropped at 17:06, just before the fifth line of position was plotted. Once the anchor was down, the team went from one-minute to six-minute fix intervals, but the plotter was still having trouble keeping up while doing mental arithmetic.

The plotter's behavior in this region can be described as opportunistic. He used three different computational orderings and several different media in computing the first twelve lines of position. Though at first glance this behavior looks unsystematic, there is a simple but powerful regularity in it. The order in which the plotter took the terms for addition depends on where the terms were in his environment and on when and with how much effort he could get access to them. For example, in LOP 8 the plotter returned to the chart table verbally rehearsing the ship's magnetic heading. He began his computation with that term. In LOP 9, where the plotter had to consult the recorder in order to establish the identity of the next relative bearing to add, he began his computation with relative bearing. In LOP 10 the plotter was again doing the calculation on his own, and again he began with ship's magnetic head. These patterns are hints to a more general organizing principle that is evident throughout this event. In the first two regions of figure 8.2, 12 out of the 15 LOPs for which the computation is initiated by the plotter begin with the ship's magnetic head, and 13 out of 18 computations initiated by the recorder begin with the relative bearing of the landmark.

This regularity appears to be a consequence of local strategies for individual cognitive economy. From the perspective of a person trying to do the addition, if one of the terms is already in working memory when it is time to begin the computation then it is most efficient to start with that term.

Consider the situation of the bearing recorder. When he does a computation while interacting with the bearing takers, he listens to, writes down, and verbally acknowledges relative bearings. These activities, although not part of the addition procedure, influence the course of that procedure because they put the relative bearing (RB) term into the working memory of the bearing recorder. With RB already in working memory, in order to do the computation in the order that supports modularization (C + V + RB), the recorder must somehow keep RB active in working memory or must over-write RB in working memory and read it again later when it is needed. If he chooses to maintain RB in working memory, then it must remain unaltered (and must not alter the other number repre-sentations present) during the reading of C, the recall of V, and the addition of C and V. This may require the recorder to maintain up to 11 digits in working memory (eight for the addition of V + C, plus up to three for RB). If the memory load of that task is too great, the recorder may choose to let RB be overwritten in working memory and read it in again later. Of course, that involves the wasted effort of overwriting and rereading RB.

In contrast to the costs of this "preferred" order, taking the terms in the order RB + C + V or RB + V + C involves lighter loads on working memory and no wasted effort. Thus, from the bearing tak-er's local perspective it was simply easier and more efficient to be-gin each computation with the relative bearing.

The plotter was in a different position. In most cases, he went to the helm station to get the ship's compass head while the relative bearings were being reported. This puts the C term into the plotter's working memory at the beginning of the fix. Notice in figure 8.2 that, except for LOPs 5–7, every LOP initiated by the plotter begins with C as the first term. But interaction with the recorder or with other representational systems can change the plotter's position in the computation. In each case where the plotter began by asking the recorder for a term to add, that term was the relative bearing and the relative bearing was taken as the first item in the addition. On closer inspection, the apparent exceptions to the rule in LOPs 5–7 are not exceptions at all. These computations were not done while the data were coming in. The observations of the three relative bearings were made while the plotter worked to determine the lo-cation of the anchor. Then he set out to compute the LOPs with all of the data in the bearing log in front of him, the relative bearings in the left columns of the page and the ship's magnetic head in the rightmost column. This interaction with the bearing log changed the temporal pattern of availability of data, which in turn changed the organization of the most efficient ordering of terms for the performance of mental arithmetic.

It is unlikely that either man was ever aware of having made a decision concerning the order in which to add the terms. Rather, each was simply trying to do the additions as correctly and as efficiently as possible. Since the two men experienced different patterns of availability of data, this principle produced characteristically different results for each of them.

The principle at work so far can be summarized as follows: Individual actors can locally minimize their workloads by allowing the sequence of terms in the sum to be driven by the availability of data in the environment. But since data become available primarily via social interactions, the computational structure is largely an unplanned side effect of this interactional structure. The interactional structure itself is chaotic because it is shaped by interference from other tasks and by social interactions with other members of the navigation team and with members of other work teams on the bridge.

After LOP 12, the recorder initiated a round of bearings on a two-minute interval. The plotter instructed him to take the fix on six-minute intervals and complained about not being able to keep up with the computations using mental arithmetic. When I asked if he had been able to keep up with the work, he said: "No, I was running it through my head and it wouldn't add. It wouldn't make numbers, so I was making making right right angles in my head to see where the hell it was at." The recorder said "You take the variation out of it." "Yes" said the plotter, "you add the, you add the magnetic head, then you add the variation." This conversation is the first evidence of reflection on the structure of the computation. The plotter explicitly named the variables: "... you add the magnetic head, then you add the variation." After this, the plotter remarked that the only way to keep up with the work would be to use a calculator. Shortly after this conversation, the plotter went to the charthouse and returned with a navigation calculator. The calculator was capable of computing a number of specialized navigation functions, but only addition and subtraction were used in what followed.

The use of the calculator eliminated the need for the intermediate sums that the plotter computed when doing mental arithmetic. In LOPs 13–15 the plotter keyed in the data. He started each LOP computation by keying in C+; then he looked for RB in the bearing book, keyed RB+, then keyed V=. Here the calculator was not only a computational device; the plotter also used it as a temporary external memory for the C term while he looked for the RB term. The immediate consequences of the introduction of the calculator were that it eliminated the production of intermediate sums (this will be important in the development of the modular solution below) and that it changed the memory requirements for the plotter by serving as an external memory. It did not change the fact that the order in which the terms were added was dependent on the pattern of availability of data in the task environment.

The dependence of the computational sequence on the availability of data is the main characteristic of events in the first region. It will survive into later regions in the behavior of the recorder, but the introduction of the calculator marks the beginning of the end of this sort of data-driven task organization for the plotter. Up until and including the first calculator round, the recorder has sometimes fed values of RB to the plotter but has done no arithmetic, mental or otherwise. That is about to change.

The following conventions are used to record the verbal and nonverbal actions of the plotter and the recorder in the transcripts below.

( )   Words enclosed in parentheses are comments or annotations of the actions observed in the video record, never verbatim transcriptions.

\#   Hash marks are used in adjacent lines of transcription to indicate simultaneity of occurrence.

/?/   This represents an unintelligible portion of an utterance.

{ }   Numbers and actions enclosed in braces denote key presses on the calculator.

{3 +}   Numbers and actions in boldface enclosed in braces are key presses on the calculator that are verbally shadowed. This example would mean that a person pressed the 3 and the + key while saying "Three plus." In addition to numbers, the most frequent key presses are +, −, =, and clear.

1 20   Spoken numbers have been transcribed mostly as numerals for convenience. If they are separated by spaces, each numeral was pronounced separately. If they are not separated by space, then they are to be read as conventional numbers.

This example could also have been transcribed "One twenty."

The following is a key to the notation for the computation:

C   The compass heading of the ship with no corrections.

D   Compass deviation. A function of heading.

V   Magnetic variation. Approximately 14° east in San Diego Harbor.

RB   The relative bearing of a landmark. This is the bearing of the landmark with respect to the ship's head.

M   Ship's magnetic heading (C+D).

T   Ship's true head (M+V)

TB   True bearing (T+RB).

( )   Terms enclosed in parenthesis were entered into the calculator with only + or − operators among them. The = operator closes the parenthesis. Thus, **(C + V + RB)** means that the three terms were added together as a group; **((C + V) + RB)** means that the = operator was applied to (C+V), which was then added to RB.

[ ]   Sums in brackets were spoken as intermediate sums. Thus, **([(V + D) + C] + RB)** denotes the following actions: key V, key +, key D, key =, key +, key C, key =, read the displayed value aloud, key +, key RB, key =.

How can we know the order in which the terms of the computation were applied? The computations involved in each line of position were reconstructed from the data available in the following way: Usually, the values of all of the variables were either present in the transcript or could be determined. In all cases, the variation was 14°. In LOP 8, for example, I had a record of the helmsman telling the chief that the ship's head was 3 3 5 degrees. The relative bearing to Silvergate was reported by the port pelorus operator as 275°. The problem was to arrange these in a way that fit with the numbers that were verbalized. Here is what the plotter said:

Is 3 3 5, 3 3 5. Oh wow. (Mumbles 3 seconds. The plotter watched the recorder write down the bearing to Silvergate. The plotter then jotted the bearing on the chart and did place value arithmetic in the margin of the chart.) 1 1 6, 60, 0, 6 from 1 is 5, 2 5 0, 2 5 0 ah, 2 5 0 would give me 2 6 4. 2 6 4, what the hell is it to? Ah, I know what it is to, it's got to be to Silvergate. Yeah. 2 6 4.

Clearly the plotter added the ship's magnetic heading, 335°, to the relative bearing of the landmark, 275° as shown below. The "1 1 6" appeared to refer to the carry digits and the sums of the leftmost two columns of the addition. It was impossible to determine which spoken 1 referred to which carry digit or to the sum of the central column. Nevertheless, it was certain that this was the sum being performed. Since this summed to more than 360, it was necessary to subtract 360 from the sum. The spoken 60 may have been the 60 of 360. Then there was the 0 which was the subtraction of the right column, followed by an entire description of the subtraction carried out in the center column: "6 from 1 is 5." Up to this point, the addition was done with paper and pencil on the margin of the chart. From here on it was conducted mentally. The outcome, 250, was rehearsed twice; then the variation was added to it to produce the final sum.

The complete reconstruction is shown below. The numbers in boldface appear explicitly in the transcript; the numbers in lightface do not appear in the transcript but can be inferred to have been present.

$$
\begin{array}{r}
{}^{1}{}^{1} \\
\mathbf{3\,3\,5} \\
\underline{2\,7\,5} \\
\mathbf{6\,1\,0} \\
\underline{3\,6\,0} \\
\end{array}
$$

$$
\mathbf{5\,0}\quad \mathbf{2\,5\,0}\quad
\begin{array}{r}
\mathbf{2\,5\,0} \\
\underline{1\,4} \\
\mathbf{2\,6\,4}
\end{array}
$$

Thus, we can infer that the addition of the correction terms for LOP 8 were taken in the order $(C+RB)+V$. Similar reconstructions were done for all LOPs in the event. In some cases it was necessary to reconstruct the actual fix itself as well in order to disambiguate unclear utterances in the tape recordings. Using this technique, it was possible to determine the exact order in which the terms were taken in all cases but three. The cases where it was not possible to make a clear determination all involved errors committed by the members of the team. In those cases I have attempted to make the most likely reconstruction.

REGION 2: EMERGENCE OF MEDIATING STRUCTURE
The most important consequence of the introduction of the calculator was that it created a new context of interaction between the

plotter and the recorder in which the plotter gave the recorder instruction in the procedure. For example in LOP 16 the plotter returned from the helm station, where he had read the compass heading and keyed in the value of C:

LOP 16:   **(C + V + RB)**

(Plotter returns from helm.)

Plotter: 2 3 1. What have we got? {231+ }

(Then he slides the calculator in front of the recorder.)
Here, add these things.
You want . . . You want the head. You want the head# which is
2 3 1

Recorder: #and
add variation.

Plotter: Plus variation.

Recorder: Oh, 2 3 1 is the head?

Plotter: 2 3 1. Here {clear **2 3 1**}

Recorder: I got it. (Recorder puts his hands on the keys.) {clear, 2 3 1}

Plotter: Plus 14.

Recorder: { + 14} OK.

Plotter: OK. (The intermediate sum was not computed.)

Recorder: { **+ 0 0 7 =**} is 2 5 2 on Silvergate.

Plotter: 2 5 2 Silvergate.

The plotter controlled the order of the arguments in this LOP. The recorder seemed surprised that he started with the ship's head.

In LOPs 17 and 18a, the plotter was busy plotting a previous bearing. The recorder initiated the computation himself by reading the RB from the book and beginning with it. In LOP 18a, the result was in error because the bearing that was reported was misread by the bearing taker. But the context of the error provided an opportunity to restructure the work. The recorder slid the calculator over in front of the plotter and began to dictate values starting with what was for him the most salient term, RB. The plotter, however, ignored the recorder and began keying in the data in the sequence C + V. The plotter made an error and cleared the calculator. The recorder, having seen the sequence in which the plotter wanted to add the terms, dictated the terms in the order (C + V + RB):

LOP 18c   **(C + V + RB)**

Recorder: 2 3 1, Chief, plus 14, plus #

Plotter: {2 3 1 + 1 4 + }   #OK, what was ah,

Recorder: The bearing was 1 5 7. (3 seconds) #OK

Plotter: {1 5 7 = }   #4 0 2

Recorder: Minus 3 60 # is

Plotter: { − #3 60 = } is 0 4 2. No it ain't. It isn't no 0 4 2. Its just not working. Look where 0 4 2 goes. (The plotter points to the chart.) If it's 0 4 2, we're sitting over on Shelter Island!

There were three more attempts to compute this LOP. In LOP 18d, the recorder made a data-entry error and passed the calculator to the plotter in frustration. In LOP 18e, the plotter made a data-entry error, cleared the calculator, and began again.

We might have thought that the importance of the introduction of the calculator would be its power as a computational device. In fact we see that using the calculator the team was neither faster nor more accurate than without it! The important contribution of the calculator was that it changed the relation of the workers to the task. When the plotter pushed the calculator over to the recorder and told him to add the terms, he engaged in a new task, that of instructing the recorder in the computation, and he organized his instructional efforts in terms of the normative computational structure, $C + D = M + V = T$. This was evident in LOP 16, where the plotter named the variables: "You want the head, which is 2 3 1.... Plus variation." Note that the recorder did not seem to learn from the explicit statements of the plotter. He returned to taking the RB first in LOPs 17, 18a, and 18b. However, once the plotter had articulated this structure it became a resource he could use to organize his own performance of the task. In LOP 18b, although the recorder had dictated the RB to him first, he keyed in $C + V$. There, the recorder verbally shadowed the plotter's keystrokes. This joint performance was the first time the recorder had taken ship's head as the first term. Once the plotter began behaving this way, the recorder was able to internalize the strategy that appeared in interpersonal work, and under certain social conditions he could use it to organize his own behavior. Thus, in LOP 18c, where the recorder took the role of dictating the values to the plotter (who was keying them in), the recorder said "2 3 1, Chief, plus 14, plus...." But the structure was not yet well established for the recorder. In the next attempt, LOP 18d, a new RB was observed and, driven by the data, the recorder began the computation with it.

The introduction of the calculator and the errors that were committed with it provided a context for instruction in which the sequence of terms could be explicitly discussed. The errors they were responding to were not sequence errors but simple key-pressing errors, yet they still served as contexts for sequence specification. The plotter appeared to learn from his own instructional statements (intended for the recorder) and changed his own behavior. Until he tried to instruct the recorder on what to do, he took the terms in the order in which they were presented by the environment. The recorder appeared to change his own behavior to fit with what the plotter *did*, not what he *said*. This newly emergent normative structure dominated the plotter's instructional efforts and came to dominate the organization of his task performance as well.

In LOP 21a, the recorder made a key-pressing error while adding the terms in the order (RB + C + V). The error drew the plotter's attention, and he turned to watch the recorder.

LOP 21b: **(C + RB + V) & ((C + V) + RB) = ((C + V) + RB + V)**

Recorder: {clear **2 2 1 # + 14** }

Plotter: #plus 14 is 2 3 5. *(C+V The plotter does it in his head.)*

Recorder: 2 3 5?

Plotter: Yeah, its 2 3 5 plus 1 1 8. **((C + V) + RB)**

Recorder: Oh. {clear}

(The recorder doesn't realize that hitting "=" would have produced 235.)

Plotter: 2 3 5 is #3 3 5, 3 4 5, how about 3 5 3. Right?

Recorder: {235 **# + 1 1 8 + 14 =**} How about 0 0 7? **((C + V) + RB + V)**

Plotter: 0 0 7.

Recorder: Chief, the computer just beat you. (The plotter glares at the recorder.) Just kidding. (They all laugh 4 seconds.) The modern technology.

Plotter: I'll modern technology you.

Here two important things happened. First, the recorder demonstrated that he could produce the normative sequence when trying to show the plotter he could do the addition correctly. Second, this was the first time the plotter had organized a properly modular computation. Unfortunately, it is also clear that the recorder did not yet understand the meaning of the intermediate sum (C + V), which is the key to the modularization. He mistook it for C alone and added in RB and V, thus generating an error. The plotter seemed intimidated by the calculator and did not challenge the result. It led to a poor fix, but he had been getting really poor fixes all along. The anchor was holding and the ship was in no danger, but at this point if they had had to rely on the quality of the fixes they would have been in trouble.

In LOP 22, the plotter failed to use the modular form of the computation. Unless they work together and make the modularized total available to each other, there is no advantage in modularization. The modularization is an instance of a much more general computational phenomenon. The construction of the compass-deviation table is part of the computation, but it is a part that was done by the navigation team days or weeks before the execution of this task. Similarly, the measurement of the variation is part of the computation, but it was done years ago by cartographers. In each case, parts of the computation that are not variable in the instance have been taken out and crystallized as artifacts (the variation printed on the chart, the deviation table). In the same way, the modular sum is a pre-computed invariant of the main computation.

The plotter performed LOP 23 with the nonstandard sequence (C + RB + V). This, however, is not a violation of the principles described above. The plotter did not get C from the helm at the beginning of the fix, as he usually did. Instead, he was busy asking whether the anchor was being hoisted at this time. The recorder announced C when the plotter returned to the table. The plotter looked in the bearing log for C. He read it aloud, and while still leaning over the book he added in the RB nearest him in the book, pointing to the place digits in it with the butt of his pencil as he added the numbers. Once again, the availability of data in the environment drove the organization of the computation.

LOP 24a: **(RB + C + V)**

Recorder: 1 1 2 plus 2 2 6 plus 14, 3 5 2 on ship's head.

(The recorder means to say "Hamm's light.")

Plotter: Which tower is he shooting for North Island Tower?

(The plotter leaves the table and goes to the port wing)
Hey, which tower are you shooting for North Island Tower?
(PW points to tower) You are? OK.

PW: Is that the right one?

Plotter: Yep.

(P returns to table)

LOP 24b: **(C + V + RB)**

Recorder: Which tower #wa—

Plotter: #And ah, what was Hamm's?

Recorder: And Hamm's was {2 2 6 **+** 1 4 **+** 1 1 2 =} 3 5 2. (5 sec)
Time 5 6 Chief.

In LOP 24a the recorder, working on his own, took the terms in
the order (RB + C + V). A few moments later, when the plotter asked
the recorder what the bearing was to Hamm's, instead of remembering it the recorder recomputed it. This time, LOP 24b, he
did it in the prescribed order, (C + V + RB). This is evidence that he
knew the sequence preferred by the plotter, but he seemed to produce it only in interactions with the plotter.

This brings us to the end of the second region. In this region we
have seen that a mediating structure is being remembered by the
plotter, but the recorder's organization of the computation is still
driven largely by the pattern of availability of data. The clear
boundary between this region and the first one is not marked by the
introduction of the calculator, but by the plotter's order "Here, add
these things." The change in computational structure follows from
a social innovation that was made possible by a technological
change rather than from the technological innovation itself.

REGION 3: PARTIAL MODULARIZATION

In the description of the computational structure of the task given
above, we noted that the true bearing is the sum of four terms:
ship's magnetic head, C; deviation, D; variation, V; and relative
bearing, RB. By now the team had computed and plotted 24 lines of
position, and the deviation term was not included in any of them.
This seems surprising, since we have ample evidence that both the
plotter and the recorder know well what deviation is and how to
use it. One can only surmise that they were so busy trying to do the
job that they forgot to include this term. Luckily, the absence of the

deviation term had no effect on the quality of the fixes plotted until LOP 22, because until then the ship was on a heading for which the deviation was near zero. Just before LOP 22, however, the ship's head swung southwest, to a heading for which there was a 3° deviation. The fix triangles started opening up and it became clear to the plotter that something was wrong. He lay the hoey on the chart from various landmarks and moved it slightly, seeing what sort of different bearings would make the triangle smaller. LOPs 25–27 are a reworking of LOPs 22–24, this time taking deviation into account.

1. Plotter: I keep getting these monstrous goddamn, these monstrous frigging goddamn triangles. I'm trying to figure out which one is fucking off.

2. Recorder: You need another round?

3. Plotter: No, no no, uh uh. 1 2 0 I know what he's doing. Let me try, let me try, (The plotter turns and moves to helm station) let me try, with my new ones, say three. (He reads the deviation card posted on compass stand.) Say three, add three to everything.

4. Recorder: Add three?

5. Plotter: Yeah.

6. Recorder: 'Cause he's using magnetic? (The recorder does not get it yet.)

LOP 25 $([(V + D) + C] + RB)$

7. Plotter: On a southwest heading add three. So its $(14 + 3 =)17$ plus 2 2, 17 plus 2 2 6 is ah, 2 3 ah

8. Recorder: Plus 2 2 6 is 3 4 is 2 4 3 $((V + D) + C)$
(The recorder is working on paper with pencil)

9. Plotter: Okay, 2 4 3 and 0 1 3 is 2 5 6. 2# 5 6 $([(V + D) + C] + RB)$

10. Recorder: #2 5 9 (this is an error)

11. Plotter: 2 5 nuh uh?

12. Recorder: 2 5 9, plus 0 1 3? It's 2 5 9.

13. Plotter: 2 5 9 that's right. OK. And plus 1 1 2 was what?

LOP 26a

14. Recorder: 1 1 2 plus 2 2 6 . . . . $(RB + C))$
(Here is clear evidence that the recorder doesn't understand the attempt to modularize.)

LOP 26b ([[(V + D) + C] + RB) & (RB + [(V + D) + C])

15. Plotter: Plus 2 4 3, 2 4 3 plus 1 1 2.   ([[(V + D) + C] + RB)

16. Recorder: 1 1 2 plus 2 4 3 is 5 5 , 3 5 5.   (RB + [(V + D) + C])

In the plotter's moment of discovery, line 3, where he said "I know what he's doing," he noticed that the geometry of the triangle was such that a small clockwise rotation of each of the lines of the previous fix would make the triangle smaller. A small error that belongs to all the LOPs suggests deviation. He went to the helm station and consulted the deviation card to determine the deviation for this heading. Although he describes the results as "much better," with deviation included, the two errors introduced by the recorder still result in a poor fix.

The plotter had compiled a new deviation table for the compass while at sea only a few days prior to this event, and the bearing recorder had demonstrated his mastery of the use of deviation in an at-sea exercise 2 months earlier. The principles of this computation are well known in the culture of navigation. I have no doubt that in an interview the plotter could describe the computation effortlessly. Their task here is not to discover these things "in the world" but to discover them in their own knowledge. Yet it takes the plotter 55 minutes and 24 lines of position to discover that he knows the proper order in which to add the terms to make the corrections.

The computation of 243° as the ship's true head and its use in LOP 26b (line 16) is the very first full modularization of the computation. The plotter has control of the computations in all three LOPs, although in LOP 26b he has to fight the recorder's strong propensity to put the RB first. The recorder clearly does not yet understand either the benefits of modularization or the necessity to add the RB last in the modular form. The structure of LOP 27 was modular too, but the value of ship's true head, while properly computed, was not correctly remembered.

Why the plotter recomputes all the lines of position for this fix instead of simply adding 3 to the earlier results he got is not so clear. It may be an attempt to eliminate any arithmetical errors that occurred in the previous round. It was, after all, a terribly big triangle. Also, all the calculations are done in this set by hand on paper with pencil rather than with the calculator. This could be a way of making sure that it was not the use of the calculator that was causing the problems.

The plotter seems to have taken the discovery of deviation and the recomputation of the bearings as an opportunity to think about the structure of the computation. The reflection that came in the wake of the introduction of the calculator led him to organize the computation in accordance with the normative form. The reflection that came with the addition of the deviation term led him to the modular structure. He never explicitly mentioned the advantages of modularization; however, if he was not aware of the advantages when he organized the computation, he must certainly have been aware of them once the computation had been performed.

The recorder computed LOP 28 while the plotter explained to the keeper of the deck log why the gyrocompass could not be restarted in time to help and why they must therefore make the remainder of the trip using magnetic bearings. The plotter's conversation was interrupted by the recorder, who checked on the procedure for using the deviation table.

LOP 28:   **([C + D] + V + RB)**

Recorder: Charles? (2 seconds) Head?

Helm: 2 2 6.

Recorder: 2 2 6

Recorder: So it's 2 2 6. You wanna add 3, right? On a southerly course? (3 seconds) Chief?

Plotter: Say again.

Recorder: You wanna add 3 to that /?/ southerly course? (pointing at the entry on the deviation table.) (2 seconds) It's 2 2 6. The magnetic head is 2 2 6.

Plotter: Yeah.

Recorder: 2 2 6 plus # 3, OK, so that makes 2 2 9. {**2 2 9** + 14}

Plotter: #right.

Recorder: {**+ 1 1 5** =} (3 seconds) 3 5 8 on Hamm's light. **([C + D] + V + RB)**

Thus, the recorder took the arguments in the right order in LOP 28 but did only a partial modularization. He computed $(C+D) = 229$ as a modular sum. Then he added V and added RB without producing the ship's true head as an intermediate sum. In LOPs 29 and 30, the recorder started with the partially modular sum and added the terms in the order $[C+D]+RB+V$. Even this partial modularization is an important step forward for the recorder. It appears to be due to two factors. First, including deviation in the computation may have made the C term more salient. Second, the recorder's location in the computation has changed. He recorded the relative bearings as usual, but he had to go to the helm station himself to get the compass heading because the plotter was otherwise occupied. At that point he had the C term in working memory and it was time to begin the computation. This change in location meant that what was best for the computation was also easiest for the recorder. This is not the best division of labor, but it is one for which there is a momentary local fit between social and computational structure. The pattern of availability of data was not running counter to the computational structure. Paradoxically, then, the extra work that took the plotter away from the chart table (a burden on the system) may have permitted the system to improve.

After one hour and twenty minutes at anchor, the *Palau* weighed anchor and began to move under its own power toward the pier. LOPs 32–33 are a turning point in the procedure. In LOP 32 there is a clear conflict of understanding between the plotter and the recorder. In LOP 33 they perform what will be the stable configuration for the first time.

LOP 32:   **([[(C + D) + V] + RB)**

1. Recorder: You want the aero beacon?

2. Plotter: Yeah, I want the aero beacon now, yeah. It's just.. 1 8 7, 8 8 , 8 7, 8 8.

3. Recorder: 0 2 0, what's the ship's head?

4. Plotter: Huh? 0 8 7. 8 7, it's # 1 west

5. Recorder: #0 8 7 it's 1 west , 7

6. Plotter: It's 8 6   **(C + D)**

7. Recorder: {**8 6**}

8. Plotter: And 14   # is 1 0 0 **((C + D) + V)**

9. Recorder: #{ **+ 14** }

10. Recorder: { **+ 1 0 0** }, hold it

11. Plotter: No, it's 1 0 0 plus whatever. **([[(C + D) + V] + RB)**

12. Recorder: 1 0, where are you getting? . . .

13. Plotter: 1 0 0 is the heading, the whole thing, #plus relative.

14. Recorder: #Oh, the whole thing. plus relative, { **+ 20 =** }, 1 20.

15. Plotter: OK

16. Recorder: 1 20 #is for North Island Tower.

LOP 33:   **([(C + D) + V] + RB)**

17. Plotter: #and Hamm's? (2 seconds) 1 0 #0 plus whatever for Hamm's.

18. Recorder: #Hamm's

19. Recorder: OK, {100 + **2 2 4** =}, 3 2 4 on #Hamm's

20. Plotter: #3 2 4.   That's   all three of 'em. I got 'em all.

21. Recorder: OK.

22. Plotter: Looks good. Right on. Perfect. Pinpoint fix.

23. Recorder: All right!

In LOP 32, the plotter works with the recorder to recompute the ship's true heading. This joint work in lines 4–16 provides the opportunity for the recorder to understand that the "whole thing" is the modular sum to which the RB can be added. The order in which the recorder added the terms still followed the pattern of data availability, but the plotter actively constructed the pattern of data availability so that the sequence produced by the recorder was the desired one. That is, the plotter acted as a mediator between the pattern of data availability in the task environment and the addition activities of the recorder.

The most salient features of region 3 were the emergence of the partial modularization of the computation and the conflicts between the plotter's newly solidified conceptual schema and the recorder's practices. In this region the plotter began to provide mediating structure that changed the pattern of data availability experienced by the recorder. In LOP 33 the recorder showed signs of using this mediating structure himself. For the recorder, the addition activity was no longer on the surface being applied opportunistically. It now lay behind a conceptual and social organization that fed it the terms of the expression in a particular order.

REGION 4: THE NEW STABLE SOLUTION

In the previous subsection, we saw how the behavior of one individual can act as a mediating device that controls the pattern of availability of data for the other. In the fourth and final region, the team discovered a division of labor in which each member could use a computational sequence that followed the availability of data in the task environment (thus minimizing memory load and wasted effort) while each simultaneously produced for the other patterns of data availability that supported the modular form of the computation. In this region the computational structure was still driven primarily by the pattern of availability of data, but the availability of data was determined by the social organization of the actions of the members of the team. Thus, the issue here is the fit between the constraints of cognitive processing (memory limitations, e.g) and the social organization of work (distribution of cognitive labor), as mediated by the structure of the computational task (modularity of addition).

In LOPs 34–36 the recorder and the plotter tuned their division of labor. They computed the modular sum jointly in LOP 34, and the recorder remembered the modular sum in LOPs 35 and 36.

LOP 34:   **([[(C + D) + V] + RB)**

Plotter: OK, what's he on? (to helm) What are ya on right now? 8, 8 5. 8 5, 0 8 5, 0 8 #4 plus 14 0 9 8.   **((C + D) + V)**

Recorder: #0 8 5 is 0 8 4 plus 14 , {**8 4 + 14 =**} that's

Plotter: OK

Recorder: 98

Plotter: 9 8 and 2 6

Recorder: 9 8 {**+ 2 6 =**} 1 2 4.   **([[(C + D) + V] + RB)**

Plotter: #1 2 4

Recorder: #1 2 4 North Island tower.

Plotter: OK

LOP 35:

Recorder: {**9 6 + 2 1 2 =**} 3 0 8 on Hamm's light. **([[(C + D) + V] + RB)**
(The recorder has misremembered the true head. It should be 98, not 96)

Plotter: OK

LOP 36:

Recorder: {98 **+ 3 5 7**}

Plotter: Damn near reciprocals.

Recorder: {**– 3 6 0 =**}

Plotter: 3 60 is #0 9 5

Recorder: ah   #0 9 5   **([[(C + D) + V] + RB)**

This is essentially the pattern of work they maintained all the way to the pier. By LOP 38 the final pattern was achieved. In this pattern, the plotter computed the modular sum alone, finding C and D at the helm station and recalling V from his long-term memory. Meanwhile, the recorder recorded the relative bearings. The plotter then added the first relative bearing to the modular sum, usually while the recorder was recording the last of the relative bearings. The plotter announced the modular sum to the recorder, and the recorder then added each of the other relative bearings to the modular sum. The only important event not included in these first 38 lines of position was the advent of a linguistic label for the ship's true head. They called it "total" in LOP 42 at 18:42. Once they had a name for it, they could pass it to each other more easily. The "publication" of the modular sum is essential to the final solution, since it acts as the bridge between the portion of the computation done by the plotter and that done by the recorder.

Discussion

It appears that four principles control the navigation team's search of the space of computational and social structures. They are (1) the advantages of operating first on the contents of working memory, which led the computational sequence to be entrained by the pattern of availability of data; (2) the use of normative computational structure, which permitted the discovery of (3) the advantages of modularization of computation; and (4) the fit of social to computational structure. Each region of the adaptation process was dominated by one of these principles. In fact, all of them, except the advantages of modularization, were present to some extent in all four regions of the adaptation history.

MEMORY LIMITATIONS AND AVAILABILITY OF DATA

In the beginning, the structure of the computation seemed to be driven exclusively by interaction between limitations of the human cognitive system (specifically memory limitations) and the availability of data in the environment (Newell and Simon 1972; Anderson 1983). Memory limitations made it advantageous to add the terms of the correction in the order in which they became available. The availability of data depended on the pattern of social interactions. This seemed to characterize the plotter's behavior until he assumeed a different relation to the computation at LOP 16. It described the recorder's behavior at least until LOP 32, and possibly to the end of the task.

At LOP 16, the introduction of the calculator gave rise to a new social arrangement (the recorder punched keys while the plotter told him which keys to press.) This gave the plotter a new relation to the computational task, which led, in turn, to the introduction of the normative computational structure. What the plotter remembered was acted out in interaction with the recorder. When the recorder took dictation from the plotter while keying in values, the plotter was mediating the task for him. The plotter was changing the recorder's relation to the task so that what was convenient for the recorder was also effective for the computation.

THE NORMATIVE COMPUTATIONAL SEQUENCE, $C + D = M$, $M + V = T$, $T + RB = TB$

There is no doubt that the plotter's computations were shaped by variants of the normative structure from LOP 16 on. There was only one exception to this (LOP 19), and in that case RB had a value that was particularly easy to handle (0 0 7). The plotter maintained this structure even when it ran counter to the pattern of availability of data, as in LOP 18b.

The recorder appeared to be capable of producing the normative sequence when in interaction with the plotter (LOPs 24b and 27), but when on his own he seemed to be driven by the availability of data. Thus, when computing the true bearings as he recorded the values of relative bearings, he always took RB as the first term. Before the discovery of the deviation term he used the sequence $(RB + C + V)$; after the inclusion of the deviation he used $(RB + C + D + V)$. In one instance, however, the plotter left the table to do another task, and the recorder computed the true bearings alone. After having recorded the relative bearings and having obtained the ship's magnetic head from the helmsman (C term in working memory), the recorder began with the C term.

The computational importance of the normative sequence is that it makes the modularization possible. Since addition is a commutative operation, there is no difference in the sum achieved by adding the terms in any of the 24 possible sequences. But if the addition is to take advantage of the modularity of the ship's true head, the terms C, D, and V will have to be added together before any of them is added to a relative bearing. The normative structure provides a rationale for doing this, and it provides culturally meaningful interpretations of the intermediate sums that are lacking from such non-normative additions as $(RB + V)$ and $(V + D)$. (See figure 8.1.)

THE MODULAR COMPUTATION

The modular organization of the computation emerges haltingly from the plotter's attempts to apply the normative form, but it seems unlikely that the plotter took up the normative form for its links to a modularized form of the computation. It is more likely that the normative form gave him a better understanding of what was going on by providing intermediate sums that have meaningful interpretations in the world of the ship. For an experienced navigator, a bearing is not simply a number; it is a body-centered feeling about a direction in space. Taking the terms in non-normative sequence results in intermediate sums that are just numbers. Taking them in normative sequence results in intermediate sums that are meaningful directions in the world of the navigator. In this form they become directions that make sense (or don't), and this gives the navigator another opportunity to detect error or to sense that the computation is going well or badly even before it is completed.

There was a hint of modularity in LOPs 18e and 18f, where the plotter computed $C + V$ and then asked for RB. Similarly, in LOP 21b he said "... it's 2 3 5 $(C + V)$ plus 1 1 8 (RB)." In each of these cases, there was only one LOP involved, so it was not possible to exploit the advantages of modularization. The first unambiguous case of modular computation was in the LOPs (25–27) that introduced the deviation term. These were performed in the non-standard sequence $([(V + D) + C] + RB)$. It is probably significant that the plotter chose to perform these calculations with paper and pencil rather than with the calculator. The paper-and-pencil computation produced, as a natural side effect, a written record of the sum $[(V + D) + C]$, which was then at hand for addition to each of the relative bearings. The written record of the modular sum in this instance was functionally similar to the verbal "publishing" of the labeled modular sum as "total" in the later fixes.

The modularization of the computation echoes the process of precomputation described in chapter 3. The modularized form of the computation captures a short-lived invariant of the environment in a temporary representation.

FIT OF SOCIAL AND COMPUTATIONAL STRUCTURE
The modular form of the computation became stable only when a new division of cognitive labor was established in LOPs 32 and 33. The pattern of availability of data produced by the division of labor in this stable configuration fit the computational structure of the problem. The plotter obtained C from the helmsman and D from the deviation table, added them, and then added the variation (easily available in memory). At the same time, the recorder recorded the

relative bearings of the landmarks. The plotter told the recorder the modular sum, which the recorder recorded, and the recorder provided the plotter with the first relative bearing. The plotter added this relative bearing to the remembered modular sum. While the plotter plotted the first LOP, the recorder then added each of the other recorded relative bearings to the modular sum. Thus, the team arrived at a division of cognitive labor in which the behavior of each of the participants provided the necessary elements in the information environment of the other just when they were needed. While each man could behave as though driven by the availability of data in the world, as a team they performed the additions in the sequence that exploited the benefits of modularization.

Adaptation by Design?

Since the work of Cyert and March (1963) organization theory has viewed routines as fundamental building blocks. Thus, the processes that change routines are very important to study. The description of the operation of the four principles that organize the performance of the task discussed above shows how a variety of solutions may be explored, but it does not in itself answer the question of how better solutions may become the routine operations of the system.

A classical view of organizational change is that an analyst looks at the behavior of the system, represents it explicitly, and plans a better solution. (See, e.g., Chandler 1966.) The better solution is expressed as an explicit description of the system's operation that is subsequently implemented in the real system by somehow altering the behavior of the participants to bring it into line with the designed solution. We often think of the organization of a system as a consequence of this sort of planning or design. We imagine an "outside" observer who observes the system's performance, represents it, operates on the representation to determine how to change the system, and then uses a channel of communication from outside the system to effect the changes (figure 8.3).

In her work on energy policy analysts, Feldman (1989) adds some complexity to the processes by which routines become stable elements of task performance. She describes organizational routines as "complex sets of interlocking behaviors held in place through common agreement on the relevant roles and expectations." She says that "any particular set of agreements about rules

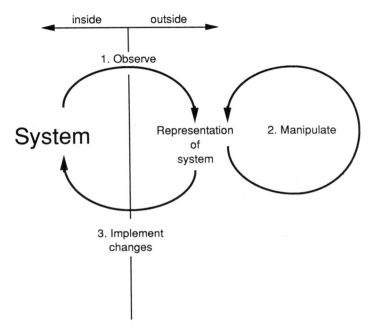

Figure 8.3 The basic design process. A representation that is "about" the entire system is created from observations of the system. This representation is manipulated in order to plan an intervention in the system.

and roles is a sort of equilibrium satisfying the demands of many different parties" (p. 136). A similar view is expressed by Nelson and Winter (1982) when they characterize routines as memory, truce, and target. This is a more subtle and interactive sense of the nature of the solutions to the problem of organization. An organization has many parts, and the operation of the whole emerges from the interactions of those parts. Each part may simultaneously provide constraints on the behavior of other parts and be constrained by the behavior of other parts. In chapter 2, I referred to this sort of system of mutually adaptive computational parts as a "cognitive ecology." This describes the sort of solution discovered by the navigation team on the *Palau*. The parties to the computation are the plotter and the bearing recorder, and the demands on them are constructed in the interactions among their cognitive processing capabilities, the structure of the computation, the availability of data, and the fit between computational and social organization. They settled into a solution that simultaneously satisfied all these constraints. In the same vein, Feldman (ibid.) writes: "Many organizations or parts of organizations must coordinate their behavior in such a way that each can cope adequately with the pressures and constraints it has to satisfy. While there may be many possible solutions to such a problem, they are not necessarily easy to find."

Given that organizations are the kinds of systems that consist of many interlocking, interacting, and mutually dependent parts, how can solutions to the organization problem be discovered? Feldman (ibid.) provides one answer "Even if one of the participants finds a new solution that will satisfy the constraints of all parties, the problems of persuading everyone else that this would be a beneficial change may still be considerable." Clearly the process described in this passage must happen frequently. Parts of the behavior of the navigation team fit this description nicely. The plotter's use of the normative computation scheme and his attempts to make that scheme explicit for the recorder are examples. But this answer is a retreat to the classical view. It posits a designer, albeit "one of the participants" who "finds a new solution" and then must "persuade everyone else" that it is a good solution. And there remain aspects of the adaptive responses of the members of the navigation team, particularly those involving the changing division of labor, that are simply not captured by *any* description that relies on explicit representation of the shape of the solution.

Adaptation and Local Design

In the analysis presented above, there are no instances of anyone's reflecting on the whole process. The plotter seems occasionally to represent the entire computation, but there is no evidence he ever imagined the structure of the division of labor. The adaptation process seemed to take place by way of local interactions, mostly of two types.

First, the members of the team put constraints on each other by presenting each other with partial computational products. When there is no previously worked out division of labor and assignment of responsibilities for various parts of the computation, team members negotiate the division of labor by doing what they can, or what is convenient, and hoping that others can do whatever else is required. These are changes that result from the interactions among the behaviors of the parts of the system as they adapt to the information environment and to the behaviors of other parts. There is no need to invoke any representation of the behavior of any part of the system to account for these adaptations. The way the computation was driven by the availability of data is an example of this kind of unreflective adaptation process. Even though they are not planned, these changes are not necessarily chaotic. If one part of the system behaves in a systematic way, another part may come to behave in a systematic way by adapting to the behavior of the first. In the interaction between the plotter and the recorder we saw that the behavior of one subsystem can be entrained by that of another.

A second adaptive process involves local design. When implicit negotiations of the division of labor fail, an actor may become aware of his inability to keep up with the computation and attempt to recruit others to take over parts of it. Thus, the most striking thing the plotter said during the search for a new configuration was something he said to the recorder while falling behind in his attempts to compute bearing corrections with a pocket calculator. He pushed the calculator at the bearing recorder and said "Here, add these things." There is no need to attribute a global awareness of the process to the plotter to account for this. He doesn't have enough time to do his own work, let alone to reflect on the overall division of labor. He is just acutely aware that he is falling behind and that he needs help to catch up. This is a case of local design. As figure 8.4 shows, design processes may be local to subsystems. This figure depicts an overall system that can change in three modes:

1. without any design activity at all, through the adaptive interactions among the subsystems
2. through local design activities in which manipulations are performed on representations of local subsystems in order to discover more adaptive relationships with the subsystem's environment (These changes may, in turn, lead to adaptive changes, either designed or not, by the other subsystems.)
3. through classical global design activities in which the representation is of the entire system of interest.

Modes 1 and 2 are processes that may lead the system to a a local minimum—a nonoptimal solution from which it is not possible to reach an optimal solution. The third mode is supposed to guard against that possibility. The response of the system to the change in its environment was eventually successful; however, it was the consequence of a large number of local interactions and adjustments, some of which led the system away from the eventual solution. Many of these adjustments appear to have been local design

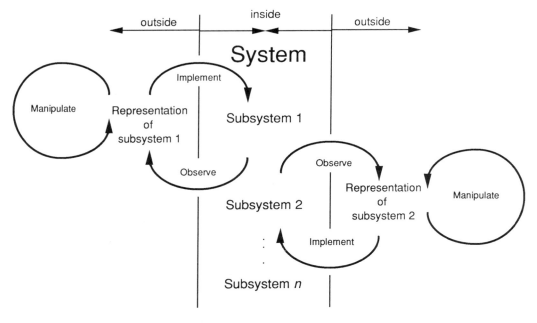

Figure 8.4 Local design activity. Subsystems interact with one another and adapt to one another's behaviors. Representations of local subsystem behavior are created and manipulated in order to plan changes to subsystem operation. These changes may trigger adaptive responses in other subsystems

decisions by the participants. Before its discovery by the system as a whole, however, the final configuration appears not to have been represented or understood by any of the participants. To the extent that the acquisition of a useful adaptation to a changing environment counts as learning, we must say that this is a case of organizational learning.

Evolution and Design

It seems to me that there is an important difference between the process of change via supervisory reflection and intervention imagined in the classical view and the process of change via local adjustment described above. It strongly resembles the difference between design and evolution (Alexander 1964).

Both evolution and design can be characterized as searches. The evolutionary search is conducted by the system in terms of itself; the design search is conducted by an "outsider" on representations of the system. The evolutionary search *is* the process of adaptation (see Weick's (1979) view of enactment); the design search precedes and guides an implementation of changes that are intended to be adaptive. Pure evolution is, in fact, a process without design (see Dawkins 1986). What we see in the case of the adaptation by the navigation team is an organizational change that is produced in part by an evolutionary process (adaptive search without representation of the search space) and in part by a process that lies between evolution and classical global-perspective design.

From this perspective, human institutions can be quite complex because they are composed of subsystems (persons) that are "aware" in the sense of having representations of themselves and their relationships with their surroundings. Whether we consider a particular change at the upper system level to be the result of evolution or the result of design depends on what we believe about the scope of the awareness of the subsystems. If we think that some of the subsystems have global awareness, and that they can represent and anticipate the consequences of possible changes, then we may view an organizational change as a result of design. If we believe that the subsystems do not form and manipulate representations of system operation, then we must view organizational change as evolutionary. What do we say when the individual subsystems only engage in local design activity—say, crying out for help when one is overworked? In that case, design is clearly involved, and the change in the local environment of the individual that adapts this way is a *designed* change. Now, that local designed change may have undesigned and unanticipated consequences for other parts of the system. It may thus provoke local adaptations by other parts of the system as all the parts seek (either by design or not) to satisfy the new environment of constraints produced by the changes in the behaviors of other parts. Ultimately, this process may produce a change in the behavior of the system as a whole. Even when many local design decisions are involved, such an adaptation at the system level appears to be evolutionary in the sense that the system-level change that resulted was never represented. I believe that most of the phenomena labeled as social or organizational "evolution" are instances of this kind of change.

Is the navigation task setting primarily the product of evolution or of design? Every participant can be both inside and outside in some sense. The changes in the organization of the navigation team were brought about by changes in the thinking of the participants of the system—that is, by changes in the agreements about rules and roles that constitute the organizational routine. To this extent, the structure of the setting is a product of design. But since the observed reorganization was never fully represented by any of the participants in the system, the actors' designs alone cannot account for the solution that was achieved. Thus, the organization of the navigation task is also a product of evolution. Although the participants may have represented and thus learned the solution after it came into being, the solution was clearly discovered by the organization before it was discovered by any of the participants.

The solution to the problem of organizing work that was discovered by the navigation team was not saved in the system. The conditions for the reproduction of this piece of knowledge are quite rare. The participants who were directly involved in this event eventually separated from the Navy without ever encountering this situation again. One of them went on to a position aboard a civilian oil tanker, so perhaps the knowledge constructed in this event will someday be reproduced in a different organizational setting.

The fact that the solution was not ultimately saved does not diminish this event's standing as an example of the processes of cultural innovation. The processes by which work is accomplished, by which people are transformed from novices into experts, and by which work practices evolve are all the same processes.

9 Cultural Cognition

The Costs of Failing to See Cognition as a Cultural Process

In this book I have tried to provide a coherent account of cognition and culture as parts of a larger system. This view is not widespread in cognitive science. Yet, there are unnoticed costs in failing to see cognition as part of a cultural process.

Marginalization of Culture

Early in the development of cognitive science, culture was relegated to a peripheral role. As Gardner (1985) pointed out, culture, history, context, and emotion were all set aside as problems to be addressed after a good understanding of individual cognition had been achieved. It is unfortunate that many anthropologists have encouraged this view by thinking of culture as some collection of things. Tylor (1871) defined culture as "that complex whole which includes knowledge, belief, art, morals, law, custom, and any other capabilities and habits acquired by man as a member of society." Goodenough (1957) gave cognitive anthropology its founding ideational definition of culture: "whatever it is one must know in order to behave appropriately in any of the roles assumed by any member of a society." This view has developed in cognitive anthropology over the years. Attempting to define a role for anthropology in cognitive science, D'Andrade (1981) proposed an intellectual distribution of labor in which psychologists would be responsible for the cognitive processes and anthropologists would be responsible for cognitive content. In this view, culture became simply a pool of ideas that are operated on by cognitive processes. Tylor's definition stresses the acquisition of cultural entities and tries to give a catalog of abilities and artifacts that constitute culture. Goodenough's definition was crucial to the birth of cognitive anthropology, but it and D'Andrade's formulation completely ignore the material aspects of culture. I reject both of these definitions.

Culture is not any collection of things, whether tangible or abstract. Rather, it is a process. It is a human cognitive process that takes place both inside and outside the minds of people. It is the process in which our everyday cultural practices are enacted. I am proposing an integrated view of human cognition in which a major component of culture is a cognitive process (it is also an energy process, but I'm not dealing with that) and cognition is a cultural process.

Anthropologists are also guilty of accepting this marginalization of culture, or even enhancing it, by granting a special place to the powers and limitations of the mind, as if these can be established without reference to culture. Anthropological structuralism tries to read the properties of minds from the structure of public representations. Sahlins (1976) criticizes it as follows: "It would seem ... that the main problem of 'reductionism' besetting modern structuralism has consisted in a mode of discourse which, by giving mind all the powers of 'law' and 'limitation,' has rather placed culture in a position of submission and dependence. The whole vocabulary of 'underlying' laws of the mind accords all force of constraint to the mental side, to which the cultural can only respond, as if the first were the active element and the latter only passive."

Marginalizing culture by reducing it to some collection of ideational contents hides the many ways in which cognition is part of the cultural process. Culture is a process, and the "things" that appear on list-like definitions of culture are residua of the process. Culture is an adaptive process that accumulates partial solutions to frequently encountered problems. It is unfortunate that cognitive science left culture, context, and history to be addressed after the understanding of the individual had matured. The understanding of the individual that has developed without consideration of cultural process is fundamentally flawed. The early researchers in cognitive science placed a bet that the modularity of human cognition would be such that culture, context, and history could be safely ignored at the outset, and then integrated in later. The bet did not pay off. These things are fundamental aspects of human cognition and cannot be comfortably integrated into a perspective that privileges abstract properties of isolated individual minds. Some of what has been done in cognitive science must now be undone so that these things can be brought into the cognitive picture.

Mistaking the Properties of the System for Those of the Individual
Another cost of failing to see the cultural nature of cognition is that it leads us to make too much of the inside/outside boundary or to assume the primacy of that boundary over other delimitations of cognitive systems.

CONSTRUCTION OF PRIMITIVE THOUGHT
A surprising side effect of the heavily drawn inside/outside boundary is that it reinforces the idea that individuals in primitive cultures have primitive minds. The firm drawing of the inside/outside boundary creates the impression that individual minds operate in isolation and encourages us to mistake the properties of complex sociocultural systems for the properties of individual minds. If one believes that technology is the consequence of cognitive capabilities, and if one further believes that the only place to look for the sources of cognitive capabilities is inside individual minds, then observed differences in level of technology between a "technologically advanced" and a "technologically primitive" culture will inevitably be seen as evidence of advanced and primitive minds. Differences in mental capacity seem necessary to account for differences in level of technology. I tried to show in chapters 2–6 that moving the boundaries of the unit of cognitive analysis out beyond the skin reveals other sources of cognitive accomplishment. These other sources are not mysterious, they simply arise from explicable effects that are not entirely internal to the individual.

Overattribution
Overlooking the cultural nature of cognition has another cost—one that may be the most interesting and far-reaching for the field of cognitive science itself. When one commits to the notion that all intelligence is inside the inside/outside boundary, one is forced to cram inside everything that is required to produce the observed behaviors. Much of cognitive science is an attribution problem. We wish to make assertions about the nature of cognitive processes that we cannot, in general, observe directly. So we make inferences on the basis of indirect evidence instead, and attribute to intelligent systems a set of structures and processes that could have produced the observed evidence. That is a venerable research strategy, and I have no objection to it in principle. However, failing to recognize

the cultural nature of cognitive processes can lead to a mis-identification of the boundaries of the system that produced the evidence of intelligence. If we fail to bound the system properly, then we may attribute the right properties to the wrong system or (worse) invent the wrong properties and attribute them to the wrong system. In this attribution game, there has been a tendency to put much more inside than should be there.

How Cognitive Science Put Symbols in the Head

If there are fundamental deficiencies in the dominant conceptions of cognition in cognitive science, how did that come about?

It is sometimes difficult to say things that are quite simple. The words we must say are simple, but sometimes it takes a lot of work to construct the conceptual framework in which those simple words have the right meanings. There are many possible readings for the sentences I want to write. In the previous chapters I tried to construct some of the conceptual background that will allow me now to say some simple things. However, one hurdle remains. Some of what I have done here departs from the mainstream of cognitive science. And some of the unexamined assumptions of the field make my words unruly. What I want to say cannot be said simply in that framework.

In order to construct a new framework, I will have to deconstruct the old one. In what follows I will give a brief "Official" History of Cognitive Science. This is a history as seen by the proponents of the currently dominant paradigm. I will then reread the history of cognitive science from a sociocultural perspective. In doing this I will identify a number of problems in contemporary cognitive science and attempt to give new meanings to some of the familiar events in its history.

The "Official" History of Cognitive Science

I begin the official history of cognitive science with a quote from Herbert Simon and Craig Kaplan (1989): "The computer was made in the image of the human."

The ideas on which cognitive science is based are so deeply ingrained in our culture that we can scarcely see how things could be otherwise. The roots of representationalism go back at least to Descartes.

Dreyfus (1992) summarizes the history of Good Old Fashioned Artificial Intelligence (GOFAI) as follows:

GOFAI is based on the Cartesian idea that all understanding consists in forming and using appropriate symbolic representations. For Descartes, these representations were complex descriptions built up out of primitive ideas or elements. Kant added the important idea that all concepts are rules for relating such elements, and Frege showed that the rules could be formalized so that they could be manipulated without intuition or interpretation.

The entities that are imagined to be inside the mind are modeled on a particular class of entities that are outside the mind: symbolic representations.

Symbolic logic has a special place in the history of cognitive science. The idea that a computer might be in some way like a person goes back to the formalization of logic and mathematics. In the early years of cognitive science, developments in information theory, neuroscience, psychology, and computer science came to have a synergistic interrelationship. In information theory the notion of a binary digit (bit) as the fundamental unit fit with speculations by McCulloch and Pitts that neurons could be characterized as on/off devices. Thus, the brain might be seen as a digital machine (this turned out to be wrong, but at the time that did not interfere with the developing synergy). Both of these ideas fit well with Turing's work showing that any function that could be explicitly specified could be computed by a class of machine called a universal machine and with his demonstration that the imaginary Turing Machine that operated on a binary code was an example of a universal machine.

The symbol-processing model of cognition has something else going for it as well: "A universal machine can be *programmed* to compute any formally specified function. This extreme plasticity in behavior is one of the reasons why computers have from the very beginning been viewed as artifacts that might be capable of exhibiting intelligence." (Pylyshyn 1989: 54) This was an essential component of the history of the field. Referring to the human cognitive architecture, Newell et al. (1989: 103) say that "the central function of the architecture is to support a system capable of universal computation." By choosing a formalism that is capable of any specifiable computation, the early theorists were surely casting a wide enough net to capture human cognition, whatever it might turn out to be. It seemed that the only viable challenge to this view would be a demonstration that human cognition might not be formally specifiable. There are many varieties of systems capable of universal computation. Newell and his colleagues and most others in the classical camp have taken what is called a "physical symbol system" as the primary architecture of human cognition. "A physical symbol system is an instance of a universal machine. Thus the symbol system hypothesis implies that intelligence will be realized by a universal computer." (Newell and Simon 1990) Newell and Simon (ibid.) define a physical symbol system this way:

A physical symbol system consists of a set of entities, called symbols, which are physical patterns that can occur as components of another type of entity called an expression (or symbol structure). Thus a symbol structure is composed of a number of instances (or tokens) of symbols related in some physical way (such as one token being next to another). At any instant of time the system will contain a collection of these symbol structures. Beside these structures, the system also contains a collection of processes that operate on expressions to produce other expressions: processes of creation, modification, reproduction, and destruction. A physical symbol system is a machine that produces through time an evolving collection of symbol structures. Such a system exists in a world of objects wider than just these symbolic expressions themselves.

According to Pylyshyn (1989), the notion of mechanism that underlies the classical concept of cognition is "concerned only with abstractly defined operations such as storing, retrieving, and altering tokens of symbolic codes."

Simon and Kaplan (1989) cite the Logic Theorist of Newell and Simon (1956) as an example of abstract intelligence and note the role of psychological research in its design:

The earliest artificial intelligence programs (for example, the Logic Theorist (Newell and Simon 1956)) are perhaps best viewed as models of abstract intelligence; but nonetheless their design was informed by psychological research on memory and problem solving—note, for example, the use of associative structures in list-processing programming languages and subsequently the frequent use of means-ends analysis for inference.

By embodying the growing knowledge of human information-processing psychology in computer programs, the early researchers were able to express their theories about cognition as working models that, in many cases, were capable of actually reproducing many important aspects of the behavior of human subjects.

Artificial intelligence (AI) and information-processing psychology thus have a synergistic relationship to each other. Information-processing psychology investigates humans as information processors via the computational metaphor of mind, while AI investigates machine implementations of intelligent processes. The operation of machines that are purportedly built in the image of humans is believed to shed light on natural human intelligence. Since the properties of abstract systems of intelligence are not dependent on the implementational details of the machines on which they run, intelligence in general (in addition to specifically human intelligence) can be investigated with this technology. The hope is that these traditions will continue to synergistically feed each other. In the most optimistic versions of the story, AI and information-processing psychology are the principal motors of scientific progress in cognitive science.

An Alternative History of Cognitive Science

Let us back up and examine the history of computers a bit more. The digital computer is a physical device that can support a mechanized version of a formal system. And it is this capacity that makes it a potential model of intelligence. Understanding computers requires an understanding of formal systems. We know that formal systems go back several thousand years in the history of our species. I do not know when the formal aspects of formal systems were first understood. I suspect that real understanding of the formal aspects of formal systems did not come until the revolutionary work on mathematics and logic at the beginning of this century that was critical to the foundation of cognitive science. Formal systems themselves are much older than our explicit understanding of them. The first arithmetic systems are at least 3000 years old, so we may take that as a minimum age of formal systems in the human experience. The idea of a formal system is that there is some world of phenomena, and some way to encode the phenomena as symbols. The symbols are manipulated by reference to their form only. We do not interpret the meanings of the symbols while they are being manipulated. The manipulation of the symbols results in some other symbolic expression. Finally, we may interpret a newly created string of symbols as meaning something about the world of phenomena.

Being able to find sets of syntactic manipulations of symbols that preserve this relationship so that we can reinterpret symbolic expressions into the world is of paramount importance. As Pylyshyn (1989) says: "One might ask how it is possible for symbolic expressions and rules to keep maintaining their semantic interpretation, to keep the semantics of the expressions coherent. It is one of the important discoveries of formal logic that one can specify rules that operate on symbolic expressions in such a way that the sequence of expressions always corresponds to a proof." If we built the right formal system, we could now describe states of affairs in the world that would have been impossible or impractical to observe directly. Such a state of affairs might be something in the future, which we cannot observe directly, but which can be predicted. I consider the mastery of formal systems to be the key to modern civilization. This is a very, very powerful idea.

The system of ship navigation that I have presented in this book is based on formal manipulations of numbers and of the symbols and lines drawn on a chart. It is a system that exploits the powerful idea of formal operations in many ways. But not all the representations that are processed to produce the computational properties of this system are inside the heads of the quartermasters. Many of them are in the culturally constituted material environment that the quartermasters share with and produce for each other.

Now, here is what I think happened. It was discovered that it is possible to build machines that can manipulate symbols. The computer is nothing more than an automated symbol manipulator. And through symbol manipulation one can not only do things we think of as intelligent, like solving logical proofs or playing chess; we know for a fact that through symbol manipulation of a certain type it is possible to compute any function that can be explicitly specified. So, in principle, the computer could be an intelligent system. The mechanical computers conceived by Charles Babbage to solve the problem of unreliability in human compilers of mathematical and navigational tables were seen by his admirers to have replaced the brain: "The wondrous pulp and fibre of the brain had been substituted by brass and iron; [Babbage] had taught wheel-work to think" (H. W. Buxton, cited in Swade 1993). Of course, a century later it would be vacuum tubes that created the "electronic brain."

But something got lost in this move. The origin myths of cognitive science place the seminal insights of Alan Turing in his observations of his own actions. Dennett (1991) describes the context of Turing's discoveries:

He was thinking self-consciously and introspectively about just how he, a mathematician, went about solving mathematical problems or performing computations, and he took the important step of trying to break down the sequence of his mental acts into their primitive components. "What do I do," he must have asked himself, "when I perform a computation? Well, first I ask myself which rule applies, and then I apply the rule, and then write down the result, and then I look at the result, and then I ask myself what to do next, and. . . ."

Originally, the model cognitive system was a person actually doing the manipulation of the symbols with his or her hands and eyes. The mathematician or logician was visually and manually interacting with a material world. A person is interacting with the symbols and that interaction does something computational. This is a case of manual manipulation of symbols.

Notice that when the symbols are in the environment of the human, and the human is manipulating the symbols, the cognitive properties of the human are not the same as the properties of the system that is made up of the human in interaction with these symbols. The properties of the human in interaction with the symbols produce some kind of computation. But that does not mean that that computation is happening inside the person's head.

John Searle's "Chinese room" thought experiment provides a good example of this effect. Imagine a room inside of which sits the philosopher Searle. Chinese people come up to the room and push strings of Chinese characters through a slot in the door. Searle slips back other strings of characters, which the Chinese take to be clever responses to their questions. Now, Searle does not understand Chinese. He doesn't know the meaning of any Chinese character. To him, the characters of written Chinese are just a bunch of elaborate squiggles. However, Searle has with him in the room baskets of Chinese characters, and he has a rulebook which says that if he gets certain sequences of characters he should create certain other sequences of characters and slide them out the slot.

Searle intends his thought experiment as a demonstration that syntax is not sufficient to produce semantics. According to Searle, the room appears to behave as though it understands Chinese; yet neither he nor anything in the room can be said to understand Chinese. There are many arguments for and against Searle's claims, and I will not review them here. Instead, I want to interpret the Chinese room in a completely different way: The Chinese room is a sociocultural cognitive system. The really nice thing about it is that it shows us very clearly that the cognitive properties of the person in the room are not the same as the cognitive properties of the room as a whole. There is John Searle with a basket of Chinese characters and a rulebook. Together he and the characters and rulebook in interaction seem to speak Chinese. But Searle himself speaks not a word of Chinese.

Let us be clear, then, on the distinction between the cognitive properties of the sociocultural system and the cognitive properties of a person who is manipulating the elements of that system.

The heart of Turing's great discovery was that the embodied actions of the mathematician and the world in which the mathematician acted could be idealized and abstracted in such a way that the mathematician could be eliminated. What remained was the essence of the application of rules to strings of symbols. For the purposes of producing the computation, the way the mathematician actually interacted with the material world is no more than an implementational detail. Pylyshyn (1989) claims that while Turing was developing the notion of the mechanically "effective procedure" he was looking "at what a mathematician does in the course of solving mathematical problems and distilling this process to its essentials." The question of what constitutes the essentials here is critical. For Turing, the essentials evidently involve the patterns of manipulations of the symbols, but they expressly do *not* involve the psychological processes which the mathematician uses in order to accomplish the manipulations. The essentials of the abstract manipulation of symbols are precisely not what the person does. What Turing modeled was the computational properties of a sociocultural system.

When the manipulation of symbols is automated, neither the cognitive processes nor the activity of the person who manipulated the symbols is modeled. The symbols themselves are dematerialized and placed inside the machine, or fed to it in a form that permits the straightforward generation of internal representations. What is important about this is that all the problems the mathematician faced when interacting with a world of material symbol tokens are avoided. That is good news, if those things are considered unimportant, because they are a nuisance to model anyway. The rulebook (or the mathematician's scribbled notations of rules) is replaced by abstract rules, also inside the computer. The mathematician who was a person interacting with a material world is neither modeled by this system nor replaced in it by something else. The person is simply absent from the system that performs automatic symbol manipulation. What is modeled is the abstract computation achieved by the manipulation of the symbols.

All that is fine if your goal is to extend the boundaries of human computational accomplishments. But it is not necessarily a model of the processes engaged in by a person doing that task. These programs produce the properties, not of the person, but of the sociocultural system. This is a nontrivial accomplishment. But the culture of cognitive science has forgotten these aspects of its past. Its creation myths do not include this sort of analysis. *The physical-symbol-system architecture is not a model of individual cognition. It is a model of the operation of a sociocultural system from which the human actor has been removed.*

Having failed to notice that the central metaphor of the physical-symbol-system hypothesis captured the properties of a sociocultural system rather than those of an individual mind, AI and information-processing psychology proposed some radical conceptual surgery for the modeled human. The brain was removed and replaced with a computer. The surgery was a success. However, there was an apparently unintended side effect: the hands, the eyes, the ears, the nose, the mouth, and the emotions all fell away when the brain was replaced by a computer.

The computer was not made in the image of the person. *The computer was made in the image of the formal manipulations of abstract symbols. And the last 30 years of cognitive science can be seen as attempts to remake the person in the image of the computer.*

It is no accident that the language of the physical-symbol-system hypothesis captures so much of what is happening in domains like ship navigation. The physical-symbol-system hypothesis is based on the operation of systems of this type. Conversely, there is nothing metaphorical about talking about the bearing record book as a memory, or about viewing the erasure of lines drawn in pencil on a chart as forgetting. Sometimes my colleagues ask me whether I feel safe metaphorically extending the language of what's happening inside people's heads to these worlds. My response is "It's not a metaphorical extension at all." The computer was made in the image of the sociocultural system, and the human was remade in the image of the computer, so the language we use for mental events is the language that we should have used for these kinds of sociocultural systems to begin with. These are not examples of metaphorical extension from the base domain of mental events to the target domain of cultural activity. Rather, the *original* source domain for the language of thought was a particular highly elaborated and culturally specific world of human activity: that of formal symbol systems.

At first, the falling away of the apparatus that connects the person to the world went unnoticed. This may have been because there was a lot of justifiable excitement about what could be done with this technology. All that remained of the person, however, was the boundary between the inside and the outside. And this boundary was not the same as the boundary of the Chinese room. The boundary that remained was assumed to be the boundary of the person—the skin or the skull. In fact, it was the boundary of the formal system. The boundary between inside and outside became the boundary between abstract symbols and the world of phenomena described by symbols. The walls of the Chinese room were mistaken for the skin of the person. And the walls of the room surrounded the symbols, so the symbols were assumed to be inside the head.

This separation between the boundaries of the formal system and the skin shows up in the language of cognitive science. "Symbol systems are an interior milieu, *protected from the external world*, in which information processing in the service of the organism can proceed." (Newell et al. 1989: 107 [my emphasis]). Or:

Act*, as is typical of many theories of cognition, focuses on the central architecture. Perception and motor behavior are assumed to take place in additional processing systems off stage. Input arrives in working (memory), which thus acts as a buffer between the unpredictable stream of environmental events and the cognitive system. (ibid.: 117)

The "off stage" metaphor of Newell et al. expresses the isolation of the cognitive system from even the sensory and motor experiences of an organism. In fact, many cognitive scientists take the word 'cognitive' as an antonym to 'perceptual' or 'motor'. Here is a typical example of this usage: "This is especially true for tasks that are primarily cognitive, in which perceptual and motor operations play only a small role in the total sequence." A strong claim about the modularity of the human cognitive system is implicit in this use of language. It places a large divide between cognition and the world of experience. But the existence of perceptual and motor processes that are distinct and separate from so-called cognitive processes is not an empirical fact: it is simply a hypothesis that was made necessary by having constructed cognition out of a mechanized formal symbol processing system. Proponents of the physical-symbol-system hypothesis point to the existence of various sensory and motor memories that can act as buffers between cognition and the world of experience as evidence of this modularity. In fact, there may be many other uses for such buffers. We are unlikely to discover these other uses, however, as long as we keep cognition isolated from the world. For example, such buffers may be essential in maintaining training signals after the disappearance of stimuli while learning is taking place.

The model of human intelligence as abstract symbol manipulation and the substitution of a mechanized formal symbol-manipulation system for the brain result in the widespread notion in contemporary cognitive science that symbols are inside the head. The alternative history I offer is not really an account of how symbols got inside the head; it is a historical account of how cognitive science put symbols inside the head. And while I believe that people do process symbols (even ones that have internal representations), I believe that it was a mistake to put symbols inside in this particular way. The mistake was to take a virtual machine enacted in the interactions of real persons with a material world and make that the architecture of cognition.

This mistake has consequences. Why did all the sensorimotor apparatus fall off the person when the computer replaced the brain? It fell off because the computer was never a model of the person to begin with. Remember that the symbols were outside, and the apparatus that fell off is exactly the apparatus that supported interaction with those symbols. When the symbols were put inside, there was no need for eyes, ears, or hands. Those are for manipulating objects, and the symbols have ceased to be material and have become entirely abstract and ideational. The notion of abstractness was necessary to bleach the material aspect out of the symbols so that they could become freed from any particular material instantiation. Calling logic and mathematics "abstract" more than misses the point of their concrete nature as human activities; it obscures it in a way that allows them to be imported into a cognitive inner sanctum. The physicality of material symbols in the environment has been replaced by the physicality (causality) of the computer; thus, while the physical is acknowledged in the physical-symbol-system hypothesis, it is rendered irrelevant by the claim that the physical aspect is an implementational detail. This idea may also help to explain the indifference that cognitive science generally shows to attempts to study implementation in real human systems.

Observe how a proponent of the classical view treats the manipulation of a computational artifact. Here Pylyshyn (1989: 56) constructs an example of manipulations of symbols that are codes for numbers:

If you can arrange for the computer to transform them systematically in the appropriate way, the transformations can correspond to useful mathematical operations such as addition or multiplication. Consider an abacus. Patterns of beads represent numbers. People learn rules for transforming these patterns of beads in such a way that the semantic interpretation of before-and-after pairs corresponds to a useful mathematical function. But there is nothing intrinsically mathematical about the rules themselves; they are just rules for moving beads around. What makes the rules useful for doing mathematics is that we are assured of a certain continuing correspondence between the formal or syntactic patterns of beads and mathematical objects (such as numbers).

There are no hands or eyes in this description. There are only the formal properties of the patterns of beads. Pylyshyn is using the example of the abacus to show how the manipulation of symbols produces computations. He provides a very nice illustration of the power of this cultural artifact. He is not interested in what the person does, or in what it means for a person to learn, to "know," or to apply a rule. Rather, he is interested in the properties of the system enacted by the person manipulating the physical beads. That is fine as a description of the computational properties of a sociocultural system, but to take this as being about cognitive processes inside the skin is to recapitulate the error of mistaking the properties of the sociocultural system for the properties of a person. It is easy to do. It is something we do in our folk psychology all the time. But when one is really careful about talking about cognition, one must carefully distinguish between the tasks that the person faces in the manipulation of symbolic tokens and the tasks that are accomplished by the manipulation of the symbolic tokens.

A failure to do this has led to a biased view of the tasks that are properly considered cognitive. Problem solving by heuristic search is taken as a representative cognitive activity. This is tailor-made for the symbol-shuffling apparatus. The definition of cognition has been unhooked from interaction with the world. Research on games and puzzles has produced some interesting insights, but the results may be of limited generality. The tasks typically chosen for laboratory studies are novel ones that are regarded by subjects as challenging or difficult. D'Andrade (1989) has likened the typical laboratory cognitive tasks to feats of athletic prowess. If we want to know about walking, studying people jumping as high as they can may not be the best approach. Such tasks are unrepresentative in another sense as well. The evolution of the material means of thought is an important component of culturally elaborated tasks. It permits a task that would otherwise be difficult to be re-coded and re-represented in a form in which it is easy to see the answer. This sort of development of material means is intentionally prohibited in puzzle tasks because to allow this sort of evolution would destroy the puzzling aspects of the puzzle. Puzzles are tasks that are preserved in the culture because they are challenging. If the performance mattered, we would learn to re-represent them in a way that removed the challenge. That would also remove their value as puzzles, of course. The point is that the tasks that are "typical" in laboratory studies of thought are drawn from a special category of cultural materials that have been isolated from the cognitive processes of the larger cultural system. This makes these tasks especially unrepresentative of human cognition.

Howard Gardner (1985) is very kind to cognitive science when he says that emotion, context, culture and history were deemphasized in early cognitive science because, although everyone believed they were important, everyone also knew that they complicated things enormously. According to Gardner, getting the program started required a simple model of cognition. The field therefore deferred consideration of affect, culture, context, and history until such time as there was a good model of how an individual worked in isolation. It was hoped that these things could be added in later. That is a charitable reading of the history, I think. I can see why there were compelling reasons to see it as it was seen, and not to notice that something is wrong when AI was producing "deaf, dumb, and blind, paraplegic agents" (Bobrow 1991) as models of human cognition.

Newell et al. (1989) seemed genuinely puzzled by the fact that no one had succeeded in integrating emotion into the system of cognition they had built. Yet this failure is completely predictable from the assumptions that underlie the construction of the symbol-manipulation model of cognition. The person was simply omitted from what was taken as the model of the cognitive system. The model of cognition came from exactly that part of the system that was material rather than human. Within this underlying theory of cognition there can be no integration of emotion, because the part of the cultural system that is the basis of the physical symbol system excludes emotion. The integration of cognition with action will remain difficult because the central hypothesis separates cognition and action by definition. History and context and culture will always be seen as add-ons to the system, rather than as integral parts of the cognitive process, because they are by definition outside the boundaries of the cognitive system.

Adherents of the physical-symbol-system hypothesis are obviously aware of the presence of a world in which action takes place, and they have attempted to take it into account. Consider the following passage from Newell and Simon's seminal 1972 book *Human Problem Solving* :

For our theory, specification of the external memories available to the problem solver is absolutely essential. These memories must be specified in the same terms as those we have used for the internal memories; symbol capacities, accessing characteristics, and read and write times. The problem solving program adopted by the information-processing system will depend on the nature of its "built in" internal STM and LTM [short-term memory and long-term memory].

From a functional viewpoint, the STM should be defined, not as an internal memory, but as the combination of (1) the internal STM and (2) the part of the visual display that is in the subject's foveal view. . . .

In short, although we have few independent data suited to defining precisely how external memory can augment STM, the two components do appear to form a single functional unit as far as the detailed specification of a problem solving information-processing system is concerned.

This is a good start on the problem, but I think it is fair to say that in the twenty years since the publication of *Human Problem Solving* the use of material structure in the problem-solving environment has not been a central topic in the physical-symbol-system research agenda. Some recent work within this tradition takes the "external world" into account (Larkin 1989; Vera and Simon 1993) but treats the world only as an extra memory on which the same sorts of operations are applied as are applied to internal memories. Structure in the world can be much more than an augment to memory. The use of cultural structures often involves, not just the same process with more memory, but altogether different processes. The overattribution of internal structure results from overlooking the coordination of what is inside with what is outside. The problem remains that the nature of the interaction with the world proposed in these systems is determined by the assumptions of the symbolic architecture that require the bridging of some gap between the inner, cognitive world and an outer world of perception and action.

These criticisms by themselves are not sufficient grounds for rejecting the notion that humans are symbol-processing systems. Newell and Simon (1990) wisely acknowledge that the physical-symbol-system hypothesis is a hypothesis and that the role of symbolic processes in cognition is an empirical question. It has proved possible to interpret much of human problem-solving behavior as if the very architecture of human cognition is symbol processing. It's a hypothesis. A lot of data can be read as failing to reject it. Yet, the hypothesis got there under suspicious circumstances. There are no plausible biological or developmental stories telling how the architecture of cognition became symbolic. We must distinguish between the proposition that the architecture of cognition is symbolic and the proposition that humans are processors of symbolic structures. The latter is indisputable, the former is not. I would like to be able to show how we got to be symbol manipulators in relation to how we work as participants in sociocultural systems, rather than assume it as an act of faith. The origins of symbolic processes have not been explored this way, though, because they were obfuscated by the creation myth that maintains that the computer was made in the image of humans.

Increasingly, the physical-symbol-system hypothesis is a perspective into which things don't fit. It was a bet or a guess, grounded in a nearly religious belief in the Platonic status of mathematics and formal systems as eternal verities rather than as historical products of human activity. This is an old dispute that lies at the heart of the developing split in cognitive science between those who feel there is more to be learned from the physical-symbol-system research and those who feel it has been exhausted. (See the special January-March 1993 issue of *Cognitive Science*.) By advocating this alternative view, I am espousing what might be called a "secular" view of cognition—one that is grounded in a secular perspective on formal systems, in contrast with the quasi-religions "cosmic truth" view put forth by the symbolists.

Why cognition became disembodied is clear from the history of the symbolic movement. An important component of the solution is to re-embody cognition, including the cognition of symbol processing.

I believe that humans actually process internal representations of symbols. But I don't believe that symbol manipulation is the architecture of cognition. Historically, we simply assumed that symbol processing was inside because we took the computer as our model of mentality. Humans (and, I suspect, most other animals) are good at detecting regularities in their environment and at constructing internal processes that can coordinate with those regularities. Humans, more than any other species, spend their time producing symbolic structure for one another. We are very good at coordinating with the regularities in the patterns of symbolic structure that we present to one another. As was described in chapter 7, the internal structures that form as a consequence of interaction with symbolic materials can be treated as symbolic representations. Ontogenetically speaking, it seems that symbols are in the world first, and only later in the head.

Studying Cognition in the Wild

Many of the foundational problems in cognitive science are consequences of our ignorance of the nature of cognition in the wild. Most of what we know about cognition was learned in laboratory experiments. Certainly, there are many things that can be learned only in closely controlled experiments. But little is known about the relationships of cognition in the captivity of the laboratory to cognition in other kinds of culturally constituted settings. The first part of the job is, therefore, a descriptive enterprise. I call this description of the cognitive task world a "cognitive ethnography." One might have assumed that cognitive anthropology would have made this sort of work its centerpiece. It has not. Studying cognition in the wild is difficult, and the outcomes are uncertain.

Cognitive systems like the one documented in this book exist in all facets of our lives. Unfortunately, few truly ethnographic studies of cognition in the wild have been performed. (Beach 1988, Frake 1985, Gladwin 1970, Goodwin 1993, Goodwin and Goodwin 1992 and 1995, Latour 1986, Lave 1988, Lave et al. 1984, Ochs et al. (in press), Scribner 1984, Suchman 1987, and Theureau 1990 are lonely exceptions to this trend.) We trust our lives to systems of this sort every day, yet this class of phenomena has somehow fallen into the crack between the established disciplines of anthropology and psychology and appears to be excluded by foundational assumptions in cognitive science. This book is an attempt to show what a natural history of a cognitive system could be like.

Among the benefits of cognitive ethnography for cognitive science is the refinement of a functional specification for the human cognitive system. What is a mind for? How confident are we that our intuitions about the cognitive nature of tasks we do on a daily basis are correct? It is a common piece of common sense that we know what those tasks are because we are human and because we engage in them daily. But I believe this is not true. In spite of the fact that we engage in cognitive activities every day, our folk and professional models of cognitive performance do not match what appears when cognition in the wild is examined carefully. I have tried to show here that the study of cognition in the wild may reveal a different sort of task world that permits a different conception of what people do with their minds.

Cognitive science was born in a reaction against behaviorism. Behaviorism had made the claim that internal mental structure was either irrelevant or nonexistent—that the study of behavior could be conducted entirely in an objective characterization of behavior itself. Cognitive science's reaction was not simply to argue that the internal mental world was important too; it took as its domain of study the internal mental environment largely separated from the external world. Interaction with the world was reduced to read and write operations conducted at either end of extensive processing

Development of the practice

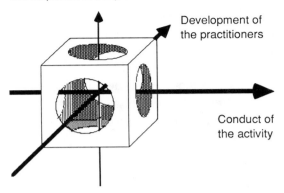

Development of
the practitioners

Conduct of
the activity

Figure 9.1   A moment of human practice.

activity. This fit the computer metaphor very well, but it made the organization of the environment in which thinking took place seem largely irrelevant. Both behaviorism and cognitivism must be wrong.

Cognition in the Intersection of Cultural Processes

The cube depicted in figure 9.1 represents any moment in navigation practice (or, in fact, any moment in any human practice). The arrows passing through the cube represent three developmental sequences of which every moment of practice is simultaneously a part. I have adopted some simple conventions to capture several aspects of the situation in this single diagram. The thickness of the arrow represents the density of interaction among the elements in that dimension. The length of the shaft of the arrow emerging from the cube represents the rate at which states in that dimension are changing. The length of the tail of the arrow going into the cube represents the duration of the relevant history of the activity in the given dimension.

It is essential to keep in mind that these things are all happening at the same time in the same activity. Having reinstated a whole human being in a culturally constituted activity, I see the following.

The conduct of the activity proceeds by the operation of functional systems that bring representational media into coordination with one another. The representational media may be inside as well as outside the individuals involved. These functional systems propagate representational state across the media. In describing the ongoing conduct of navigation tasks, it is possible to identify a number of cognitive systems, some subsuming others. One may focus on the processes internal to a single individual, on an individual in coordination with a set of tools (chapter 3), or on a group of individuals in interaction with one another and with a set of tools (chapter 4). Each system produces identifiable cognitive properties, and in each case the properties of the system are explained by reference to processes that transform states inside the system (chapter 5). The structured representational media in the system interact in the conduct of the activity. Each medium is put to use in an operational environment constituted by other media. As indicated in figure 9.1, the conduct of the activity itself has a relatively short history. An entry into a harbor, for example, involves a few hours of preparation and takes about an hour to complete. Changes in this dimension happen quickly, and the elements of the task performance are in relatively intense interaction with one another. The conduct of the activity creates elements of representational structure that survive beyond the end of the task. These elements—the logbooks, pencil marks on charts, the quartermasters' memories of the events—are the operational residua of the process.

In this adaptive system, the media may be changed by the very processes that constitute the conduct of the activity. The operations of the navigation team produce a structured experience for the participants that contains opportunities for individual learning (chapter 6). As a consequence of their participation in the task performance, the quartermasters may acquire internal organization that permits them to coordinate with the structure of their surroundings. In this way, learning can be seen as the propagation of organization through an adaptive system (chapter 7). The development of the practitioners themselves takes years. Through a career, a quartermaster gradually acquires the skills that are exercised in the performance of the job. Changes to the organization of the internal media that the quartermasters bring to the job take place more slowly than the changes to the states that the media support. That is, it takes longer to learn how to plot a fix, for example, than it does to plot a fix. But since most learning in this setting happens in the doing, the changes to internal media that permit them to be coordinated with external media happen in the same processes that bring the media into coordination with one another. The changes to the quartermasters' skills and the knowledge produced by this process are the mental residua of the process.

The setting of navigation work evolves over time as partial solutions to frequently encountered problems are crystallized and saved in the material and conceptual tools of the trade and in the the social organization of the work. The development of the practice takes place over centuries (chapter 2). The very same processes that constitute the conduct of the activity and that produce changes in the individual practitioners of navigation also produce changes in the social, material, and conceptual aspects of the setting. The example given in chapter 8 illustrates the creation in interaction of a new concept and a shared lexical label for it (the "total" in the modular form of the true-bearing computation). The microgenesis of the cultural elements that make up the navigation setting is visible in the details of the ongoing practice.

All this happens simultaneously in cognition in the wild. It is in this sense that cognition is a fundamentally cultural process.

References

Alexander, C. 1964. *Notes on the Synthesis of Form*. Harvard University Press.

Anderson, J. 1983. *Architecture of Cognition*. Harvard University Press.

Asimov, I. 1982. *Foundation's Edge*. Ballantine.

Aveni, A. F. 1981. Tropical archeoastronomy. *Science* 213 (4504): 161–170.

Bateson, G. 1972. *Steps to an Ecology of Mind*. Ballantine.

Beach, K. 1988. The role of external mnemonic symbols in acquiring an occupation. In M. M. Gruneberg, P. E. Morris, and R. N. Sykes (eds.), *Practical Aspects of Memory: Current Research and Issues*, volume 1. Wiley.

Bearden, B., and Wedertz, B. 1978. *The Bluejacket's Manual* (twentieth edition). U.S. Naval Institute.

Benedict, R. 1946. *The Chrysanthemum and the Sword*. Meridian.

Bobrow, D. 1991. Dimensions of interaction. *AAAI Magazine*, fall: 64–80.

Boster, J. S. 1985. Requiem for the omniscient informant: There's life in the old girl yet. In J. Dougherty (ed.), *Directions in Cognitive Anthropology*. University of Illinois Press.

Boster, J. S. 1990. The information economy model applied to biological similarity judgement. In L. Resnick, J. Levine, and S. Teasley (eds.), *Perspectives on Socially Shared Cognition*. APA Press.

Bowditch, N. 1977. *American Practical Navigator (An Epitome of Navigation)*. U.S. Defense Mapping Agency Hydrographic Center.

Buckhout, R. 1982. Eyewitness testimony. In U. Neisser (ed.), *Memory Observed: Remembering in Natural Contexts*. Freeman

Chandler, A. 1966. *Strategy and Structure*. Harvard University Press.

Chandrasekaran, B. 1981. Natural and social system metaphors for distributed problem solving: Introduction to the issue. *IEEE Transaction on Systems, Man, and Cybernetics* 11: 1–5.

Cole, M., and Griffin, P. 1980. Cultural amplifiers reconsidered. In D. R. Olson (ed.), *The Social Foundations of Language and Thought*. Norton.

Cotter, C. 1983a. A brief historical survey of British navigation manuals. *Journal of Navigation* 36 (2): 237–248.

Cotter, C. 1983b. A brief history of sailing directions. *Journal of Navigation* 36 (2): 249–261.

Cutler, A., and McShane, R. 1975. *Trachtenberg Speed Mathematics Self-Taught*. Doubleday.

Cyert, R. M., and March, J. G. 1963. *A Behavioral Theory of the Firm*. Prentice-Hall.

D'Andrade, R. G. 1981. The cultural part of cognition. *Cognitive Science* 5: 179–195.

D'Andrade, R. G. 1989. Cultural cognition. In M. Posner (ed.), *Foundations of Cognitive Science*. MIT Press.

Dawkins, R. 1986. *The Blind Watchmaker*. Norton.

Dennett, D. C. 1991. *Consciousness Explained*. Little, Brown.

Dreyfus, H. L. 1992. *What Computers Still Can't Do: A Critique of Artificial Reason* (second edition). MIT Press.

Feldman, M. S. 1989. *Order without Design*. University of California Press.

Finney, B. R. 1979. *Hokulea: The Way to Tahiti*. Dodd, Mead.

Finney, B. R. 1991. Myth, experiment, and the reinvention of Polynesian voyaging. *American Anthropologist* 93(2): 383–404.

Fleck, L. 1935. *The Genesis and Development of a Scientific Fact*. University of Chicago Press, 1979.

Frake, C. 1985. Cognitive maps of time and tide among medieval seafarers. *Man* 20: 254–270.

Fuson, R. H. 1987. *The Log of Christopher Columbus*. International Marine.

Gardner, H. 1985. *The Mind's New Science*. Basic Books.

Geertz, C. 1983. *Local Knowledge: Further Essays in Interpretive Anthropology*. Basic Books.

Gelman, R., and Gallistel, C. R. 1978. *The Child's Understanding of Number*. Harvard University Press.

Gentner, D., and Grudin, J. 1985. The evolution of mental metaphors in psychology: A ninety-year retrospective. *American Psychologist* 40: 181–192.

Gladwin, T. 1970. *East is a Big Bird*. Harvard University Press.

Goodenough, W. 1953. *Native Astronomy in the Central Carolines*. University of Pennsylvania.

Goodenough, W. 1957. Cultural anthropology and linguistics. In Report of the Seventh Annual Round Table Meeting in Linguistics and Language Study (Language and Linguistics monograph 9), Georgetown University.

Goodwin, C. 1993. Perception, Technology and Interaction on a Scientific Research Vessel. Research report, University of South Carolina.

Goodwin, C. 1994. Professional vision. *American Anthropologist* 96 (2): 606–633.

Goodwin, C., and Goodwin, M. H. 1995. Formulating planes: Seeing as situated activity. In D. Middleton and Y. Engestrom (eds.), *Cognition and Communication at Work*. Cambridge University Press.

Goody, J. 1977. *The Domestication of the Savage Mind*. Cambridge University Press.

Grudin, J. 1988. Why CSCW applications fail: Problems in the design and evaluation of organizational interfaces. In Proceedings of the CSCW'88 Conference on Computer-Supported Cooperative Work, Portland, Oregon.

Hastie, R., and Kumar, P. 1979. Person memory: Personality traits as organizing principles in memory for behavior. *Journal of Personality and Social Psychology* 37: 25–38.

Hewson, J. B. 1983. *A history of the Practice of Navigation* (second edition). Brown, Son and Ferguson.

Hutchins, E. 1983. Understanding Micronesian navigation. In D. Gentner and A. L. Stevens (eds.), *Mental Models*. Erlbaum.

Hutchins, E. 1991. The social organization of distributed cognition. In L. Resnick, J. Levine, and Stephanie Teasley (eds.), *Perspectives on Socially Shared Cognition*. APA Press.

Hutchins, E., and Hinton, G. E. 1984. Why the islands move. *Perception* 13: 629–632.

Hutchins, E., Hollan, J., and Norman, D. A. 1986. Direct manipulation interfaces. In D. A. Norman and S. Draper (eds.), *User Centered System Design: New Perspectives in Human-Computer Interaction*. Erlbaum.

Ifrah, G. 1987. *From One to Zero: A Universal History of Numbers*. Penguin.

Kann, E. 1978. *Leningrad in Three Days*. Progress.

Kirsh, D. 1990. When is information explicitly represented? In P. Hanson (ed.), *Information, Thought, and Content*. UBC Press.

Kyselka, W. 1987. *An Ocean in Mind*. University of Hawaii Press.

Langacker, R. 1987. *Foundations of Cognitive Grammar*, volume 1. Stanford University Press.

Lantz, D., and Stefflre, V. 1964. Language and cognition revisited. *Journal of Abnormal and Social Psychology* 69 (5): 472–481.

Larkin, J. 1989. Display-based problem solving. In D. Klahr and K. Kotovsky (eds.), *Complex Information Processing: The Impact of Herbert A. Simon*. Erlbaum.

Latour, B. 1986. Visualization and cognition: Thinking with eyes and hands. *Knowledge and Society* 6: 1–40.

Latour, B. 1987. *Science in Action*. Harvard University Press.

Lave, J. 1988. *Cognition in Practice*. Cambridge University Press.

Lave, J., Murtaugh, M., and de la Rocha, O. 1984. The dialectic of arithmetic in grocery shopping. In B. Rogoff and J. Lave (eds.), *Everyday Cognition: Its Development in Social Context*. Harvard University Press.

Law, J. 1987. Technology and heterogeneous engineering: the case of the Portuguese expansion. In W. E. Bijker, T. P. Hughes, and T. Pinch (eds.), *The Social Construction of Technological Systems*. MIT Press.

Levinson, S. 1990. Interactional Biases in Human Thinking. Working paper 3, Project Group in Cognitive Anthropology, Max Planck Gesellschaft, Berlin.

Lewis, D. 1972. *We the Navigators*. University of Hawaii Press.

Lewis, D. 1976. A return voyage between Puluwat and Saipan using Micronesian navigational techniques. In B. R. Finney (ed.), *Pacific Navigation and Voyaging*. Polynesian Society.

Lewis, D. 1978. *The Voyaging Stars: Secrets of Pacific Island Navigators*. Norton.

Lord, C., Lepper, M., and Ross, L. 1979. Biased assimilation and attitude polarization: The effects of prior theories on subsequently considered evidence. *Journal of Personality and Social Psychology* 37: 2098–2110.

Maloney, E. 1985. *Dutton's Navigation and Piloting* (fourteenth edition). Naval Institute Press.

Marr, D. 1982. *Vision: A Computational Investigation into the Human Representation and Processing of Visual Information*. Freeman.

Miyake, N. 1986. Constructive interaction and the iterative process of understanding. *Cognitive Science* 10 (2): 151–177.

National Maritime Museum. 1976. *The Planispheric Astrolabe*. Her Majesty's Stationery Office.

Neisser, U. 1976. *Cognition and Reality*. Freeman.

Nelson, R., and Winter, S. 1982. *An Evolutionary Theory of Economic Change*. Harvard University Press.

Newell, A. 1973. You can't play 20 questions with nature and win. In W. G. Chase (ed.), *Visual Information Processing*. Academic Press.

Newell, A., and Simon, H. A. 1972. *Human Problem Solving*. Prentice-Hall.

Newell, A., and Simon, H. A. 1990. Computer science as empirical inquiry: Symbols and search. In J. L. Garfield (ed.), *Foundations of Cognitive Science: The Essential Readings*. Paragon House.

Newell, A., Rosenbloom, P. S., and Laird, J. E. 1989. Symbolic architectures for cognition. In M. Posner (ed.), *Foundations of Cognitive Science*. MIT Press.

Nickerson, R., and Adams, M. J. 1979. Long term memory for a common object. *Cognitive Psychology* 11: 287–307.

Norman, D. A. 1981. Categorization of action slips. *Psychological Review* 88: 1–15.

Norman, D.A. 1983. Design rules based on analyses of human error. *Communications of the Association of Computing Machinery* 4: 254–258.

Norman, D.A. 1986. Cognitive engineering. In D. A. Norman and S. Draper (eds.), *User Centered System Design: New Perspectives in Human-Computer Interaction*. Erlbaum.

Norman, D. A. 1987. *The Psychology of Everyday Things*. Basic Books.

Norman, D. A. 1991. Approaches to the study of intelligence. *Artificial Intelligence* 47 (1–3): 327–346.

Norman, D. A. 1993. *Things That Make Us Smart*. Addison-Wesley.

Ochs, E., Jacoby, S., and Gonzalez, P. 1994. Interpretive journeys: How physicists talk and travel through graphic space. *Configurations* 2 (1): 151–171.

Perrow, C. 1984. *Normal Accidents*. Basic Books.

Pollatsek, A., and Rayner, K. 1989. Reading. In M. Posner (ed.), *Foundations of Cognitive Science*. MIT Press.

Pylyshyn, Z. W. 1989. Computing in cognitive science. In M. Posner (ed.), *Foundations of Cognitive Science*. MIT Press.

Reisberg, D. 1987. External representations and the advantages of externalizing one's thoughts. In program of ninth annual conference, Cognitive Science Society.

Riesenberg, S. 1972. The organization of navigational knowledge on Puluwat. *Journal of the Polynesian Society* 1 (81): 19–55.

Roberts, J. 1964. The self-management of cultures. In W. Goodenough (ed.), *Explorations in Cultural Anthropology: Essays in Honor of George Peter Murdock*. McGraw-Hill.

Romney, A. K. , Weller, S. C., and Batchelder, W. H. 1986. Culture as consensus: A theory of culture and informant accuracy. *American Anthropologist* 88 (2): 313–338.

Rumelhart, D. E., Smolensky, P., McClelland, J. L., and Hinton, G. E. 1986. Schemata and sequential thought processes in PDP models. In J. L. McClelland, D. E. Rumelhart, and the PDP Research Group (eds.), *Parallel Distributed Processing: Explorations in the Microstructure of Cognition*, volume 2. MIT Press.

Sahlins, M. 1976. *Culture and Practical Reason*. University of Chicago Press.

Sarfert, E. 1911. Zur kenntnis der schiffahrtskunde der Karoliner. *Korrespondenzblatt der Deutschen Gesellschaft für Anthropologie, Ethnologie und Urgeschichte* 42: 131–136.

Schück, A. 1882. Die astronomischen, geographischen und nautischen kennitnisse der Derwohoner der Karolinen und Marshall Inseln im Westlichen Grossen Ozean. *Aus Allen Welttheilen* 13 : 51–57, 242–243.

Schwartz, T. 1978. The size and shape of a culture. In F. Barth (ed.), *Scale and Social Organization*. Universitetsforlaget (Oslo).

Scribner, S. 1984. Studying working intelligence. In B. Rogoff and J. Lave (eds.), *Everyday Cognition: Its Development in Social Context*. Harvard University Press.

Searle, J. R. 1990. Is the brain's mind a computer program? *Scientific American* 262 (1): 26–31.

Segal, L. 1990. Effects of cockpit design on crew communication. In Editor, *Contemporary Ergonomics*. Taylor and Francis.

Simon, H. A. 1981. *The Sciences of the Artificial* (second edition). MIT Press.

Simon, H. A., and Kaplan, C. A. 1989. Foundations of cognitive science. In M. Posner (ed.), Foundations of Cognitive Science. MIT Press.

Suchman, L. 1987. *Plans and Situated Actions: The Problem of Human-Machine Communication*. Cambridge University Press.

Swade, D. D. 1993. Redeeming Charles Babbage's mechanical computer. *Scientific American* 268 (2), 86–91.

Taylor, E. G. R. 1971. *The Haven Finding Art*. American Elsevier.

Taylor, F. J. 1984. Residue arithmetic: a tutorial with examples. *IEEE Computer*.

Theureau, J. 1990. Introduction a l'etude du cours d'action: Un programme de recherche en ergonomie st anthropologie cognitive. Laboratoire Communication et Travail, Université Paris-Nord.

Tweney, R., Doherty, M., and Mynatt C. 1981. *On Scientific Thinking*. Columbia University Press.

Tylor, E. B. 1871. *Primitive Culture*. Murray.

Vera, J., and Simon, H. 1993. Situated action: A symbolic interpretation. *Cognitive Science* 17 (1): 7–48.

Vygotsky, L. S. 1978. *Mind in Society: The Development of Higher Psychological Processes*. Harvard University Press.

Wason, P. 1968. Reasoning about a rule. *Quarterly Journal of Experimental Psychology* 20: 273–281.

Wason, P., and Johnson-Laird, P. 1972. *Psychology of Reasoning: Structure and Content*. Batsford.

Waters, D. 1976. Science and the Techniques of Navigation in the Renaissance. Maritime Monographs and Reports, National Maritime Museum, London.

Weick, K. E. 1979. *Social Psychology of Organizing*. Addison-Wesley.

Wertsch, James, V. 1985. *Vygotsky and the Social Formation of Mind*. Harvard University Press.

Wickens, C., and Flach, J. 1988. Information processing. In E. Wiener and D. Nagel (eds.), *Human Factors in Aviation*. Academic Press.

Zhang, J. 1992. Distributed Representation: The Interaction between Internal and External Information. Technical report 9201, Department of Cognitive Science, University of California, San Diego.

Index